akahashi

The spotlight on Rumiko Takahashi's career began in 1978 when she won an honorable mention in Shogakukan's annual New Comic Artist Contest for *Those Selfish Aliens*. Later that same year, her boy-meets-alien comedy series, *Urusei Yatsura*, was serialized in *Weekly Shonen Sunday*. This phenomenally successful manga series was adapted into anime and spawned a TV series and half a dozen theatrical incredibly popular in their own right. Takahashi follow of her debut series with one blockbuster hit after another—*M* ran from 1980 to 1987, *Ranma ½* from 1987 to 1996, and *Inuyasha* 1996 to 2008. Other notable works include *Mermaid Saga*, *Rumic Theater*, and *One-Pound Gospel*.

Takahashi won the prestigious Shogakukan Manga Award twice in her career, once for *Urusei Yatsura* in 1981 and the second time for *Inuyasha* in 2002. A majority of the Takahashi canon has been adapted into other media such as anime, live-action TV series, and film. Takahashi's manga, as well as the other formats her work has been adapted into, have continued to delight generations of fans around the world. Distinguished by her wonderfully endearing characters, Takahashi's work adeptly incorporates a wide variety of elements such as comedy, romance, fantasy, and martial arts. While her series are difficult to pin down into one simple genre, the signature style she has created has come to be known as the "Rumic World." Rumiko Takahashi is an artist who truly represents the very best from the world of manga.

RIN-NE
VOLUME 2
Shonen Sunday Edition

STORY AND ART BY
Rumiko Takahashi

Original Japanese edition "KYOUKAI NO RINNE"
published by SHOGAKUKAN Inc.

Translation/Christine Dashiell
Touch-up Art & Lettering/Evan Waldinger
Design/Yukiko Whitley
Editor/Mike Montesa

VP, Production/Alvin Lu
VP, Sales & Product Marketing/Gonzalo Ferreyra
VP, Creative/Linda Espinosa
Publisher/Hyoe Narita

Printed in the U.S.A.

Published by VIZ Media, LLC
P.O. Box 77010
San Francisco, CA 94107

10 9 8 7 6 5 4 3 2 1
First printing, January 2010

www.viz.com
WWW.SHONENSUNDAY.COM

PARENTAL ADVISORY
RIN-NE is rated T+ for Older Teen and is recommended for ages 16 and up.

T+ FOR OLDER TEEN
ratings.viz.com

Story and Art by
Rumiko Takahashi

RIN-NE

Characters

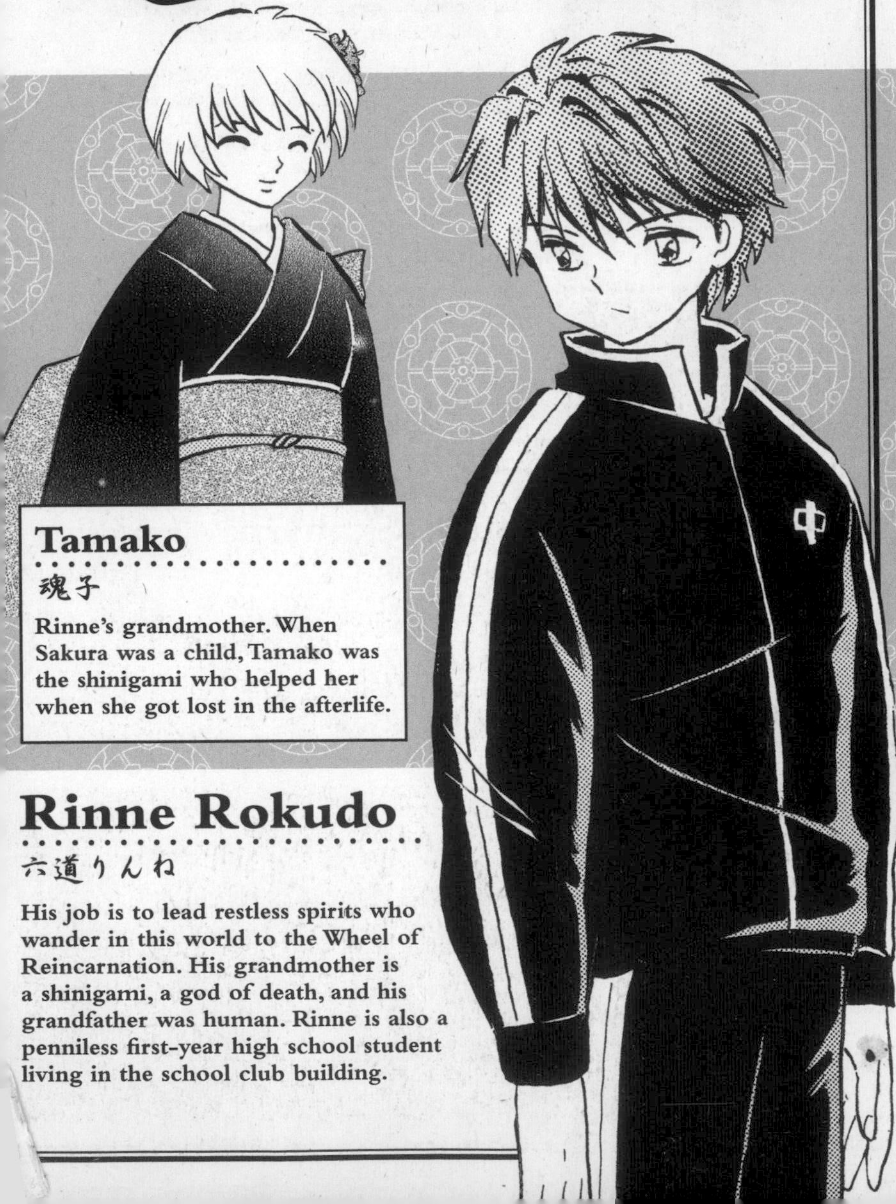

Tamako

魂子

Rinne's grandmother. When Sakura was a child, Tamako was the shinigami who helped her when she got lost in the afterlife.

Rinne Rokudo

六道りんね

His job is to lead restless spirits who wander in this world to the Wheel of Reincarnation. His grandmother is a shinigami, a god of death, and his grandfather was human. Rinne is also a penniless first-year high school student living in the school club building.

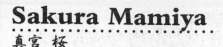

Sakura Mamiya

真宮 桜

When she was a child, Sakura gained the ability to see ghosts after getting lost in the afterlife. Somehow, she's wound up helping Rinne with his work.

Rokumon

六文

One of the Black Cats that help shinigami do their work. He is Rinne's loyal Black Cat by Contract.

The Story So Far

When she was a child, Sakura Mamiya was spirited away to the afterlife and has had the ability to see ghosts ever since. Now she's a high school student, and one day she sees a boy she thinks is a ghost but actually isn't. His name is Rinne Rokudo, and it turns out he's also her classmate. The earthbound spirit of a lovestruck boy has been pestering Sakura on her way home from school, and Rinne helps this spirit to pass on.

Rinne is a shinigami...sort of. His job is to lead spirits who have lingering attachments to this world to the Wheel of Reincarnation so that they may be reborn.

Since meeting Rinne, Sakura's after-school activities are really out of this world!

Contents

CHAPTER 9: NUPTIAL CUPS

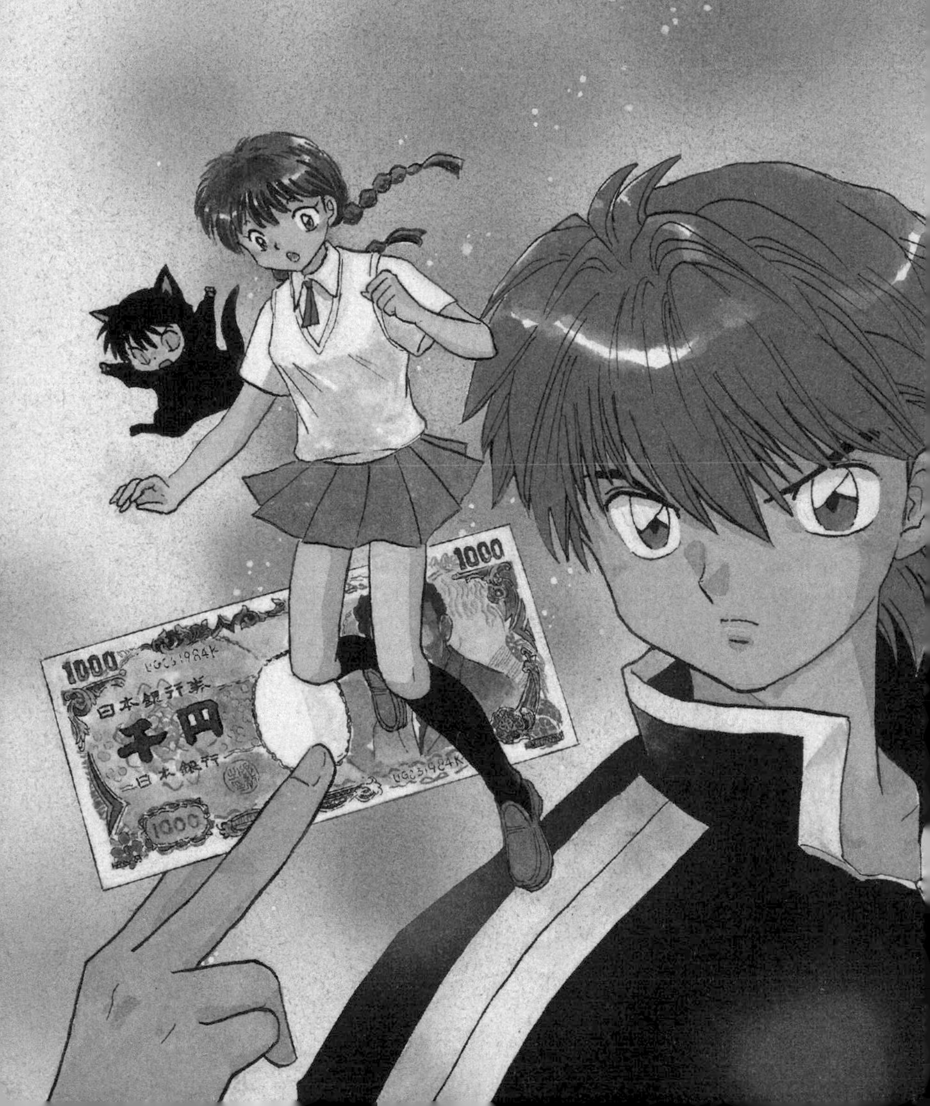

1000
日本銀行券
千円
日本銀行
1000

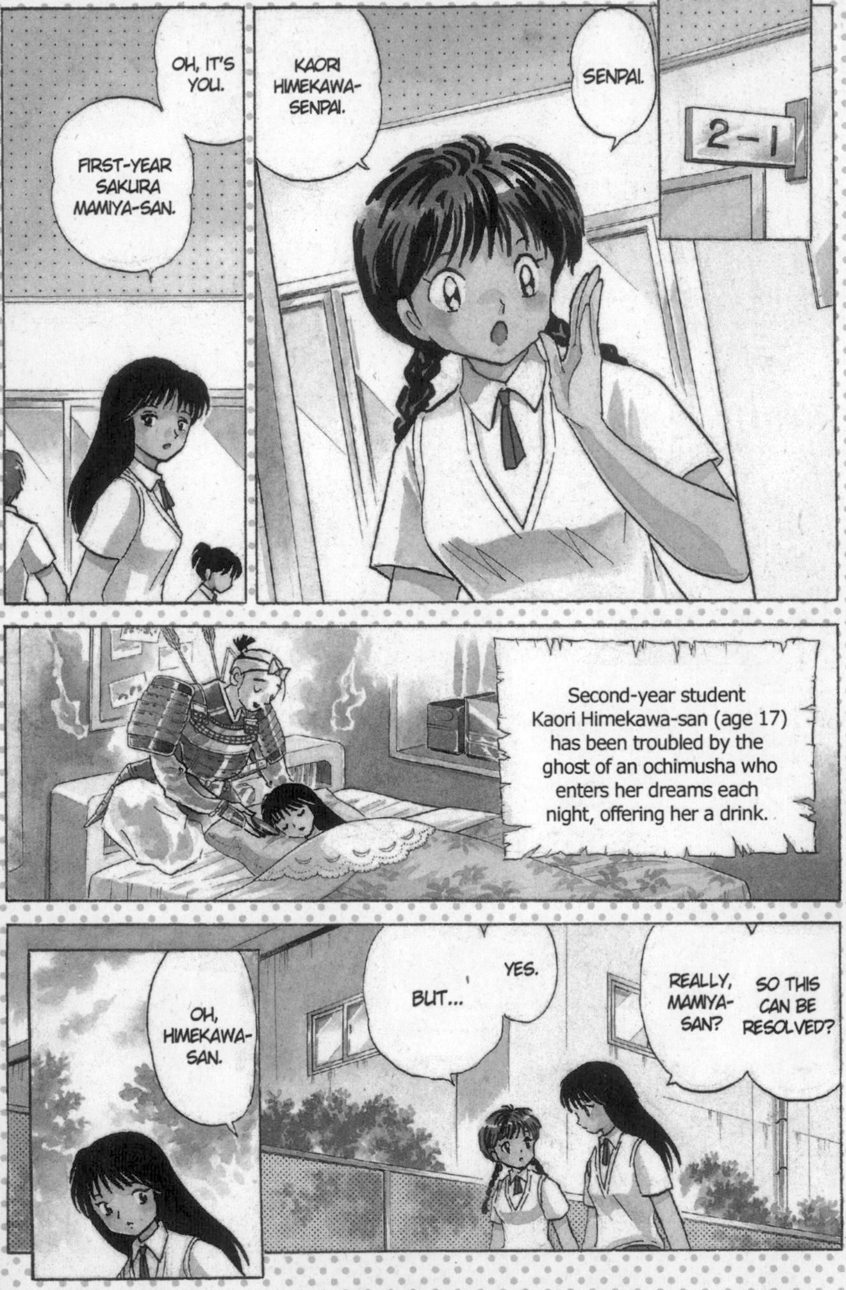
SENPAI.
KAORI HIMEKAWA-SENPAI.
OH, IT'S YOU.
FIRST-YEAR SAKURA MAMIYA-SAN.
2-1
Second-year student Kaori Himekawa-san (age 17) has been troubled by the ghost of an ochimusha who enters her dreams each night, offering her a drink.
REALLY, MAMIYA-SAN? SO THIS CAN BE RESOLVED?
YES.
BUT...
OH, HIMEKAWA-SAN.

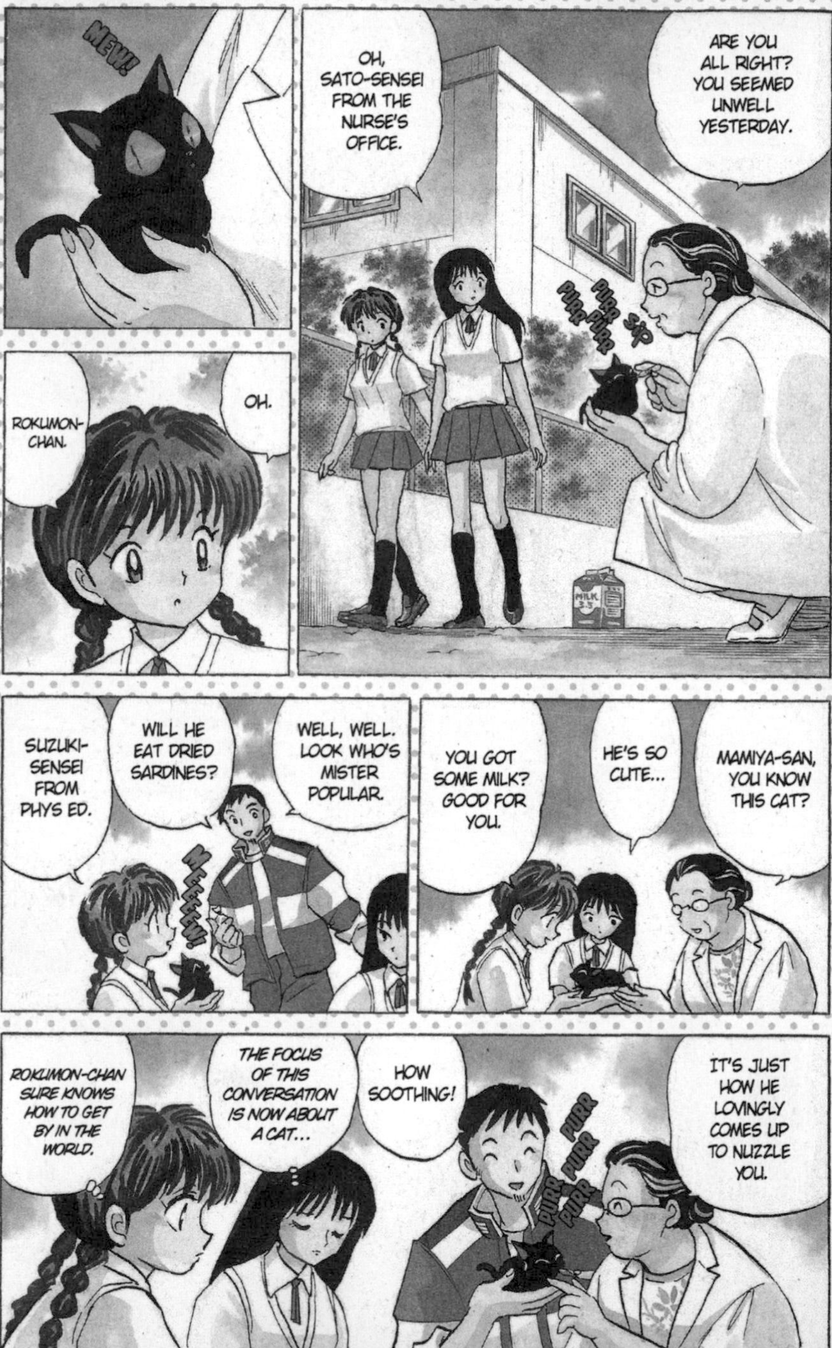
ARE YOU ALL RIGHT? YOU SEEMED UNWELL YESTERDAY.
OH, SATO-SENSEI FROM THE NURSE'S OFFICE.
PURR PURR PURR SIP
MEW!
OH.
ROKUMON-CHAN.
MAMIYA-SAN, YOU KNOW THIS CAT?
HE'S SO CUTE...
YOU GOT SOME MILK? GOOD FOR YOU.
WELL, WELL. LOOK WHO'S MISTER POPULAR.
WILL HE EAT DRIED SARDINES?
SUZUKI-SENSEI FROM PHYS ED.
MEEEEW!
IT'S JUST HOW HE LOVINGLY COMES UP TO NUZZLE YOU.
PURR PURR PURR PURR
HOW SOOTHING!
THE FOCUS OF THIS CONVERSATION IS NOW ABOUT A CAT...
ROKUMON-CHAN SURE KNOWS HOW TO GET BY IN THE WORLD.

RIN-NE

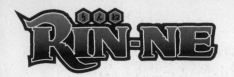

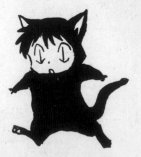

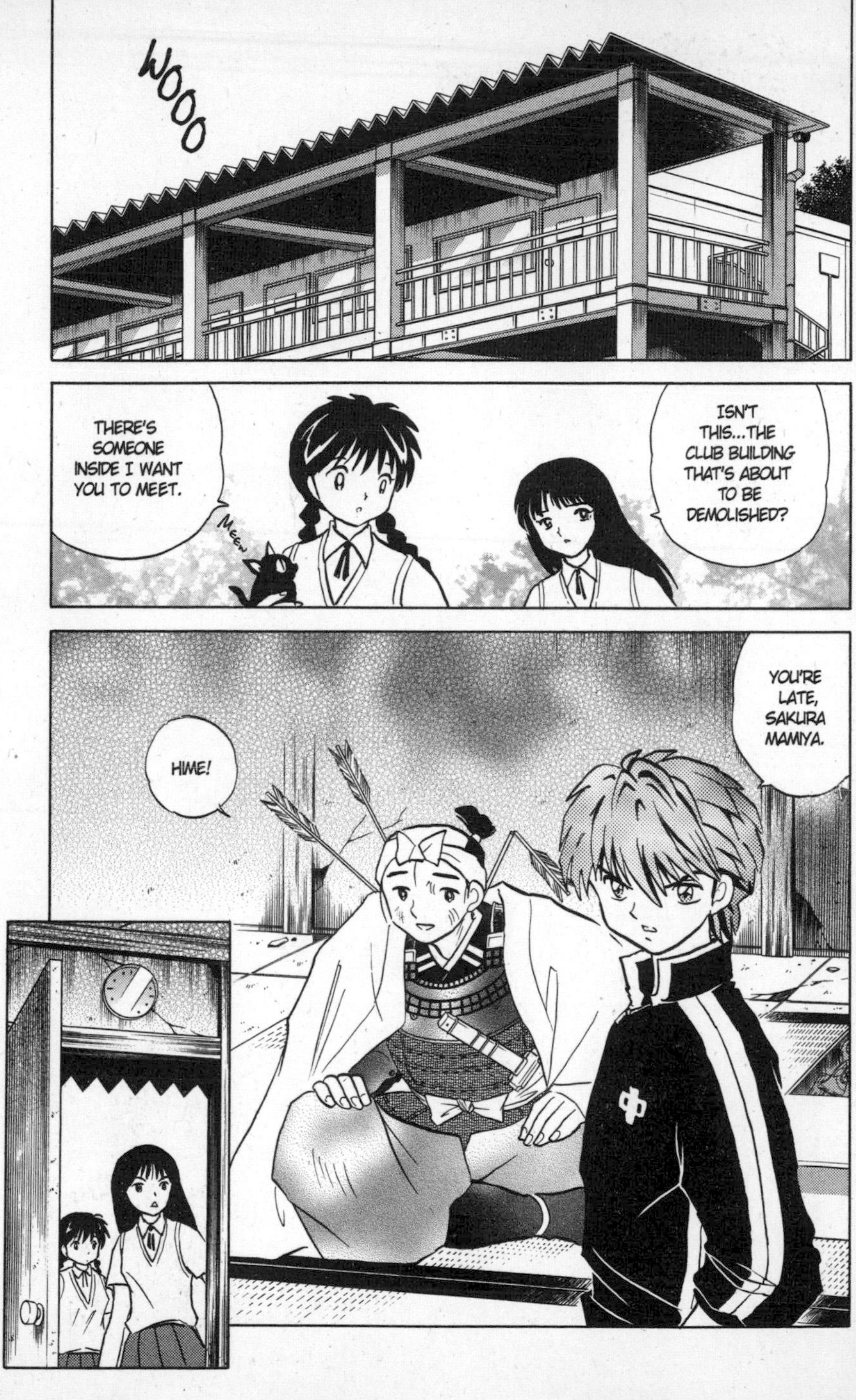
WOOO
ISN'T THIS...THE CLUB BUILDING THAT'S ABOUT TO BE DEMOLISHED?
THERE'S SOMEONE INSIDE I WANT YOU TO MEET.
MEEW
YOU'RE LATE, SAKURA MAMIYA.
HIME!

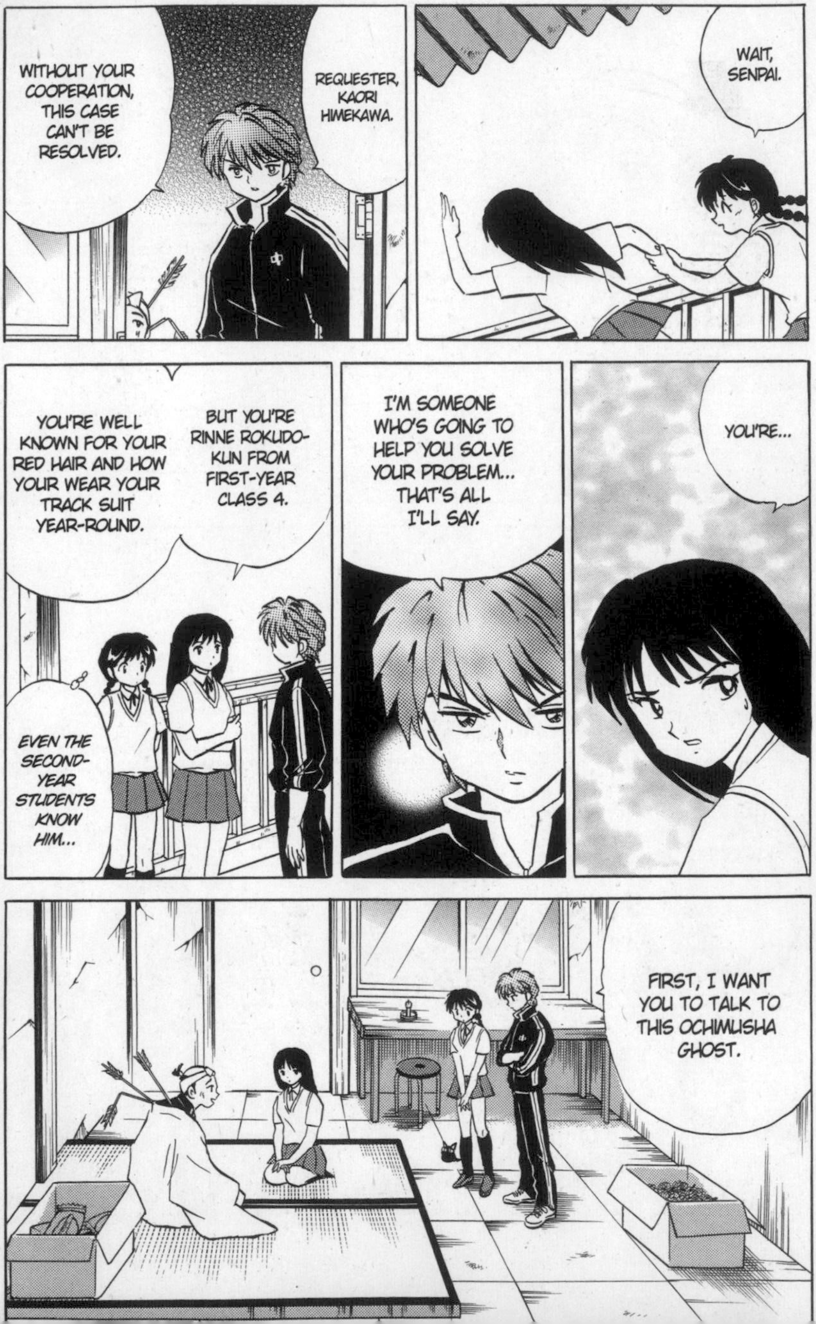
WAIT, SENPAI.
REQUESTER, KAORI HIMEKAWA.
WITHOUT YOUR COOPERATION, THIS CASE CAN'T BE RESOLVED.
YOU'RE...
I'M SOMEONE WHO'S GOING TO HELP YOU SOLVE YOUR PROBLEM... THAT'S ALL I'LL SAY.
BUT YOU'RE RINNE ROKUDO-KUN FROM FIRST-YEAR CLASS 4.
YOU'RE WELL KNOWN FOR YOUR RED HAIR AND HOW YOUR WEAR YOUR TRACK SUIT YEAR-ROUND.
EVEN THE SECOND-YEAR STUDENTS KNOW HIM...
FIRST, I WANT YOU TO TALK TO THIS OCHIMUSHA GHOST.

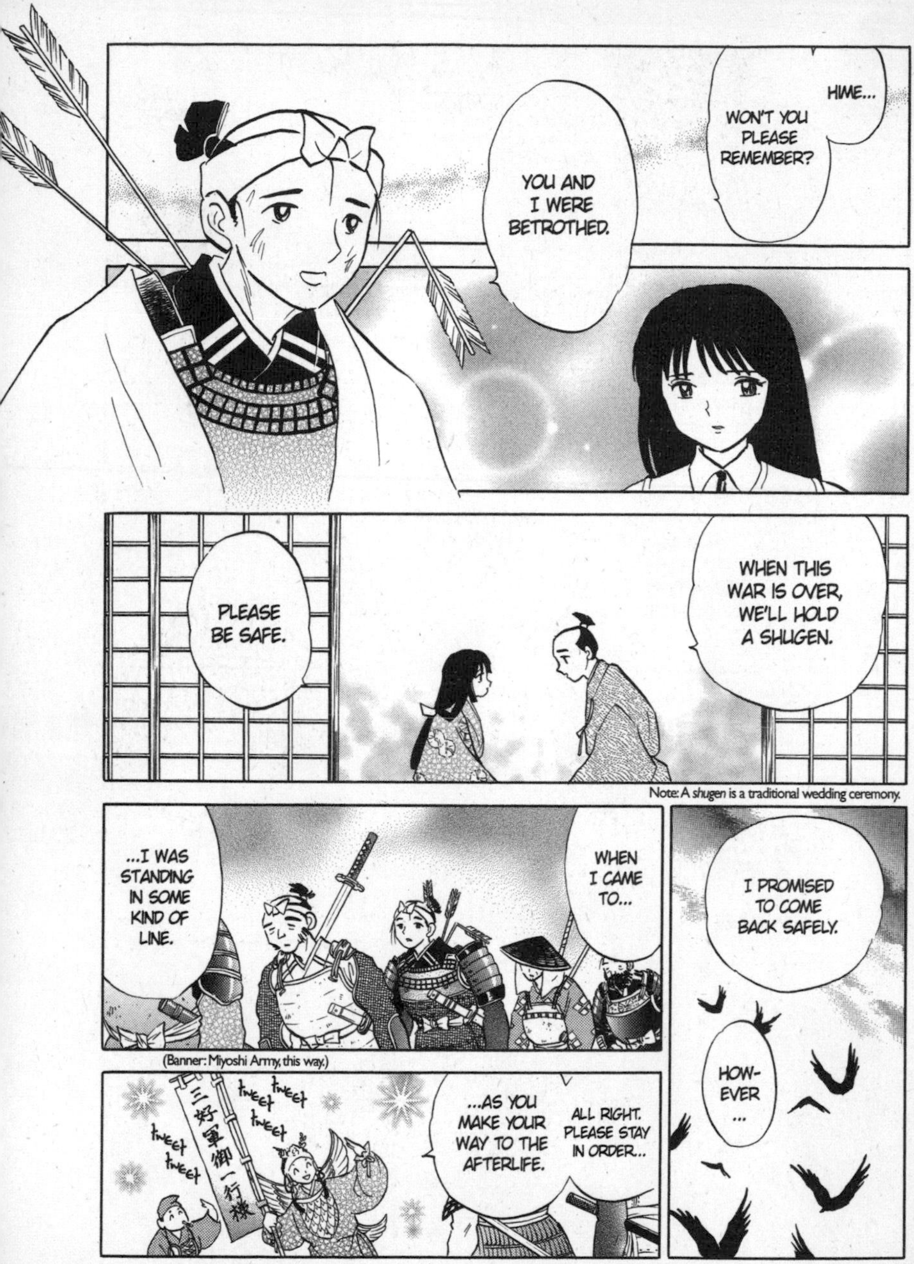
HIME... WON'T YOU PLEASE REMEMBER?
YOU AND I WERE BETROTHED.
WHEN THIS WAR IS OVER, WE'LL HOLD A SHUGEN.
PLEASE BE SAFE.
I PROMISED TO COME BACK SAFELY.
HOW-EVER...
WHEN I CAME TO...
...I WAS STANDING IN SOME KIND OF LINE.
ALL RIGHT. PLEASE STAY IN ORDER...
...AS YOU MAKE YOUR WAY TO THE AFTERLIFE.
tweet tweet
tweet
tweet tweet
三好軍御一行様
Note: A *shugen* is a traditional wedding ceremony.

(Banner: Miyoshi Army, this way.)

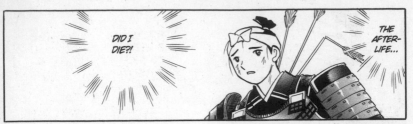

THE AFTER-LIFE...
DID I DIE?!
BUT I CANNOT PASS AWAY.
HIME IS WAITING FOR ME.
I FLED THE LINE OF THE DEAD AND HEADED FOR MY HOMELAND.
I HAD NO IDEA HOW MUCH TIME HAD PASSED.
BY THE TIME I REACHED MY HOME...
...HIME WAS NOWHERE TO BE SEEN.
SO YOU ENDED UP NOT SEEING HER FOR HUNDREDS OF YEARS.
THE POOR THING.
UM...
WHAT DOES ALL THIS MEAN?

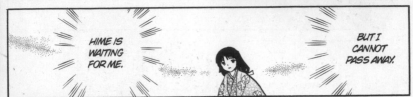

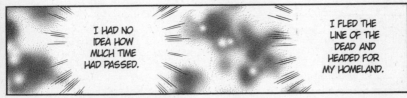

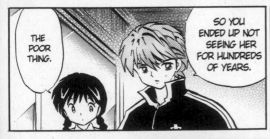

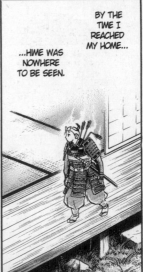

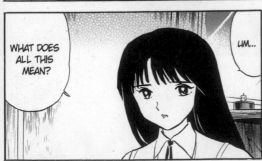

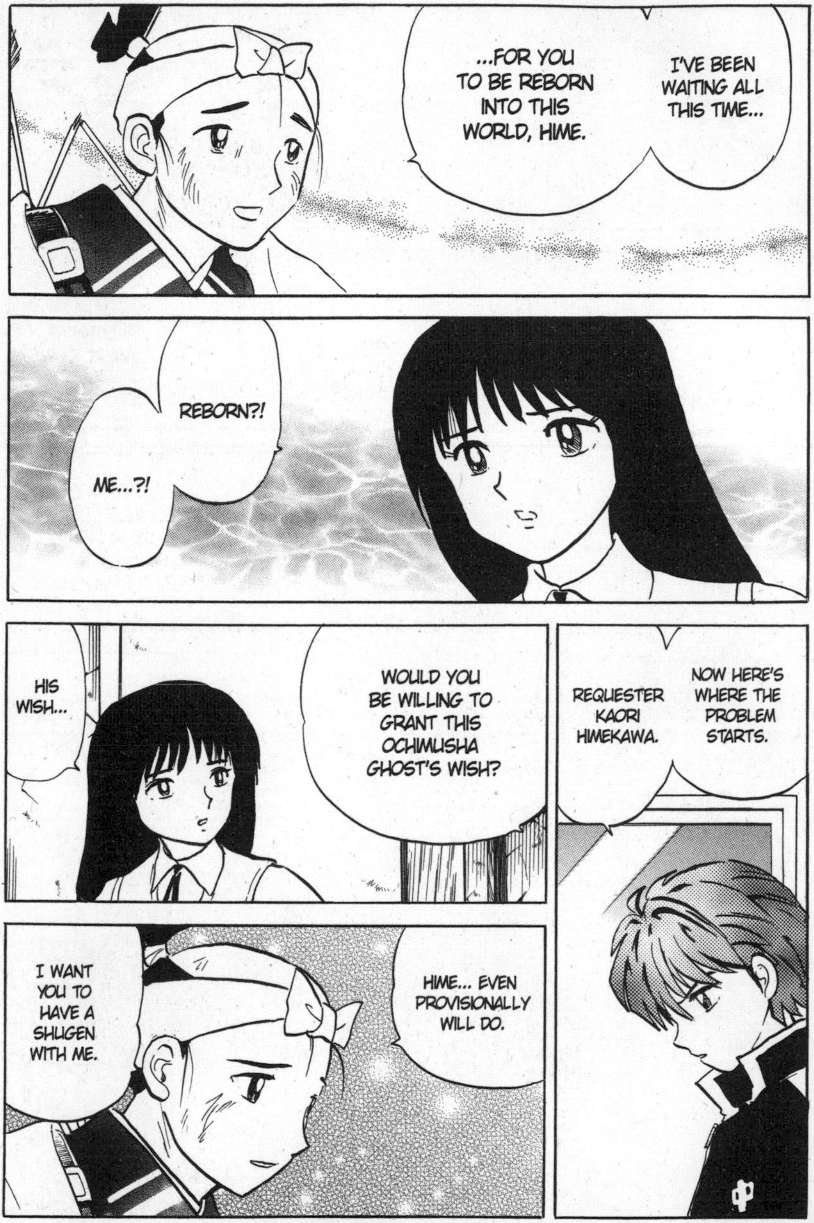
I'VE BEEN WAITING ALL THIS TIME...
...FOR YOU TO BE REBORN INTO THIS WORLD, HIME.
REBORN?!
ME...?!
NOW HERE'S WHERE THE PROBLEM STARTS.
REQUESTER KAORI HIMEKAWA.
WOULD YOU BE WILLING TO GRANT THIS OCHIMUSHA GHOST'S WISH?
HIS WISH...
HIME... EVEN PROVISIONALLY WILL DO.
I WANT YOU TO HAVE A SHUGEN WITH ME.

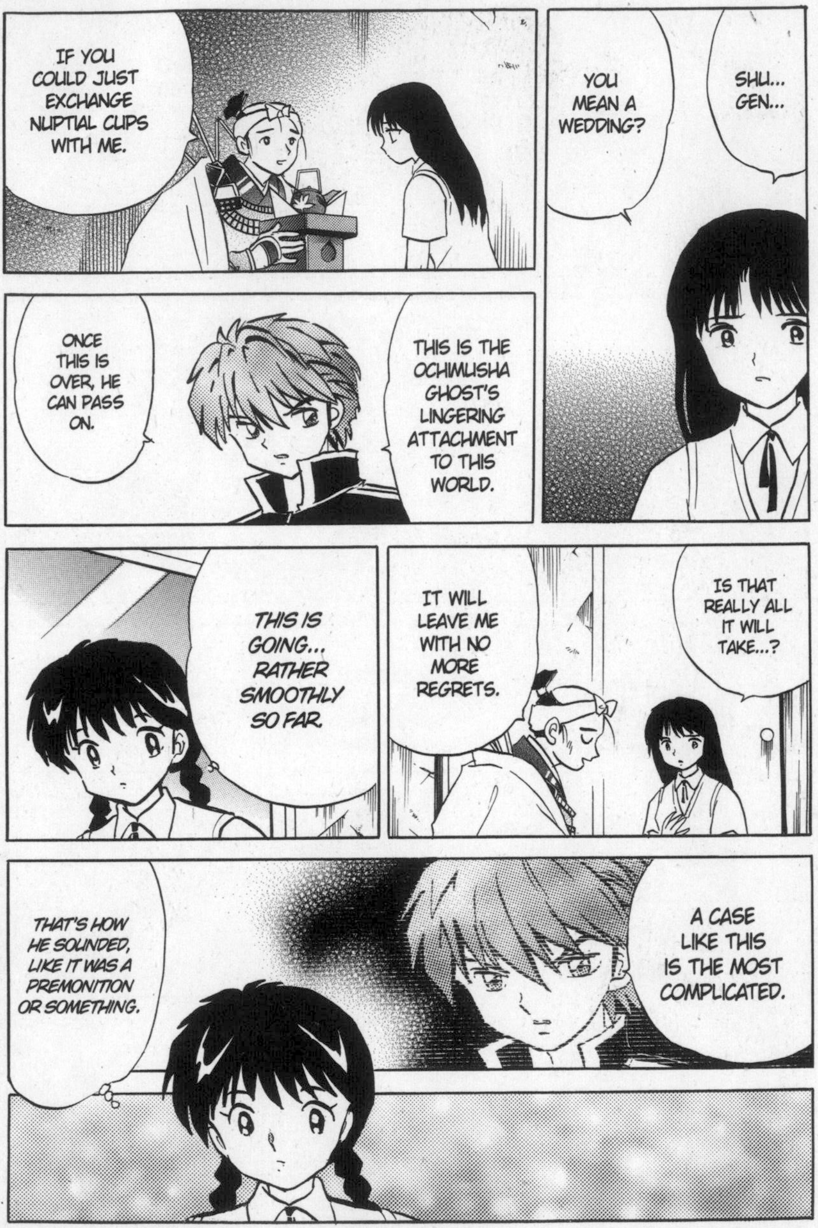
SHU... GEN...
YOU MEAN A WEDDING?
IF YOU COULD JUST EXCHANGE NUPTIAL CUPS WITH ME.
THIS IS THE OCHIMUSHA GHOST'S LINGERING ATTACHMENT TO THIS WORLD.
ONCE THIS IS OVER, HE CAN PASS ON.
IS THAT REALLY ALL IT WILL TAKE...?
IT WILL LEAVE ME WITH NO MORE REGRETS.
THIS IS GOING... RATHER SMOOTHLY SO FAR.
A CASE LIKE THIS IS THE MOST COMPLICATED.
THAT'S HOW HE SOUNDED, LIKE IT WAS A PREMONITION OR SOMETHING.

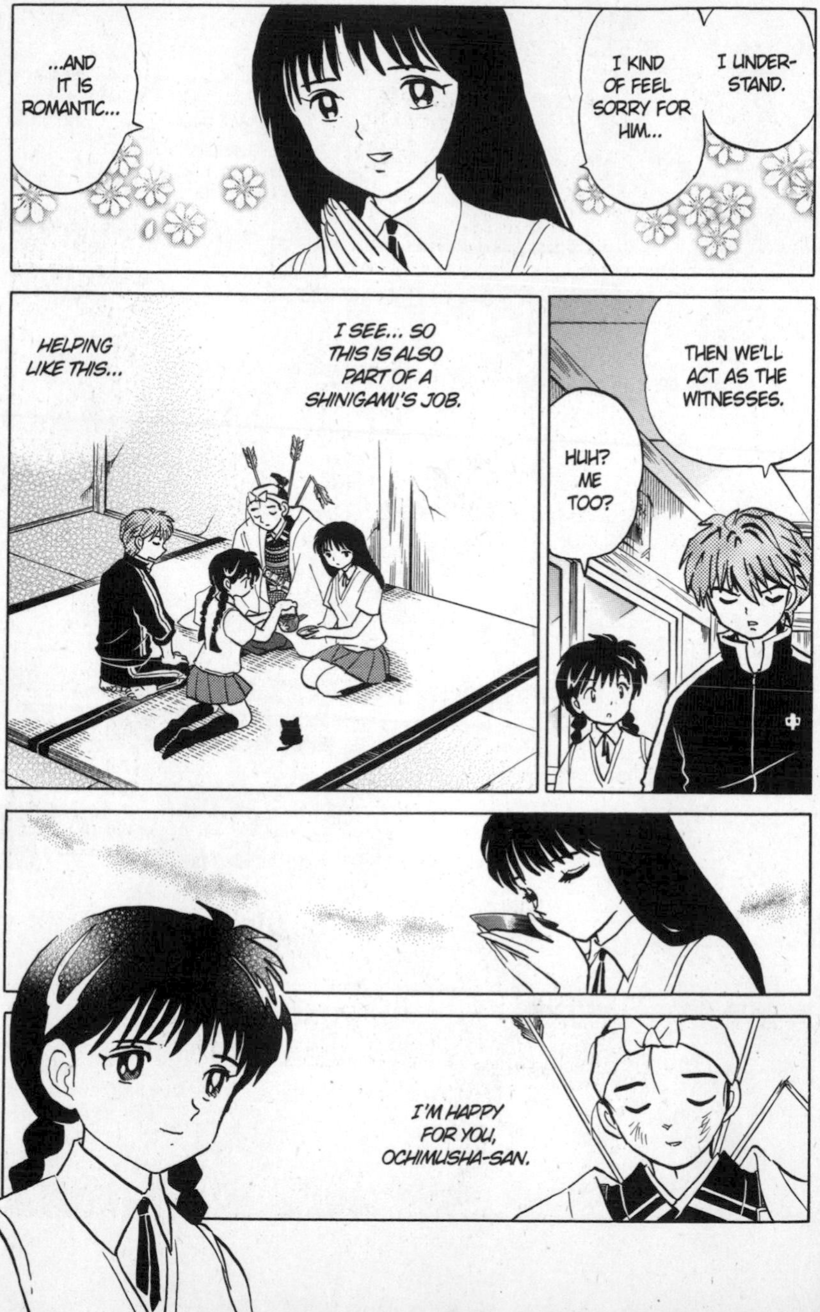
I UNDER-STAND.
I KIND OF FEEL SORRY FOR HIM...
...AND IT IS ROMANTIC...
THEN WE'LL ACT AS THE WITNESSES.
HUH? ME TOO?
I SEE... SO THIS IS ALSO PART OF A SHINIGAMI'S JOB.
HELPING LIKE THIS...
I'M HAPPY FOR YOU, OCHIMUSHA-SAN.

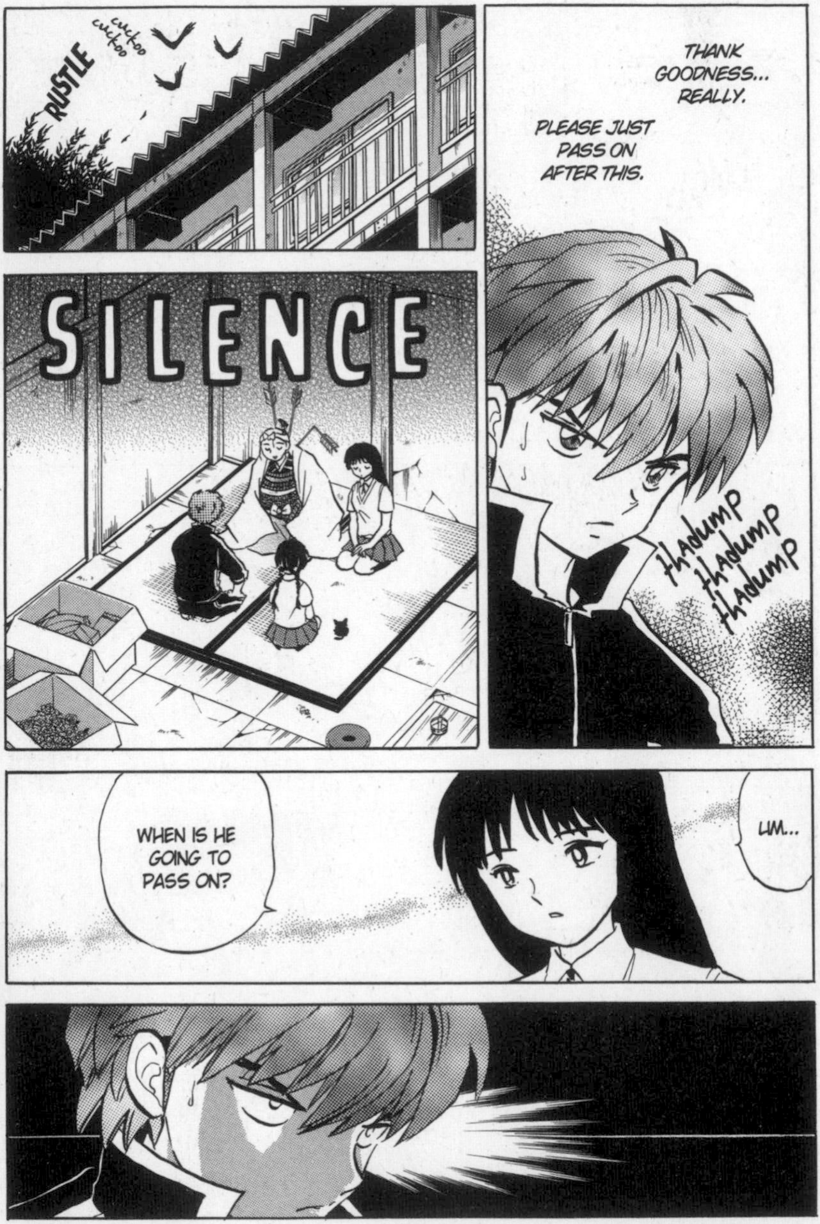
THANK GOODNESS... REALLY.
PLEASE JUST PASS ON AFTER THIS.
thadump thadump thadump
RUSTLE
cuckoo cuckoo
SILENCE
UM...
WHEN IS HE GOING TO PASS ON?

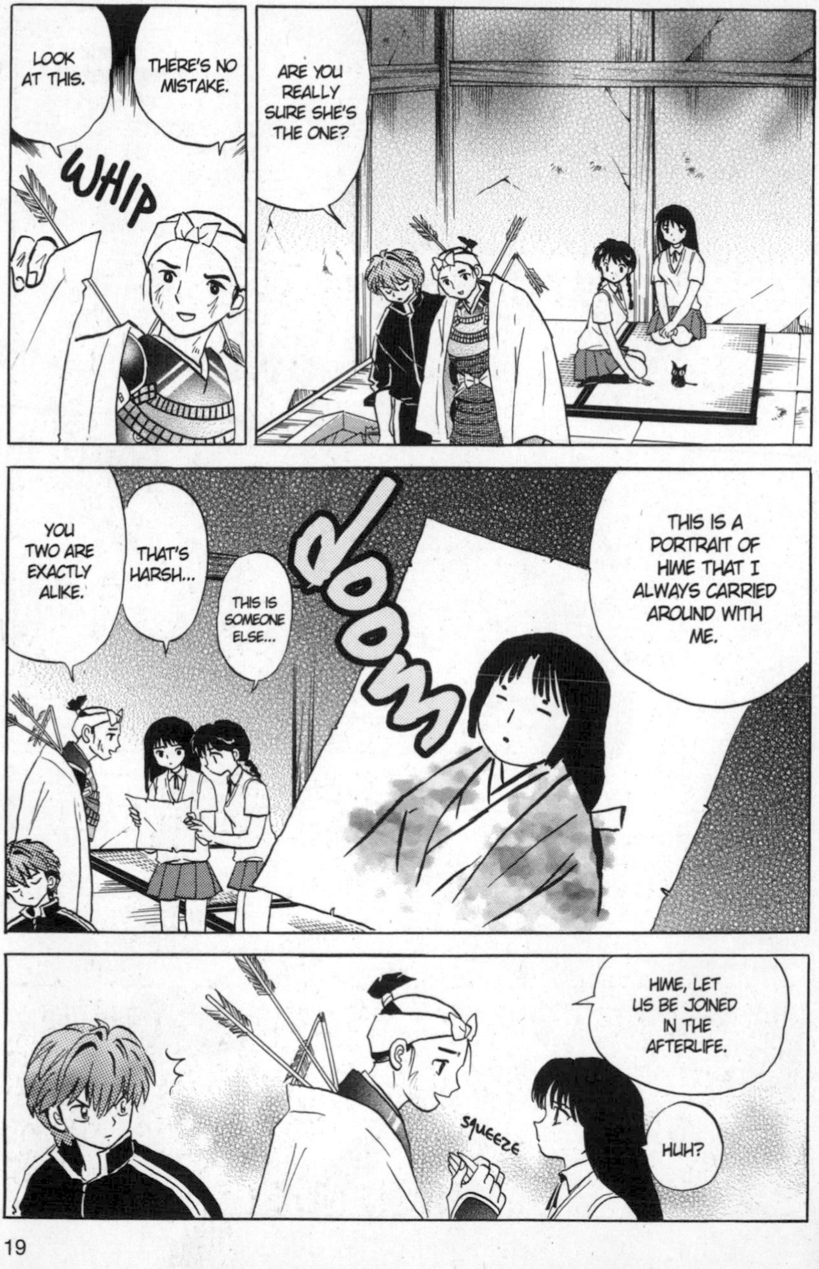
ARE YOU REALLY SURE SHE'S THE ONE?
THERE'S NO MISTAKE.
LOOK AT THIS.
WHIP
THIS IS A PORTRAIT OF HIME THAT I ALWAYS CARRIED AROUND WITH ME.
DOOM
THIS IS SOMEONE ELSE...
THAT'S HARSH...
YOU TWO ARE EXACTLY ALIKE.
HIME, LET US BE JOINED IN THE AFTERLIFE.
HUH?
SQUEEZE

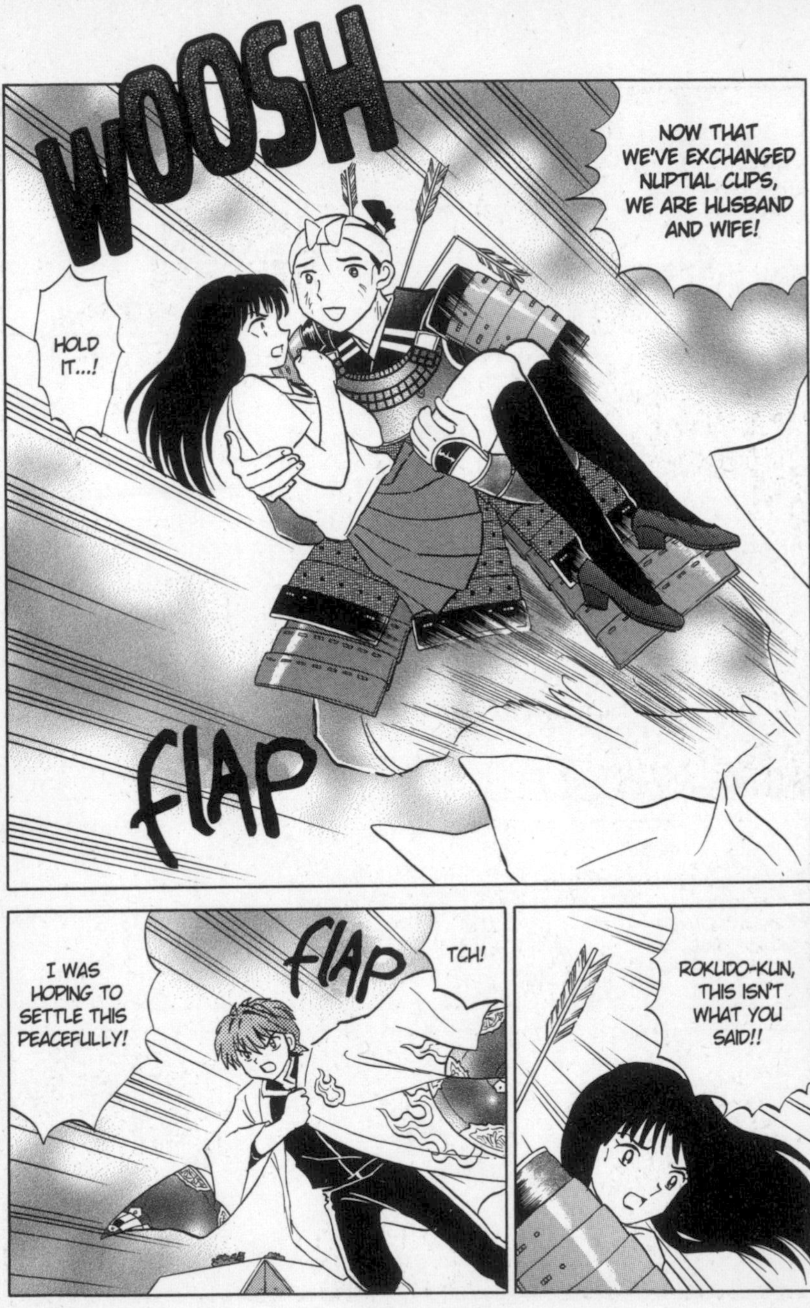
WOOSH
NOW THAT WE'VE EXCHANGED NUPTIAL CUPS, WE ARE HUSBAND AND WIFE!
HOLD IT...!
FLAP
ROKUDO-KUN, THIS ISN'T WHAT YOU SAID!!
TCH!
FLAP
I WAS HOPING TO SETTLE THIS PEACEFULLY!

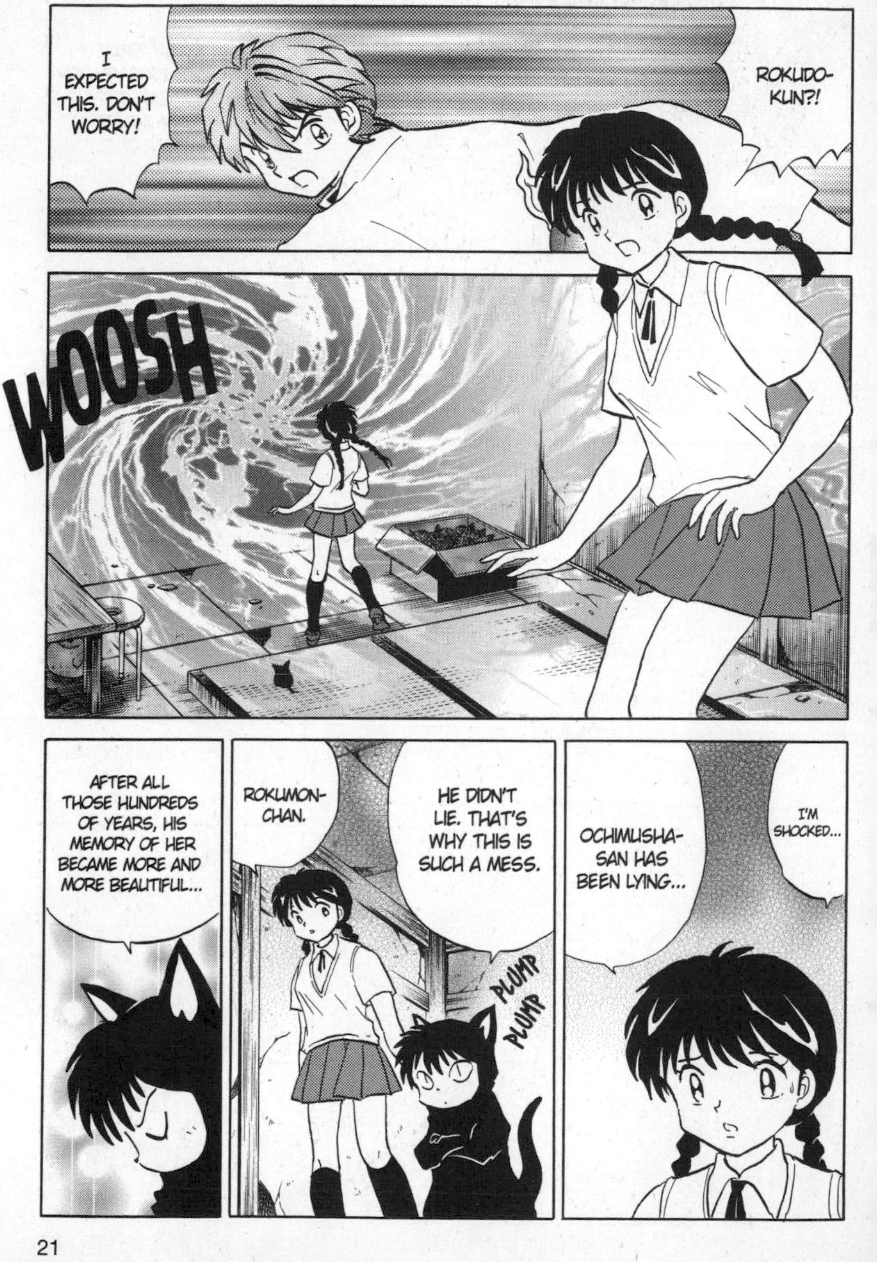
ROKUDO-KUN?!
I EXPECTED THIS. DON'T WORRY!
WOOSH
I'M SHOCKED...
OCHIMUSHA-SAN HAS BEEN LYING...
HE DIDN'T LIE. THAT'S WHY THIS IS SUCH A MESS.
ROKUMON-CHAN.
PLUMP PLUMP
AFTER ALL THOSE HUNDREDS OF YEARS, HIS MEMORY OF HER BECAME MORE AND MORE BEAUTIFUL...

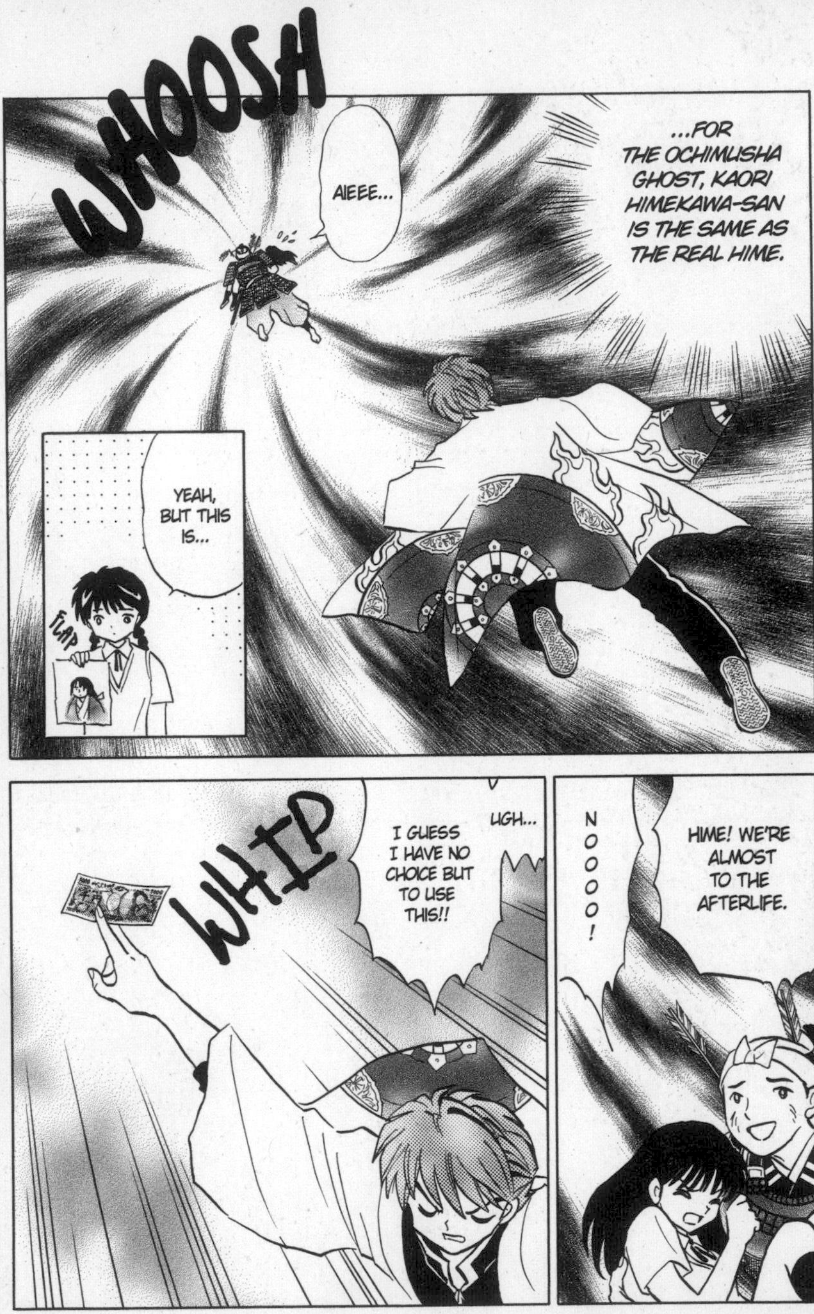
...FOR THE OCHIMUSHA GHOST, KAORI HIMEKAWA-SAN IS THE SAME AS THE REAL HIME.
AIEEE...
WHOOSH
YEAH, BUT THIS IS...
FLAP
HIME! WE'RE ALMOST TO THE AFTERLIFE.
NOOOOO!
UGH...
I GUESS I HAVE NO CHOICE BUT TO USE THIS!!
WHIP

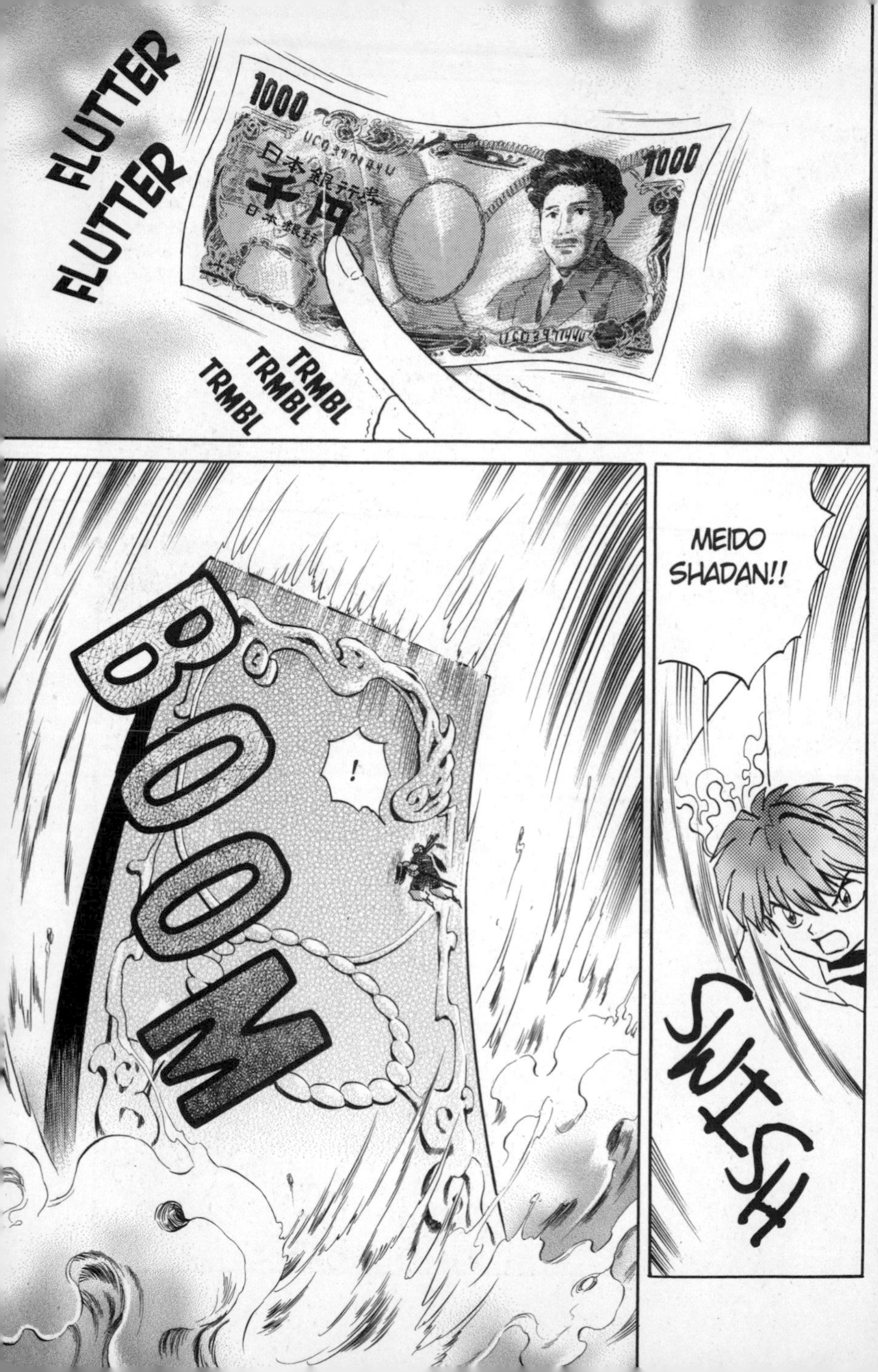
FLUTTER
FLUTTER
1000
日本銀行券
千円
日本銀行
1000
TRMBL
TRMBL
TRMBL
MEIDO SHADAN!!
SWISH
BOOM
!

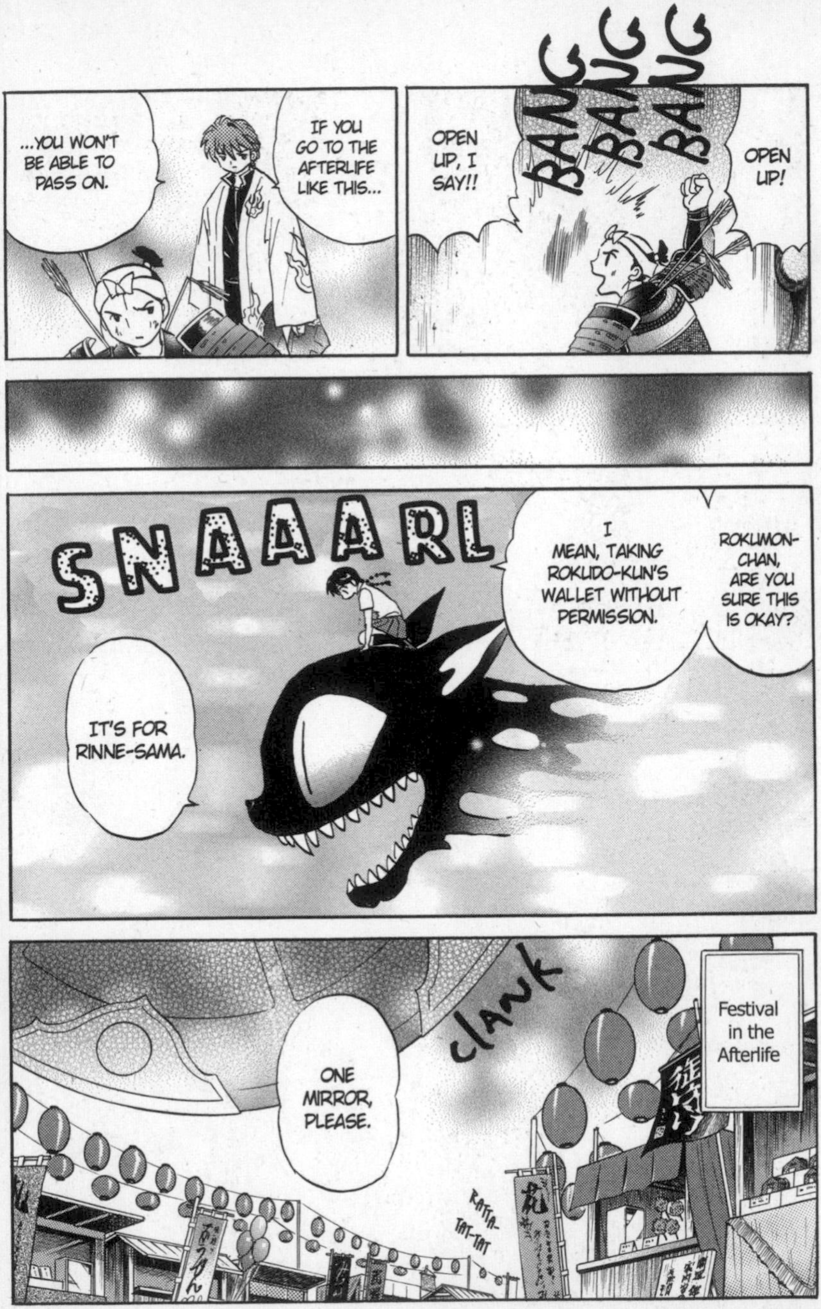
BANG BANG BANG
OPEN UP!
OPEN UP, I SAY!!
IF YOU GO TO THE AFTERLIFE LIKE THIS...
...YOU WON'T BE ABLE TO PASS ON.
ROKUMON-CHAN, ARE YOU SURE THIS IS OKAY?
I MEAN, TAKING ROKUDO-KUN'S WALLET WITHOUT PERMISSION.
SNAAARL
IT'S FOR RINNE-SAMA.
Festival in the Afterlife
clank
ONE MIRROR, PLEASE.
RATTA-TAT-TAT

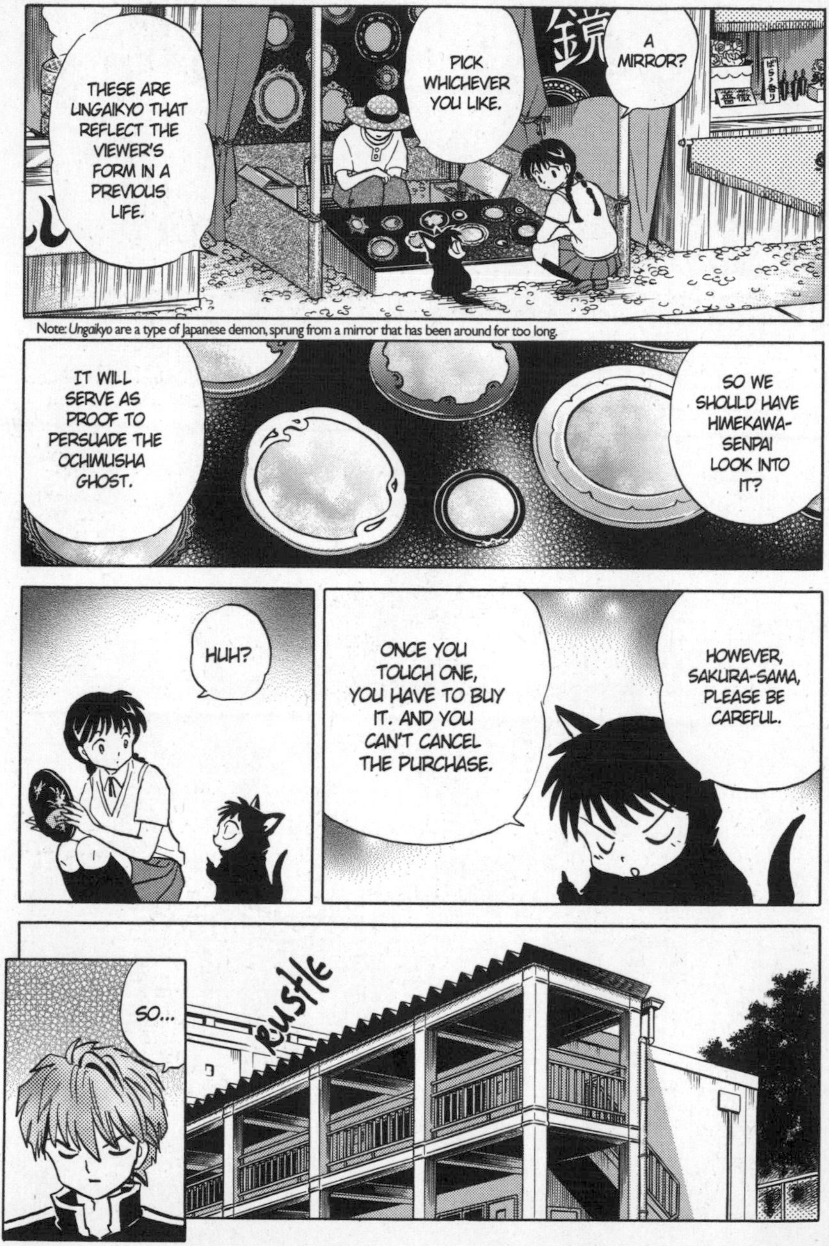

鏡
A MIRROR?
PICK WHICHEVER YOU LIKE.
THESE ARE UNGAIKYO THAT REFLECT THE VIEWER'S FORM IN A PREVIOUS LIFE.
SO WE SHOULD HAVE HIMEKAWA-SENPAI LOOK INTO IT?
IT WILL SERVE AS PROOF TO PERSUADE THE OCHIMUSHA GHOST.
HOWEVER, SAKURA-SAMA, PLEASE BE CAREFUL.
ONCE YOU TOUCH ONE, YOU HAVE TO BUY IT. AND YOU CAN'T CANCEL THE PURCHASE.
HUH?
Rustle
SO...

Note: *Ungaikyo* are a type of Japanese demon, sprung from a mirror that has been around for too long.

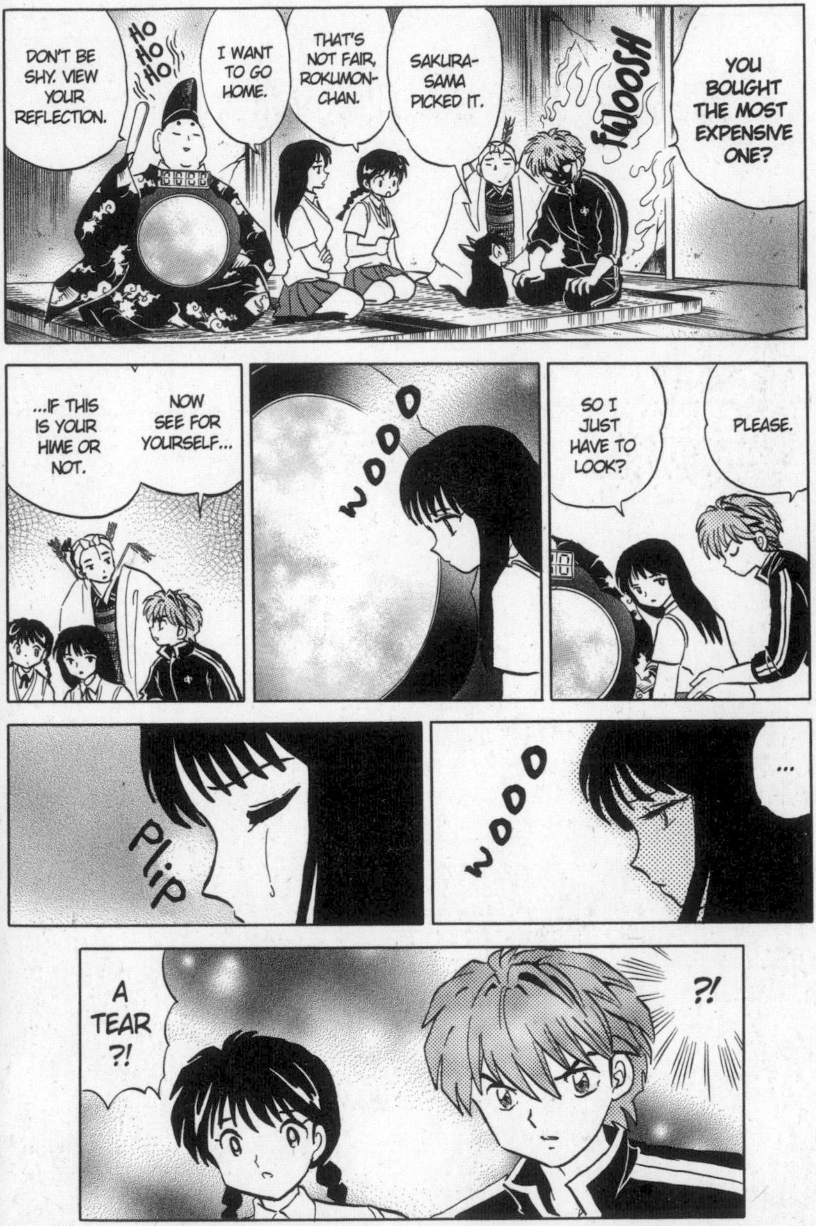
YOU BOUGHT THE MOST EXPENSIVE ONE?
FWOOSH
SAKURA-SAMA PICKED IT.
THAT'S NOT FAIR, ROKUMON-CHAN.
I WANT TO GO HOME.
HO HO HO
DON'T BE SHY. VIEW YOUR REFLECTION.
PLEASE.
SO I JUST HAVE TO LOOK?
WOOD
NOW SEE FOR YOURSELF...
...IF THIS IS YOUR HIME OR NOT.
...
WOOD
Plip
?!
A TEAR ?!

CHAPTER 10: REUNION

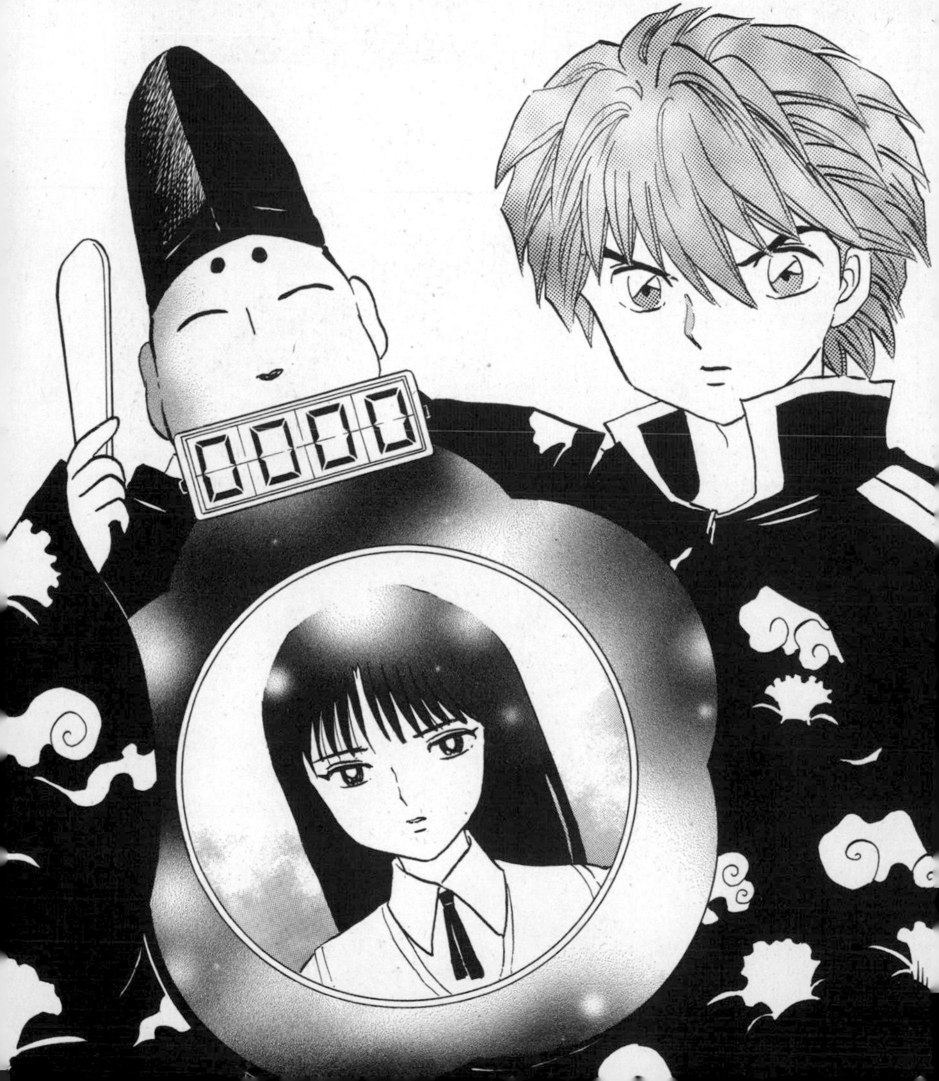
0000

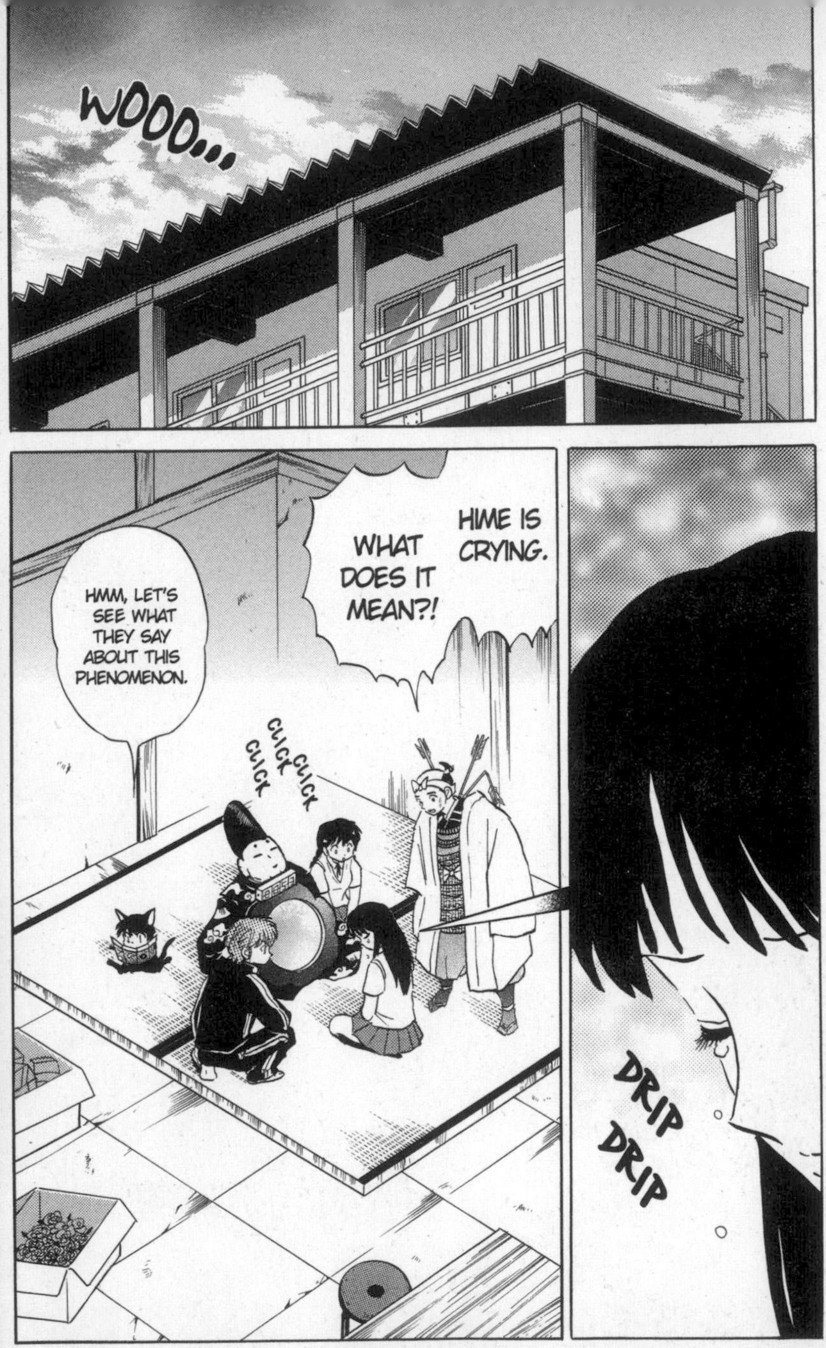
WOOO...
DRIP DRIP
HIME IS CRYING.
WHAT DOES IT MEAN?!
HMM, LET'S SEE WHAT THEY SAY ABOUT THIS PHENOMENON.
CLICK CLICK CLICK

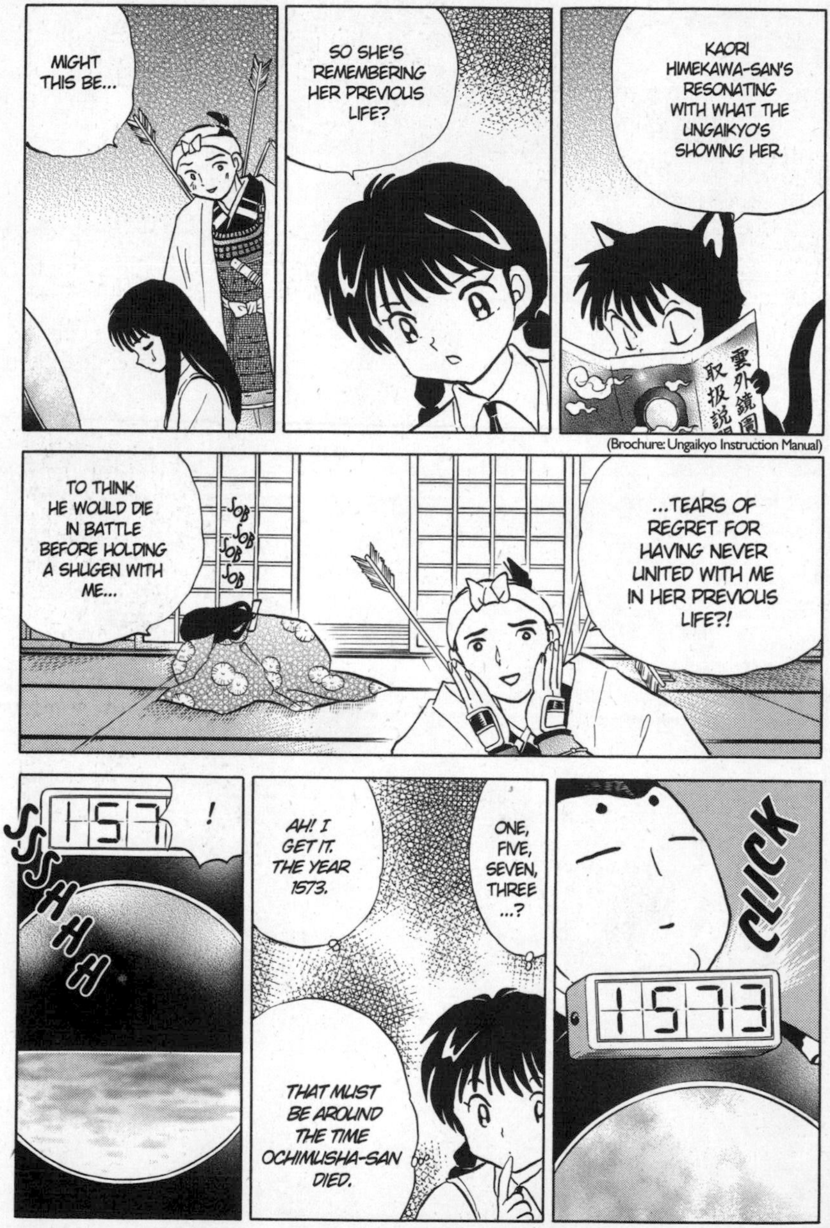
KAORI HIMEKAWA-SAN'S RESONATING WITH WHAT THE UNGAIKYO'S SHOWING HER.
(Brochure: Ungaikyo Instruction Manual)
SO SHE'S REMEMBERING HER PREVIOUS LIFE?
MIGHT THIS BE...
...TEARS OF REGRET FOR HAVING NEVER UNITED WITH ME IN HER PREVIOUS LIFE?!
TO THINK HE WOULD DIE IN BATTLE BEFORE HOLDING A SHUGEN WITH ME...
SOB SOB SOB SOB
CLICK
1573
ONE, FIVE, SEVEN, THREE ...?
AH! I GET IT. THE YEAR 1573.
THAT MUST BE AROUND THE TIME OCHIMUSHA-SAN DIED.
157 !
SSSHHHH

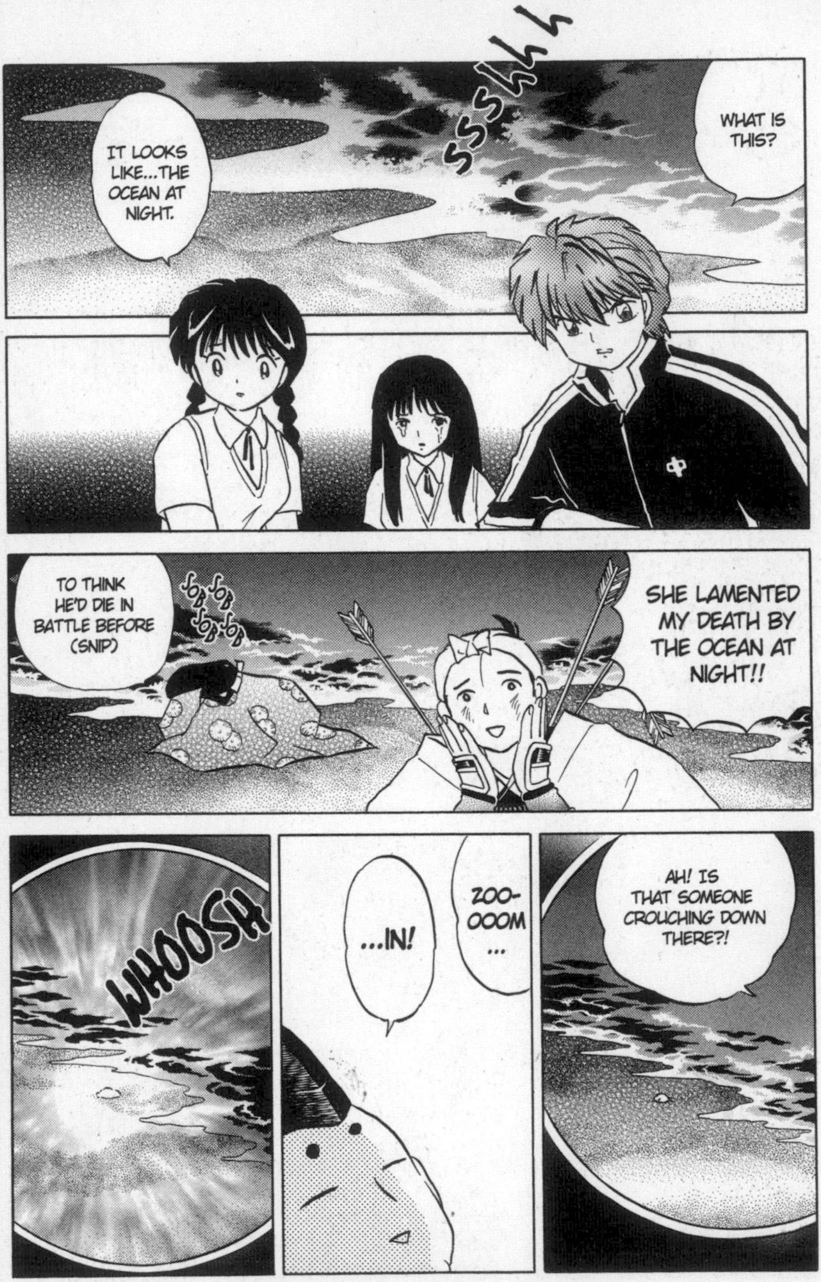
WHAT IS THIS?
IT LOOKS LIKE...THE OCEAN AT NIGHT.
SHE LAMENTED MY DEATH BY THE OCEAN AT NIGHT!!
SOB SOB SOB SOB
TO THINK HE'D DIE IN BATTLE BEFORE (SNIP)
AH! IS THAT SOMEONE CROUCHING DOWN THERE?!
ZOO-OOOM ...
...IN!
WHOOSH

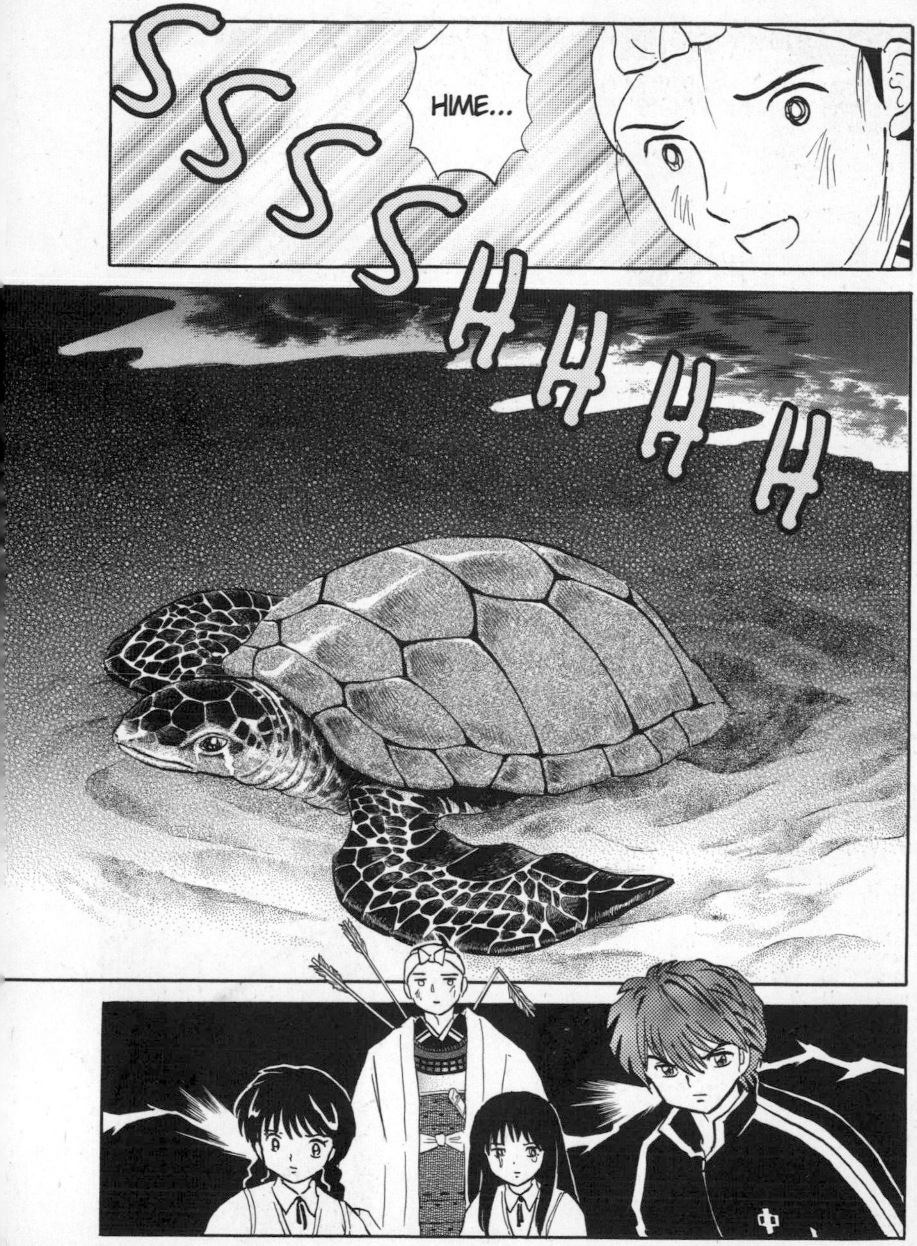
HIME...
SSSSHHHHH

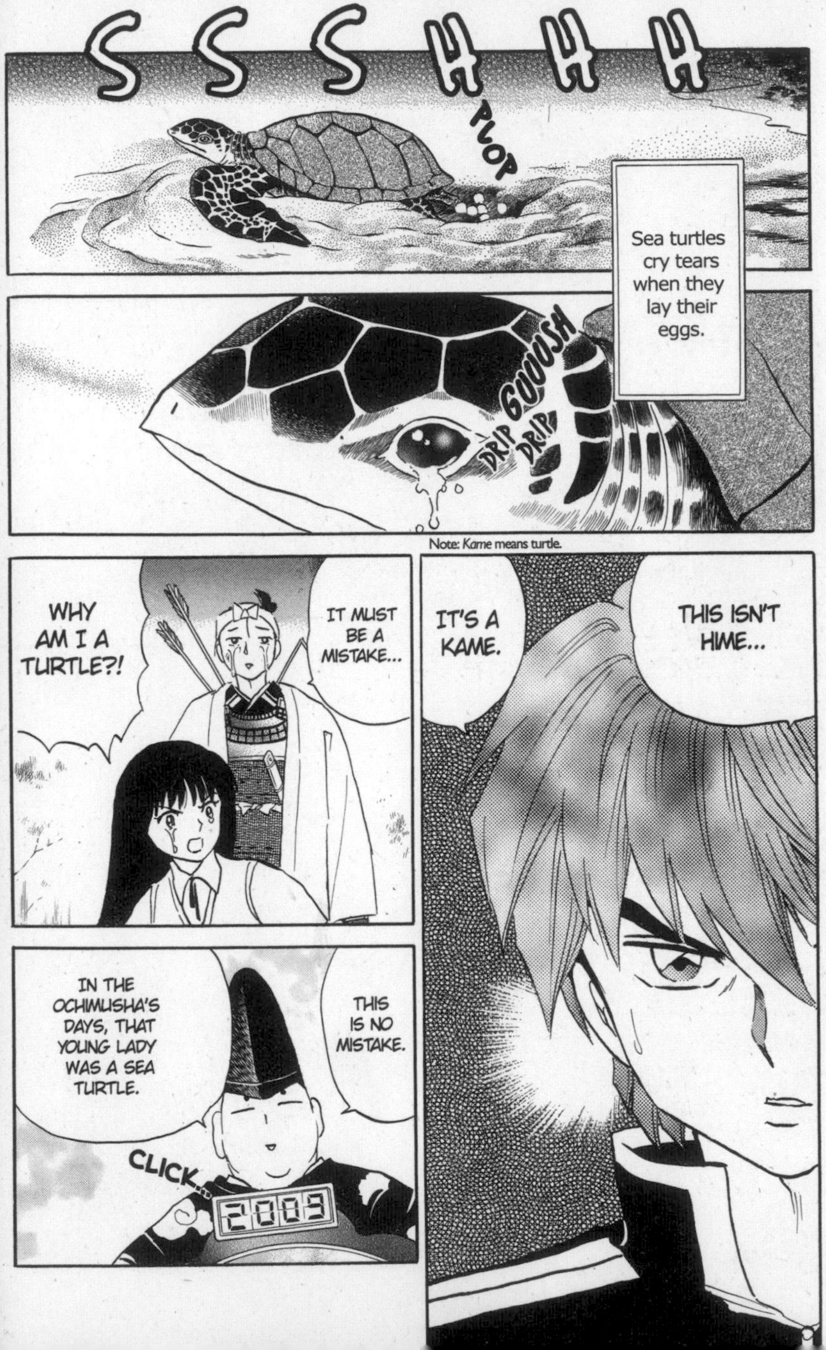
SSSHHH
PLOP
Sea turtles cry tears when they lay their eggs.
GOUUSH
DRIP DRIP
THIS ISN'T HIME...
IT'S A KAME.
IT MUST BE A MISTAKE...
WHY AM I A TURTLE?!
THIS IS NO MISTAKE.
IN THE OCHIMUSHA'S DAYS, THAT YOUNG LADY WAS A SEA TURTLE.
CLICK...
2003

Note: *Kame* means turtle.

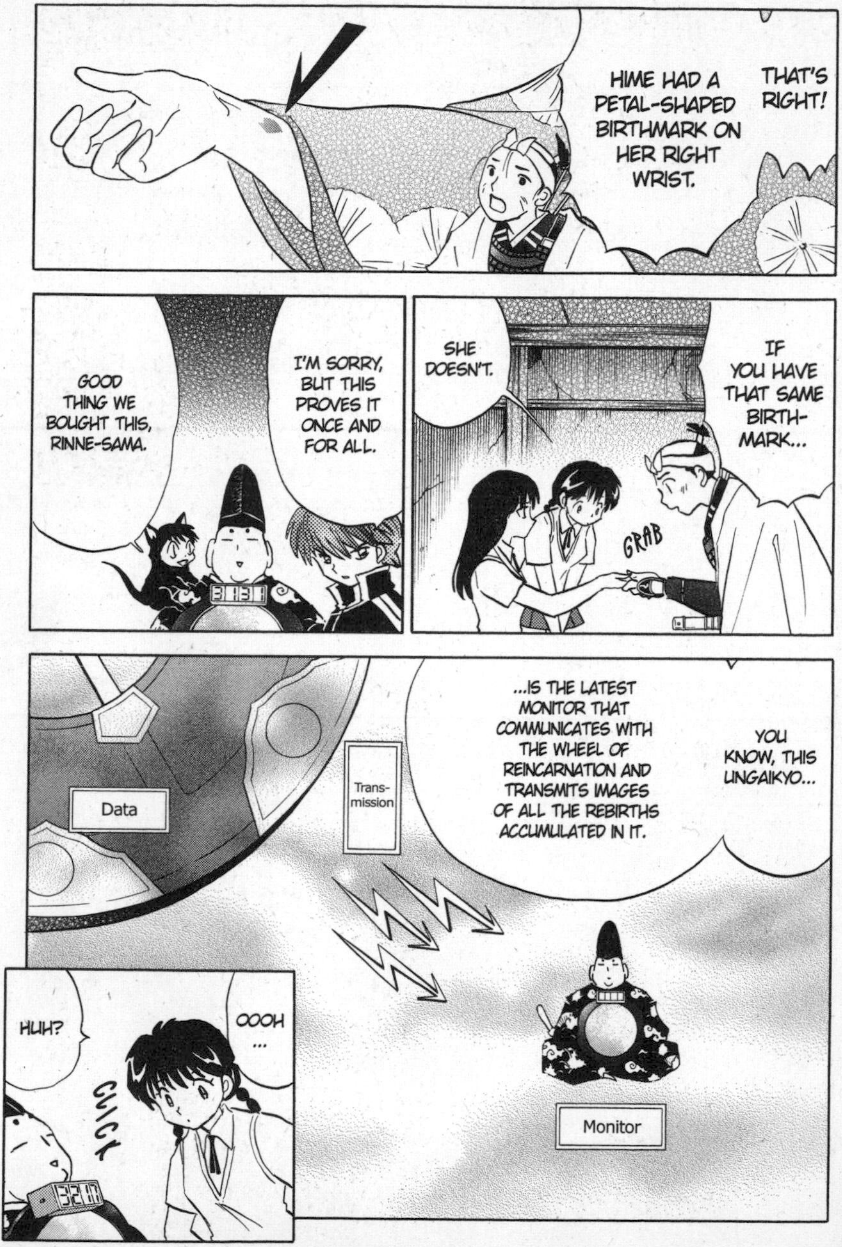
THAT'S RIGHT!
HIME HAD A PETAL-SHAPED BIRTHMARK ON HER RIGHT WRIST.
IF YOU HAVE THAT SAME BIRTH-MARK...
SHE DOESN'T.
GRAB
I'M SORRY, BUT THIS PROVES IT ONCE AND FOR ALL.
GOOD THING WE BOUGHT THIS, RINNE-SAMA.
YOU KNOW, THIS UNGAIKYO...
...IS THE LATEST MONITOR THAT COMMUNICATES WITH THE WHEEL OF REINCARNATION AND TRANSMITS IMAGES OF ALL THE REBIRTHS ACCUMULATED IN IT.
Transmission
Data
Monitor
OOOH ...
HUH?
CLICK

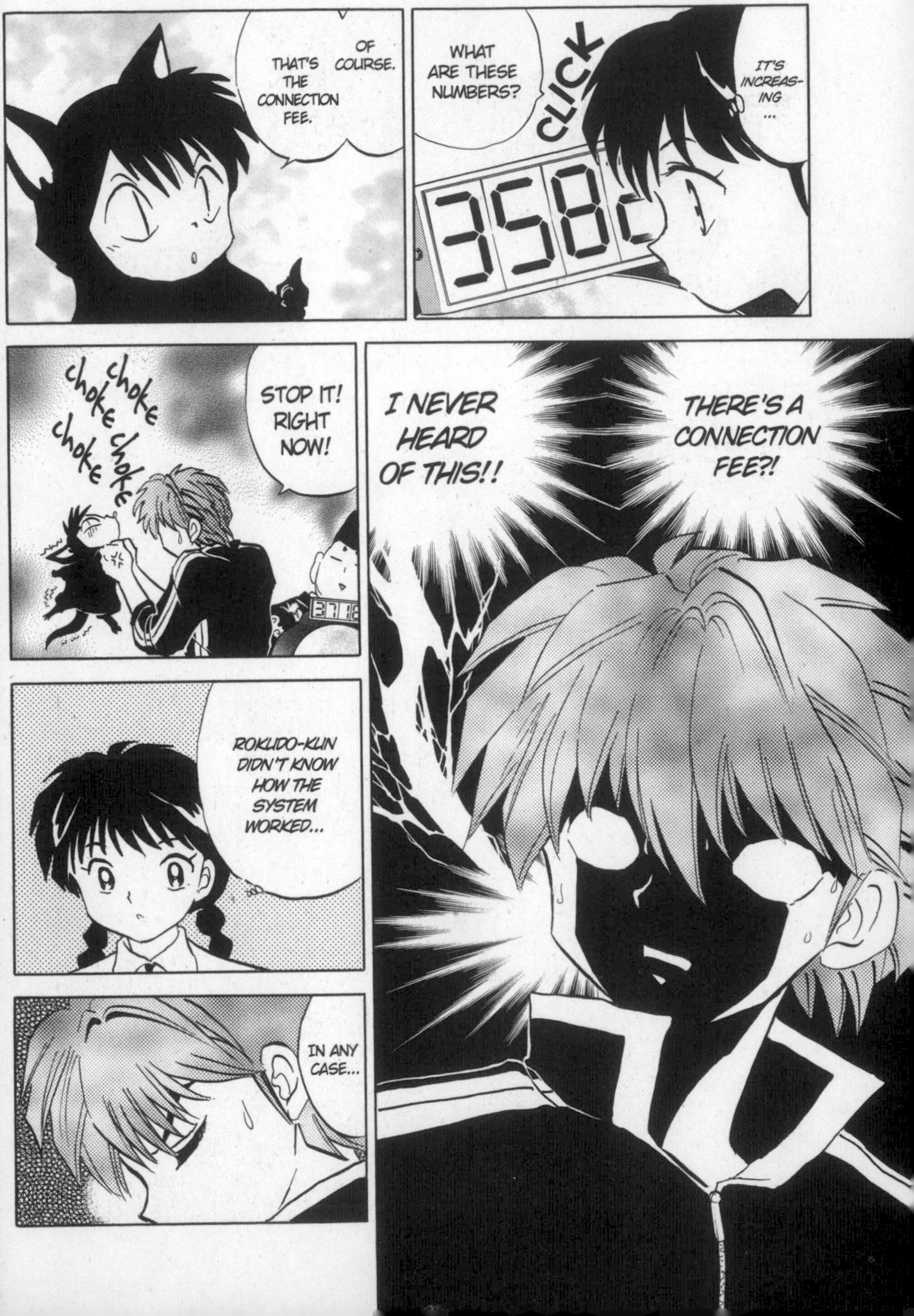
IT'S INCREASING...
CLICK
WHAT ARE THESE NUMBERS?
358
OF COURSE. THAT'S THE CONNECTION FEE.
THERE'S A CONNECTION FEE?!
I NEVER HEARD OF THIS!!
STOP IT! RIGHT NOW!
choke choke choke choke
ROKUDO-KUN DIDN'T KNOW HOW THE SYSTEM WORKED...
IN ANY CASE...

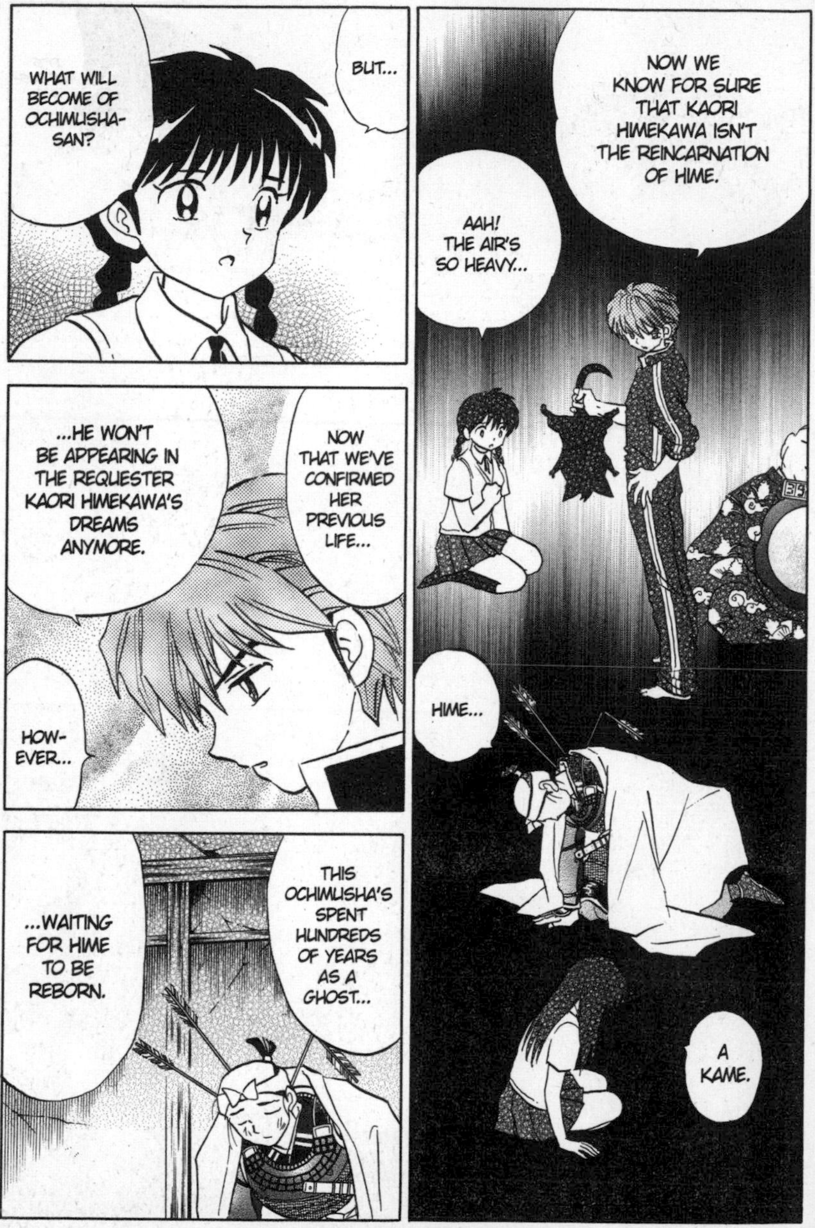
NOW WE KNOW FOR SURE THAT KAORI HIMEKAWA ISN'T THE REINCARNATION OF HIME.
AAH! THE AIR'S SO HEAVY...
HIME...
A KAME.
BUT...
WHAT WILL BECOME OF OCHIMUSHA-SAN?
NOW THAT WE'VE CONFIRMED HER PREVIOUS LIFE...
...HE WON'T BE APPEARING IN THE REQUESTER KAORI HIMEKAWA'S DREAMS ANYMORE.
HOW-EVER...
THIS OCHIMUSHA'S SPENT HUNDREDS OF YEARS AS A GHOST...
...WAITING FOR HIME TO BE REBORN.

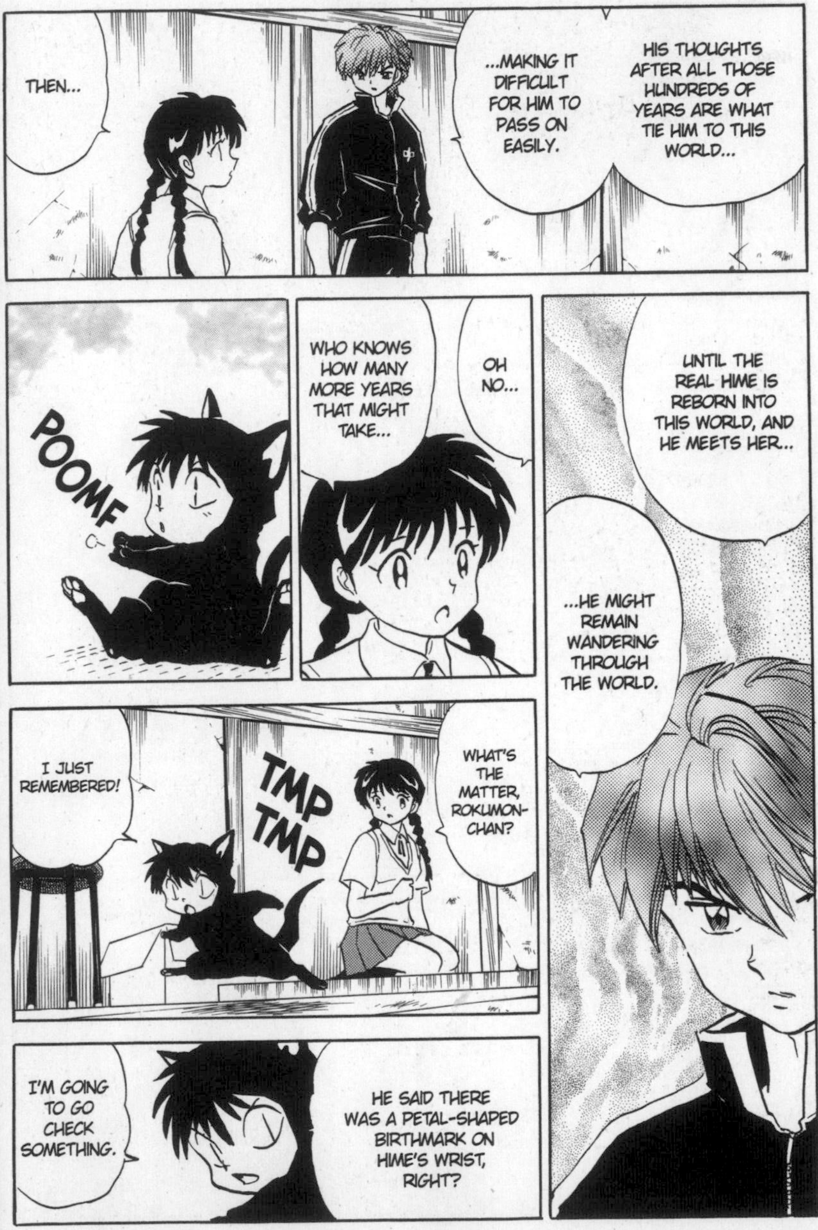
HIS THOUGHTS AFTER ALL THOSE HUNDREDS OF YEARS ARE WHAT TIE HIM TO THIS WORLD...
...MAKING IT DIFFICULT FOR HIM TO PASS ON EASILY.
THEN...
UNTIL THE REAL HIME IS REBORN INTO THIS WORLD, AND HE MEETS HER...
...HE MIGHT REMAIN WANDERING THROUGH THE WORLD.
OH NO...
WHO KNOWS HOW MANY MORE YEARS THAT MIGHT TAKE...
POOMF
WHAT'S THE MATTER, ROKUMON-CHAN?
TMP TMP
I JUST REMEMBERED!
HE SAID THERE WAS A PETAL-SHAPED BIRTHMARK ON HIME'S WRIST, RIGHT?
I'M GOING TO GO CHECK SOMETHING.

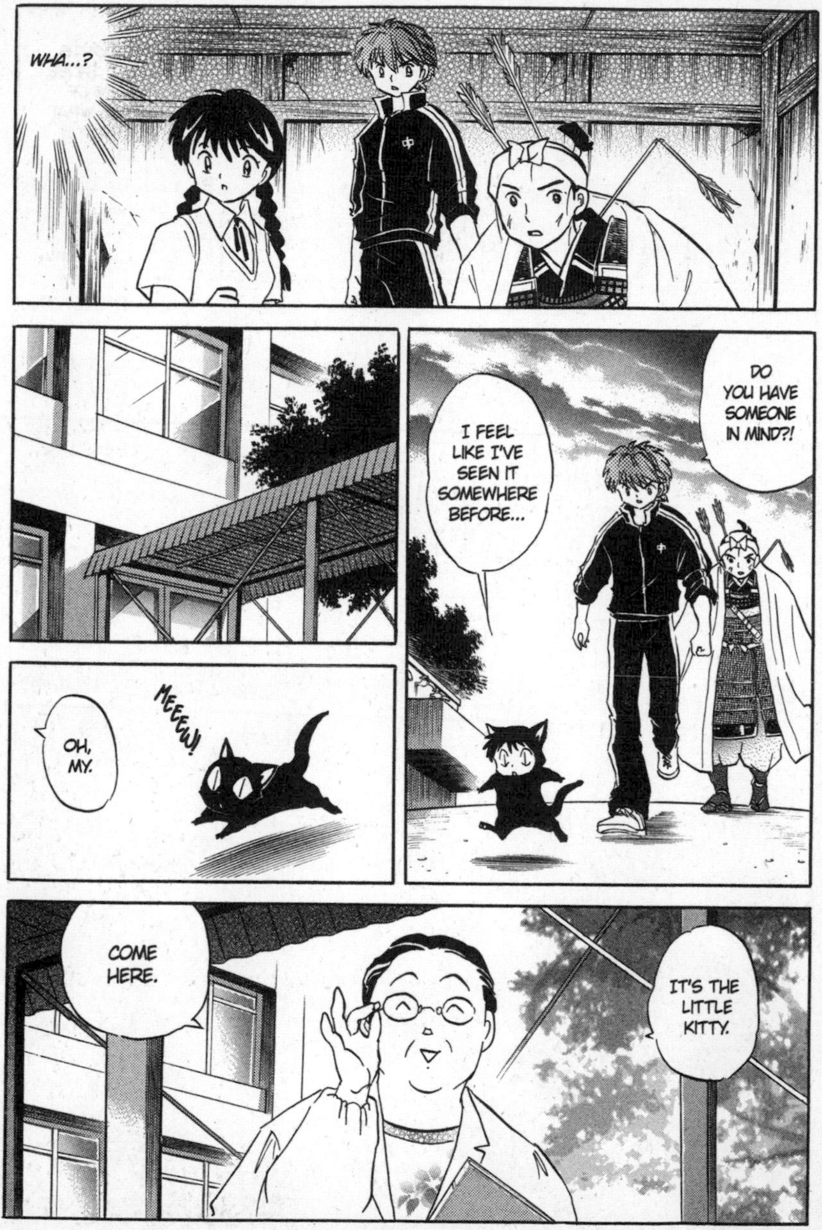
WHA...?
DO YOU HAVE SOMEONE IN MIND?!
I FEEL LIKE I'VE SEEN IT SOMEWHERE BEFORE...
MEEEW!
OH, MY.
IT'S THE LITTLE KITTY.
COME HERE.

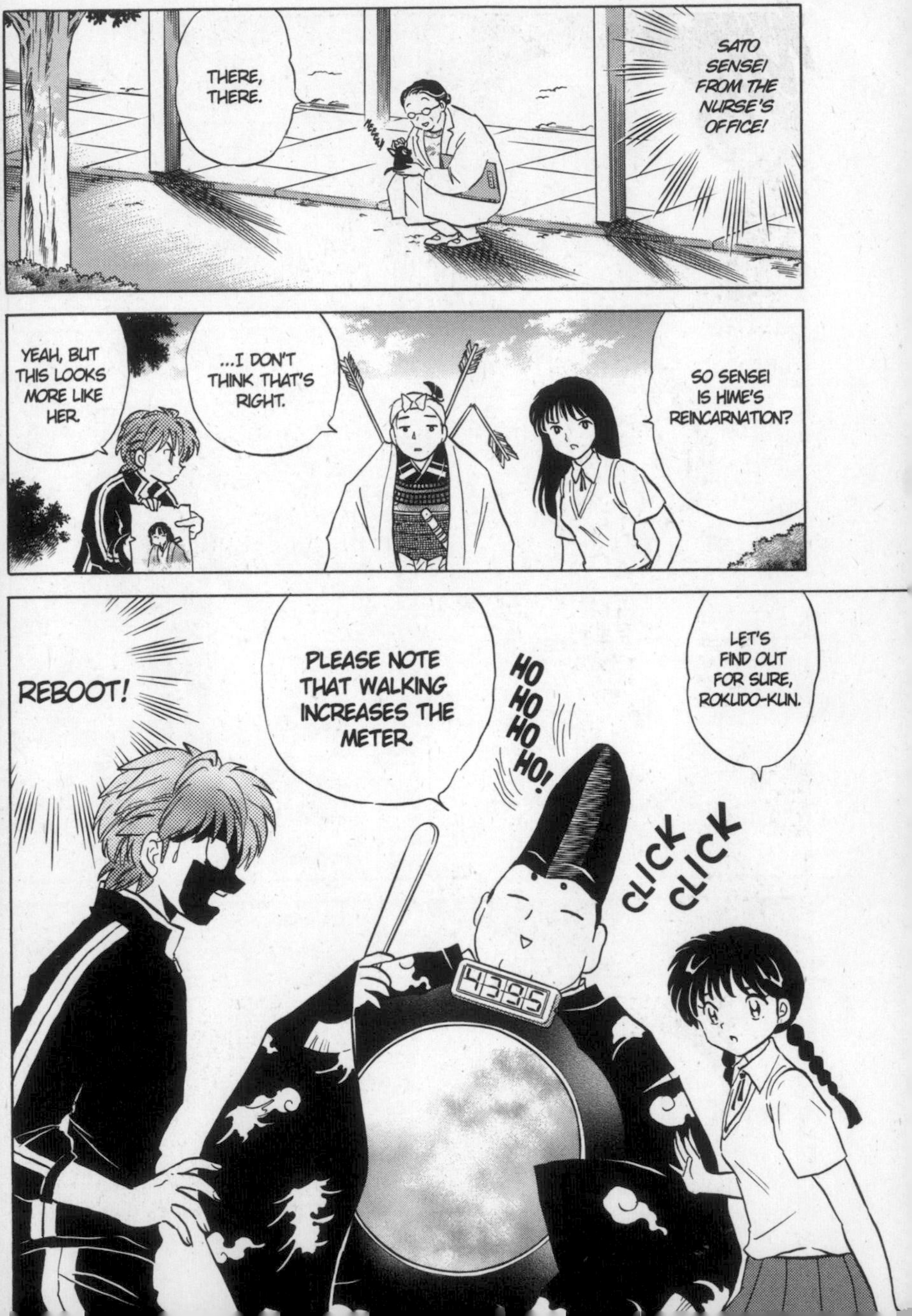
SATO SENSEI FROM THE NURSE'S OFFICE!
THERE, THERE.
SO SENSEI IS HIME'S REINCARNATION?
...I DON'T THINK THAT'S RIGHT.
YEAH, BUT THIS LOOKS MORE LIKE HER.
LET'S FIND OUT FOR SURE, ROKUDO-KUN.
CLICK CLICK
HO HO HO HO HO!
PLEASE NOTE THAT WALKING INCREASES THE METER.
REBOOT!

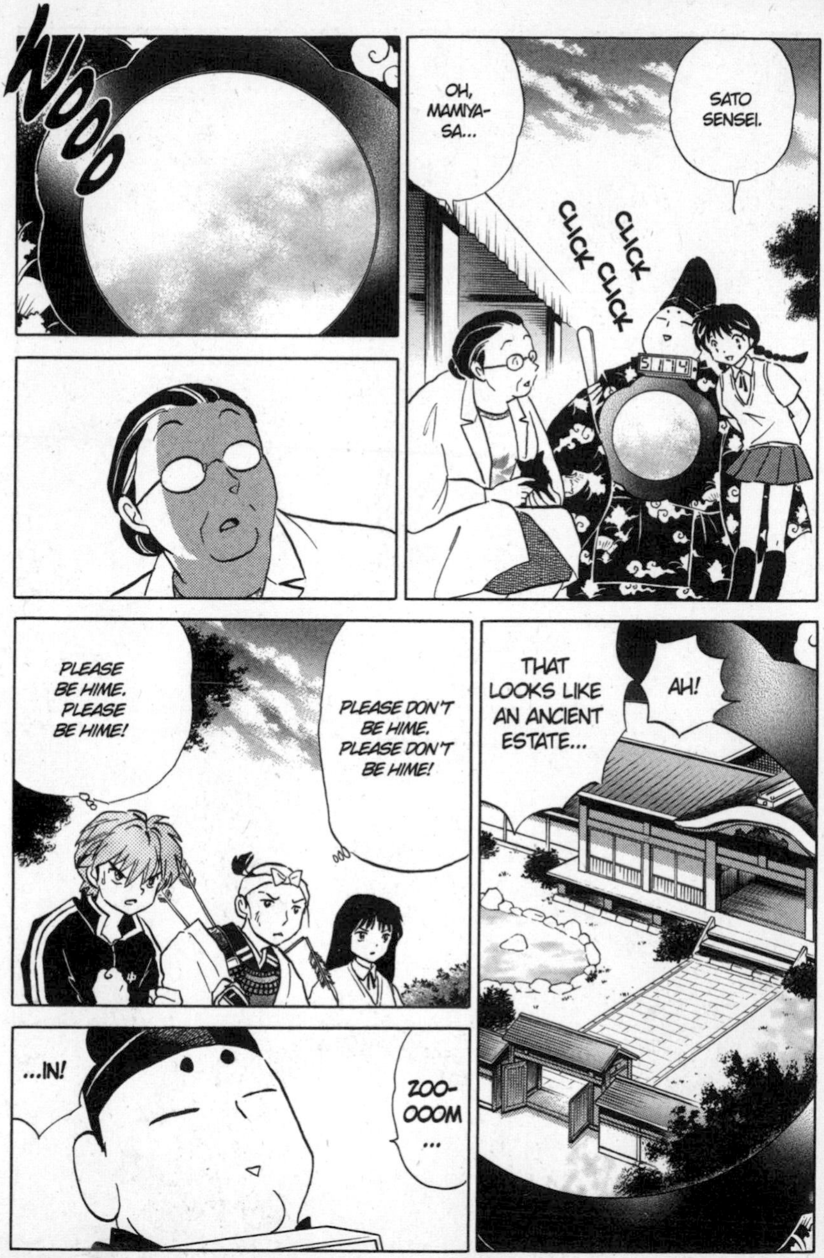
SATO SENSEI.
OH, MAMIYA-SA...
CLICK CLICK
CLICK
WOOO
AH!
THAT LOOKS LIKE AN ANCIENT ESTATE...
PLEASE DON'T BE HIME. PLEASE DON'T BE HIME!
PLEASE BE HIME. PLEASE BE HIME!
ZOO-OOOM ...
...IN!

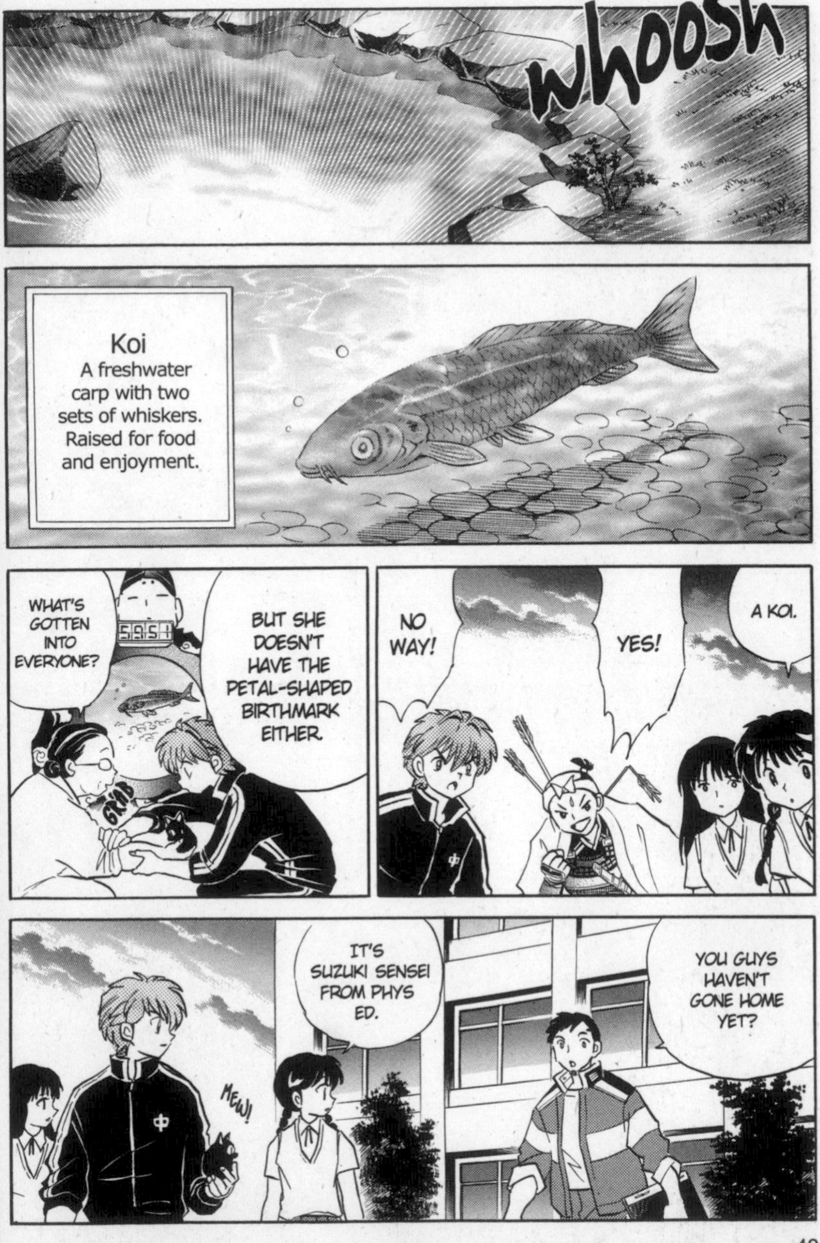
whoosh
Koi
A freshwater carp with two sets of whiskers. Raised for food and enjoyment.
A KOI.
YES!
NO WAY!
BUT SHE DOESN'T HAVE THE PETAL-SHAPED BIRTHMARK EITHER.
WHAT'S GOTTEN INTO EVERYONE?
GRAB
YOU GUYS HAVEN'T GONE HOME YET?
IT'S SUZUKI SENSEI FROM PHYS ED.
MEW!

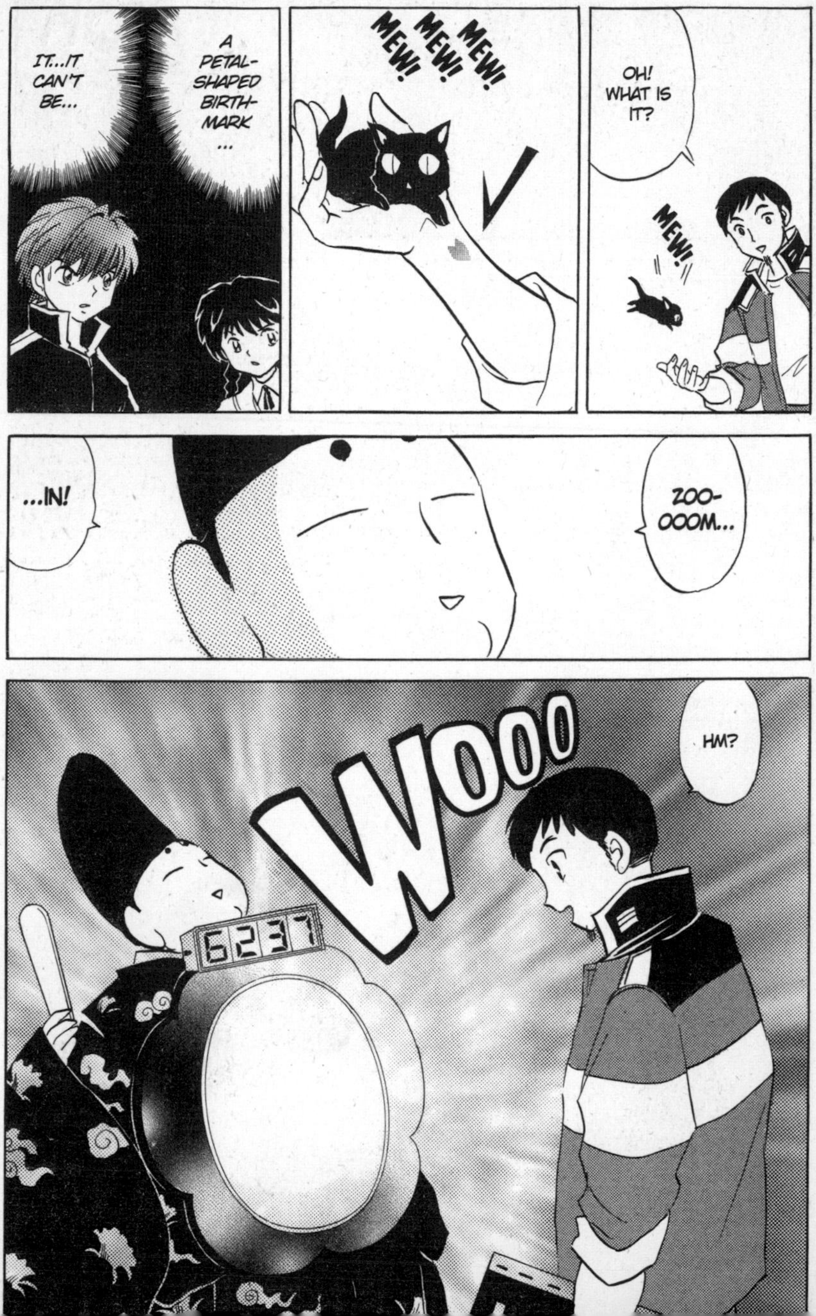
OH! WHAT IS IT?
MEW!
MEW! MEW! MEW!
A PETAL-SHAPED BIRTH-MARK ...
IT...IT CAN'T BE...
ZOO-OOOM...
...IN!
HM?
WOOO
6237

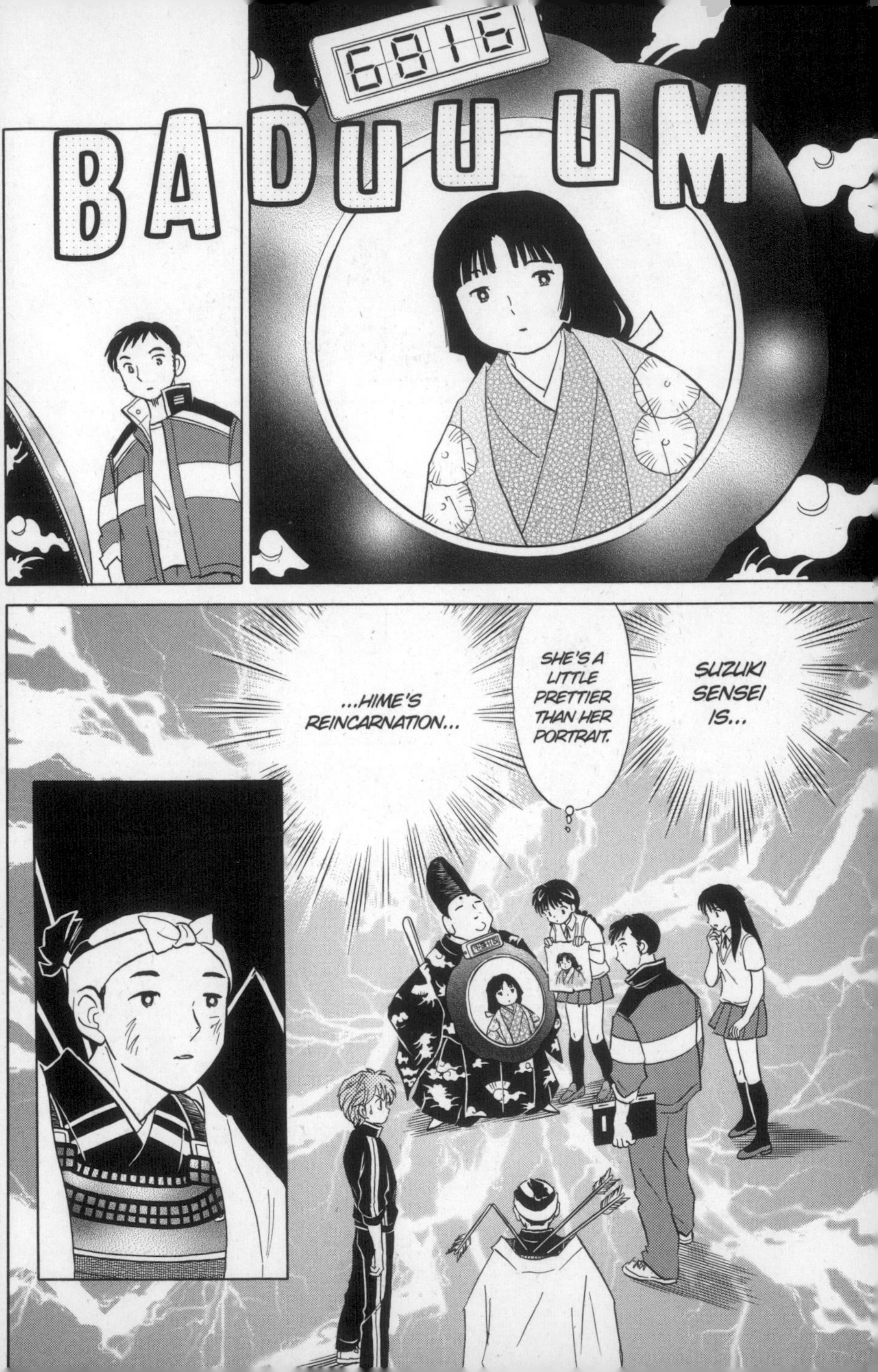
6816
BADUUUM
SUZUKI SENSEI IS...
SHE'S A LITTLE PRETTIER THAN HER PORTRAIT.
...HIME'S REINCARNATION...

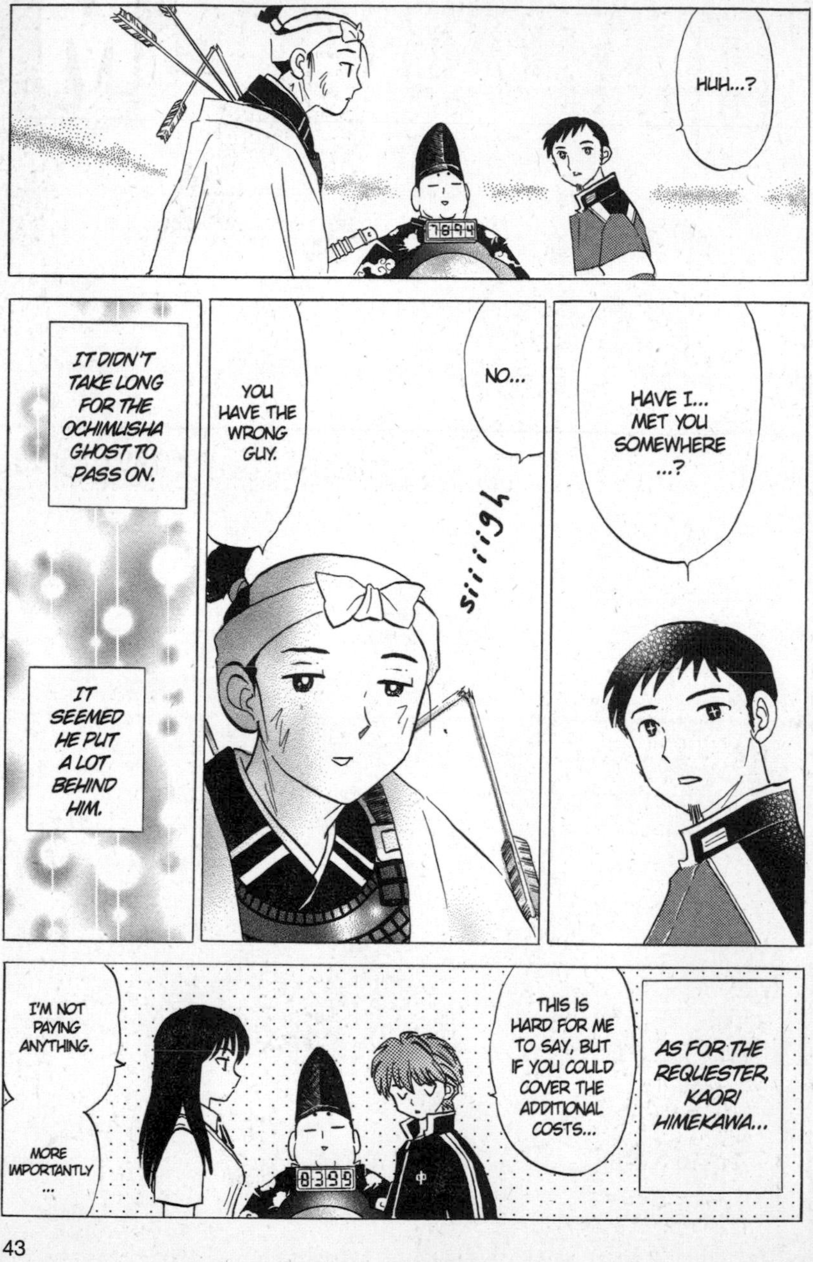
HUH...?
HAVE I... MET YOU SOMEWHERE ...?
NO...
YOU HAVE THE WRONG GUY.
siiiiigh
IT DIDN'T TAKE LONG FOR THE OCHIMUSHA GHOST TO PASS ON.
IT SEEMED HE PUT A LOT BEHIND HIM.
AS FOR THE REQUESTER, KAORI HIMEKAWA...
THIS IS HARD FOR ME TO SAY, BUT IF YOU COULD COVER THE ADDITIONAL COSTS...
I'M NOT PAYING ANYTHING.
MORE IMPORTANTLY ...

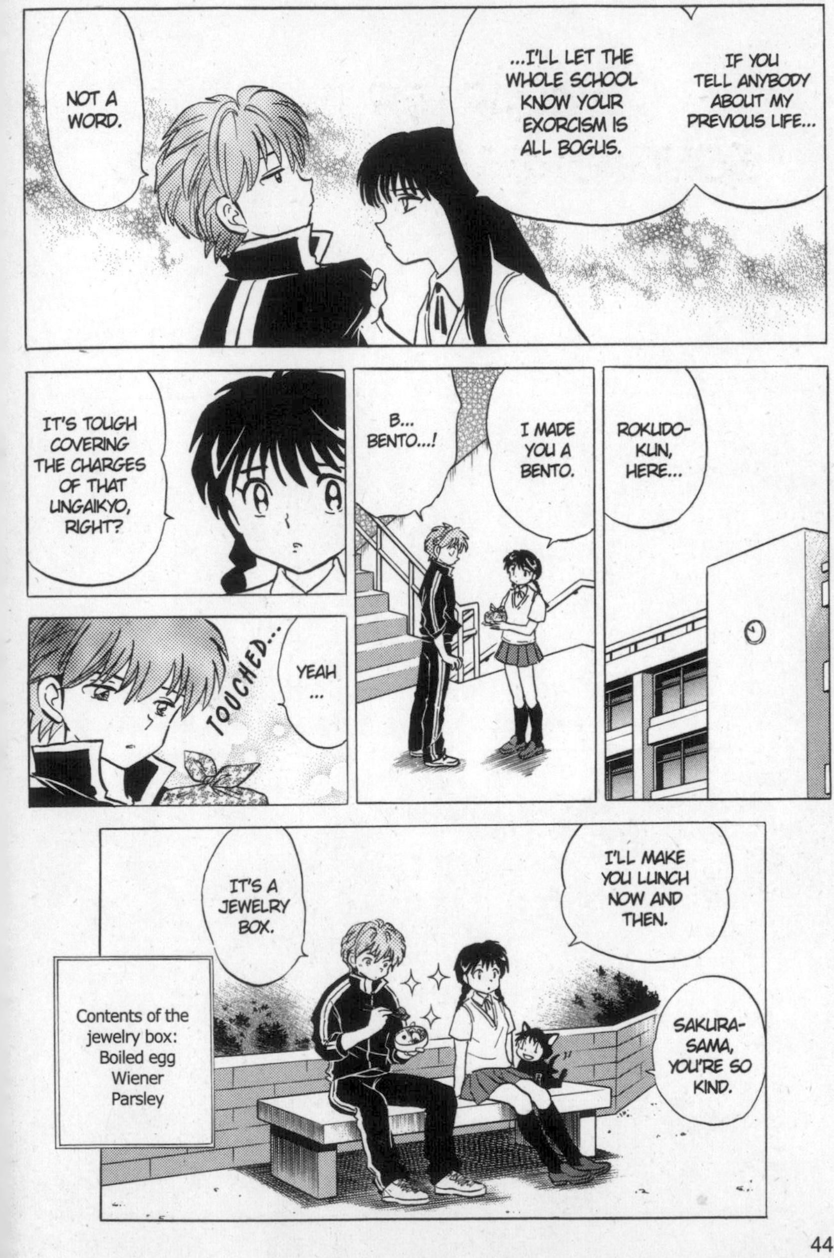
IF YOU TELL ANYBODY ABOUT MY PREVIOUS LIFE...
...I'LL LET THE WHOLE SCHOOL KNOW YOUR EXORCISM IS ALL BOGUS.
NOT A WORD.
ROKUDO-KUN, HERE...
I MADE YOU A BENTO.
B... BENTO...!
IT'S TOUGH COVERING THE CHARGES OF THAT UNGAIKYO, RIGHT?
YEAH ...
TOUCHED...
I'LL MAKE YOU LUNCH NOW AND THEN.
SAKURA-SAMA, YOU'RE SO KIND.
IT'S A JEWELRY BOX.
Contents of the jewelry box: Boiled egg Wiener Parsley

CHAPTER 11: SONGSTRESS OF THE POOL

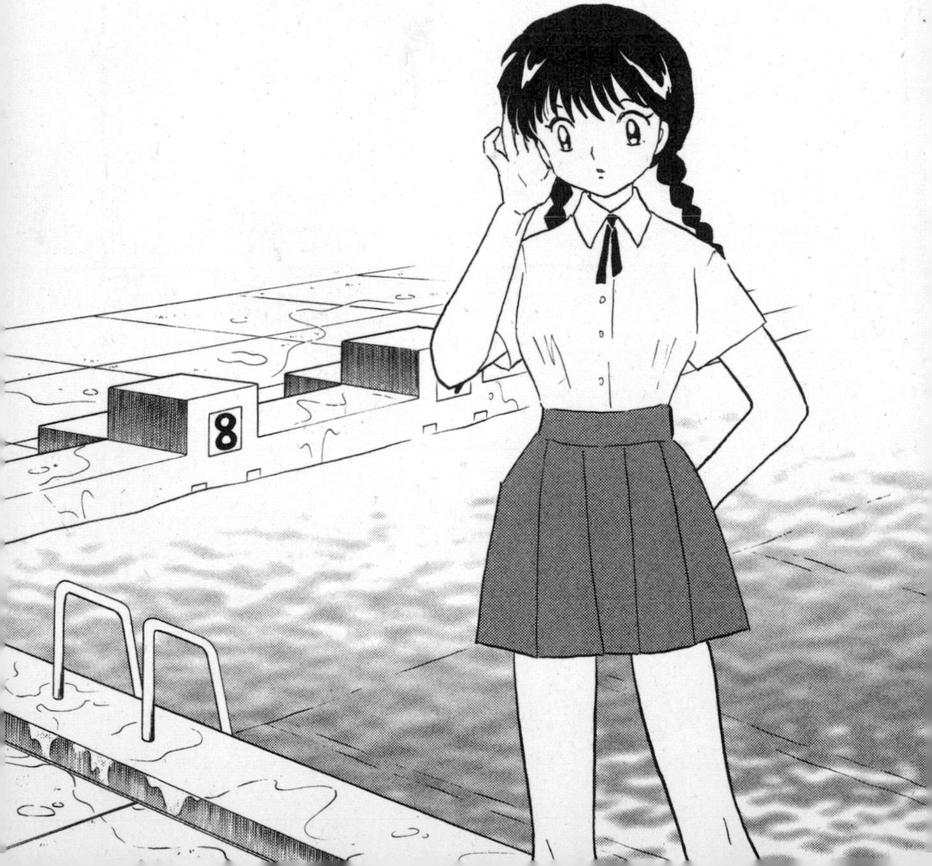
8

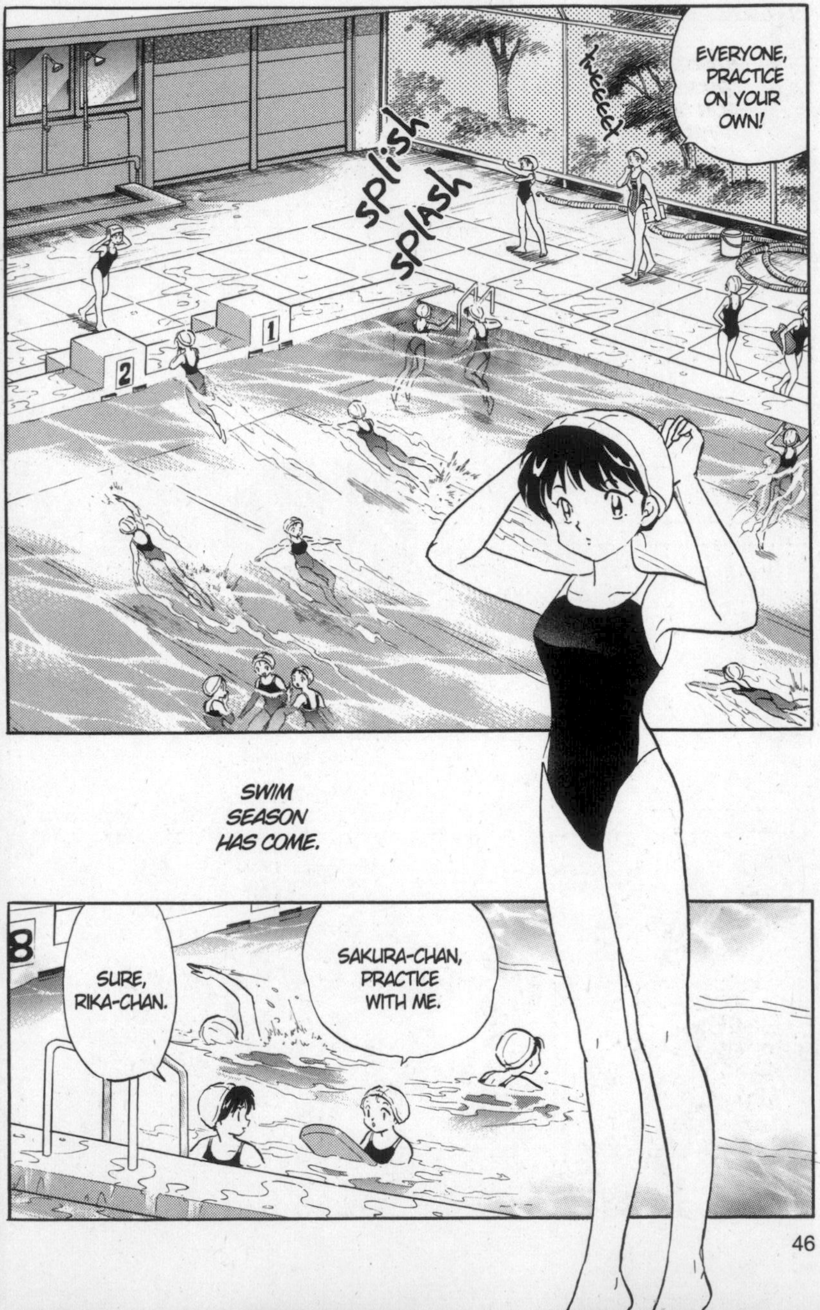
EVERYONE, PRACTICE ON YOUR OWN!
tweeeet
splish splash
SWIM SEASON HAS COME.
SAKURA-CHAN, PRACTICE WITH ME.
SURE, RIKA-CHAN.

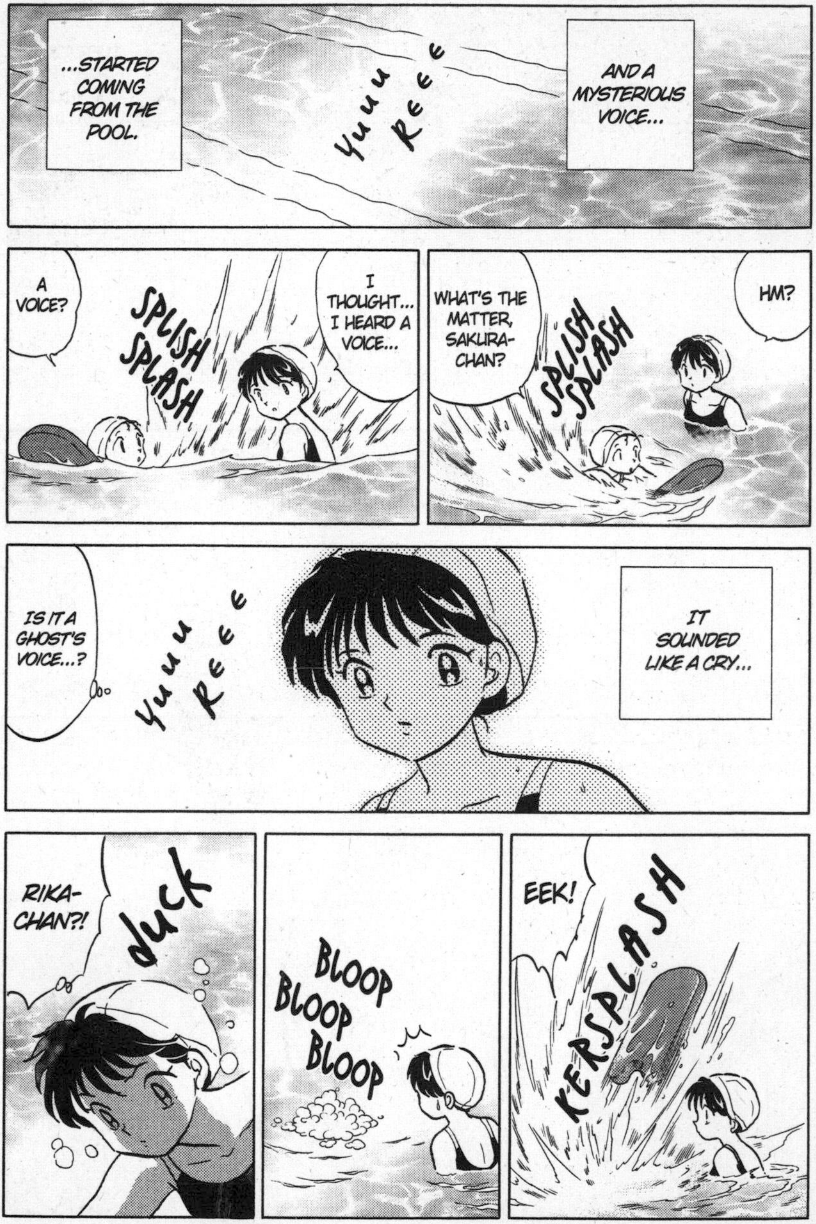
AND A MYSTERIOUS VOICE...
Yuuu Reeee
...STARTED COMING FROM THE POOL.
HM?
SPLISH SPLASH
WHAT'S THE MATTER, SAKURA-CHAN?
I THOUGHT... I HEARD A VOICE...
SPLISH SPLASH
A VOICE?
IT SOUNDED LIKE A CRY...
Yuuu Reeee
IS IT A GHOST'S VOICE...?
EEK!
KERSPLASH
BLOOP BLOOP BLOOP
duck
RIKA-CHAN?!

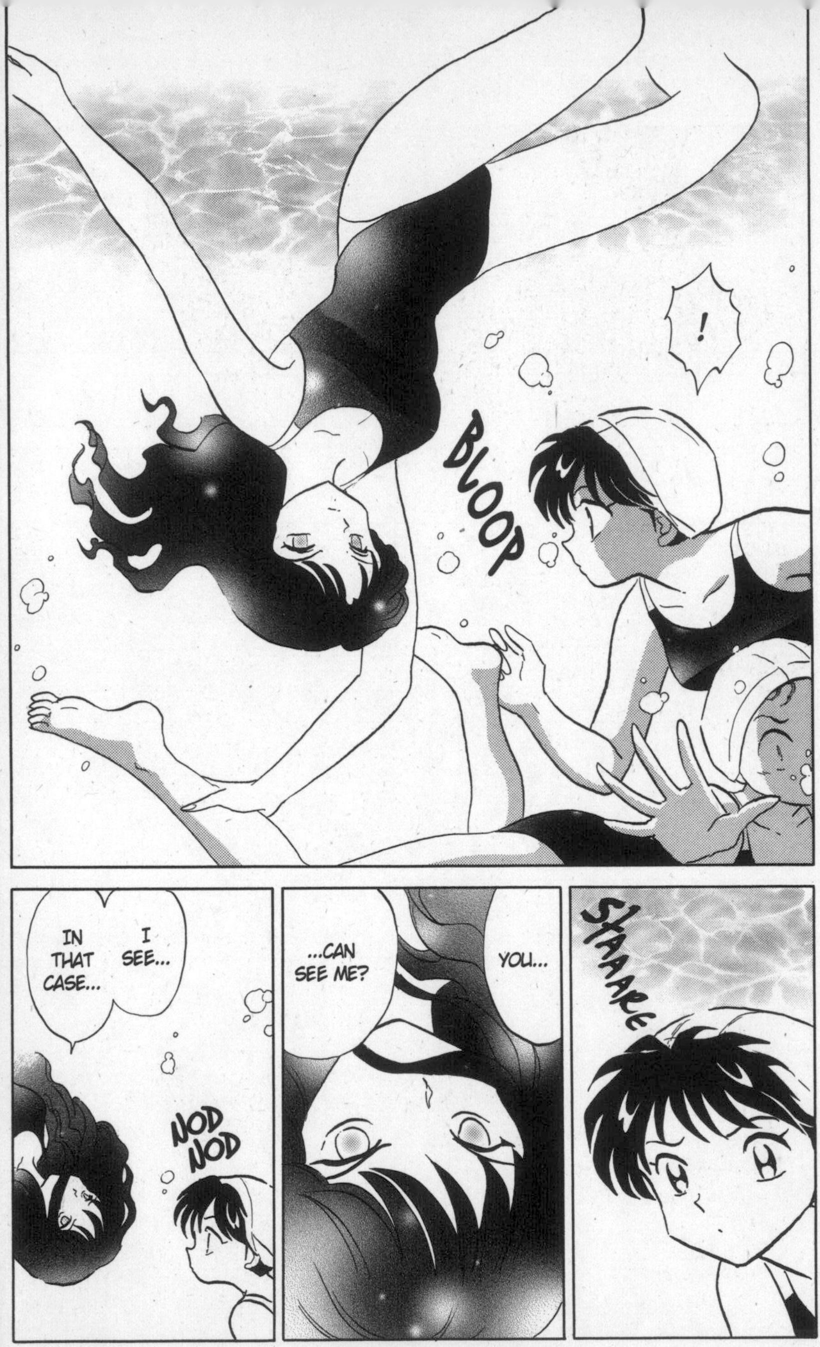
!
BLOOP
STAAAARE
YOU...
...CAN SEE ME?
I SEE... IN THAT CASE...
NOD NOD

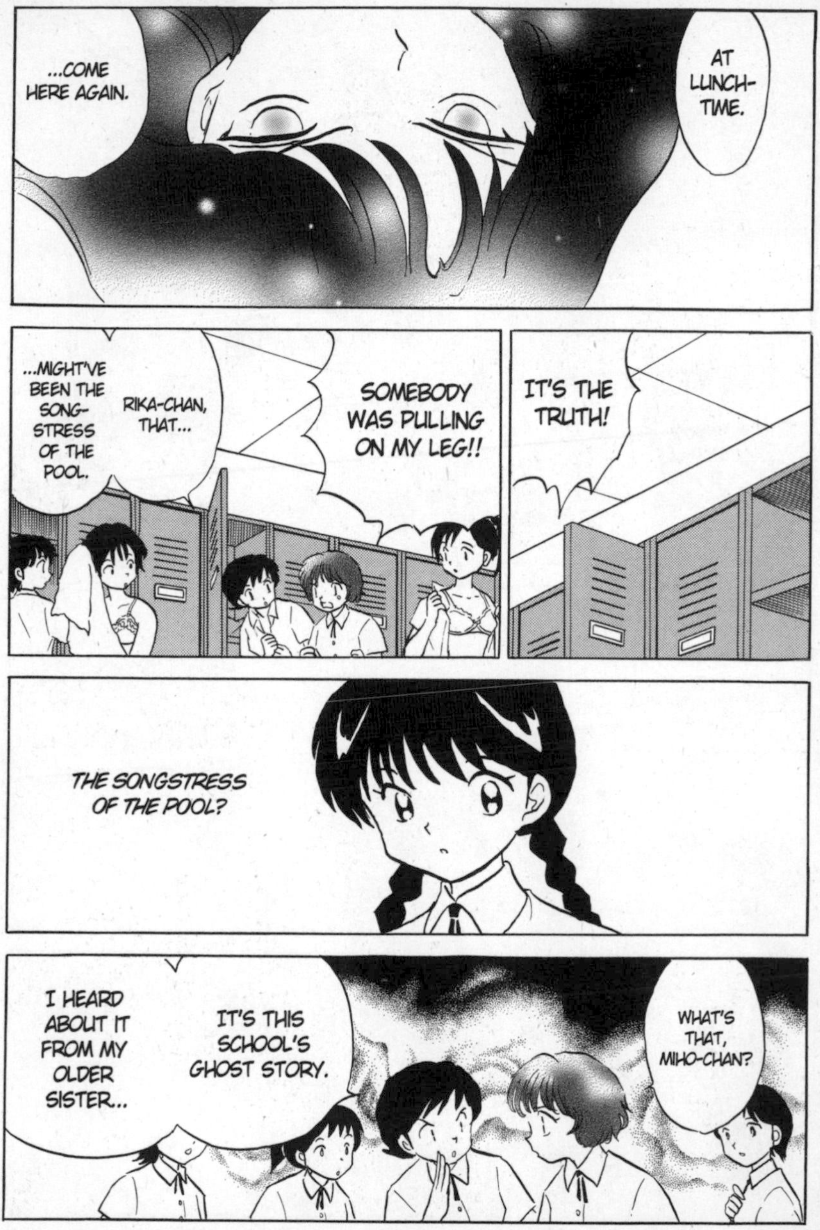
AT LUNCH-TIME.
...COME HERE AGAIN.
IT'S THE TRUTH!
SOMEBODY WAS PULLING ON MY LEG!!
RIKA-CHAN, THAT...
...MIGHT'VE BEEN THE SONG-STRESS OF THE POOL.
THE SONGSTRESS OF THE POOL?
WHAT'S THAT, MIHO-CHAN?
IT'S THIS SCHOOL'S GHOST STORY.
I HEARD ABOUT IT FROM MY OLDER SISTER...

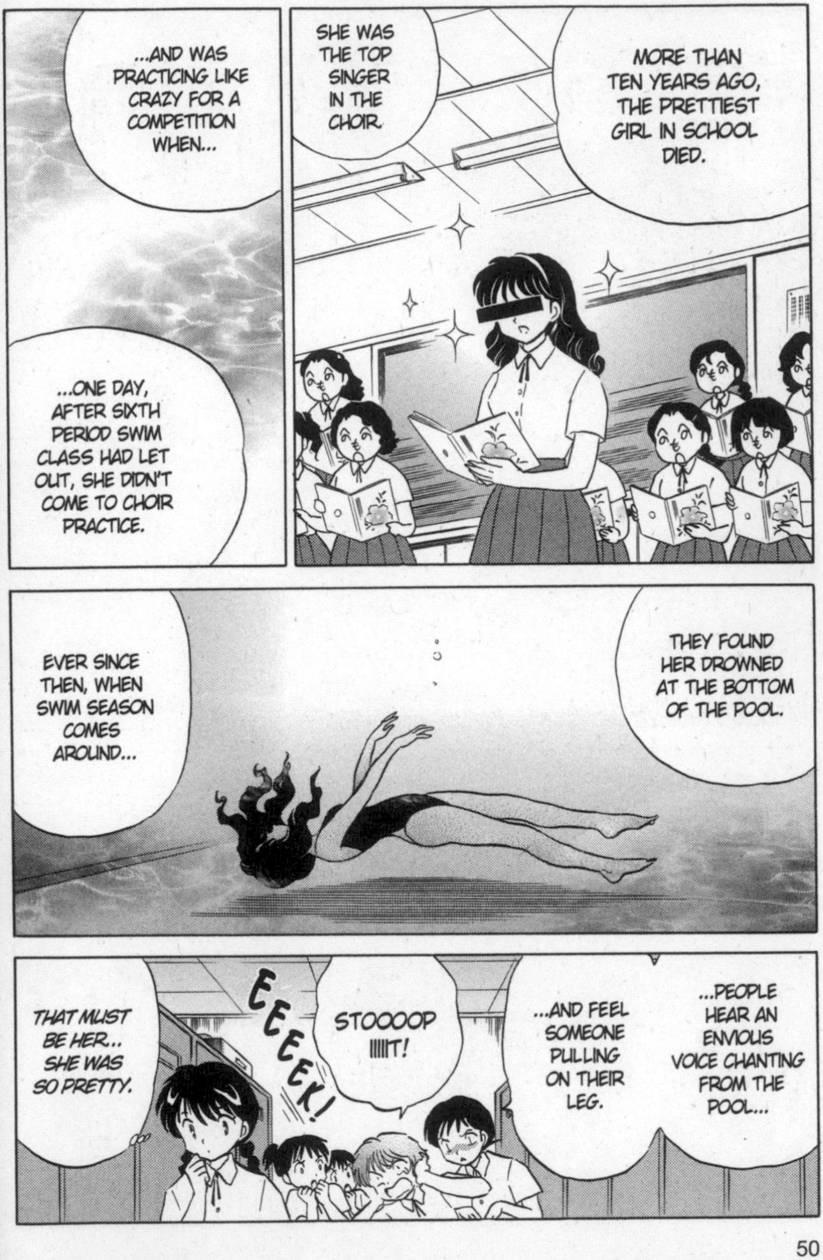
MORE THAN TEN YEARS AGO, THE PRETTIEST GIRL IN SCHOOL DIED.
SHE WAS THE TOP SINGER IN THE CHOIR.
...AND WAS PRACTICING LIKE CRAZY FOR A COMPETITION WHEN...
...ONE DAY, AFTER SIXTH PERIOD SWIM CLASS HAD LET OUT, SHE DIDN'T COME TO CHOIR PRACTICE.
THEY FOUND HER DROWNED AT THE BOTTOM OF THE POOL.
EVER SINCE THEN, WHEN SWIM SEASON COMES AROUND...
...PEOPLE HEAR AN ENVIOUS VOICE CHANTING FROM THE POOL...
...AND FEEL SOMEONE PULLING ON THEIR LEG.
STOOOOP IIIIIT!
EEEEEK!
THAT MUST BE HER... SHE WAS SO PRETTY.

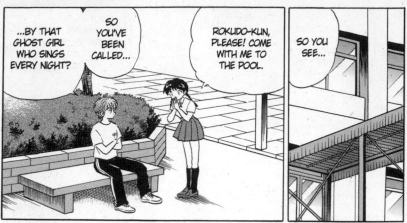

SO YOU SEE...
ROKUDO-KUN, PLEASE! COME WITH ME TO THE POOL.
SO YOU'VE BEEN CALLED...
...BY THAT GHOST GIRL WHO SINGS EVERY NIGHT?
YOU KNOW HER?
NO, BUT I CAN HEAR HER.
AND...
...THERE WAS A REQUEST FROM RIKA IN THE WEATHER HUTCH.
GETTING PULLED DOWN BY THE LEG REALLY FREAKED HER OUT. AND THAT STINGY RIKA...
...ACTUALLY GAVE ME AN OFFERING OF 300 YEN!
HMPH.
CRUSH
THAT SHOULD DO IT.

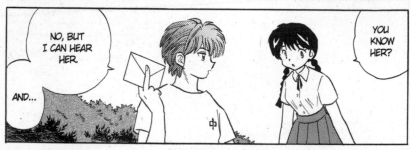

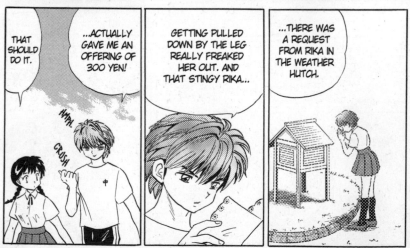

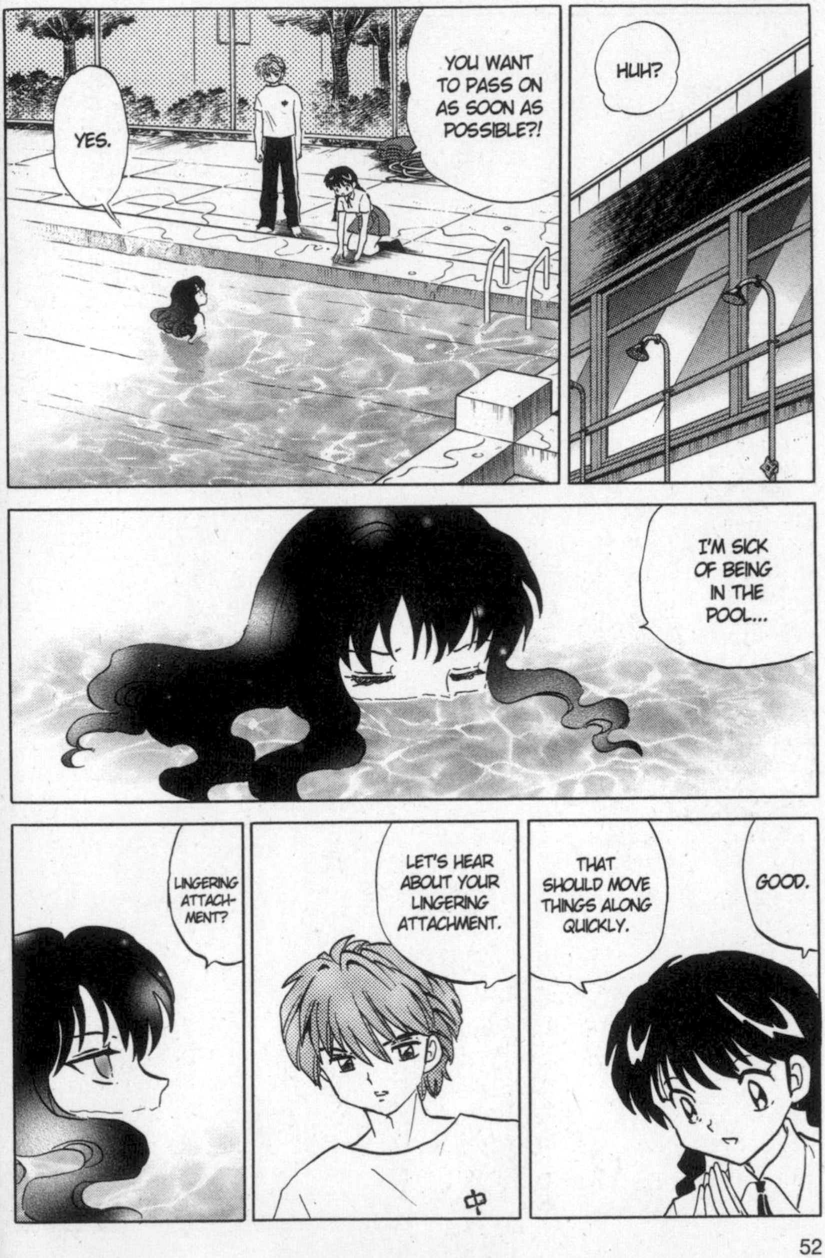
HUH?
YOU WANT TO PASS ON AS SOON AS POSSIBLE?!
YES.
I'M SICK OF BEING IN THE POOL...
GOOD.
THAT SHOULD MOVE THINGS ALONG QUICKLY.
LET'S HEAR ABOUT YOUR LINGERING ATTACHMENT.
LINGERING ATTACH-MENT?

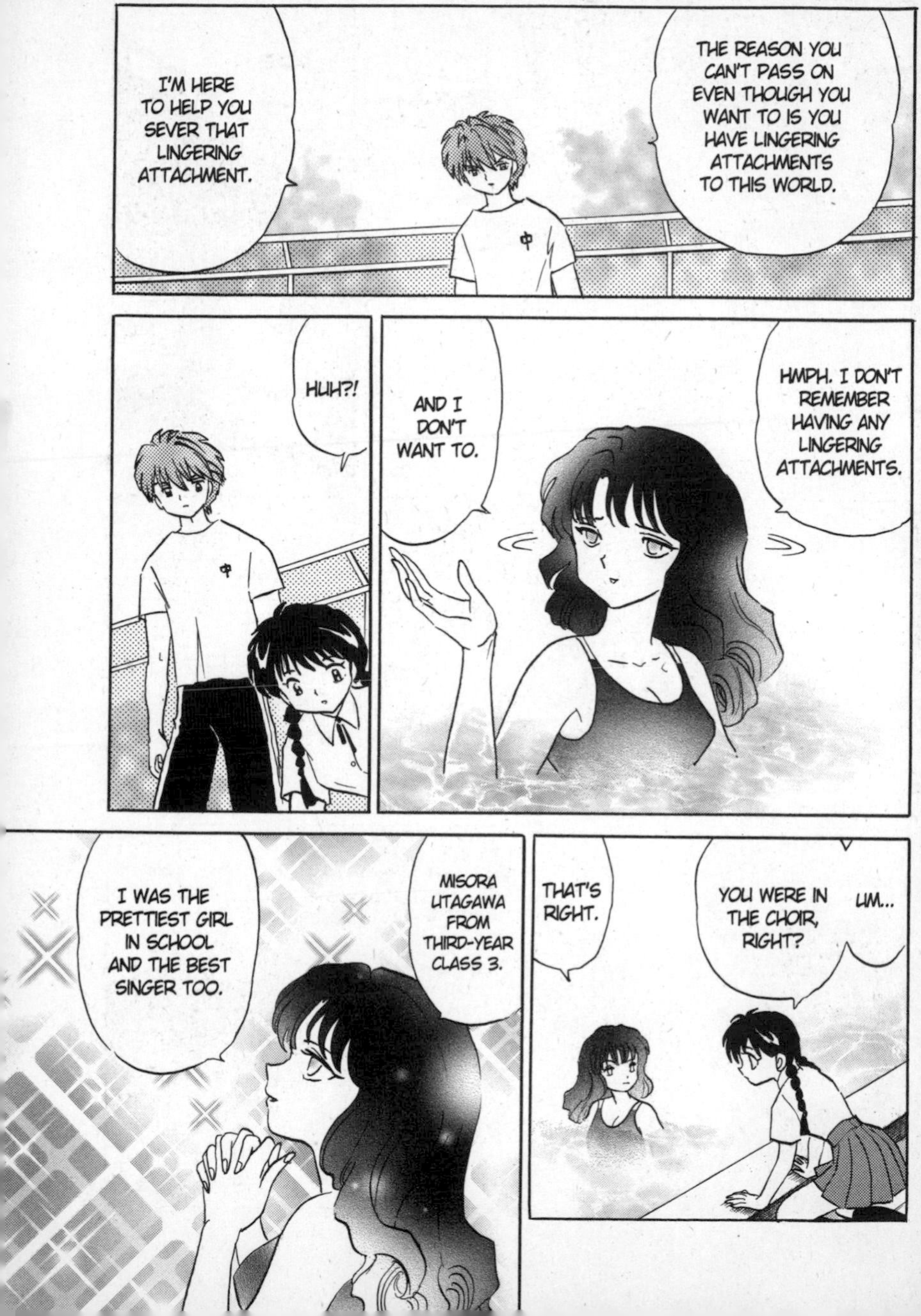
THE REASON YOU CAN'T PASS ON EVEN THOUGH YOU WANT TO IS YOU HAVE LINGERING ATTACHMENTS TO THIS WORLD.
I'M HERE TO HELP YOU SEVER THAT LINGERING ATTACHMENT.
HMPH. I DON'T REMEMBER HAVING ANY LINGERING ATTACHMENTS.
AND I DON'T WANT TO.
HUH?!
UM...
YOU WERE IN THE CHOIR, RIGHT?
THAT'S RIGHT.
MISORA UTAGAWA FROM THIRD-YEAR CLASS 3.
I WAS THE PRETTIEST GIRL IN SCHOOL AND THE BEST SINGER TOO.

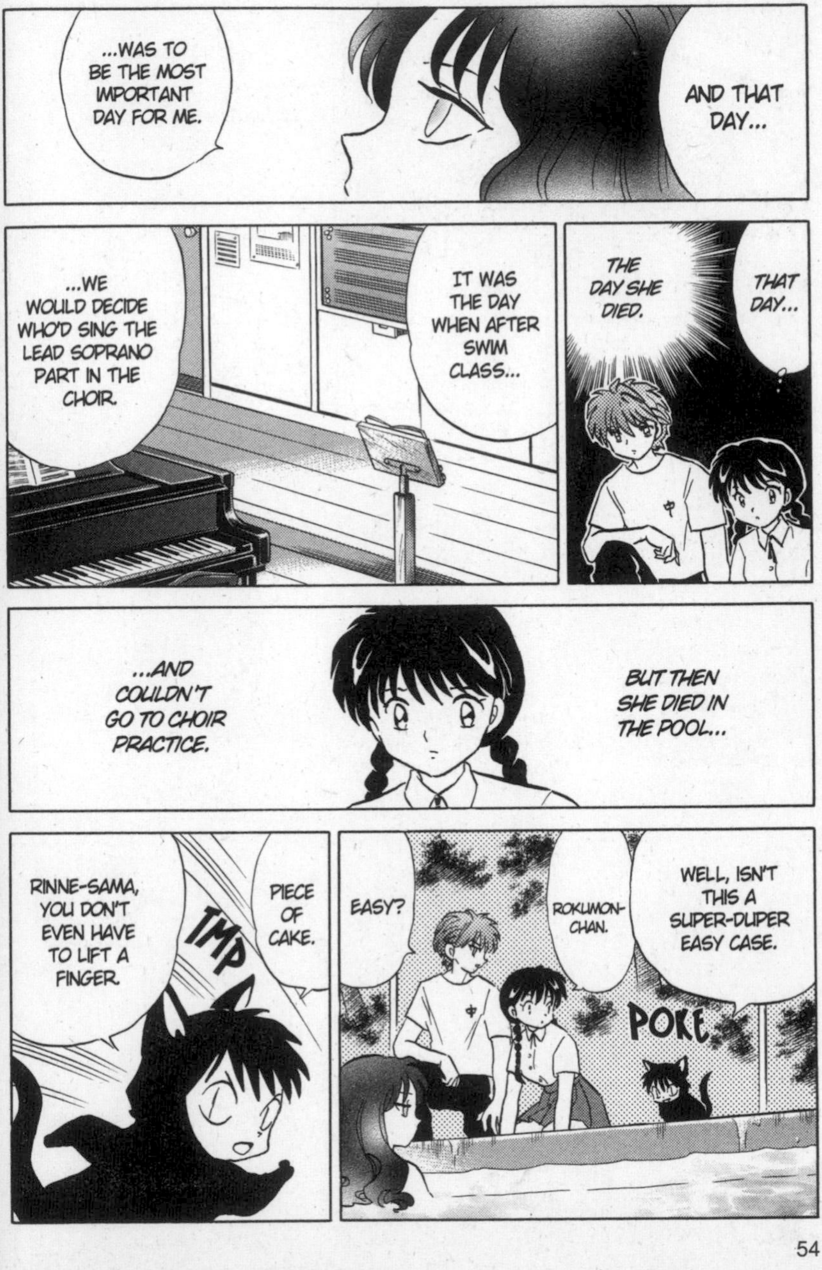
AND THAT DAY...
...WAS TO BE THE MOST IMPORTANT DAY FOR ME.
THAT DAY...
THE DAY SHE DIED.
IT WAS THE DAY WHEN AFTER SWIM CLASS...
...WE WOULD DECIDE WHO'D SING THE LEAD SOPRANO PART IN THE CHOIR.
BUT THEN SHE DIED IN THE POOL...
...AND COULDN'T GO TO CHOIR PRACTICE.
WELL, ISN'T THIS A SUPER-DUPER EASY CASE.
POKE
ROKUMON-CHAN.
EASY?
PIECE OF CAKE.
TMP
RINNE-SAMA, YOU DON'T EVEN HAVE TO LIFT A FINGER.

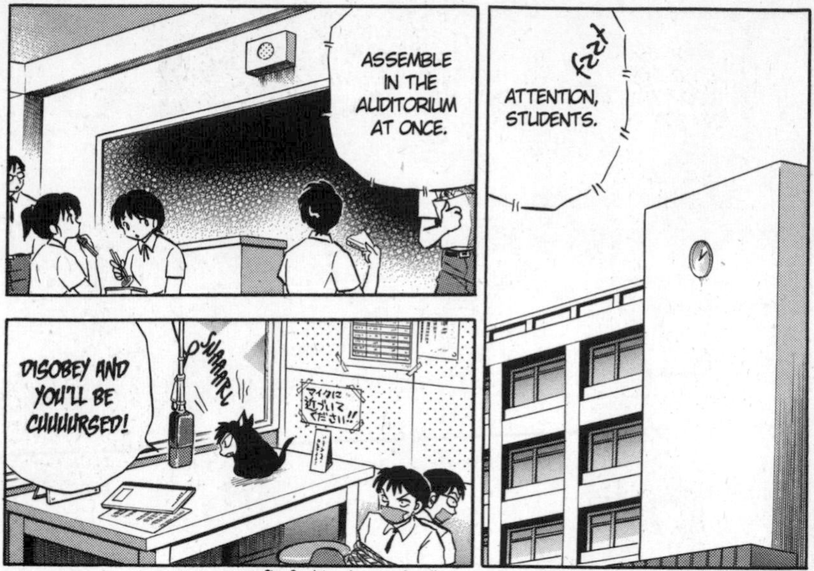
fzzzt
ATTENTION, STUDENTS.
ASSEMBLE IN THE AUDITORIUM AT ONCE.
DISOBEY AND YOU'LL BE CUUUURSED!
SWAAAR!
マイクに近づいてください!!

Sign: Speak into the microphone!!

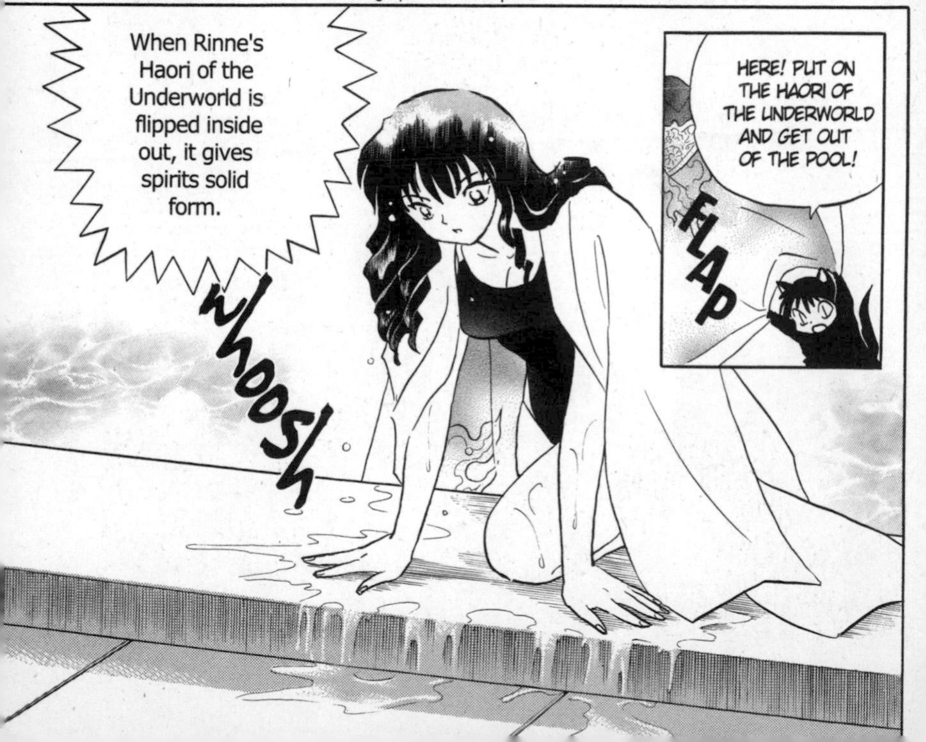
HERE! PUT ON THE HAORI OF THE UNDERWORLD AND GET OUT OF THE POOL!
FLAP
When Rinne's Haori of the Underworld is flipped inside out, it gives spirits solid form.
WHOOSH

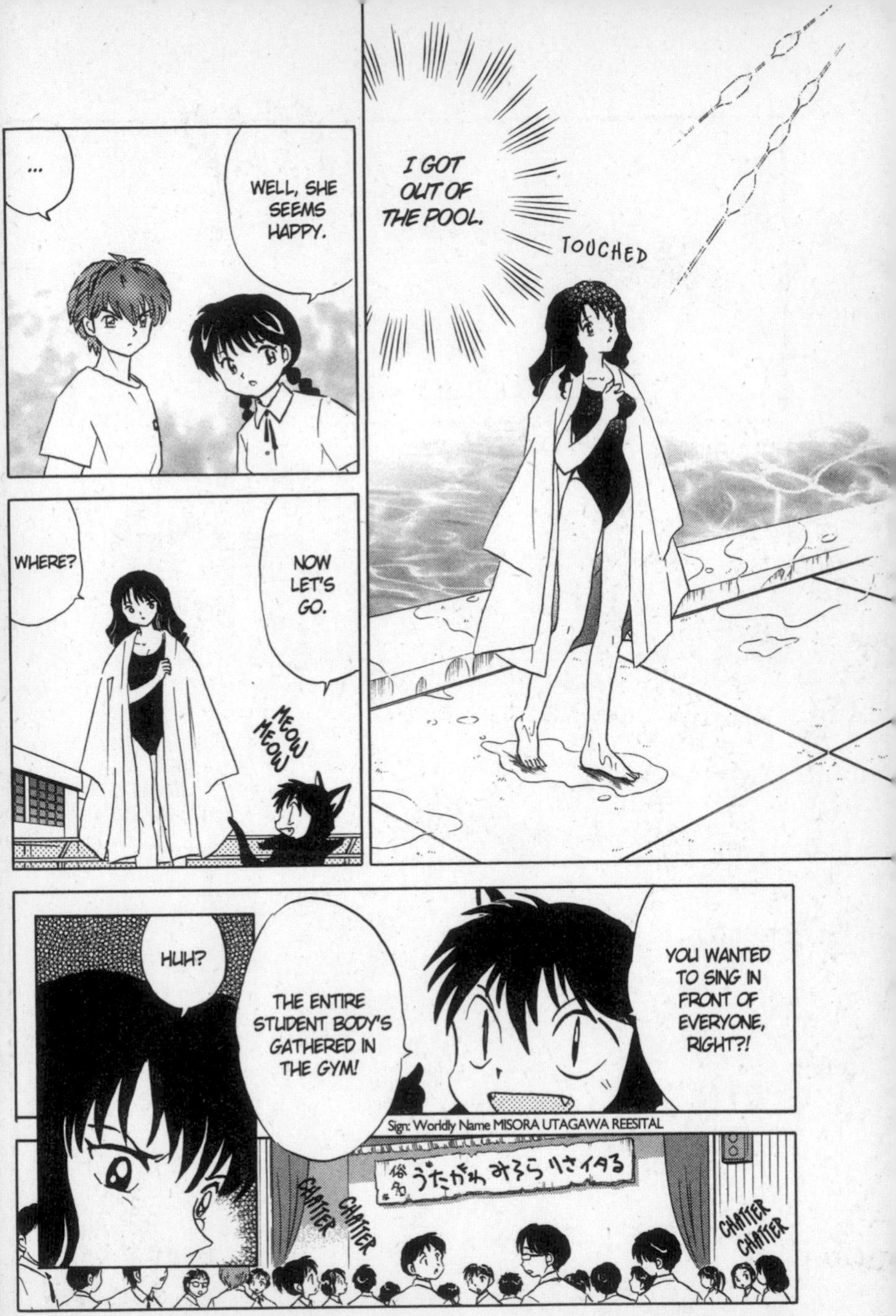
I GOT OUT OF THE POOL.
TOUCHED
WELL, SHE SEEMS HAPPY.
...
NOW LET'S GO.
WHERE?
MEOW MEOW
YOU WANTED TO SING IN FRONT OF EVERYONE, RIGHT?!
THE ENTIRE STUDENT BODY'S GATHERED IN THE GYM!
HUH?
Sign: Worldly Name MISORA UTAGAWA REESITAL
俗名 うたがわ みそら りさイタる
CHATTER CHATTER
CHATTER CHATTER

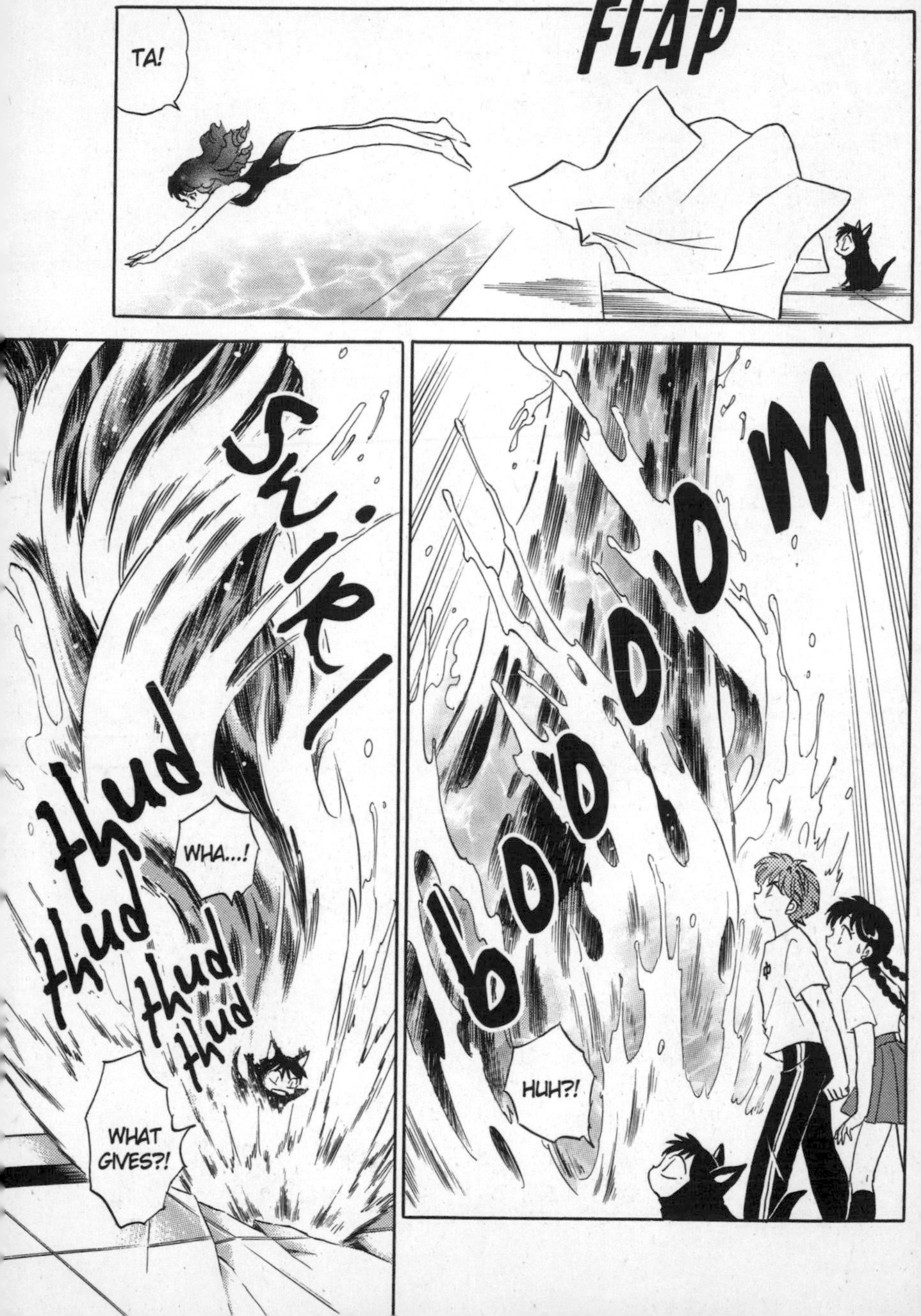
FLAP
TA!
BOOOOM
HUH?!
SWIRL
thud thud thud thud
WHA...!
WHAT GIVES?!

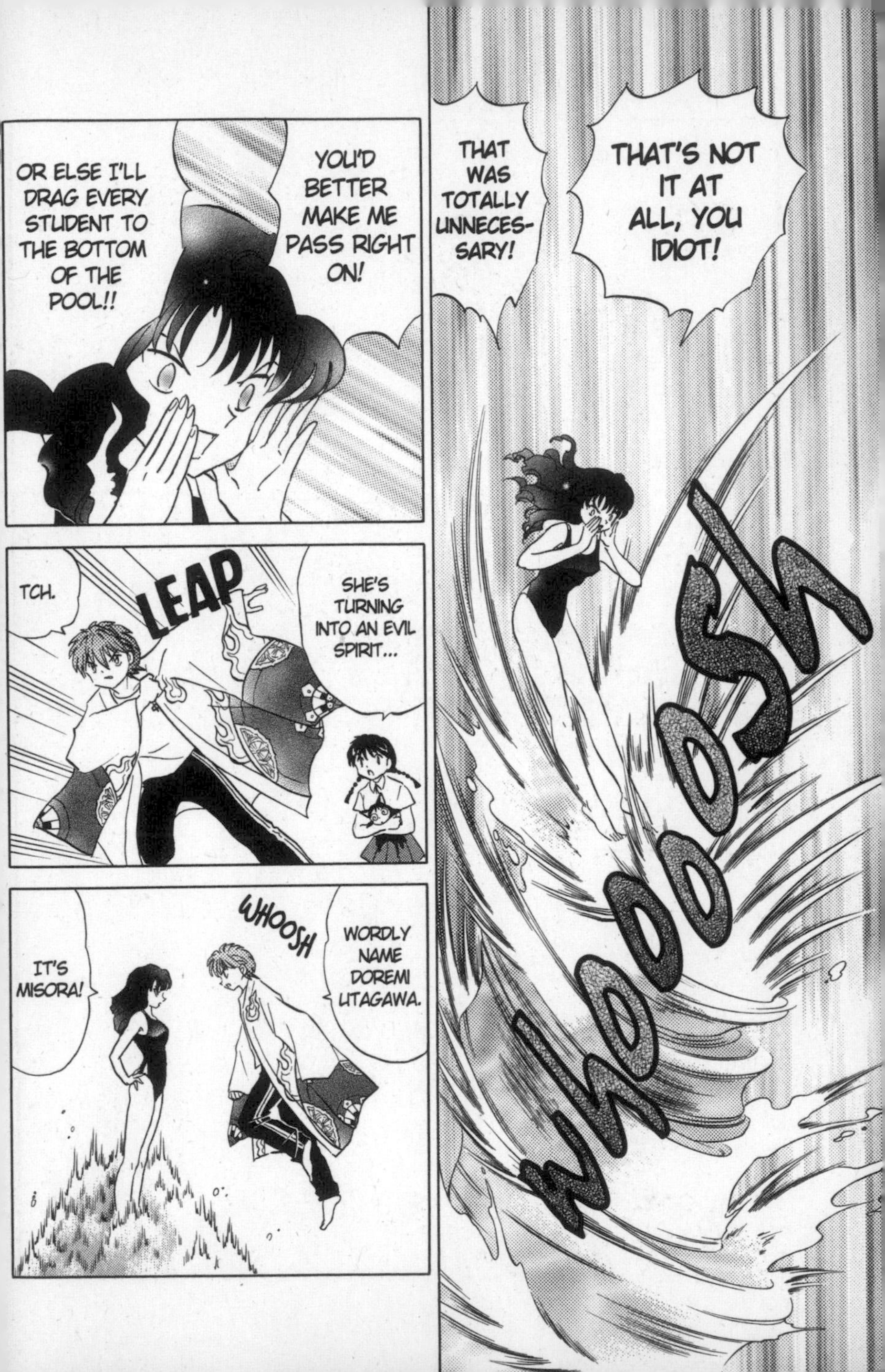
THAT'S NOT IT AT ALL, YOU IDIOT!
THAT WAS TOTALLY UNNECES-SARY!
WHOOOOSH
YOU'D BETTER MAKE ME PASS RIGHT ON!
OR ELSE I'LL DRAG EVERY STUDENT TO THE BOTTOM OF THE POOL!!
SHE'S TURNING INTO AN EVIL SPIRIT...
LEAP
TCH.
WHOOSH
WORDLY NAME DOREMI UTAGAWA.
IT'S MISORA!

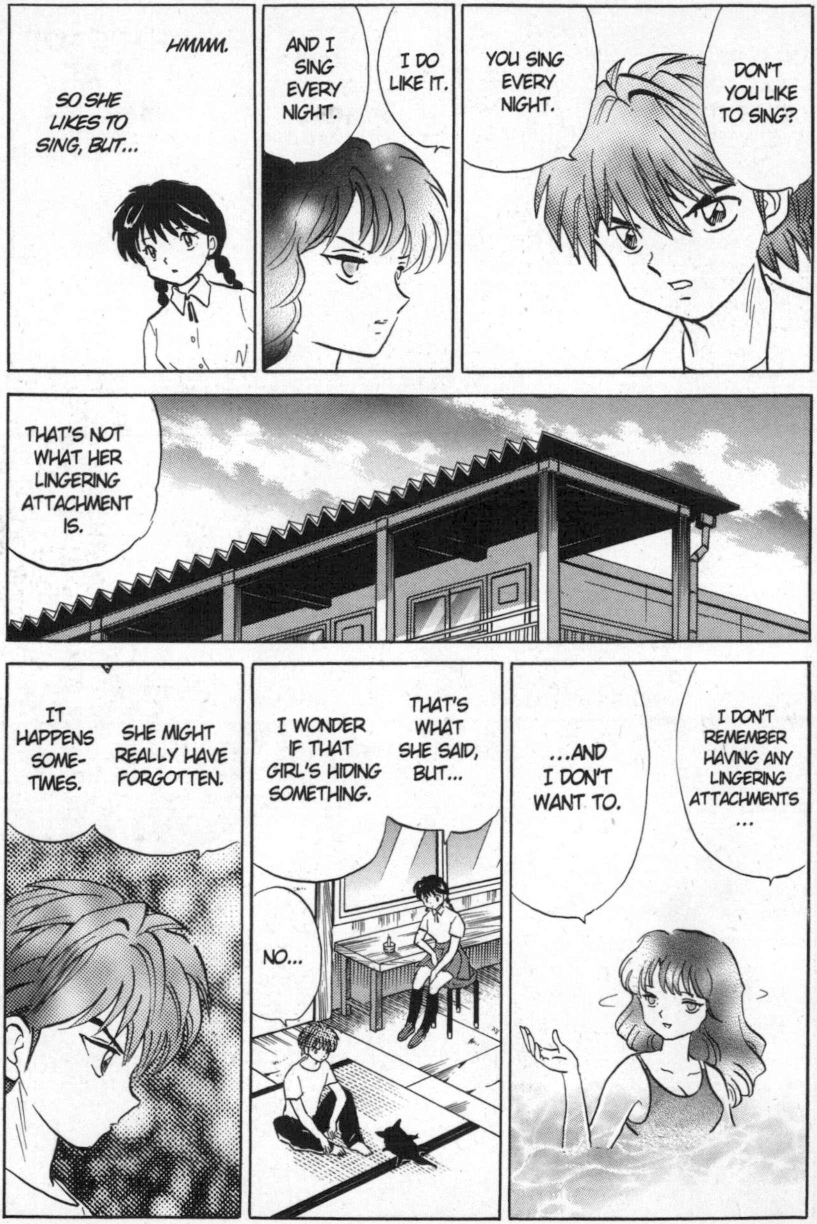
DON'T YOU LIKE TO SING?
YOU SING EVERY NIGHT.
I DO LIKE IT.
AND I SING EVERY NIGHT.
HMMM.
SO SHE LIKES TO SING, BUT...
THAT'S NOT WHAT HER LINGERING ATTACHMENT IS.
I DON'T REMEMBER HAVING ANY LINGERING ATTACHMENTS...
...AND I DON'T WANT TO.
THAT'S WHAT SHE SAID, BUT...
I WONDER IF THAT GIRL'S HIDING SOMETHING.
NO...
SHE MIGHT REALLY HAVE FORGOTTEN.
IT HAPPENS SOMETIMES.

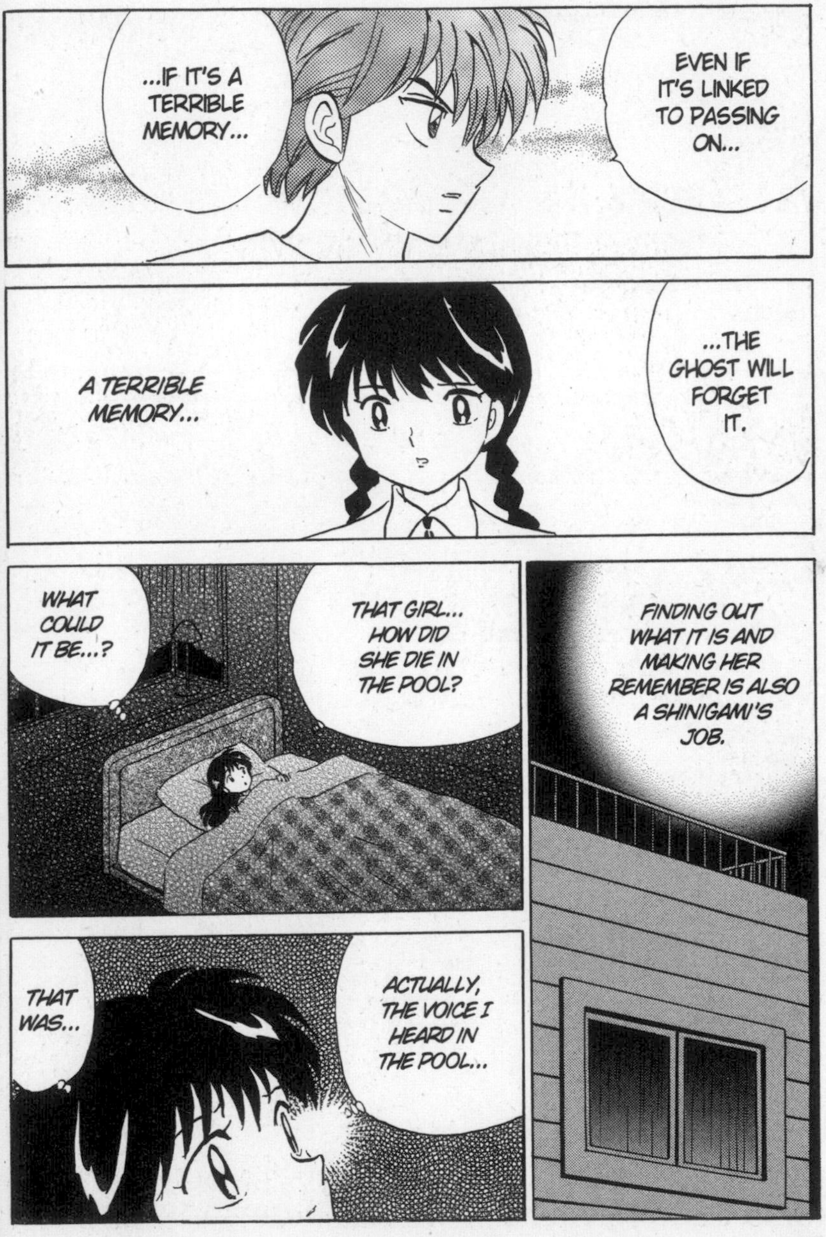
EVEN IF IT'S LINKED TO PASSING ON...
...IF IT'S A TERRIBLE MEMORY...
...THE GHOST WILL FORGET IT.
A TERRIBLE MEMORY...
FINDING OUT WHAT IT IS AND MAKING HER REMEMBER IS ALSO A SHINIGAMI'S JOB.
THAT GIRL... HOW DID SHE DIE IN THE POOL?
WHAT COULD IT BE...?
ACTUALLY, THE VOICE I HEARD IN THE POOL...
THAT WAS...

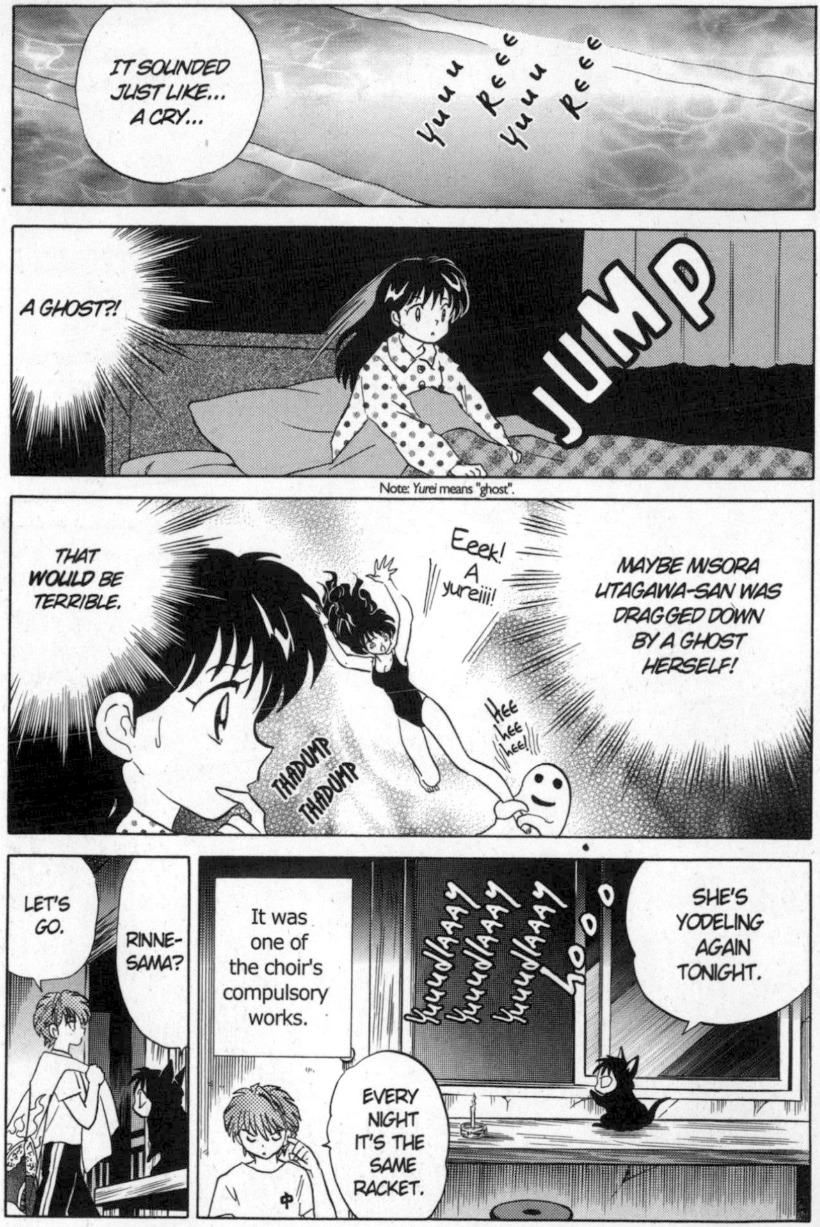
Yuuu Reee Yuuu Reee
IT SOUNDED JUST LIKE... A CRY...
JUMP
A GHOST?!
MAYBE MISORA UTAGAWA-SAN WAS DRAGGED DOWN BY A GHOST HERSELF!
Eeek! A yureiii!
Heee heee heee!
THADUMP THADUMP
THAT WOULD BE TERRIBLE.
SHE'S YODELING AGAIN TONIGHT.
Yuuudlaaay Yuuudlaaay Yuuudlaaay Hooo
It was one of the choir's compulsory works.
EVERY NIGHT IT'S THE SAME RACKET.
RINNE-SAMA?
LET'S GO.

Note: *Yurei* means "ghost".

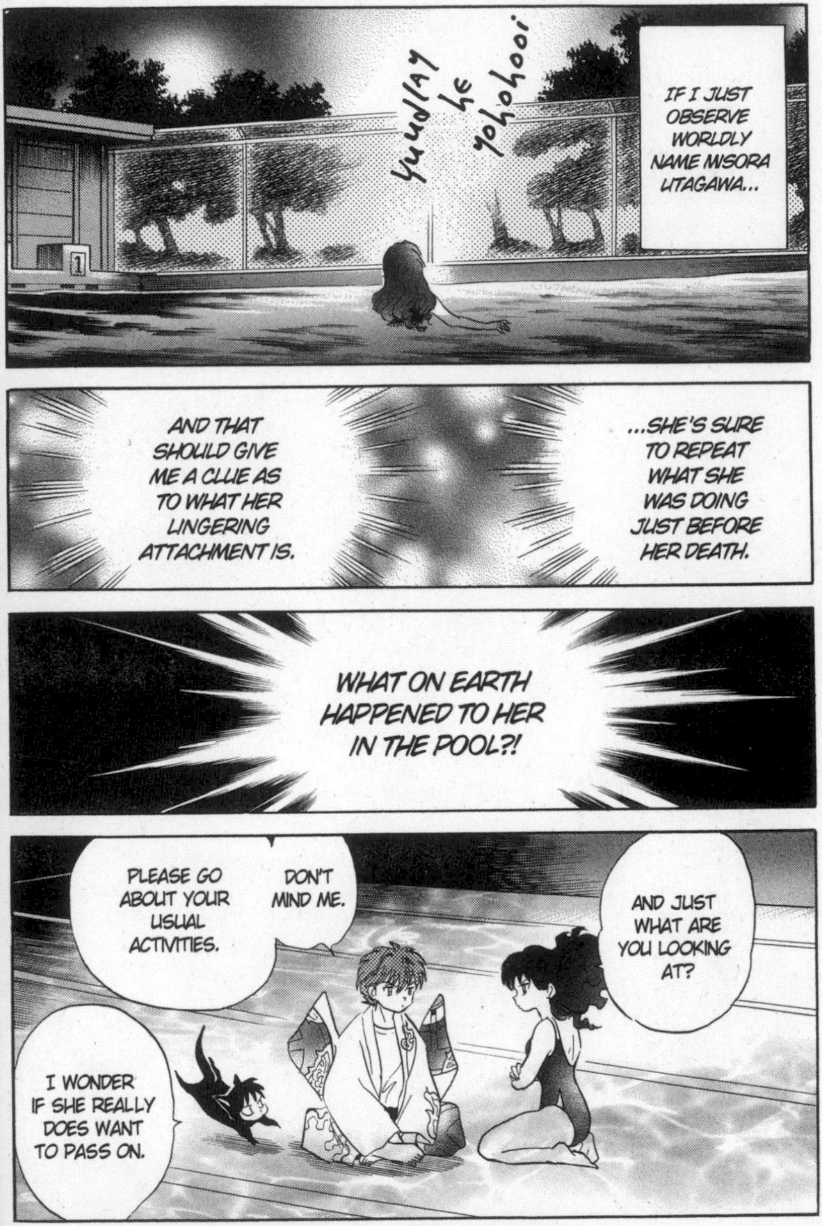
IF I JUST OBSERVE WORLDLY NAME MISORA UTAGAWA...
yudlay he yohohooi
...SHE'S SURE TO REPEAT WHAT SHE WAS DOING JUST BEFORE HER DEATH.
AND THAT SHOULD GIVE ME A CLUE AS TO WHAT HER LINGERING ATTACHMENT IS.
WHAT ON EARTH HAPPENED TO HER IN THE POOL?!
AND JUST WHAT ARE YOU LOOKING AT?
DON'T MIND ME.
PLEASE GO ABOUT YOUR USUAL ACTIVITIES.
I WONDER IF SHE REALLY DOES WANT TO PASS ON.

CHAPTER 12: SOMETHING LOST

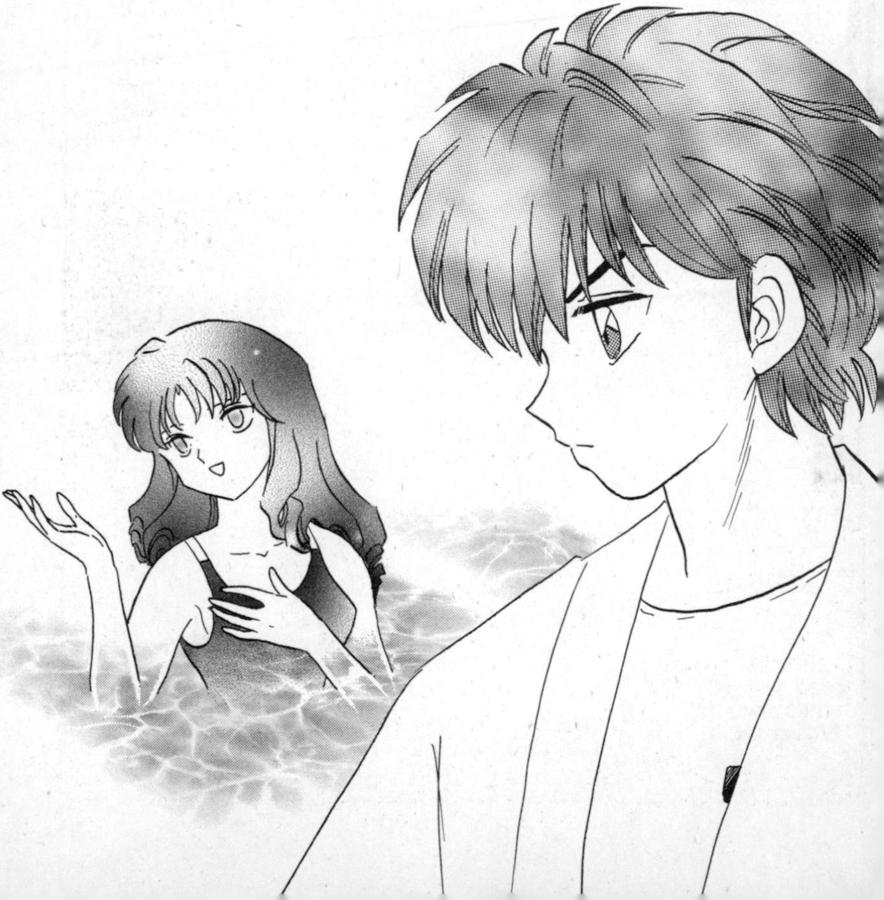

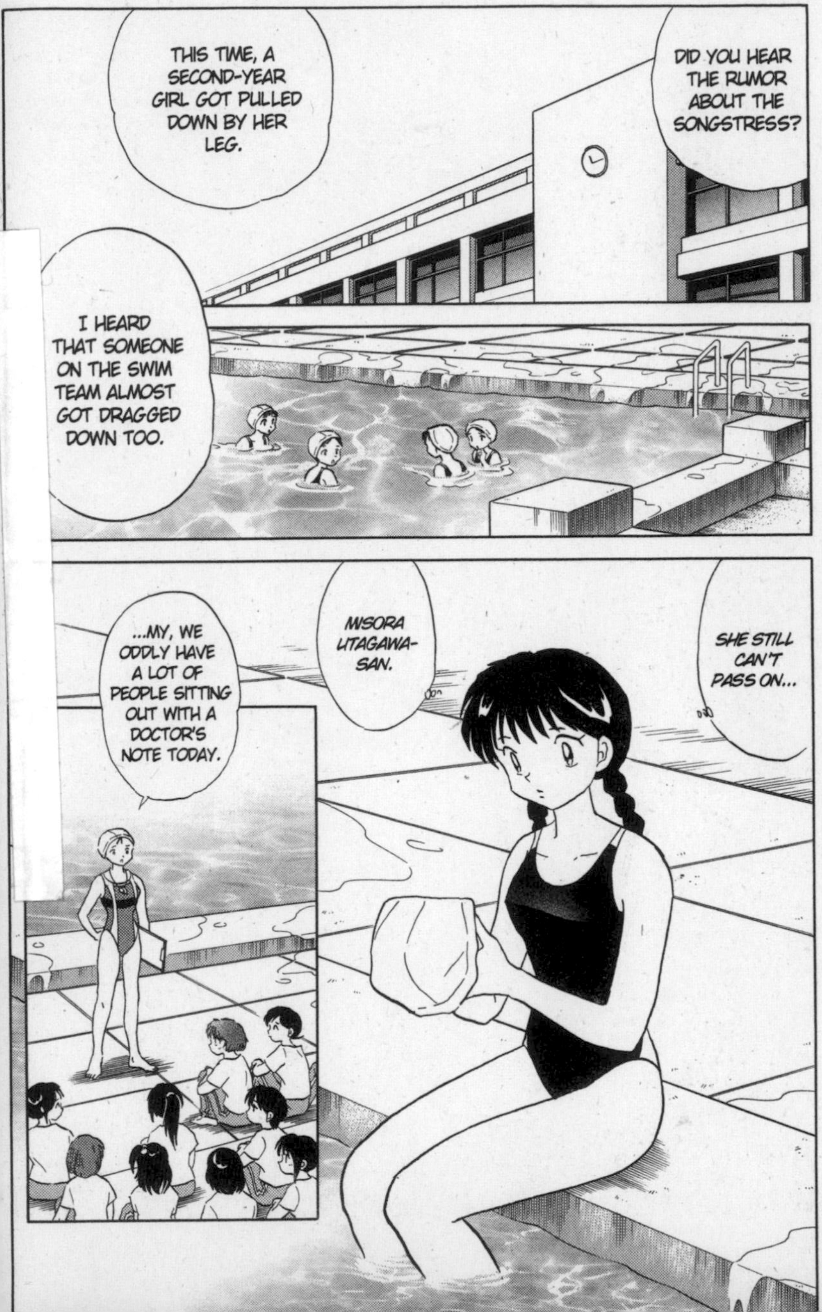
DID YOU HEAR THE RUMOR ABOUT THE SONGSTRESS?
THIS TIME, A SECOND-YEAR GIRL GOT PULLED DOWN BY HER LEG.
I HEARD THAT SOMEONE ON THE SWIM TEAM ALMOST GOT DRAGGED DOWN TOO.
SHE STILL CAN'T PASS ON...
MISORA UTAGAWA-SAN.
...MY, WE ODDLY HAVE A LOT OF PEOPLE SITTING OUT WITH A DOCTOR'S NOTE TODAY.

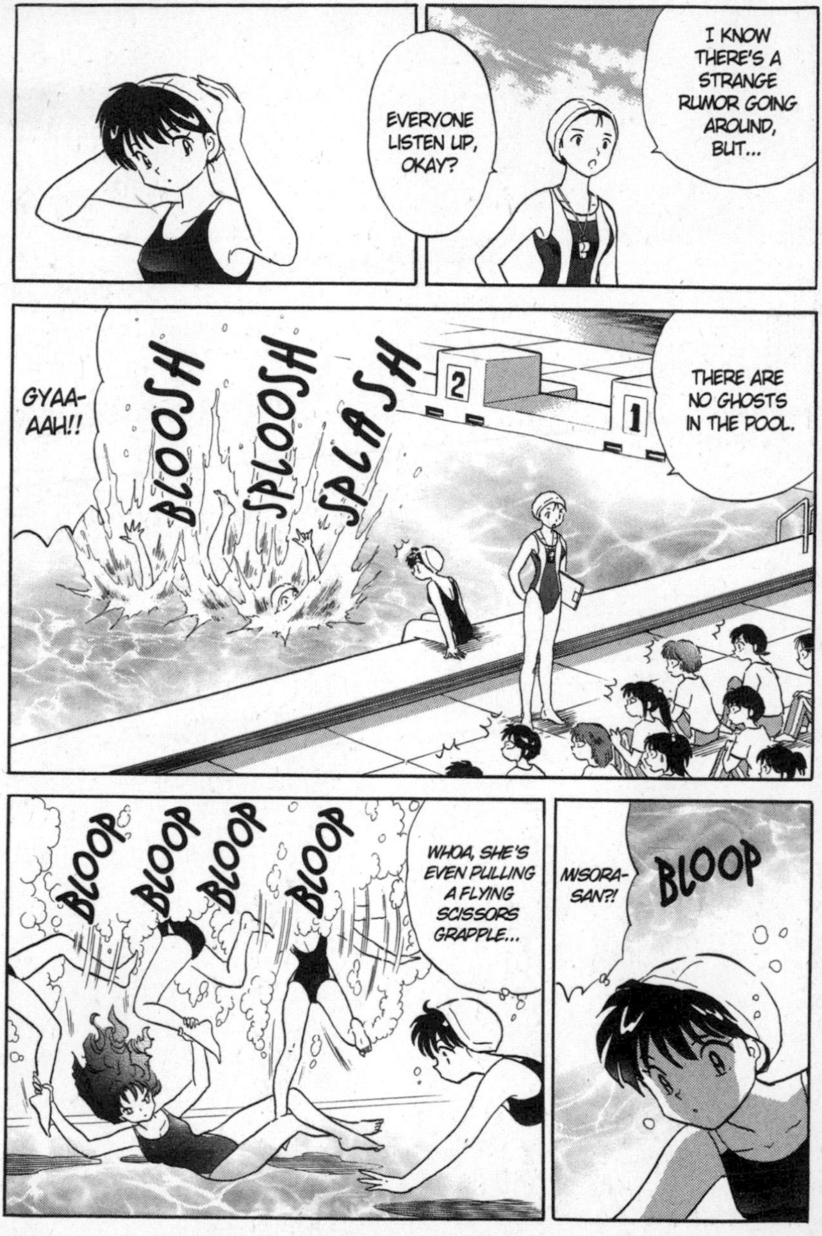
I KNOW THERE'S A STRANGE RUMOR GOING AROUND, BUT...
EVERYONE LISTEN UP, OKAY?
THERE ARE NO GHOSTS IN THE POOL.
SPLASH
SPLOOSH
BLOOSH
GYAA-AAH!!
BLOOP
MISORA-SAN?!
WHOA, SHE'S EVEN PULLING A FLYING SCISSORS GRAPPLE...
BLOOP
BLOOP
BLOOP
BLOOP

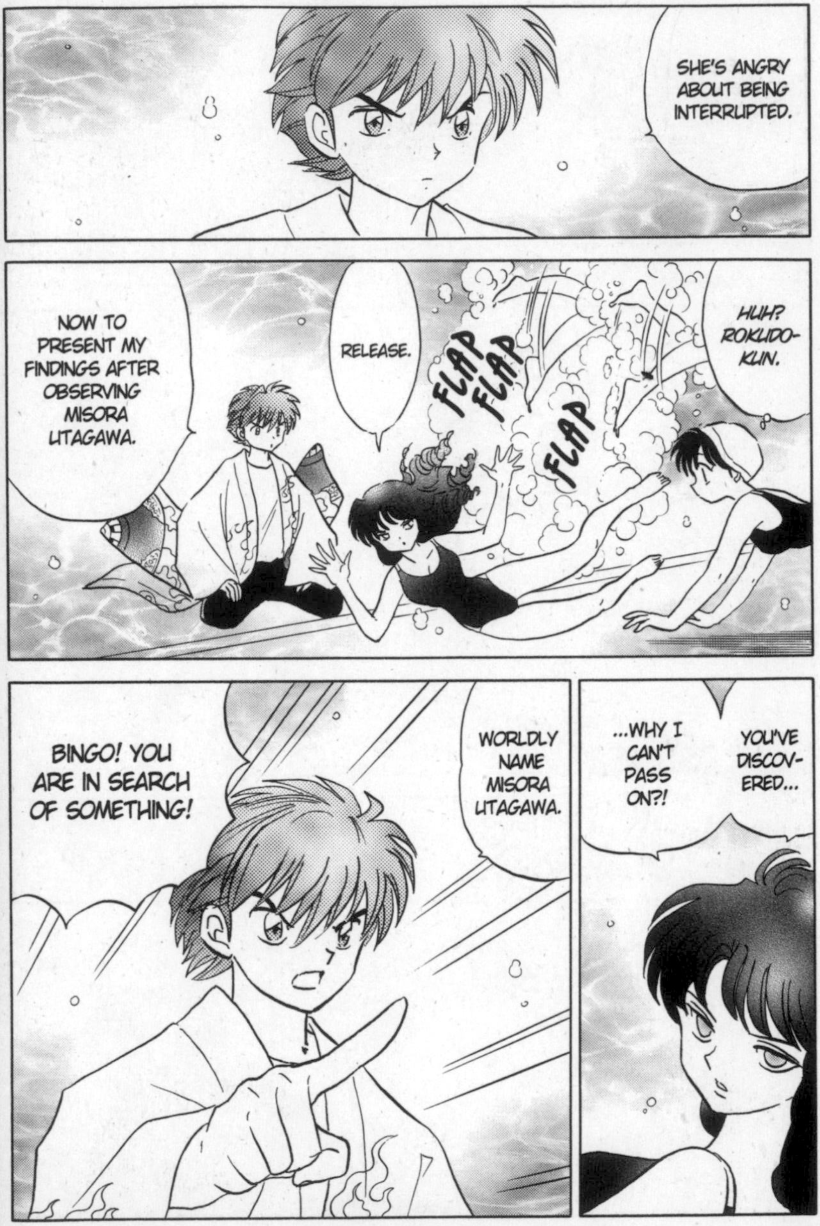
SHE'S ANGRY ABOUT BEING INTERRUPTED.
HUH? ROKUDO-KUN.
FLAP
FLAP FLAP
RELEASE.
NOW TO PRESENT MY FINDINGS AFTER OBSERVING MISORA UTAGAWA.
YOU'VE DISCOV-ERED...
...WHY I CAN'T PASS ON?!
WORLDLY NAME MISORA UTAGAWA.
BINGO! YOU ARE IN SEARCH OF SOMETHING!

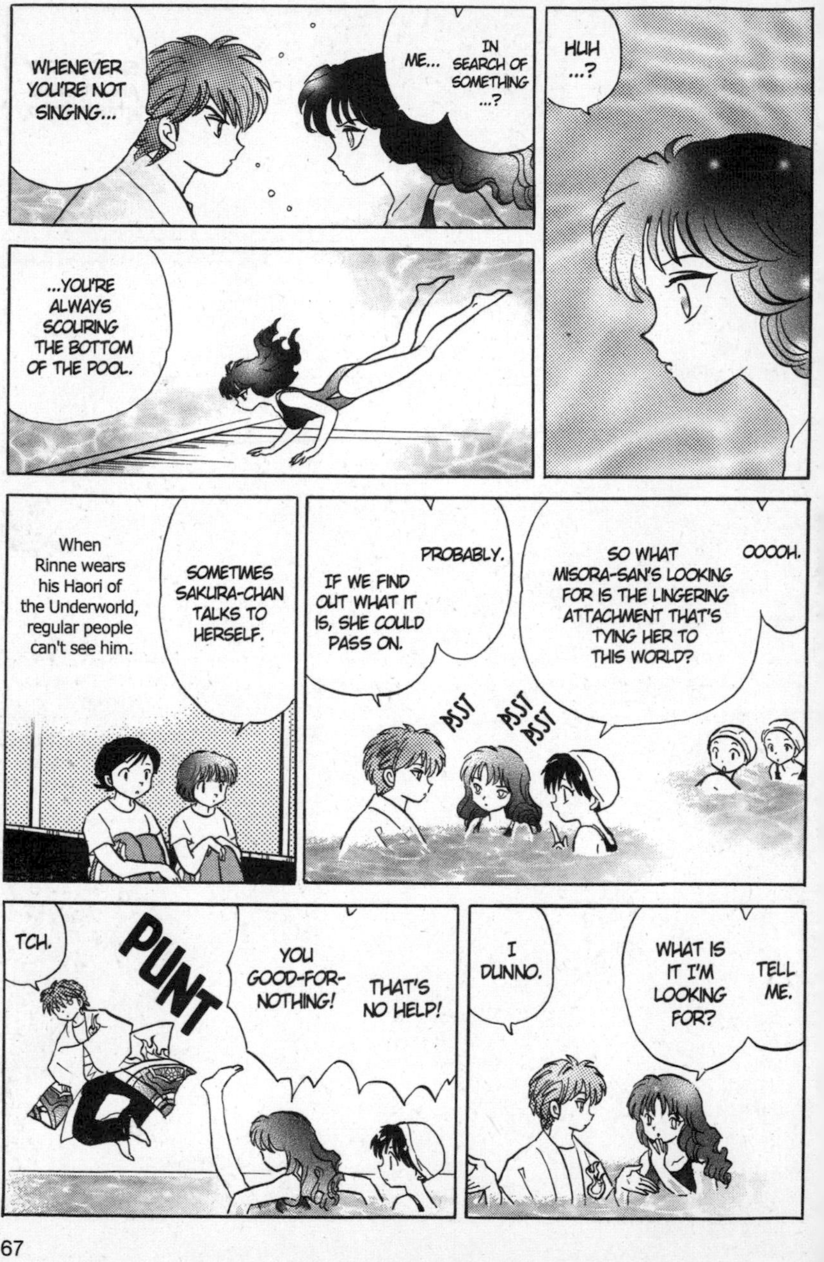
HUH ...?
ME... IN SEARCH OF SOMETHING ...?
WHENEVER YOU'RE NOT SINGING...
...YOU'RE ALWAYS SCOURING THE BOTTOM OF THE POOL.
OOOOH.
SO WHAT MISORA-SAN'S LOOKING FOR IS THE LINGERING ATTACHMENT THAT'S TYING HER TO THIS WORLD?
PROBABLY.
IF WE FIND OUT WHAT IT IS, SHE COULD PASS ON.
PSST
PSST PSST
SOMETIMES SAKURA-CHAN TALKS TO HERSELF.
When Rinne wears his Haori of the Underworld, regular people can't see him.
TELL ME.
WHAT IS IT I'M LOOKING FOR?
I DUNNO.
THAT'S NO HELP!
YOU GOOD-FOR-NOTHING!
PUNT
TCH.

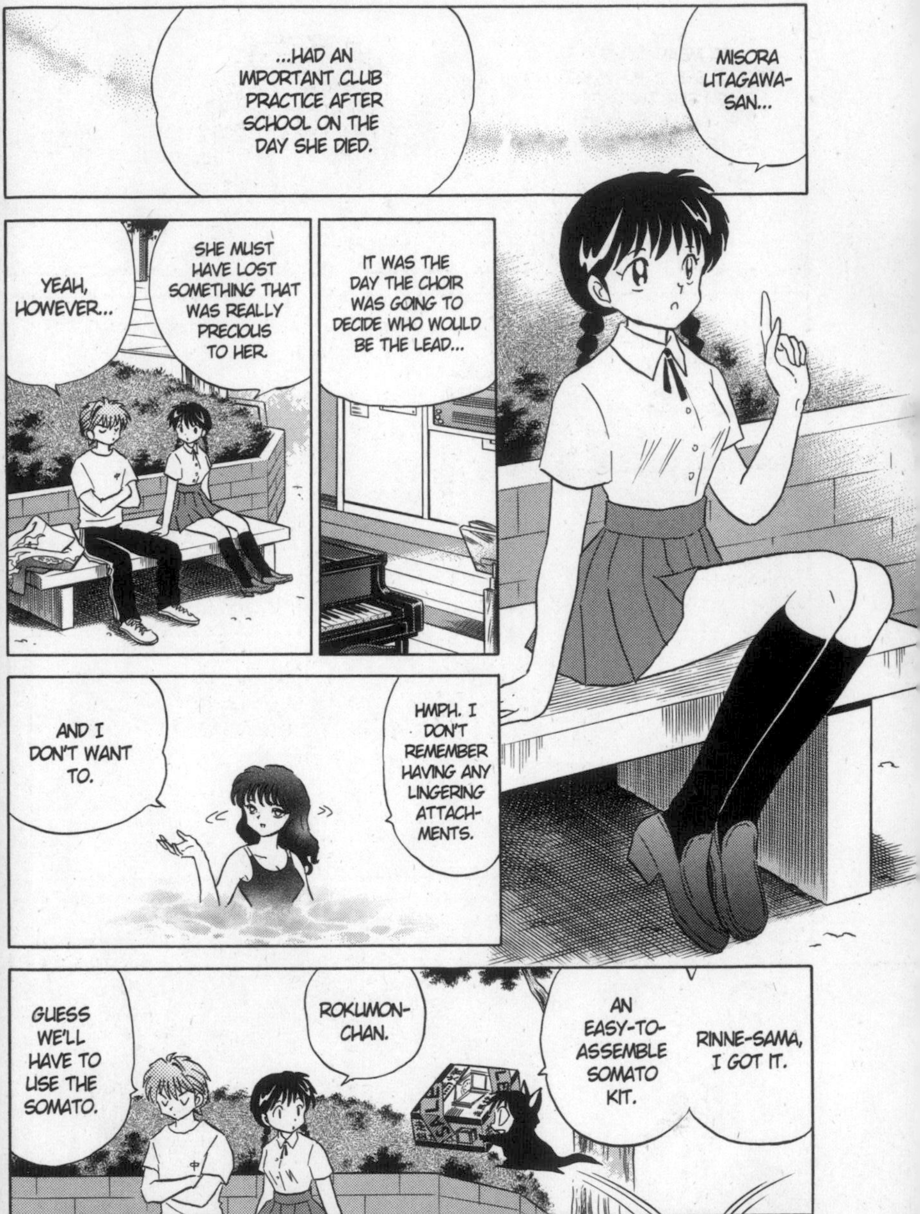
MISORA UTAGAWA-SAN...
...HAD AN IMPORTANT CLUB PRACTICE AFTER SCHOOL ON THE DAY SHE DIED.
IT WAS THE DAY THE CHOIR WAS GOING TO DECIDE WHO WOULD BE THE LEAD...
SHE MUST HAVE LOST SOMETHING THAT WAS REALLY PRECIOUS TO HER.
YEAH, HOWEVER...
HMPH. I DON'T REMEMBER HAVING ANY LINGERING ATTACH-MENTS.
AND I DON'T WANT TO.
RINNE-SAMA, I GOT IT.
AN EASY-TO-ASSEMBLE SOMATO KIT.
ROKUMON-CHAN.
GUESS WE'LL HAVE TO USE THE SOMATO.
Note: A *somato* is a revolving lantern.

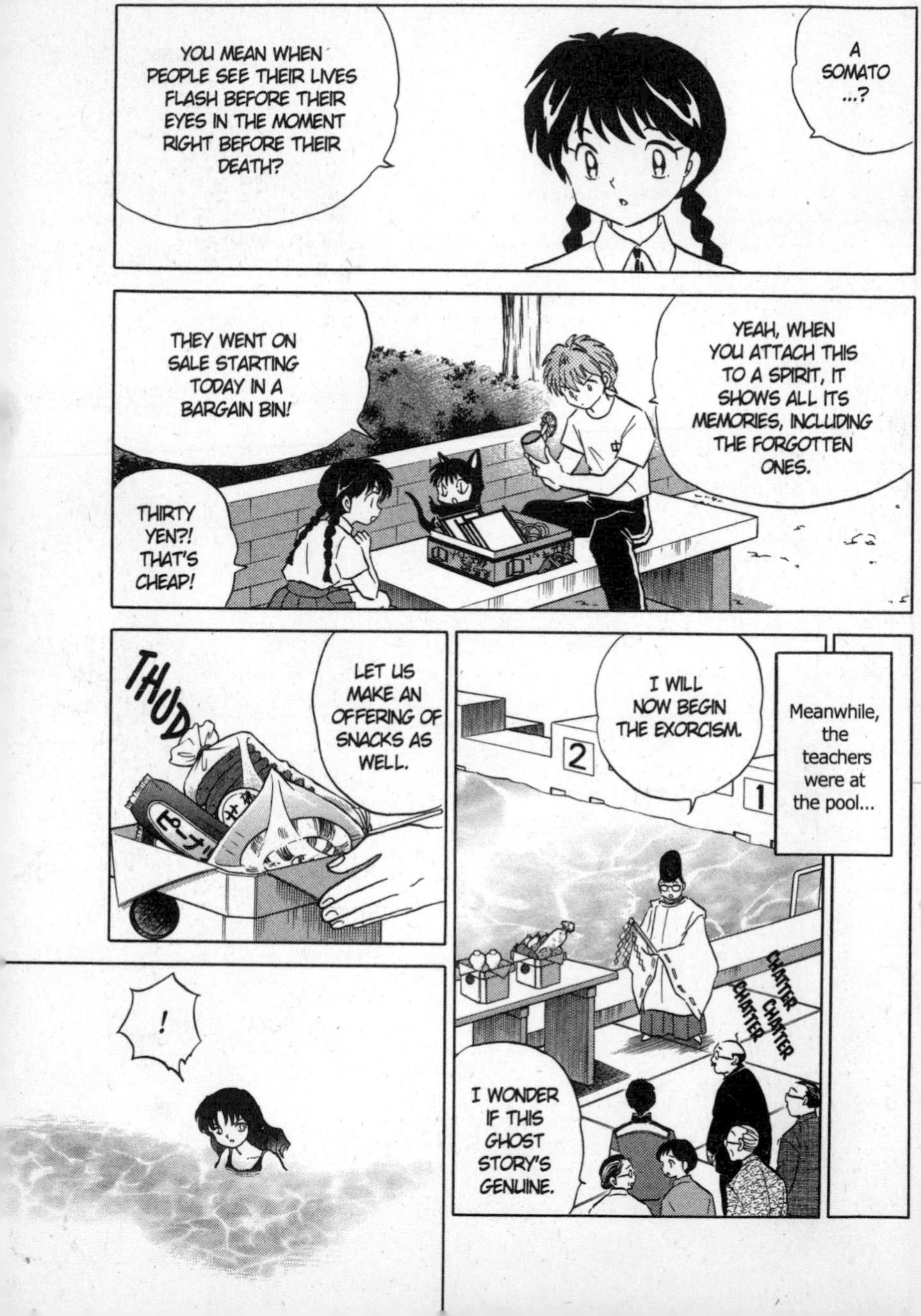
A SOMATO ...?
YOU MEAN WHEN PEOPLE SEE THEIR LIVES FLASH BEFORE THEIR EYES IN THE MOMENT RIGHT BEFORE THEIR DEATH?
YEAH, WHEN YOU ATTACH THIS TO A SPIRIT, IT SHOWS ALL ITS MEMORIES, INCLUDING THE FORGOTTEN ONES.
THEY WENT ON SALE STARTING TODAY IN A BARGAIN BIN!
THIRTY YEN?! THAT'S CHEAP!
Meanwhile, the teachers were at the pool...
I WILL NOW BEGIN THE EXORCISM.
CHATTER CHATTER CHATTER
I WONDER IF THIS GHOST STORY'S GENUINE.
LET US MAKE AN OFFERING OF SNACKS AS WELL.
THUD
!

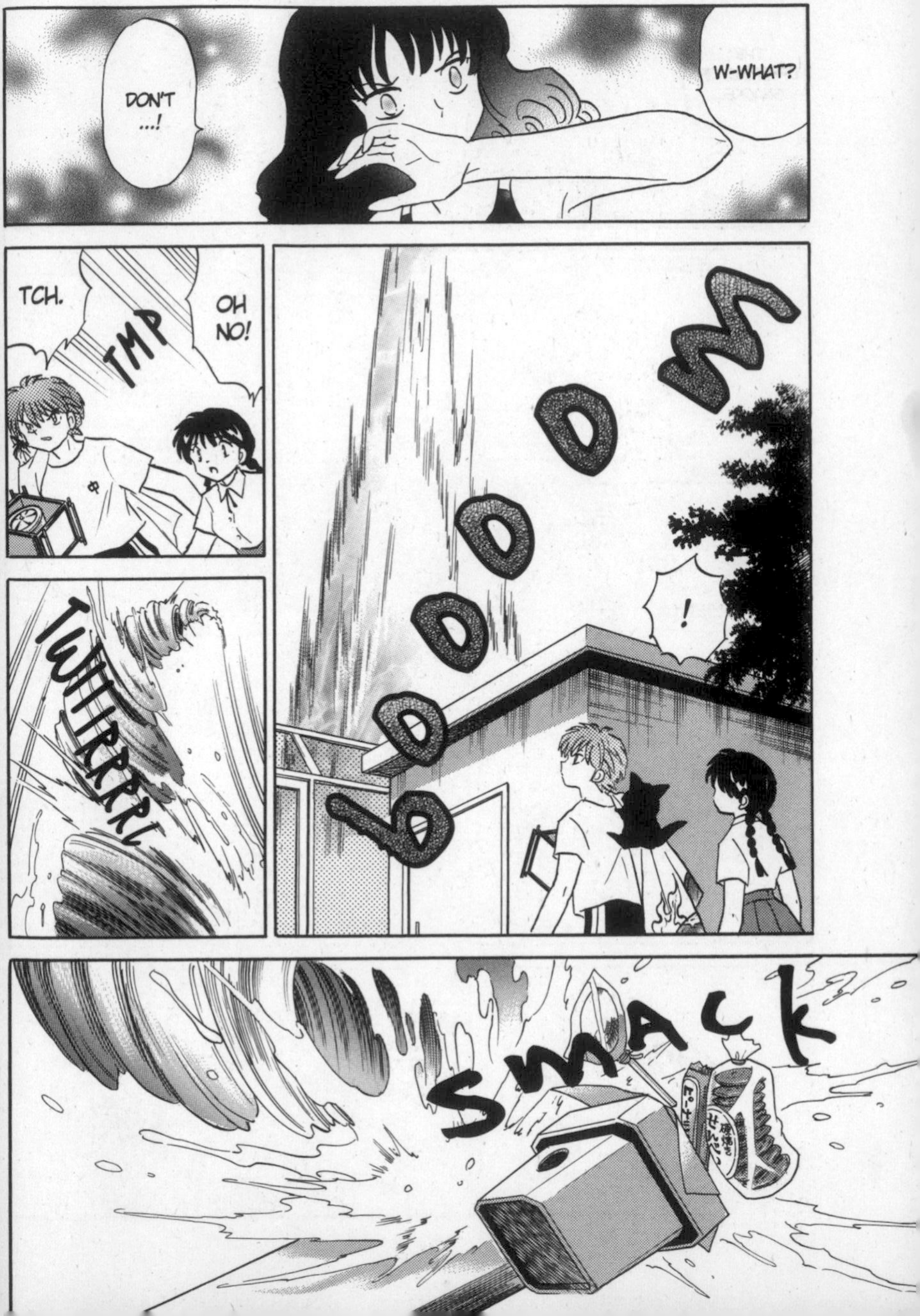
W-WHAT?
DON'T ...!
DOOOOM
!
OH NO!
TMP
TCH.
TWHIRRRRL
SMACK

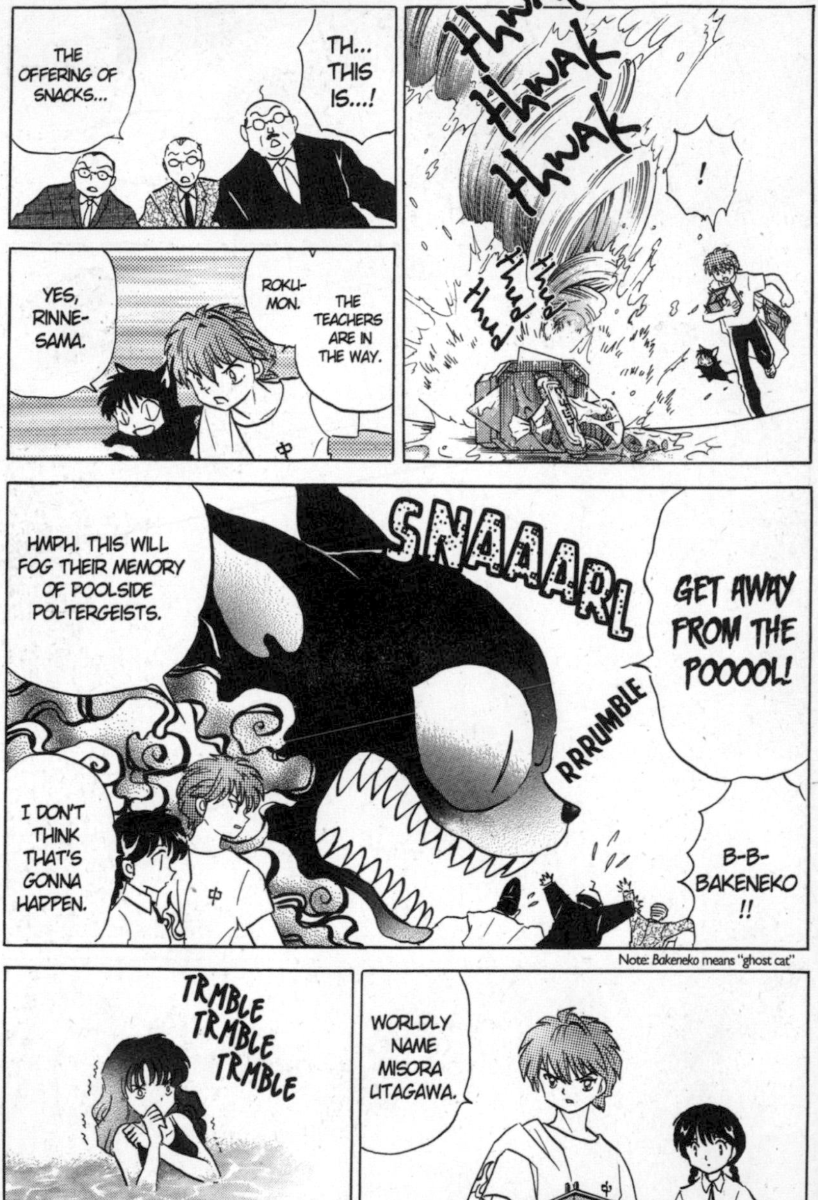
thwak thwak thwak
!
thud thud thud
TH... THIS IS...!
THE OFFERING OF SNACKS...
ROKU-MON.
THE TEACHERS ARE IN THE WAY.
YES, RINNE-SAMA.
GET AWAY FROM THE POOOOL!
SNAAARL
HMPH. THIS WILL FOG THEIR MEMORY OF POOLSIDE POLTERGEISTS.
RRRUMBLE
B-B-BAKENEKO!!
I DON'T THINK THAT'S GONNA HAPPEN.
WORLDLY NAME MISORA UTAGAWA.
TRMBLE TRMBLE TRMBLE

Note: *Bakeneko* means "ghost cat"

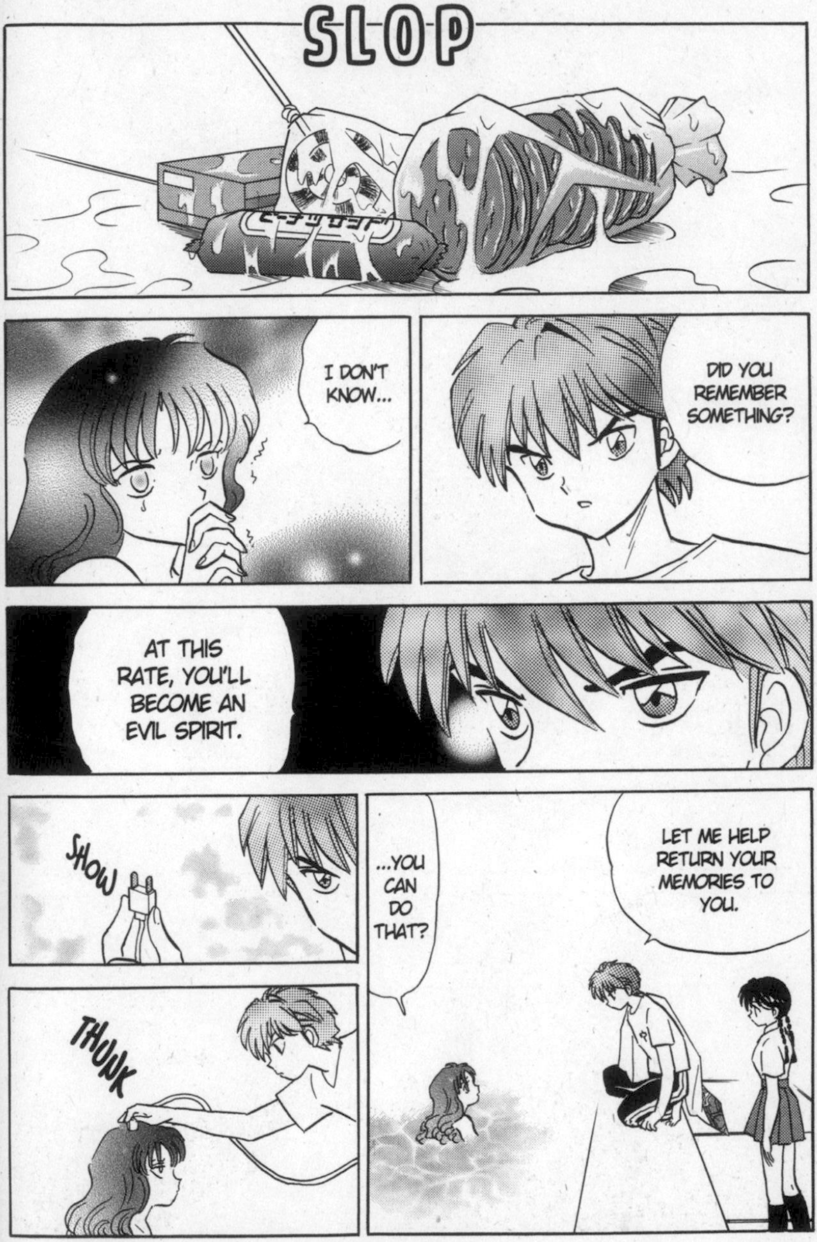
SLOP
DID YOU REMEMBER SOMETHING?
I DON'T KNOW...
AT THIS RATE, YOU'LL BECOME AN EVIL SPIRIT.
LET ME HELP RETURN YOUR MEMORIES TO YOU.
...YOU CAN DO THAT?
SHOW
THUNK

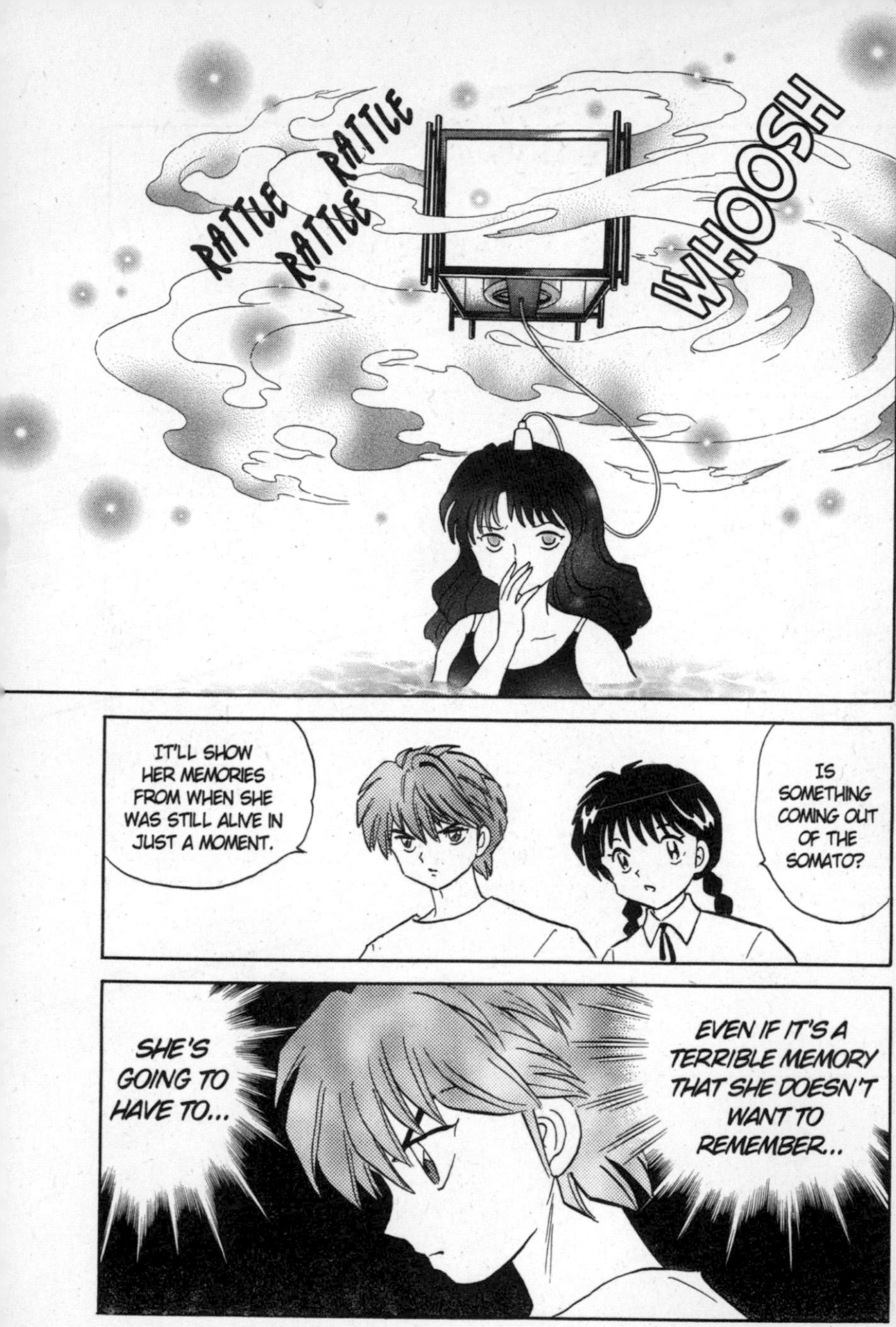
WHOOSH
RATTLE RATTLE
RATTLE
IS SOMETHING COMING OUT OF THE SOMATO?
IT'LL SHOW HER MEMORIES FROM WHEN SHE WAS STILL ALIVE IN JUST A MOMENT.
EVEN IF IT'S A TERRIBLE MEMORY THAT SHE DOESN'T WANT TO REMEMBER...
SHE'S GOING TO HAVE TO...

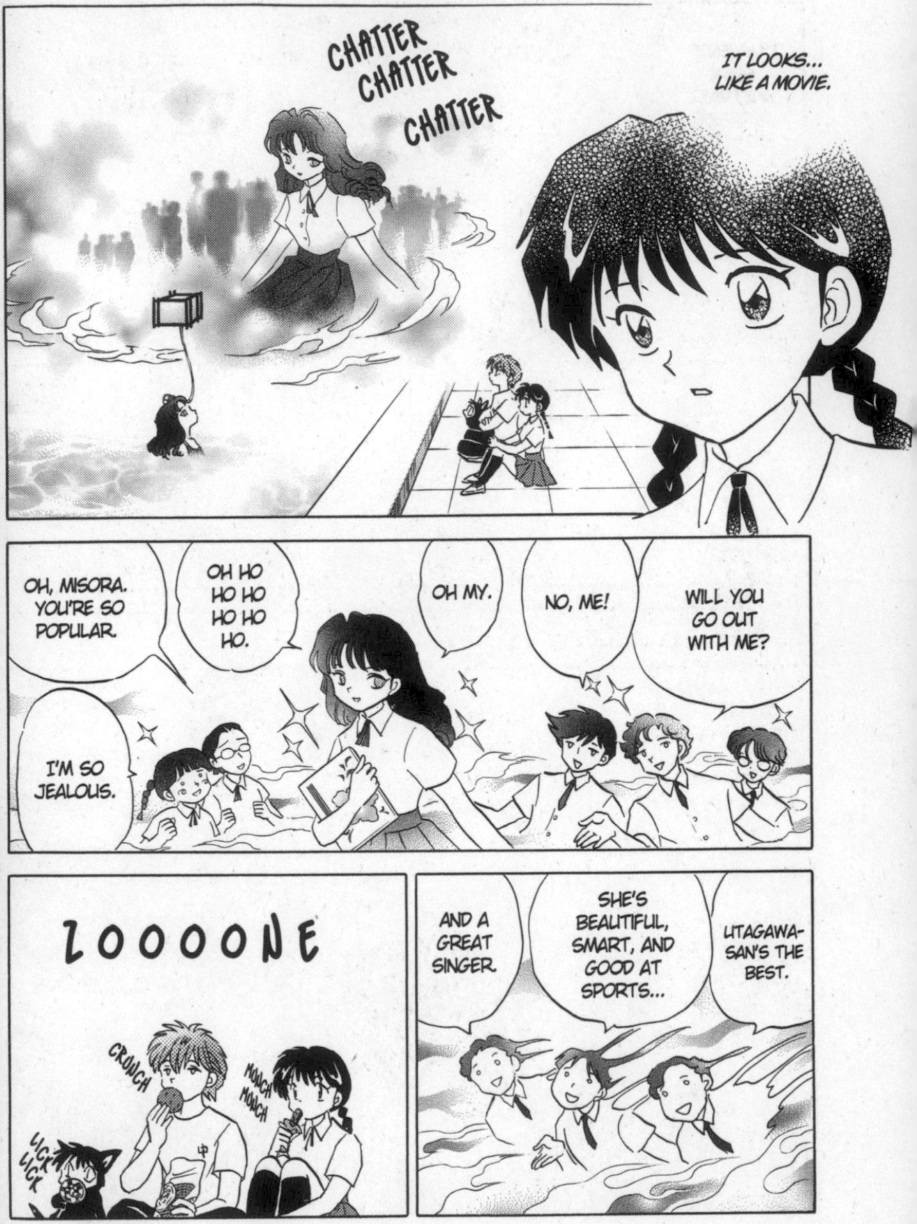
IT LOOKS... LIKE A MOVIE.
CHATTER CHATTER CHATTER
WILL YOU GO OUT WITH ME?
NO, ME!
OH MY.
OH HO HO HO HO HO HO.
OH, MISORA. YOU'RE SO POPULAR.
I'M SO JEALOUS.
UTAGAWA-SAN'S THE BEST.
SHE'S BEAUTIFUL, SMART, AND GOOD AT SPORTS...
AND A GREAT SINGER.
ZOOOONE
CRUNCH
MONCH MONCH
LICK LICK

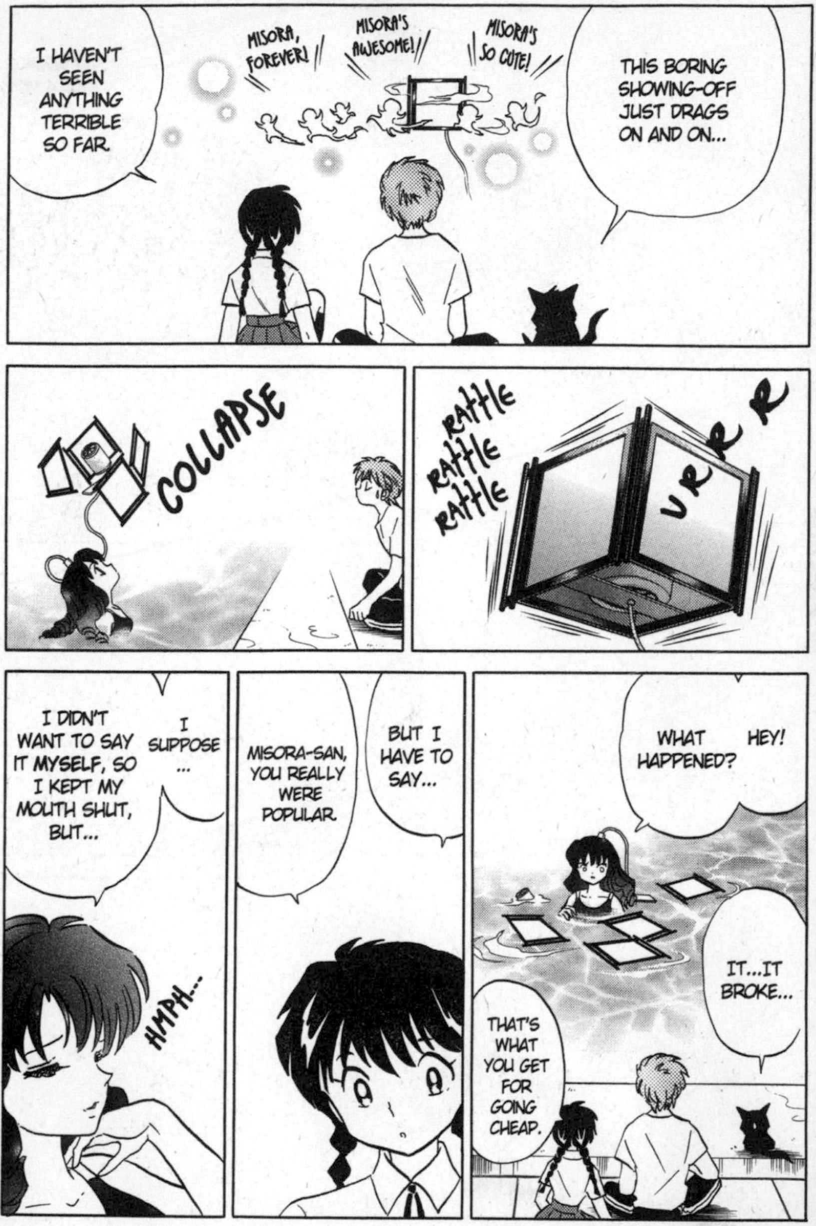
THIS BORING SHOWING-OFF JUST DRAGS ON AND ON...
MISORA'S SO CUTE!
MISORA'S AWESOME!
MISORA, FOREVER!
I HAVEN'T SEEN ANYTHING TERRIBLE SO FAR.
URRR
RATTLE RATTLE RATTLE
COLLAPSE
HEY!
WHAT HAPPENED?
IT...IT BROKE...
THAT'S WHAT YOU GET FOR GOING CHEAP.
BUT I HAVE TO SAY...
MISORA-SAN, YOU REALLY WERE POPULAR.
I SUPPOSE ...
I DIDN'T WANT TO SAY IT MYSELF, SO I KEPT MY MOUTH SHUT, BUT...
HMPH...

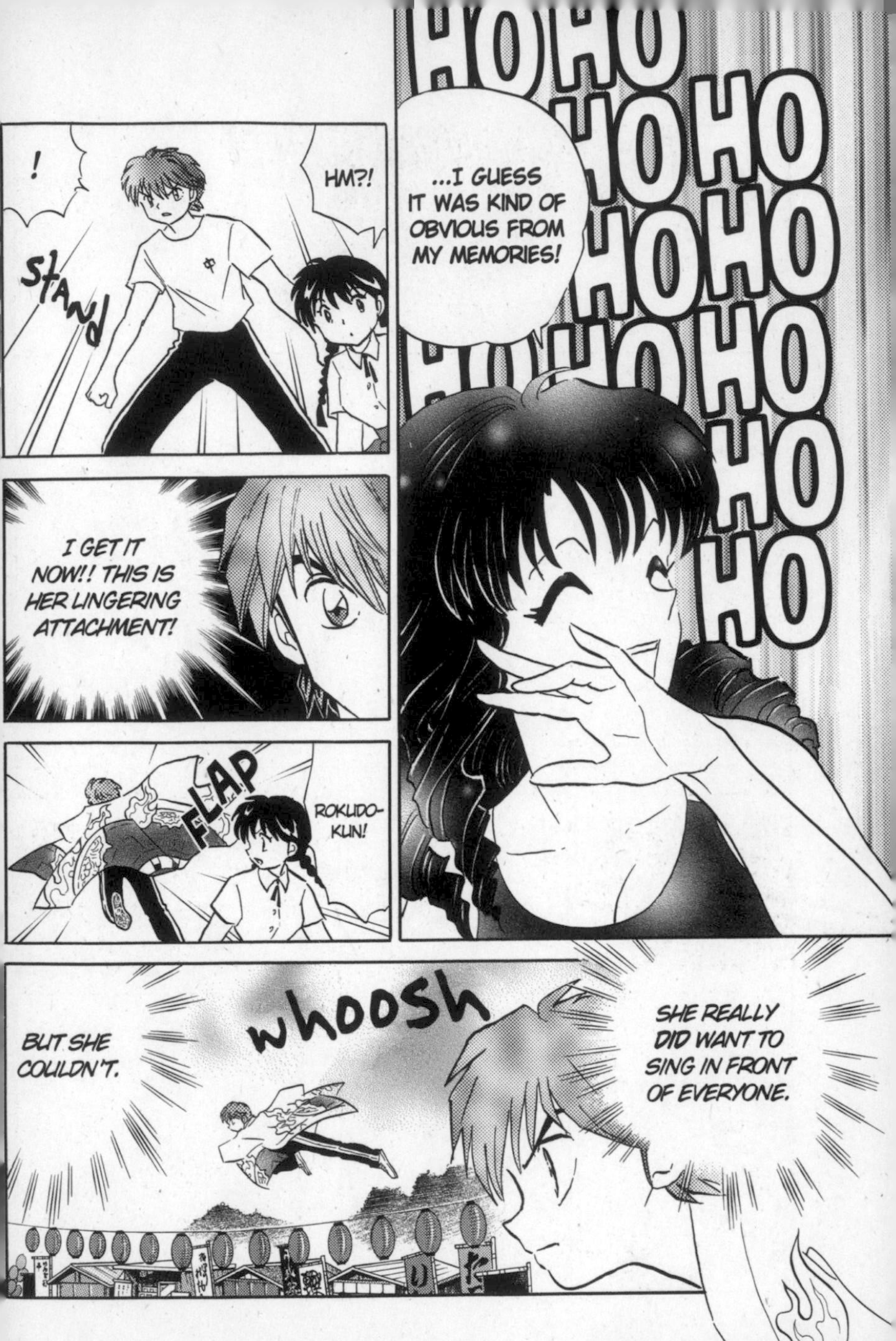
HOHO
HOHO
HOHO
HOHO
HOHOHO
HO
HO
...I GUESS IT WAS KIND OF OBVIOUS FROM MY MEMORIES!
!
HM?!
stand
I GET IT NOW!! THIS IS HER LINGERING ATTACHMENT!
FLAP
ROKUDO-KUN!
SHE REALLY DID WANT TO SING IN FRONT OF EVERYONE.
whoosh
BUT SHE COULDN'T.

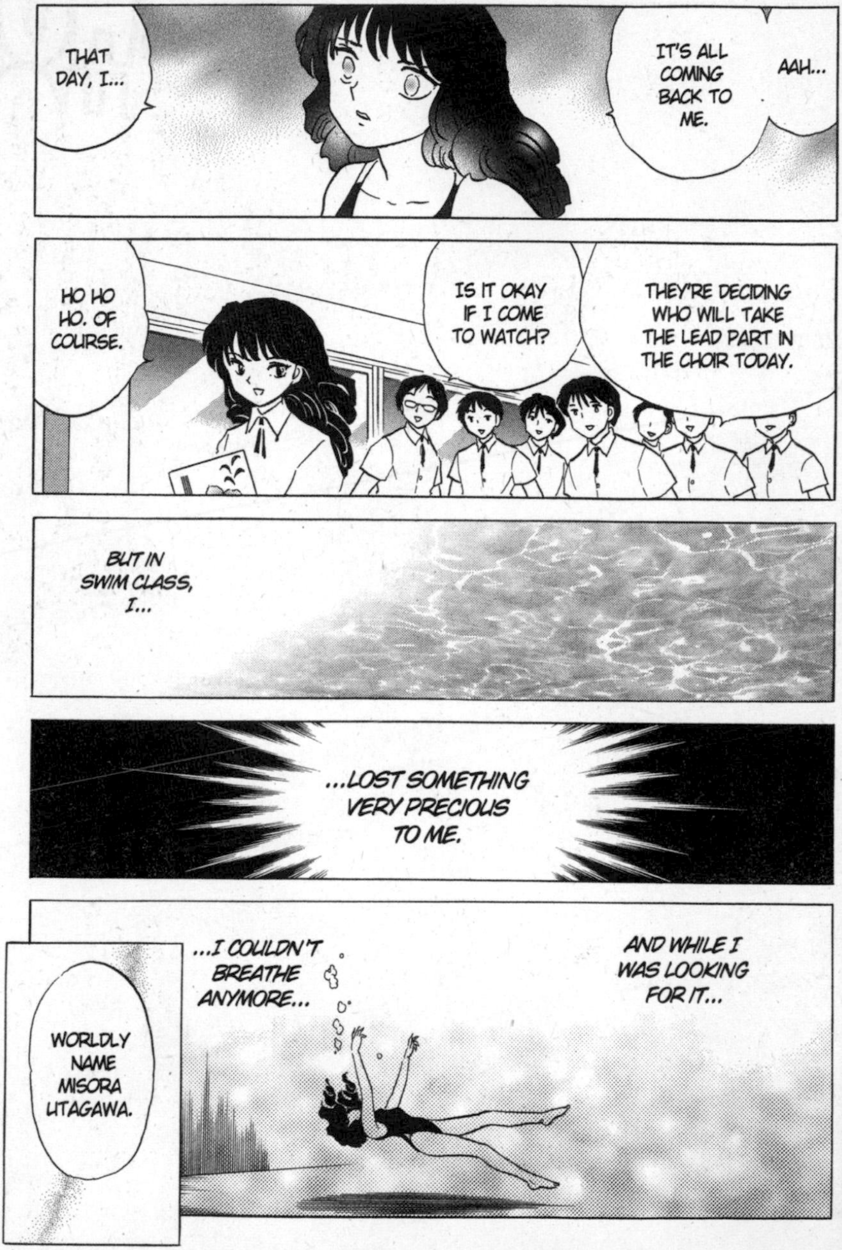
AAH...
IT'S ALL COMING BACK TO ME.
THAT DAY, I...
THEY'RE DECIDING WHO WILL TAKE THE LEAD PART IN THE CHOIR TODAY.
IS IT OKAY IF I COME TO WATCH?
HO HO HO. OF COURSE.
BUT IN SWIM CLASS, I...
...LOST SOMETHING VERY PRECIOUS TO ME.
AND WHILE I WAS LOOKING FOR IT...
...I COULDN'T BREATHE ANYMORE...
WORLDLY NAME MISORA UTAGAWA.

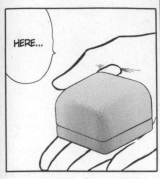

HERE...

WHAT IS IT?

SWFF

TWINKLE TWINKLE

THIS... THIS IS...

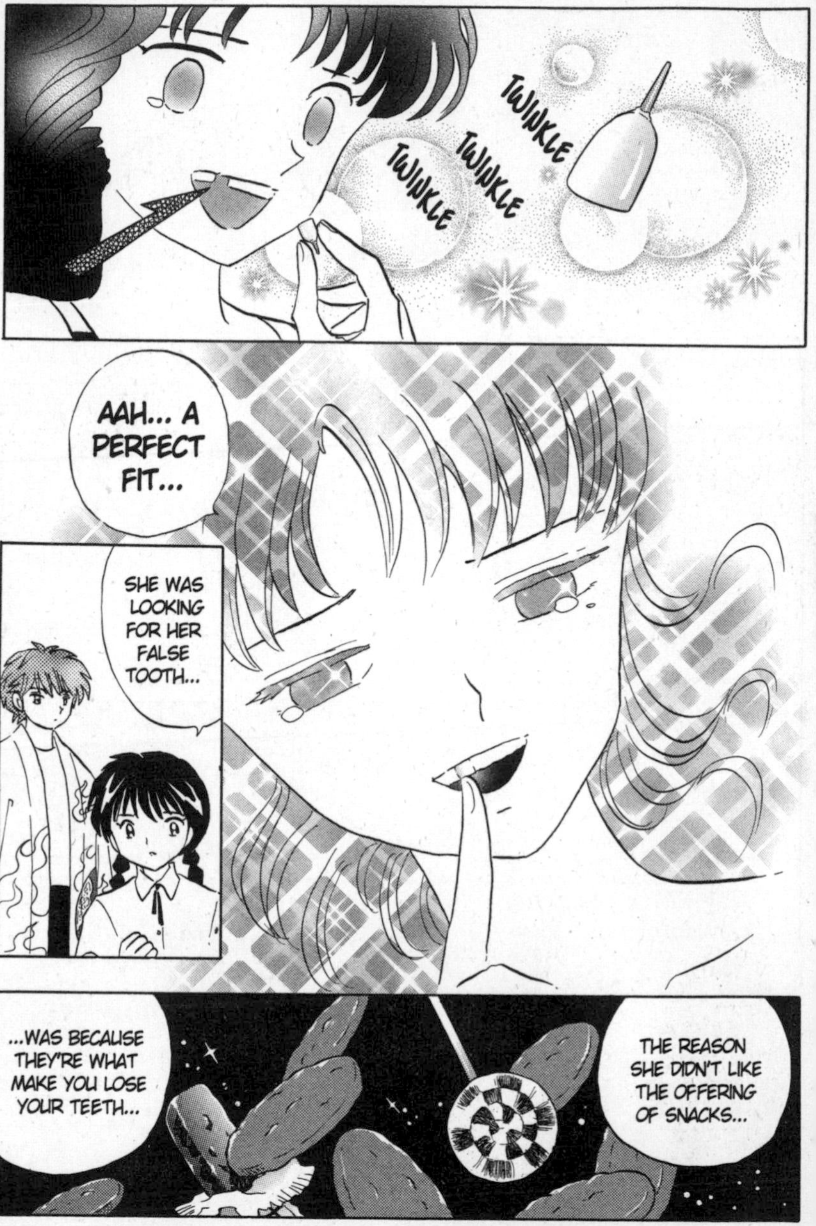
TWINKLE
TWINKLE
TWINKLE
AAH... A PERFECT FIT...
SHE WAS LOOKING FOR HER FALSE TOOTH...
THE REASON SHE DIDN'T LIKE THE OFFERING OF SNACKS...
...WAS BECAUSE THEY'RE WHAT MAKE YOU LOSE YOUR TEETH...

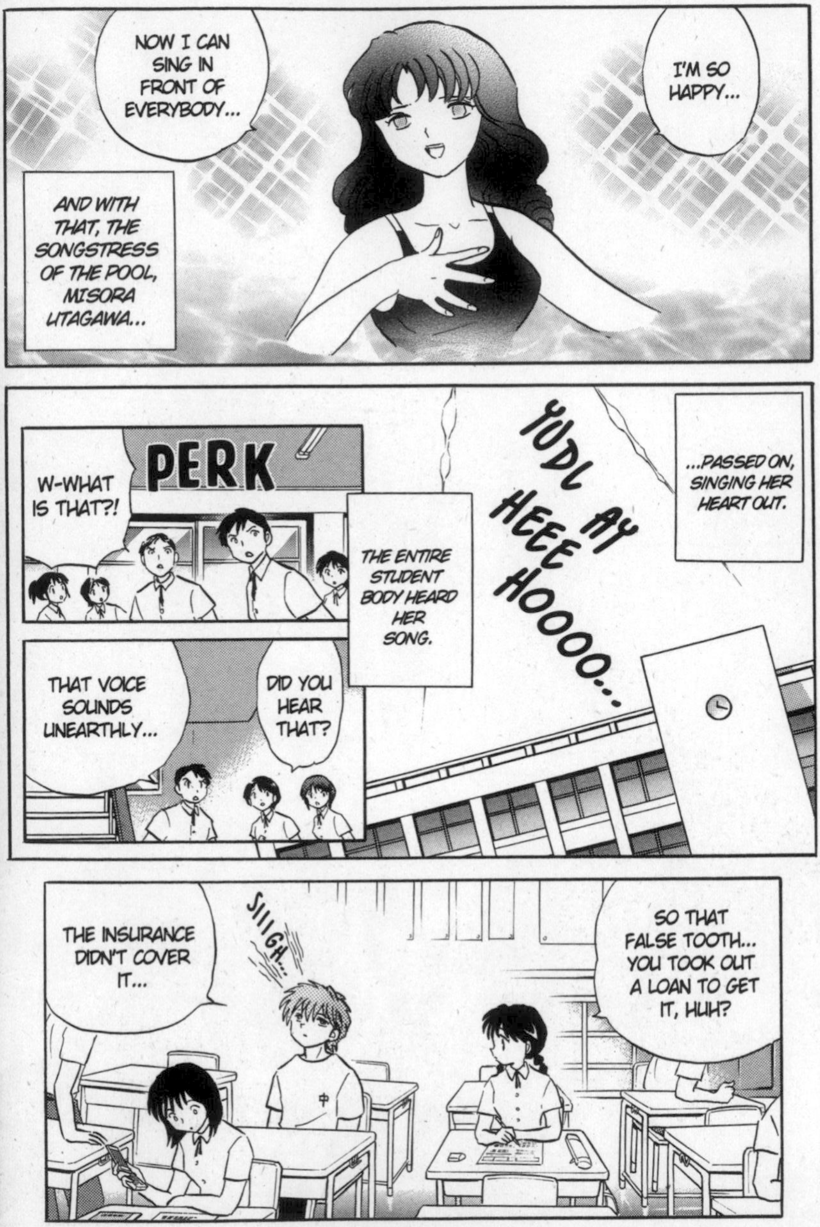
I'M SO HAPPY...
NOW I CAN SING IN FRONT OF EVERYBODY...
AND WITH THAT, THE SONGSTRESS OF THE POOL, MISORA UTAGAWA...
...PASSED ON, SINGING HER HEART OUT.
YUDL AY HEEE HOOOO...
THE ENTIRE STUDENT BODY HEARD HER SONG.
PERK
W-WHAT IS THAT?!
DID YOU HEAR THAT?
THAT VOICE SOUNDS UNEARTHLY...
SO THAT FALSE TOOTH... YOU TOOK OUT A LOAN TO GET IT, HUH?
SIIIGH...
THE INSURANCE DIDN'T COVER IT...

CHAPTER 13: CURSE

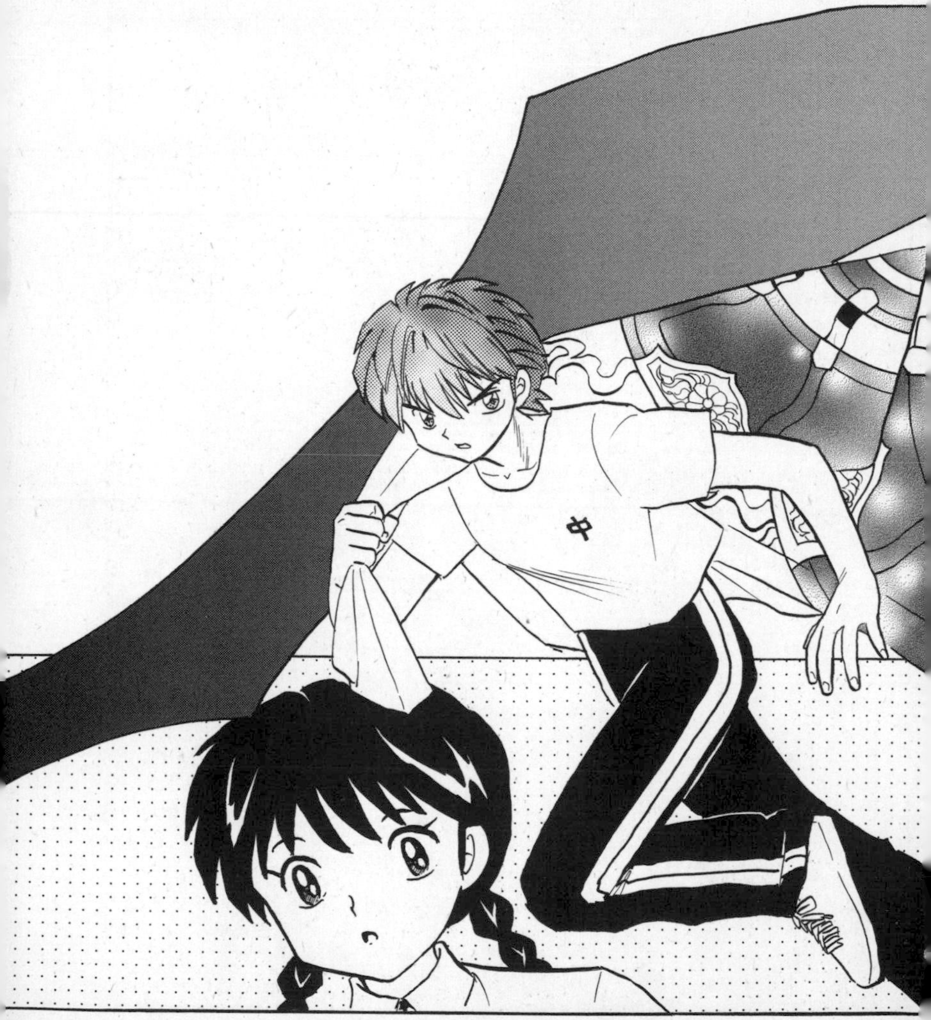

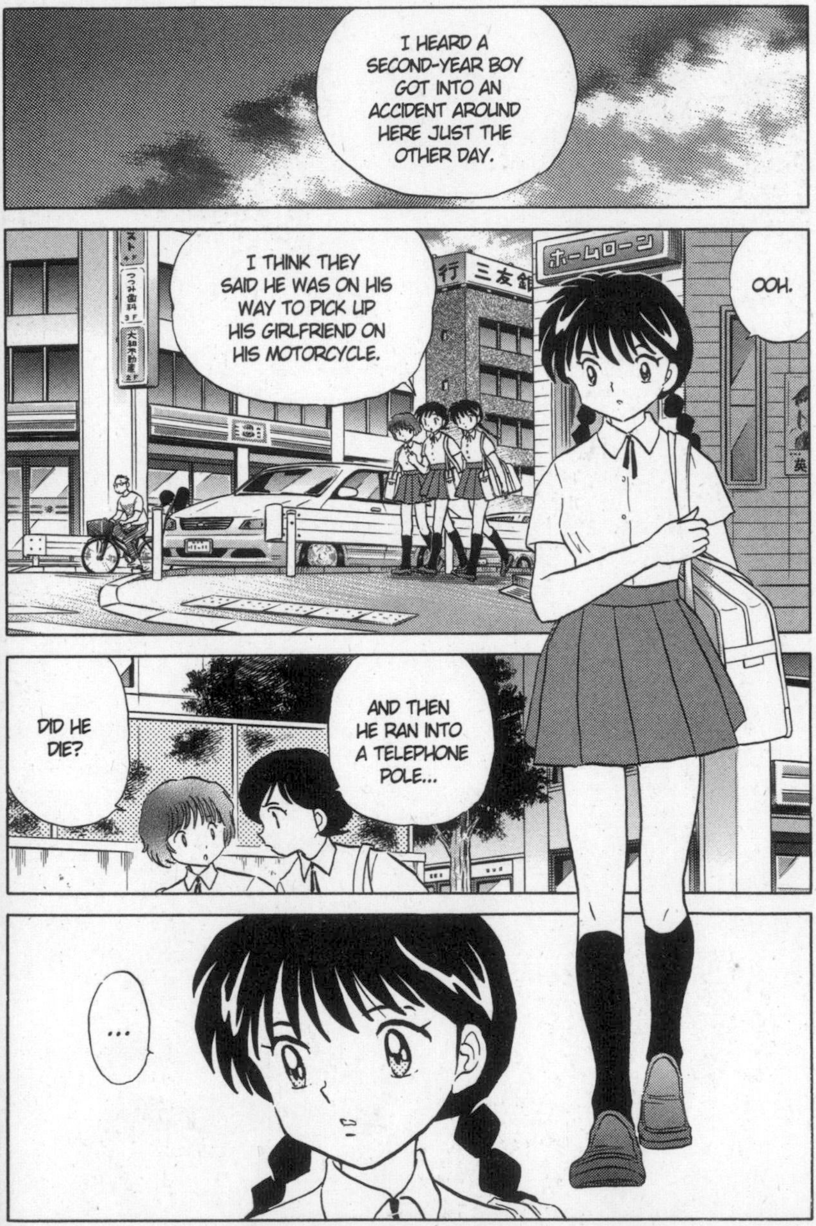
I HEARD A SECOND-YEAR BOY GOT INTO AN ACCIDENT AROUND HERE JUST THE OTHER DAY.
ホームローン
I THINK THEY SAID HE WAS ON HIS WAY TO PICK UP HIS GIRLFRIEND ON HIS MOTORCYCLE.
OOH.
AND THEN HE RAN INTO A TELEPHONE POLE...
DID HE DIE?
...

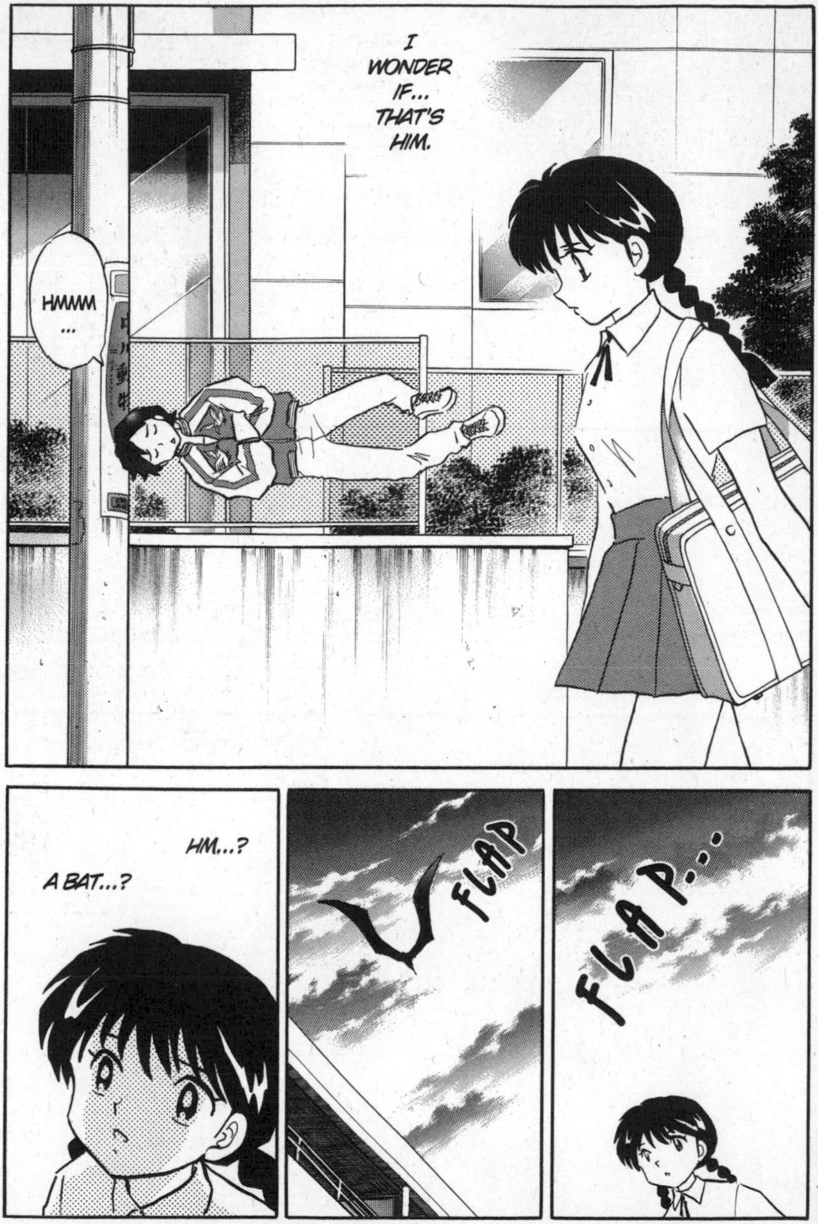
I WONDER IF... THAT'S HIM.
HMMM ...
FLAP...
FLAP
HM...?
A BAT...?

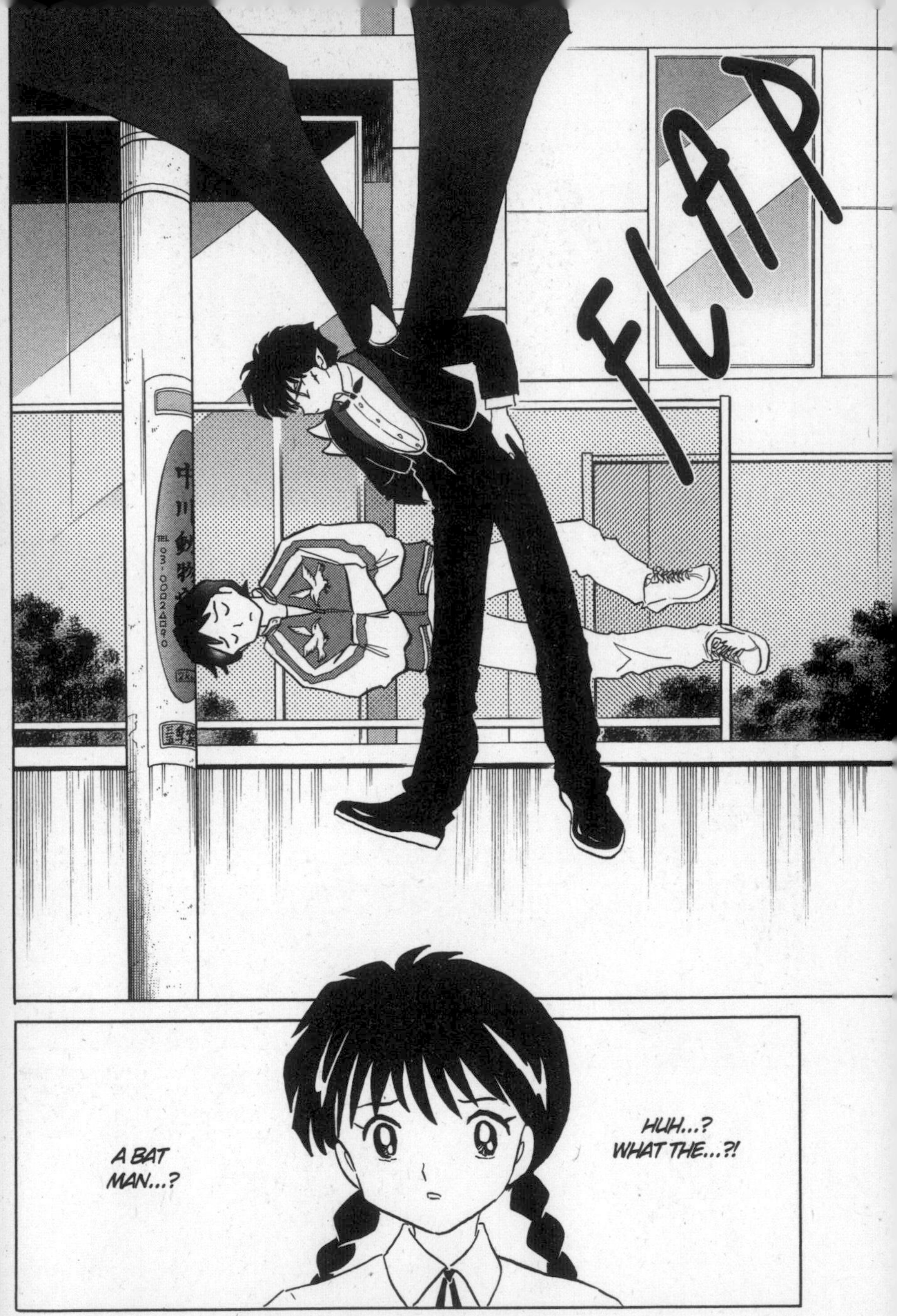
FLAP
HUH...? WHAT THE...?!
A BAT MAN...?

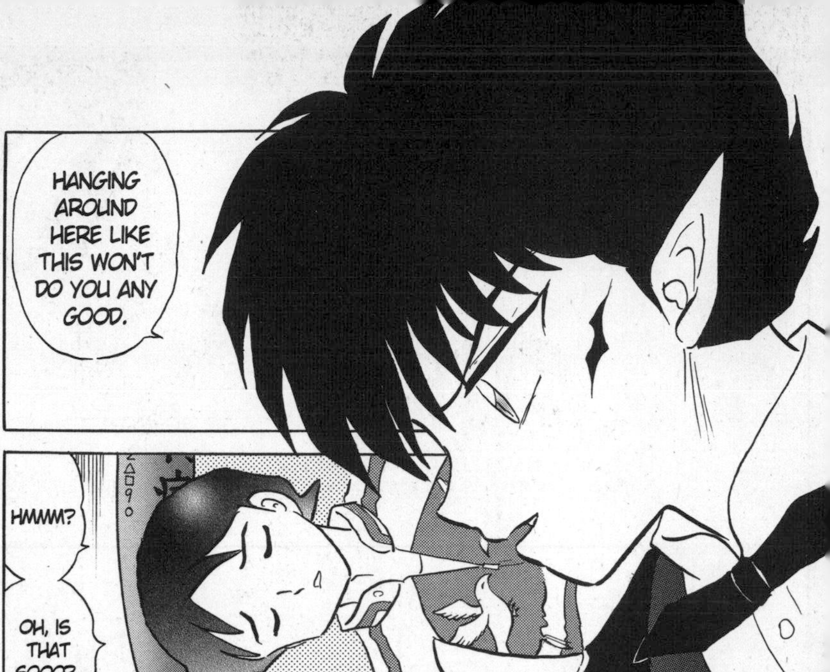
HANGING AROUND HERE LIKE THIS WON'T DO YOU ANY GOOD.
HMMMM?
OH, IS THAT SOOO?
YOU'LL CURSE THEM, GOT IT?!
GOT IT?!
HMMM ?
OOOH, OKAY.
GOOD. THAT'S A PROMISE.
SWFF
SQUEAK SQUEAK

Note: Kanji reads "curss," a miswriting of the kanji character for the word "curse"

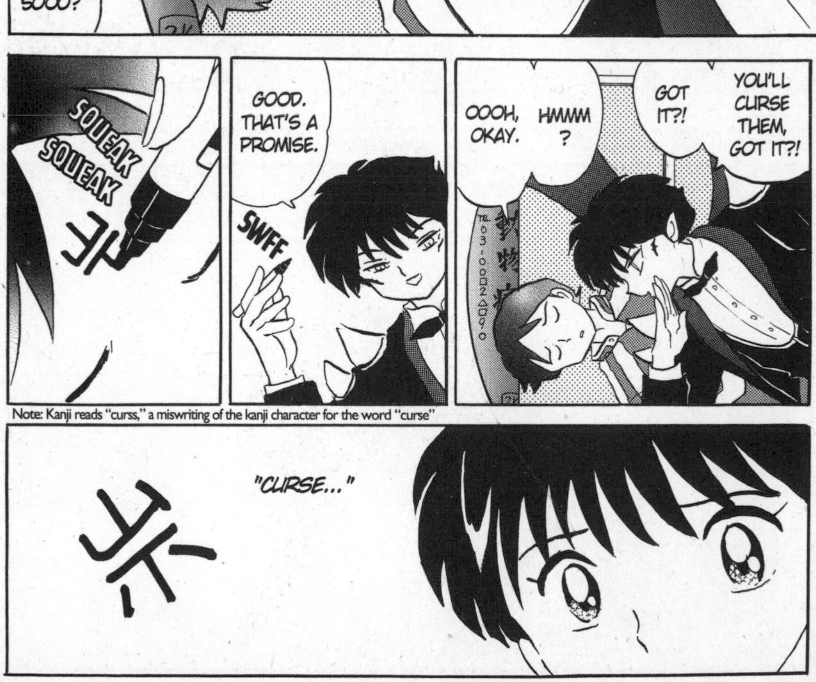
"CURSE..."

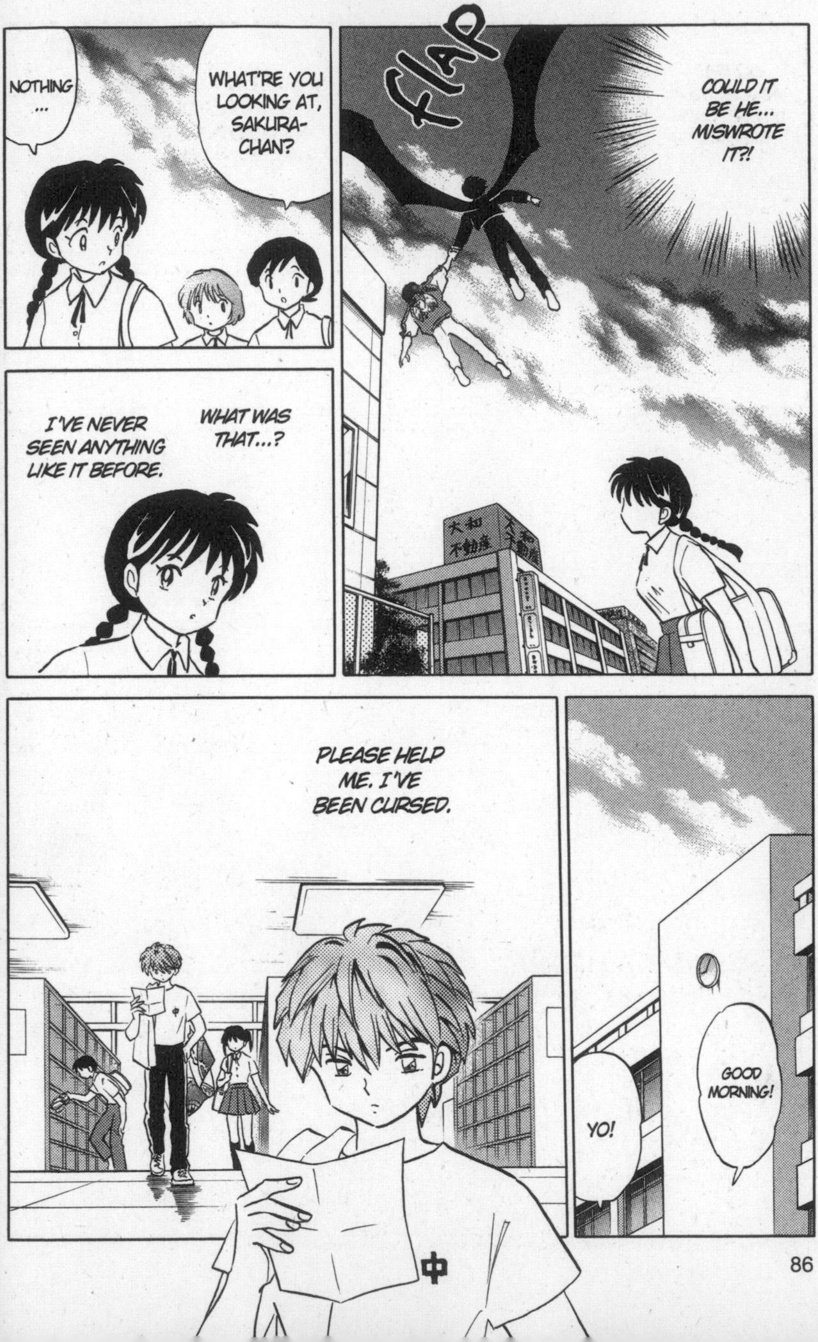
FLAP
COULD IT BE HE... MISWROTE IT?!
WHAT'RE YOU LOOKING AT, SAKURA-CHAN?
NOTHING ...
WHAT WAS THAT...?
I'VE NEVER SEEN ANYTHING LIKE IT BEFORE.
GOOD MORNING!
YO!
PLEASE HELP ME. I'VE BEEN CURSED.

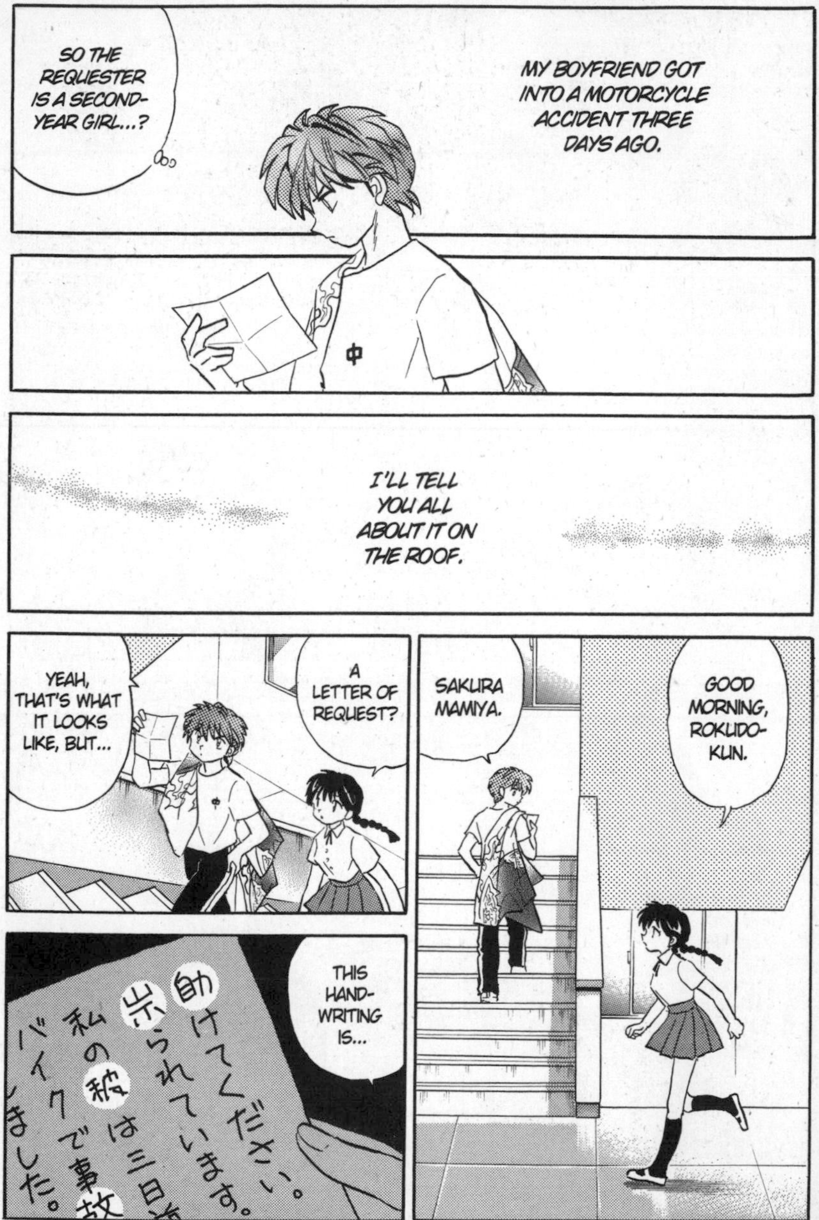
MY BOYFRIEND GOT INTO A MOTORCYCLE ACCIDENT THREE DAYS AGO.
SO THE REQUESTER IS A SECOND-YEAR GIRL...?
I'LL TELL YOU ALL ABOUT IT ON THE ROOF.
GOOD MORNING, ROKUDO-KUN.
SAKURA MAMIYA.
A LETTER OF REQUEST?
YEAH, THAT'S WHAT IT LOOKS LIKE, BUT...
THIS HAND-WRITING IS...
助けてください。
祟られています。
私の彼は三日前
バイクで事故
しました。
Letter: Please **hellp** me. I've been **curssed**. My **boifrend** got into a motorcycle **axident** three days ago.

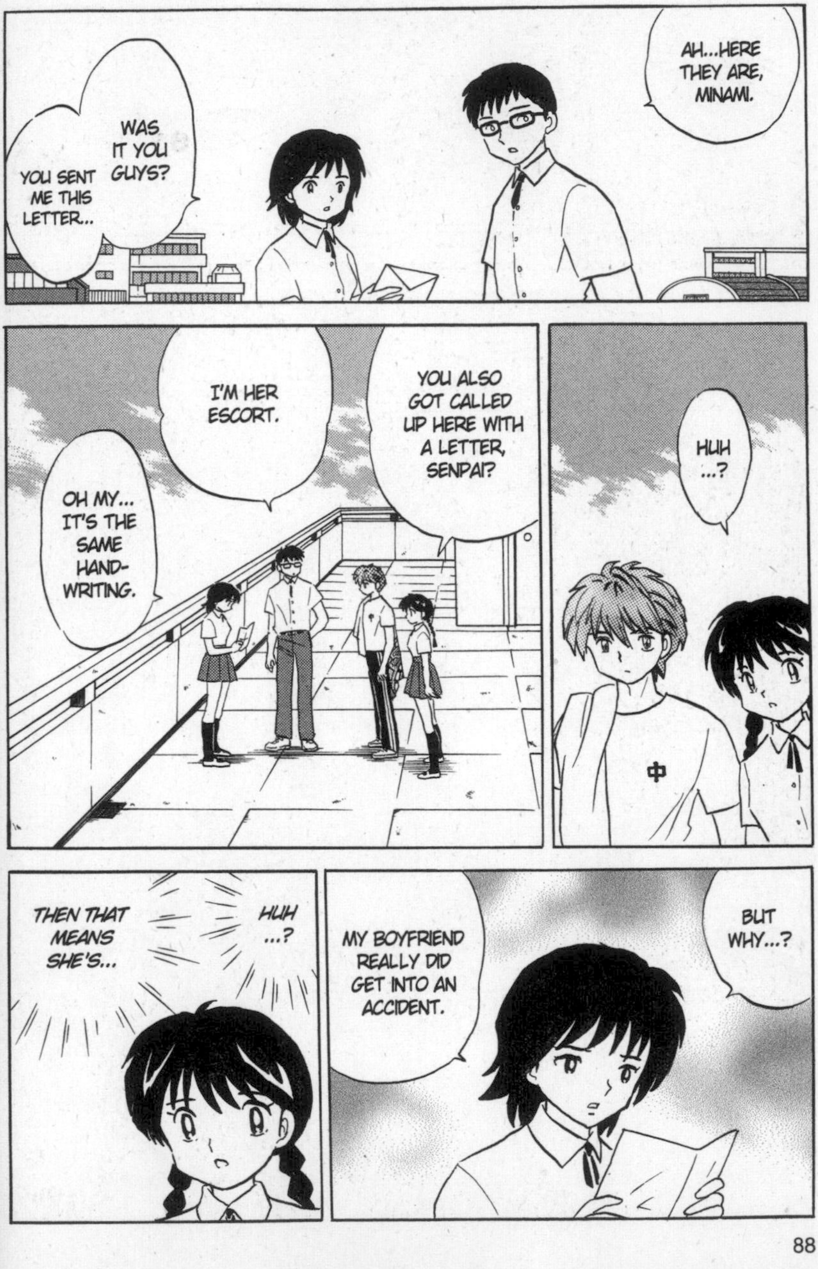
AH...HERE THEY ARE, MINAMI.
WAS IT YOU GUYS?
YOU SENT ME THIS LETTER...
HUH ...?
YOU ALSO GOT CALLED UP HERE WITH A LETTER, SENPAI?
I'M HER ESCORT.
OH MY... IT'S THE SAME HAND-WRITING.
BUT WHY...?
MY BOYFRIEND REALLY DID GET INTO AN ACCIDENT.
HUH ...?
THEN THAT MEANS SHE'S...

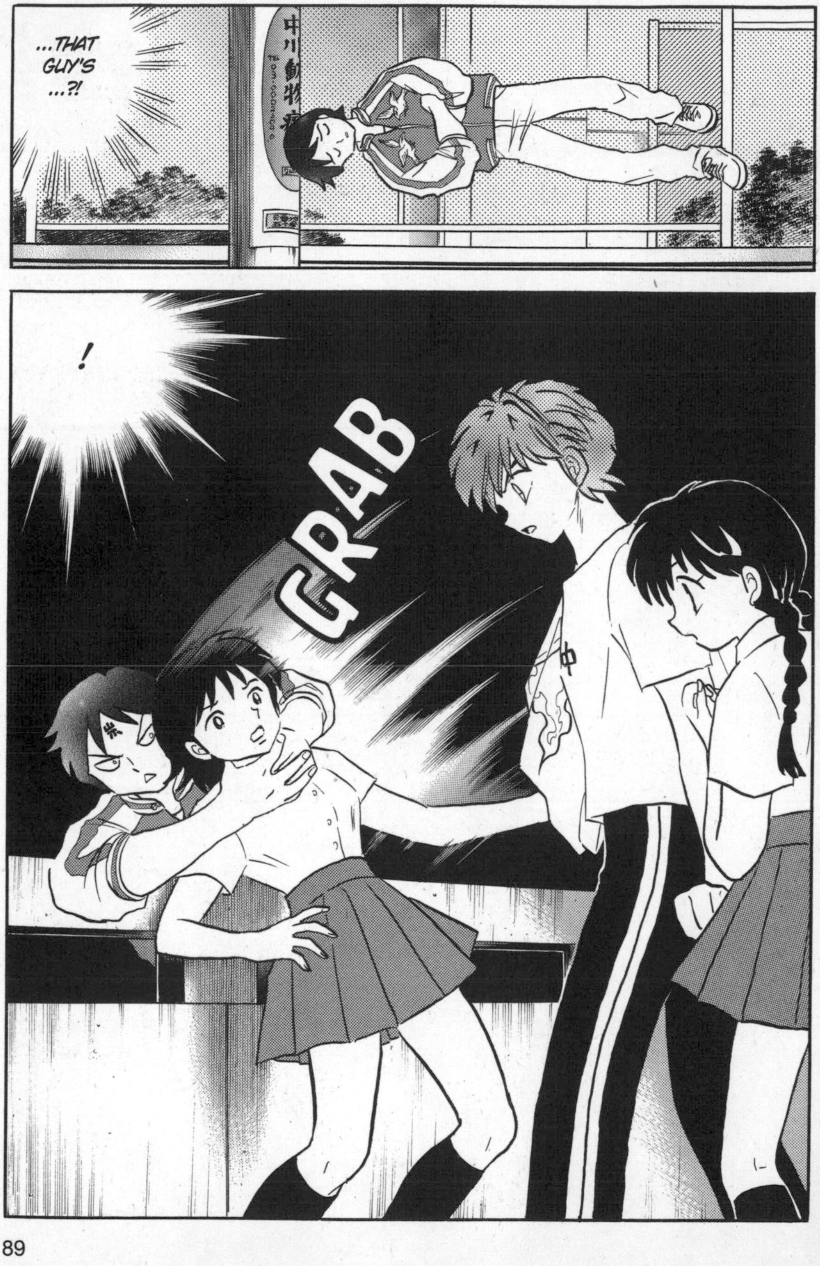
...THAT GUY'S ...?!
!
GRAB

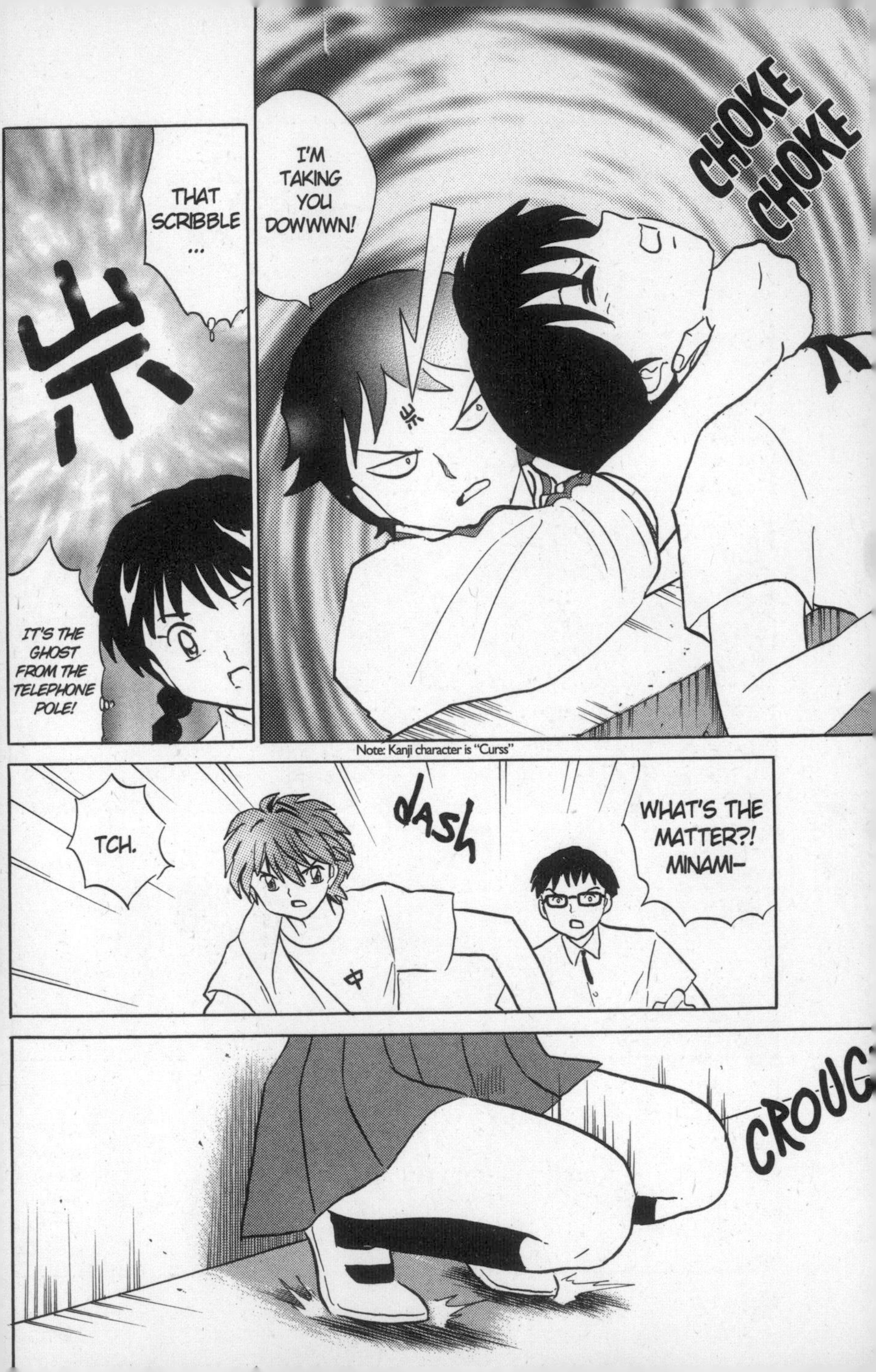
CHOKE CHOKE
I'M TAKING YOU DOWWWN!
THAT SCRIBBLE ...
IT'S THE GHOST FROM THE TELEPHONE POLE!
WHAT'S THE MATTER?! MINAMI-
dash
TCH.
CROUC
Note: Kanji character is "Curss"

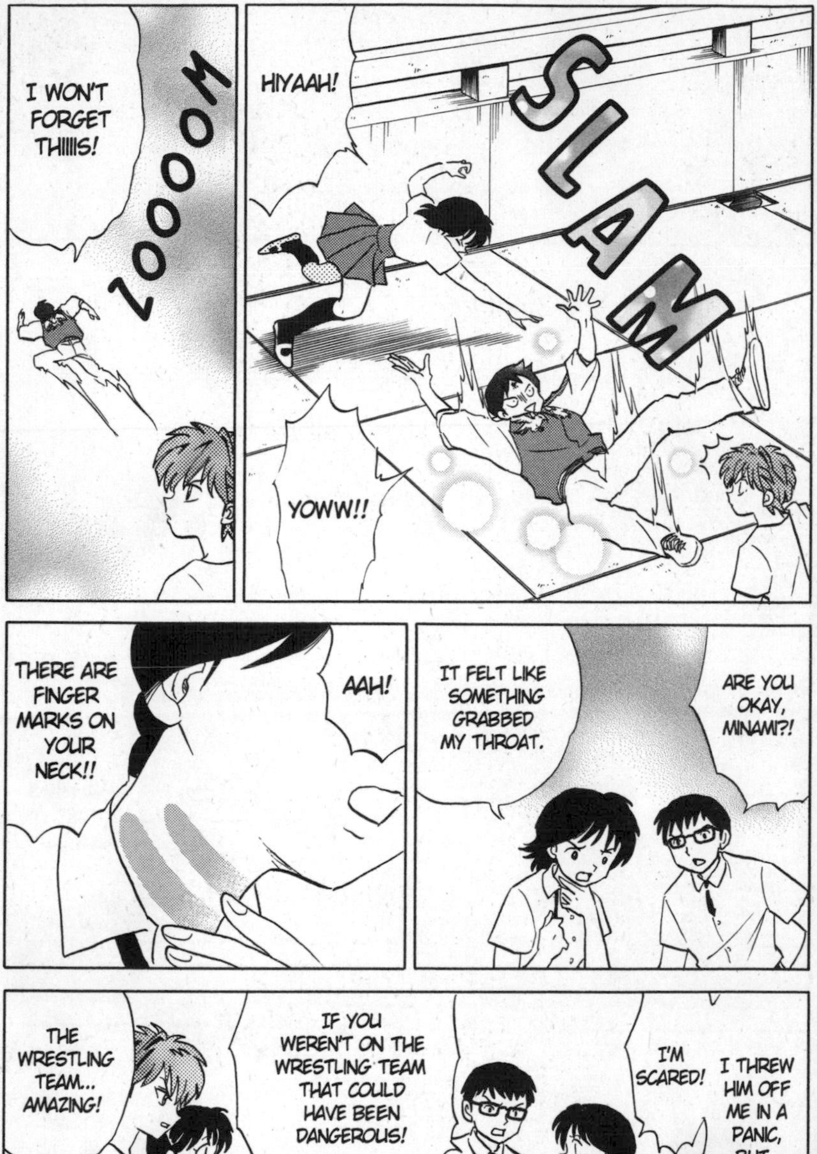
HIYAAH!
SLAM
YOWW!!
ZOOOOM
I WON'T FORGET THIIIIS!
ARE YOU OKAY, MINAMI?!
IT FELT LIKE SOMETHING GRABBED MY THROAT.
AAH!
THERE ARE FINGER MARKS ON YOUR NECK!!
I THREW HIM OFF ME IN A PANIC, BUT...
I'M SCARED!
IF YOU WEREN'T ON THE WRESTLING TEAM THAT COULD HAVE BEEN DANGEROUS!
THE WRESTLING TEAM... AMAZING!

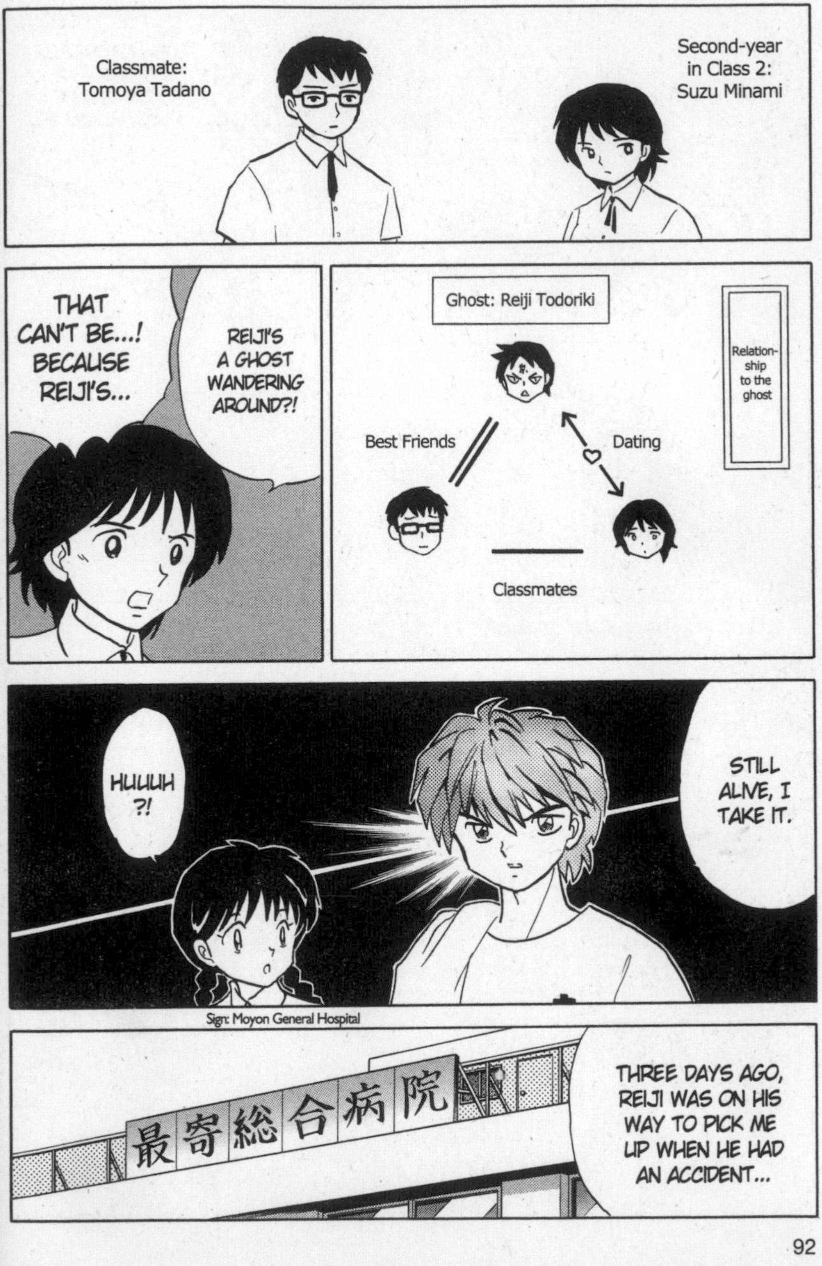
Second-year in Class 2: Suzu Minami
Classmate: Tomoya Tadano
Relationship to the ghost
Ghost: Reiji Todoriki
Dating
Best Friends
Classmates
REIJI'S A GHOST WANDERING AROUND?!
THAT CAN'T BE...! BECAUSE REIJI'S...
STILL ALIVE, I TAKE IT.
HUUUH ?!
Sign: Moyon General Hospital
THREE DAYS AGO, REIJI WAS ON HIS WAY TO PICK ME UP WHEN HE HAD AN ACCIDENT...
最寄総合病院

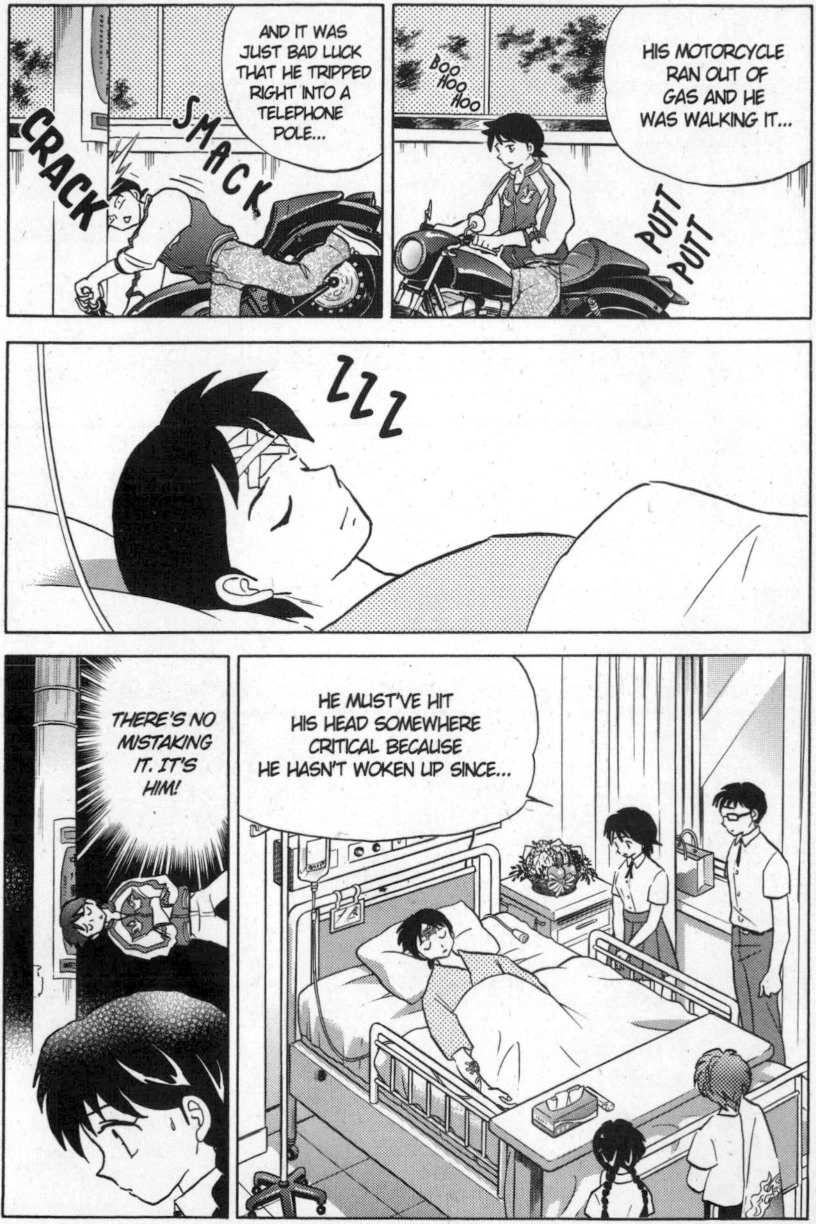

HIS MOTORCYCLE RAN OUT OF GAS AND HE WAS WALKING IT...
BOO HOO HOO
PUTT PUTT
AND IT WAS JUST BAD LUCK THAT HE TRIPPED RIGHT INTO A TELEPHONE POLE...
SMACK
CRACK
ZZZ
HE MUST'VE HIT HIS HEAD SOMEWHERE CRITICAL BECAUSE HE HASN'T WOKEN UP SINCE...
THERE'S NO MISTAKING IT. IT'S HIM!

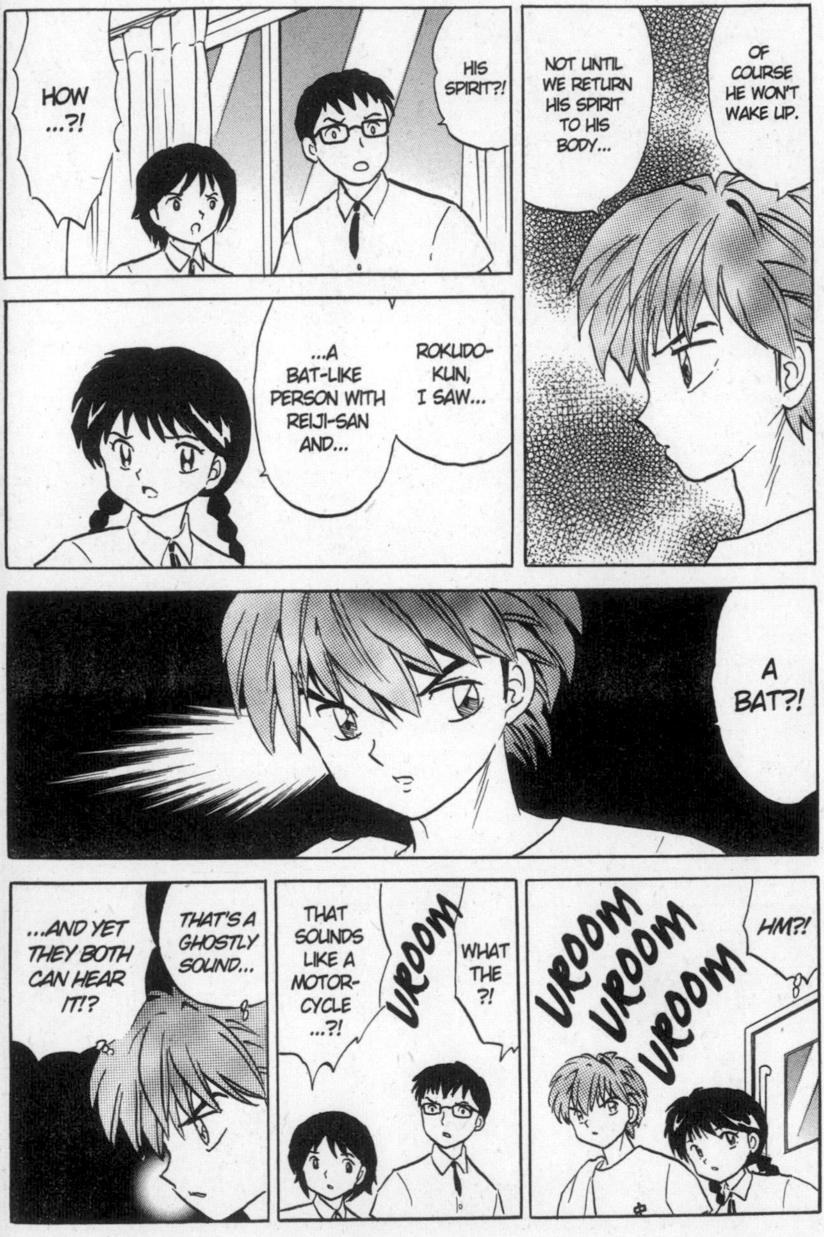
OF COURSE HE WON'T WAKE UP.
NOT UNTIL WE RETURN HIS SPIRIT TO HIS BODY...
HIS SPIRIT?!
HOW ...?!
ROKUDO-KUN, I SAW...
...A BAT-LIKE PERSON WITH REIJI-SAN AND...
A BAT?!
HM?!
VROOM VROOM VROOM
WHAT THE ?!
VROOM
THAT SOUNDS LIKE A MOTOR-CYCLE ...?!
THAT'S A GHOSTLY SOUND...
...AND YET THEY BOTH CAN HEAR IT!?

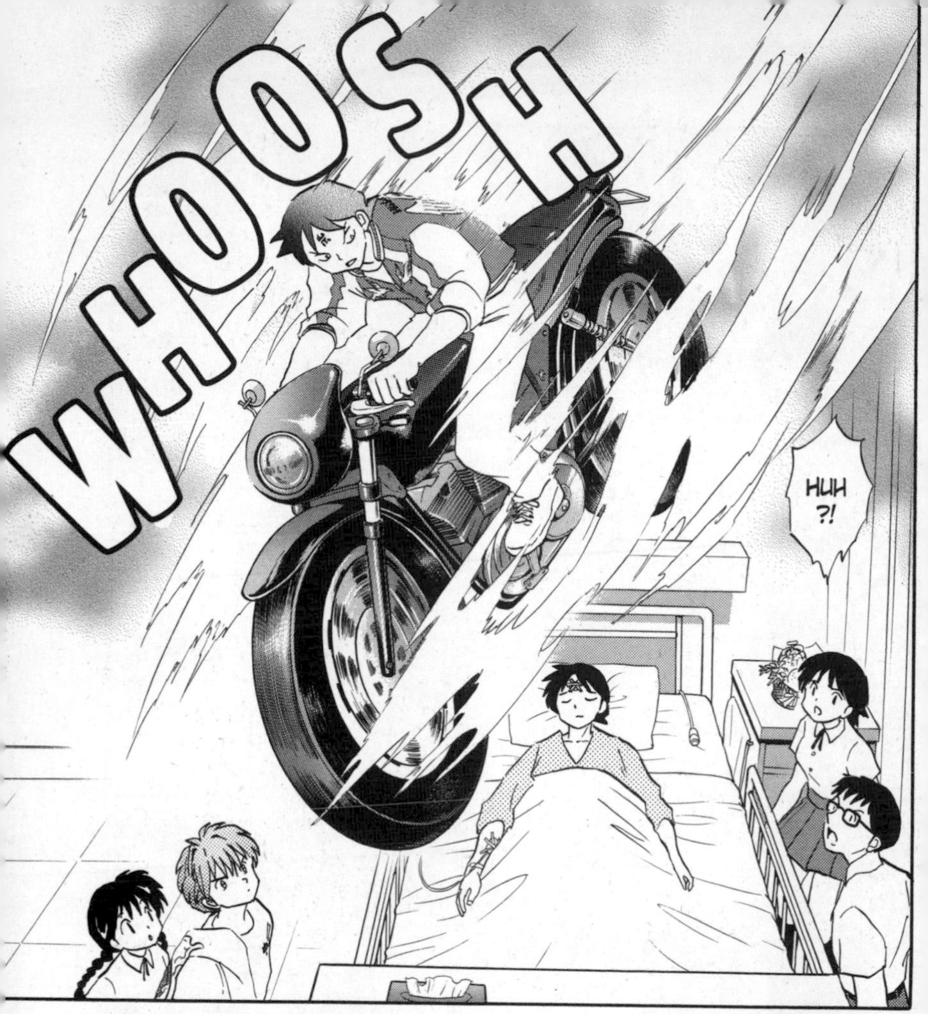
WHOOSH
HUH ?!

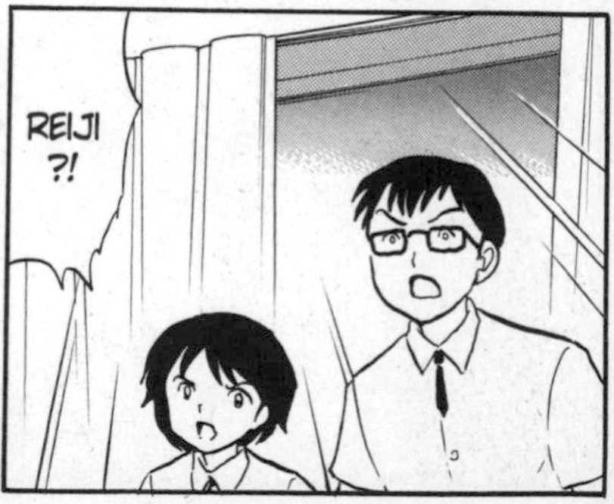
REIJI ?!

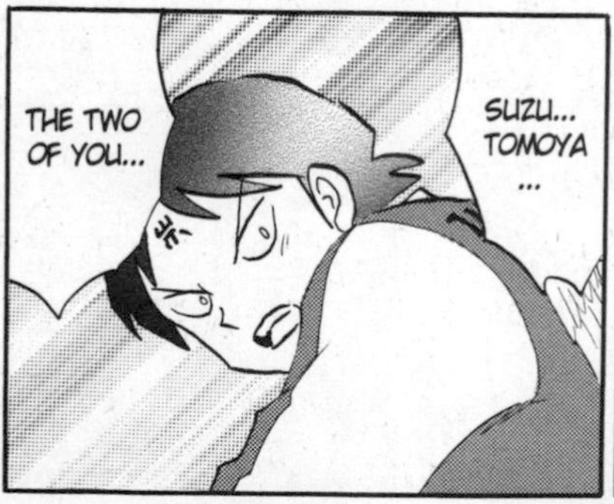
SUZU... TOMOYA ...
THE TWO OF YOU...

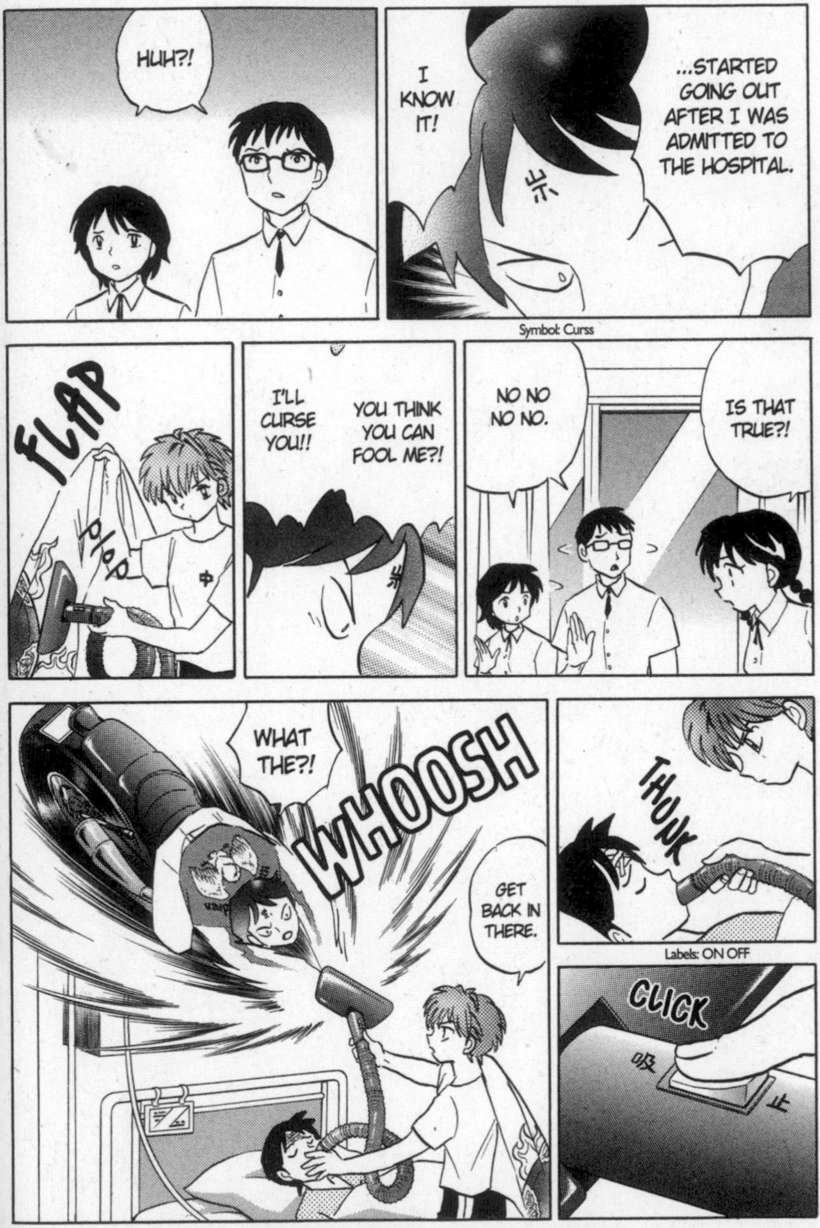
...STARTED GOING OUT AFTER I WAS ADMITTED TO THE HOSPITAL.
I KNOW IT!
HUH?!
Symbol: Curss
IS THAT TRUE?!
NO NO NO NO.
YOU THINK YOU CAN FOOL ME?!
I'LL CURSE YOU!!
FLAP
PLOP
THUNK
Labels: ON OFF
CLICK
WHAT THE?!
WHOOSH
GET BACK IN THERE.

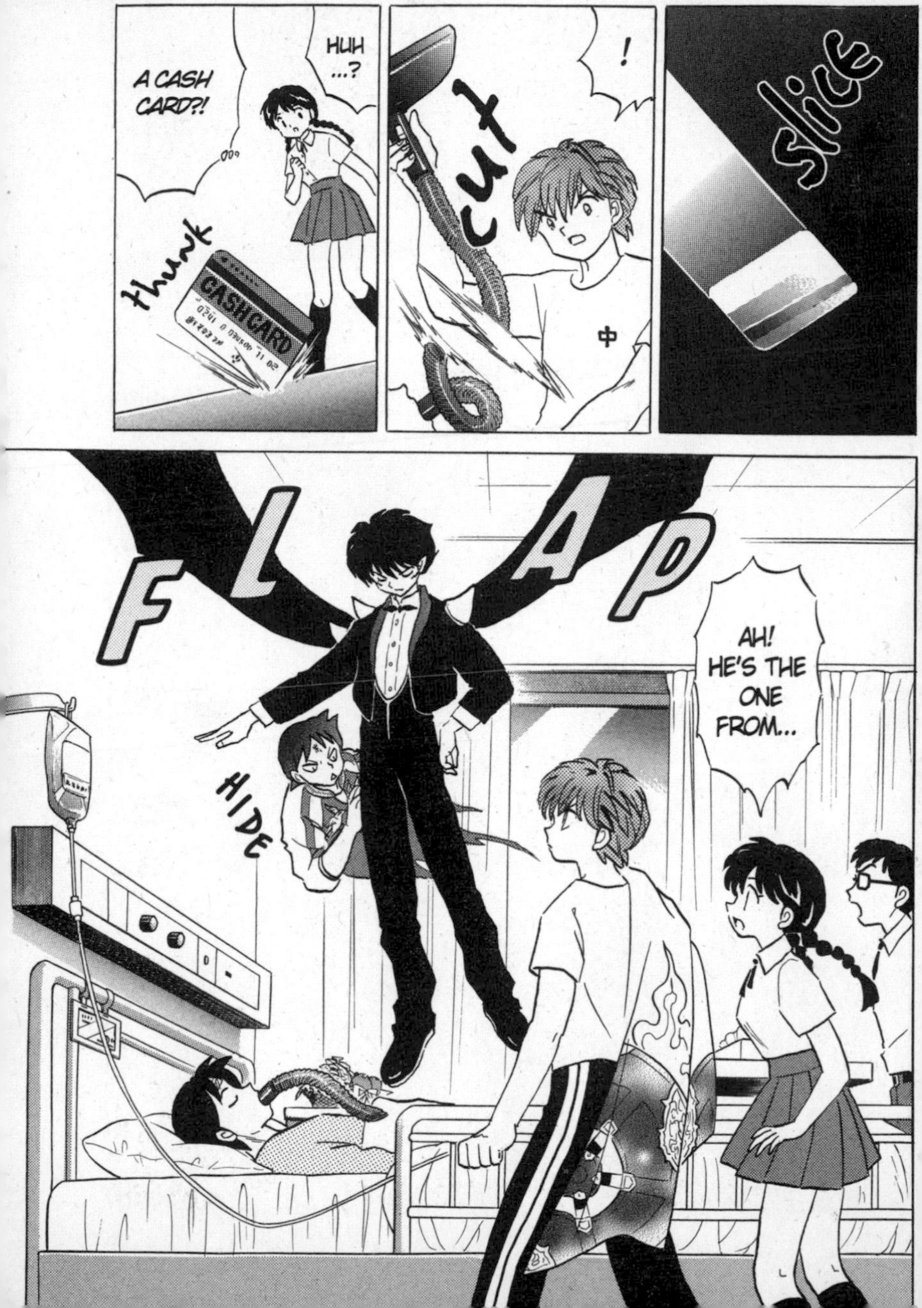
slice
!
cut
HUH ...?
A CASH CARD?!
thunk
CASH CARD
FLAP
AH! HE'S THE ONE FROM...
HIDE

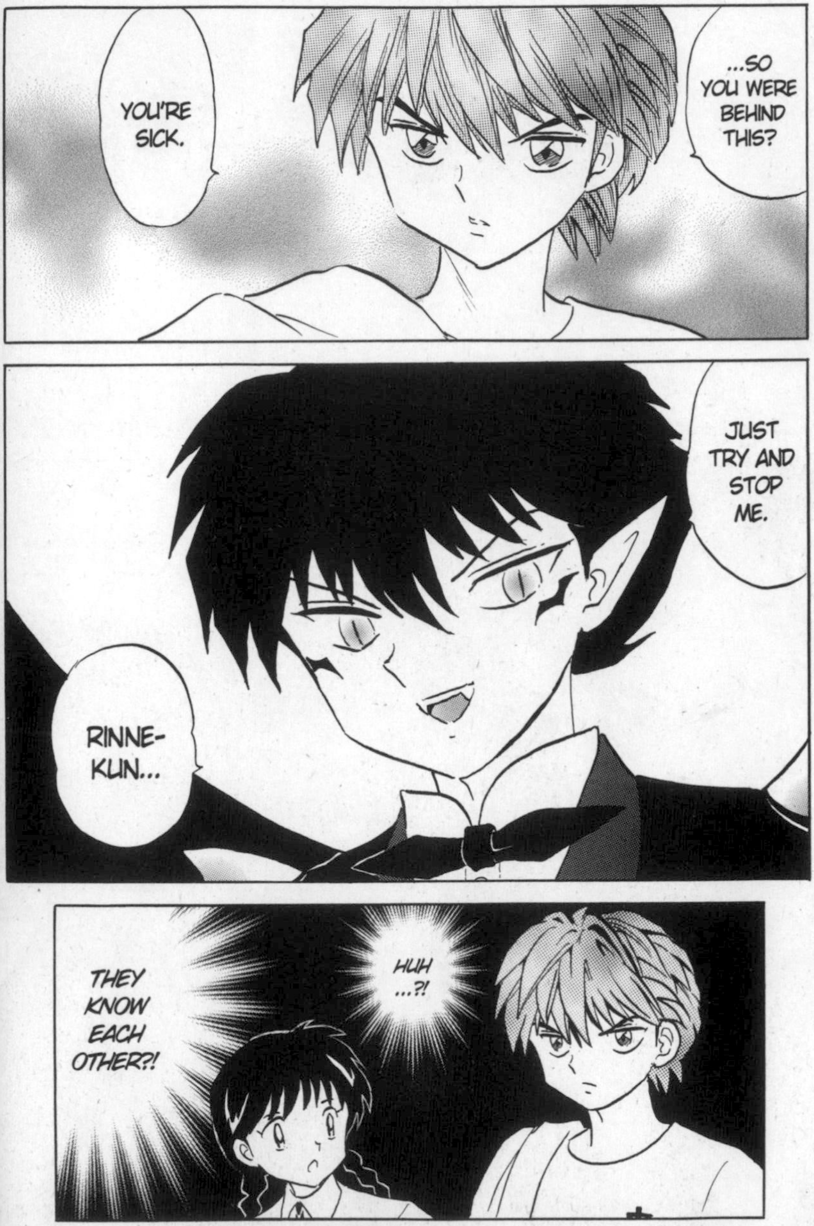
...SO YOU WERE BEHIND THIS?
YOU'RE SICK.
JUST TRY AND STOP ME.
RINNE-KUN...
HUH ...?!
THEY KNOW EACH OTHER?!

CHAPTER 14: DUEL AT THE RABBIT HUTCH

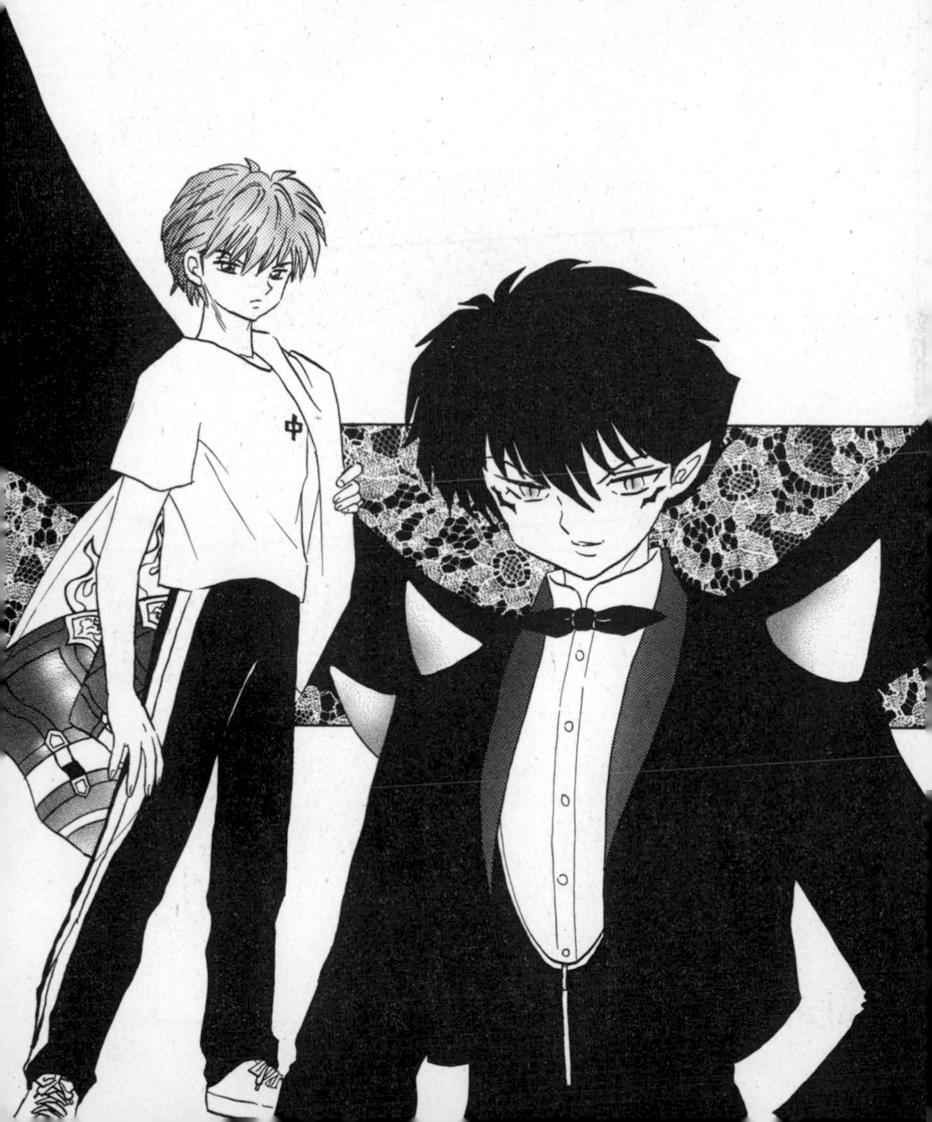

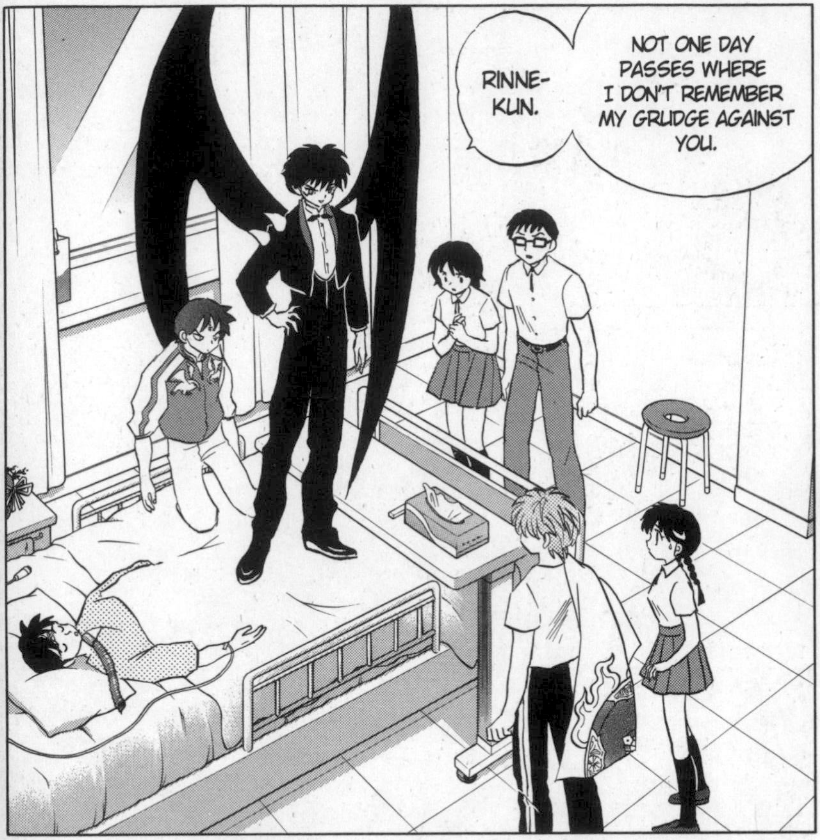
NOT ONE DAY PASSES WHERE I DON'T REMEMBER MY GRUDGE AGAINST YOU.
RINNE-KUN.
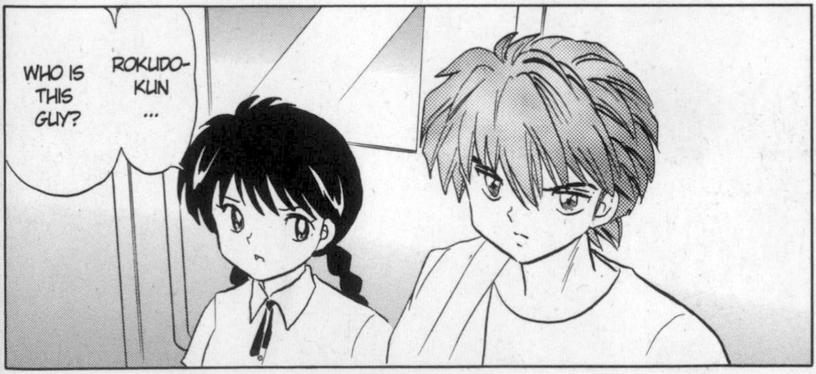
ROKUDO-KUN ...
WHO IS THIS GUY?

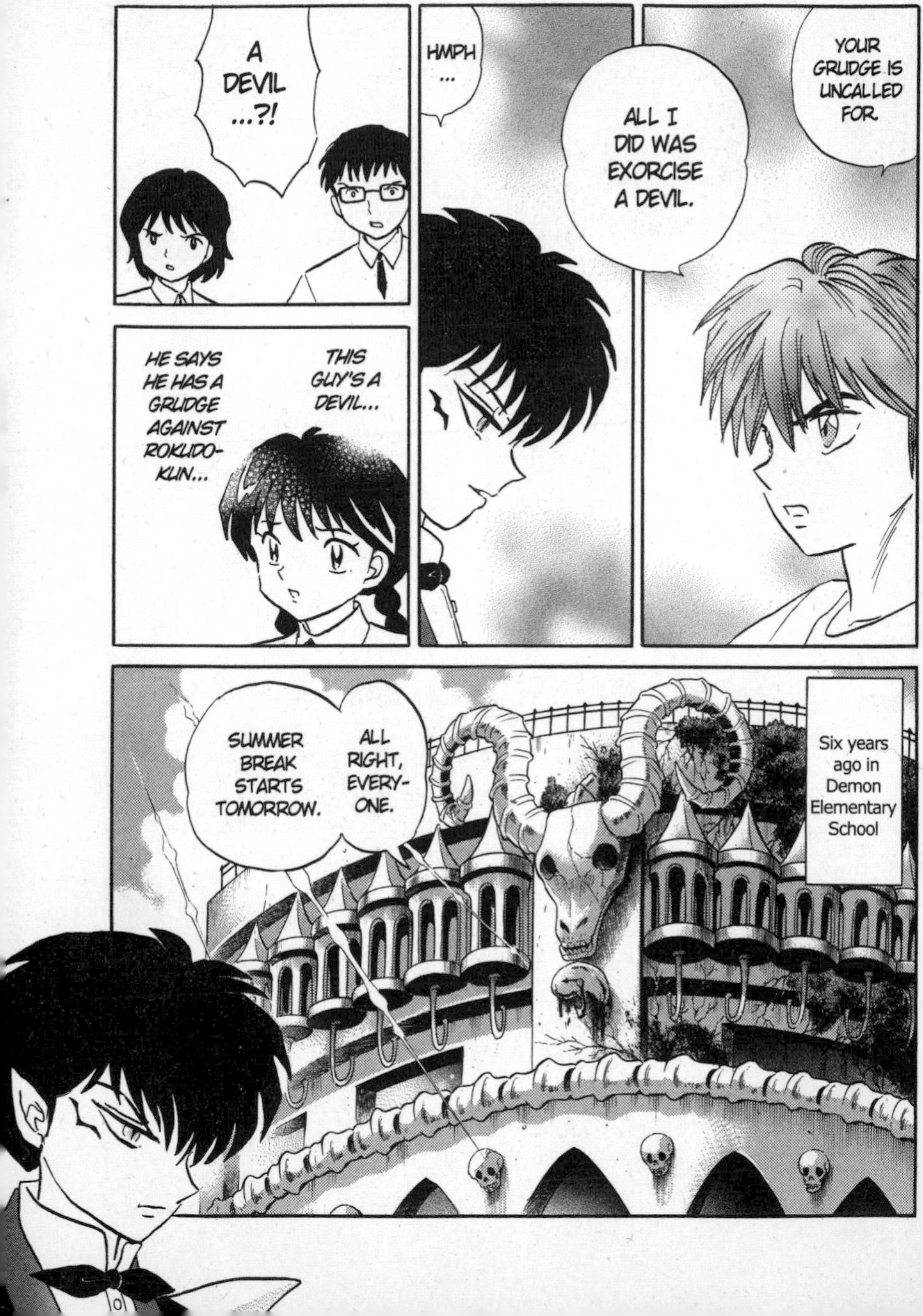
YOUR GRUDGE IS UNCALLED FOR.
ALL I DID WAS EXORCISE A DEVIL.
HMPH ...
A DEVIL ...?!
THIS GUY'S A DEVIL...
HE SAYS HE HAS A GRUDGE AGAINST ROKUDO-KUN...
Six years ago in Demon Elementary School
ALL RIGHT, EVERY-ONE.
SUMMER BREAK STARTS TOMORROW.

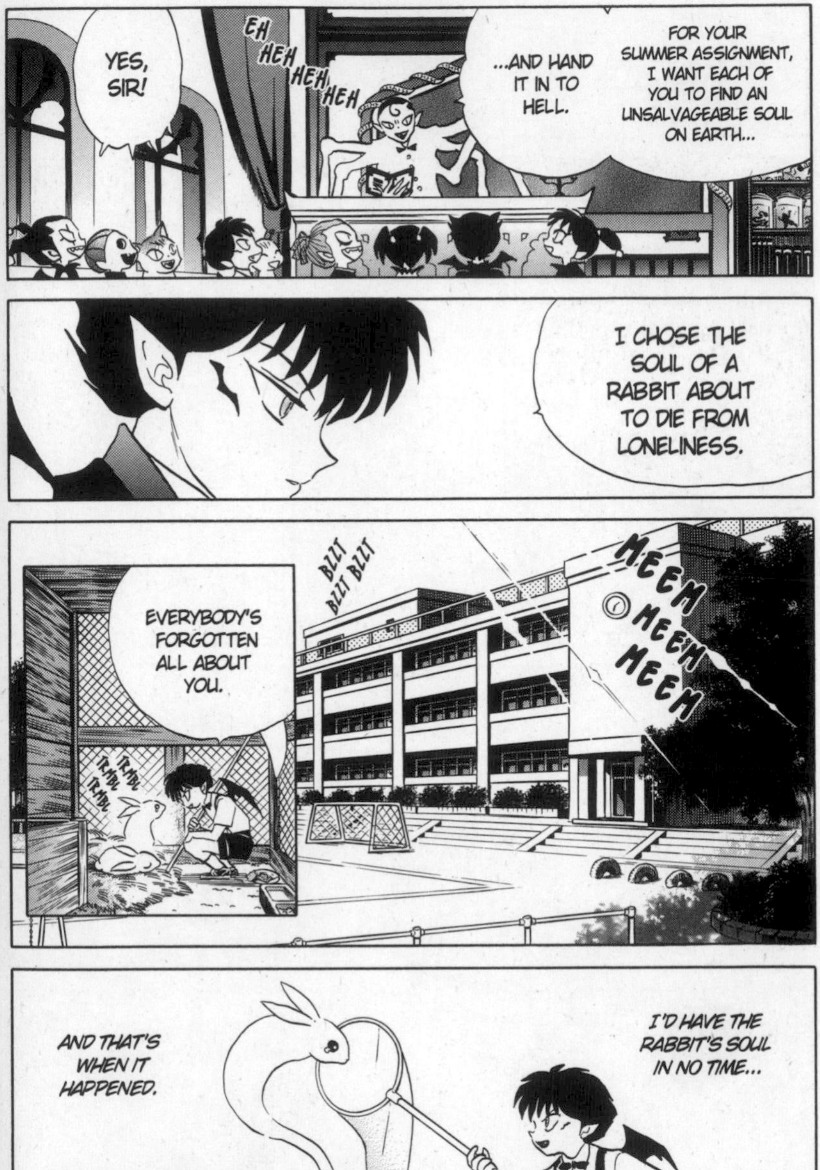
FOR YOUR SUMMER ASSIGNMENT, I WANT EACH OF YOU TO FIND AN UNSALVAGEABLE SOUL ON EARTH...
...AND HAND IT IN TO HELL.
EH HEH HEH HEH
YES, SIR!
I CHOSE THE SOUL OF A RABBIT ABOUT TO DIE FROM LONELINESS.
MEEM MEEM MEEM
BZZT BZZT BZZT
EVERYBODY'S FORGOTTEN ALL ABOUT YOU.
TRMBL TRMBL TRMBL
I'D HAVE THE RABBIT'S SOUL IN NO TIME...
AND THAT'S WHEN IT HAPPENED.

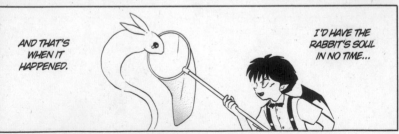

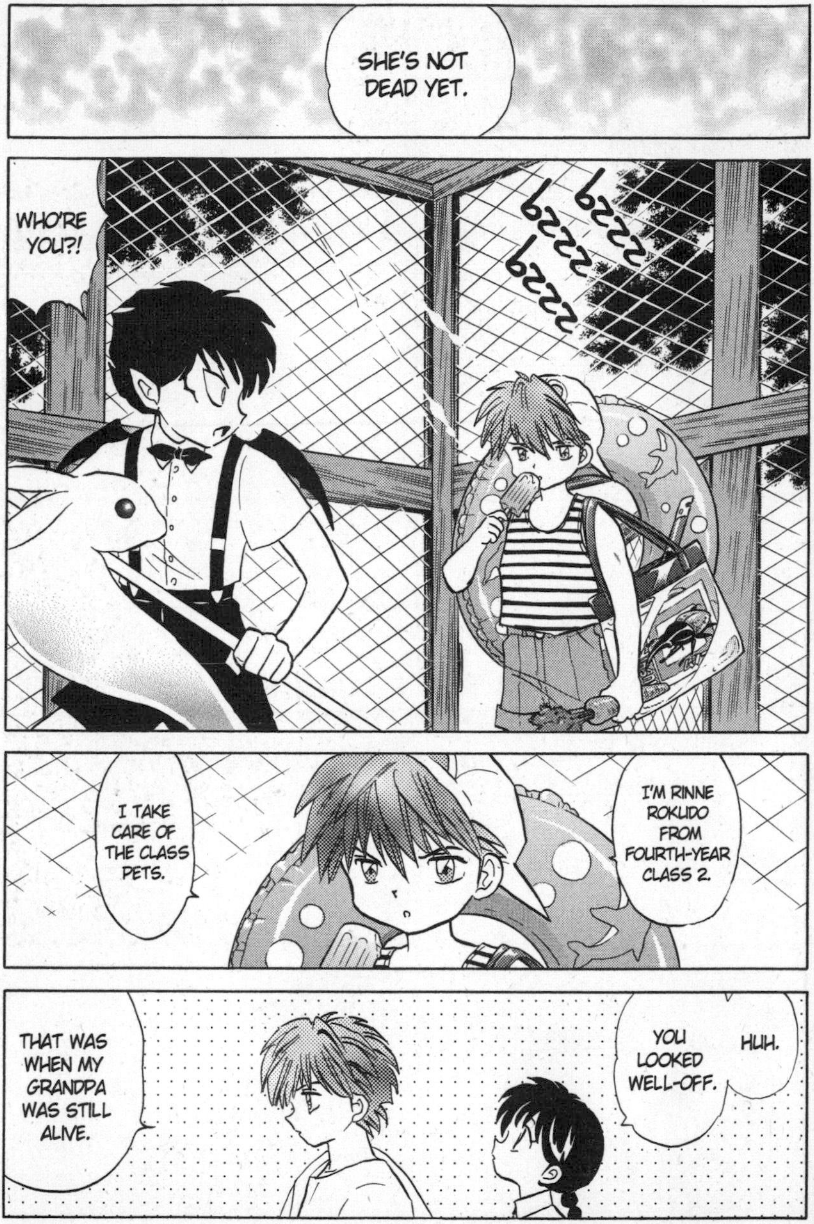
SHE'S NOT DEAD YET.
bzzzz
bzzzz
bzzzz
WHO'RE YOU?!
I'M RINNE ROKUDO FROM FOURTH-YEAR CLASS 2.
I TAKE CARE OF THE CLASS PETS.
HUH.
YOU LOOKED WELL-OFF.
THAT WAS WHEN MY GRANDPA WAS STILL ALIVE.

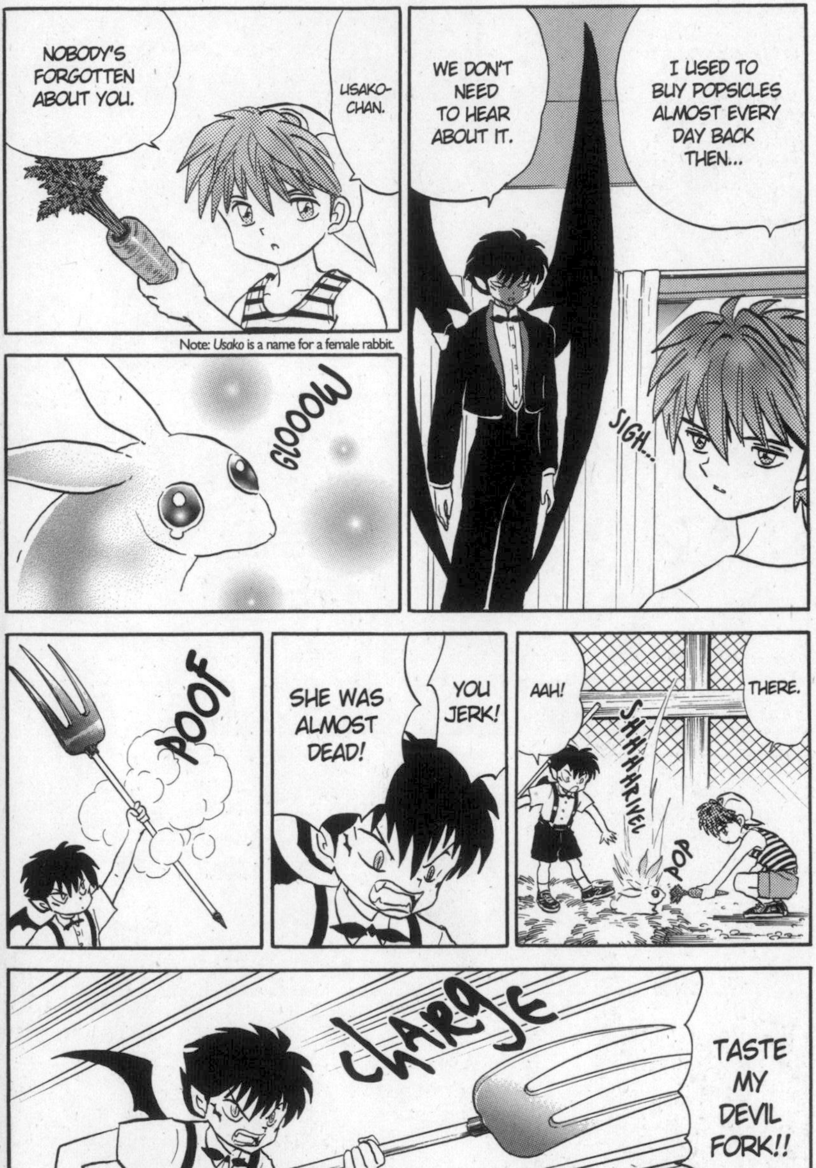
I USED TO BUY POPSICLES ALMOST EVERY DAY BACK THEN...
WE DON'T NEED TO HEAR ABOUT IT.
SIGH...
USAKO-CHAN.
NOBODY'S FORGOTTEN ABOUT YOU.
GLOOOW
THERE.
AAH!
SHHHHRIVEL
POP
YOU JERK!
SHE WAS ALMOST DEAD!
POOF
TASTE MY DEVIL FORK!!
CHARGE
Note: *Usako* is a name for a female rabbit.

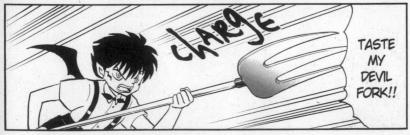

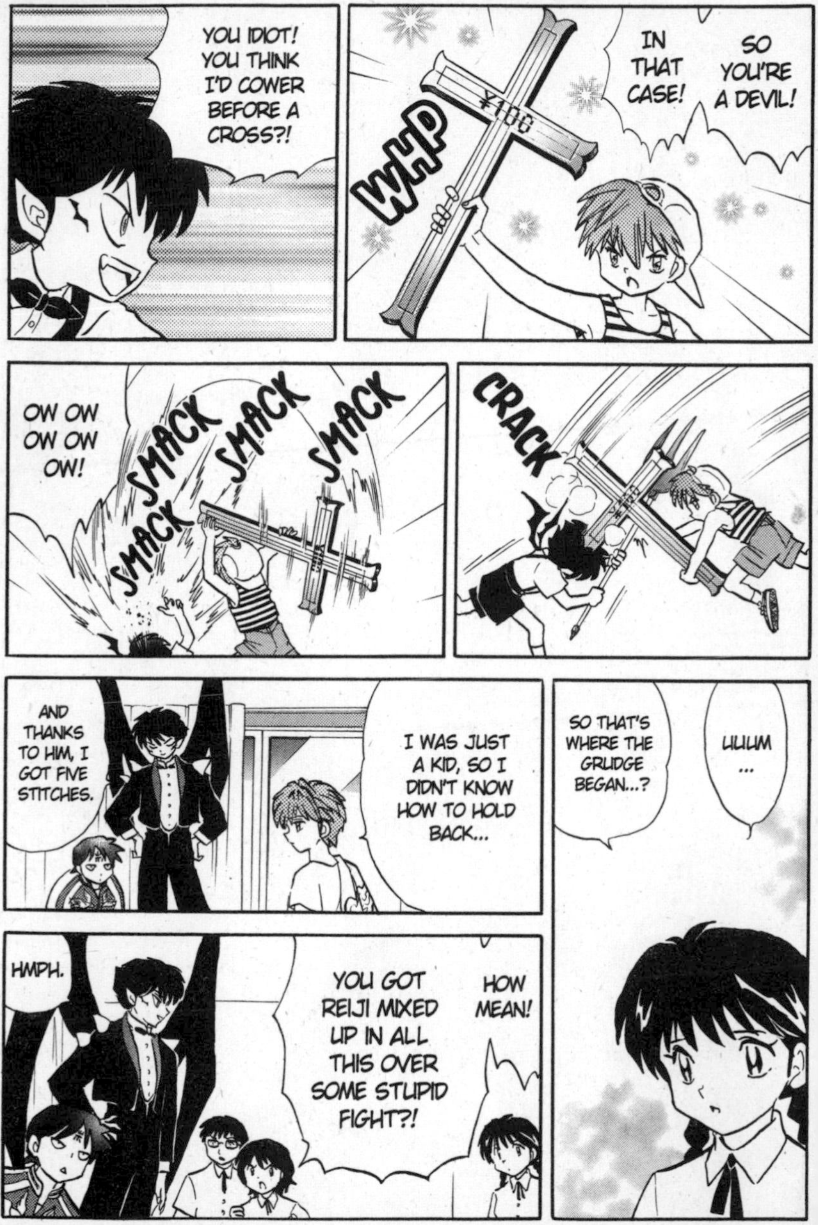
SO YOU'RE A DEVIL!
IN THAT CASE!
¥100
WHP
YOU IDIOT! YOU THINK I'D COWER BEFORE A CROSS?!
CRACK
SMACK SMACK SMACK SMACK
OW OW OW OW OW!
UUUM ...
SO THAT'S WHERE THE GRUDGE BEGAN...?
I WAS JUST A KID, SO I DIDN'T KNOW HOW TO HOLD BACK...
AND THANKS TO HIM, I GOT FIVE STITCHES.
HOW MEAN!
YOU GOT REIJI MIXED UP IN ALL THIS OVER SOME STUPID FIGHT?!
HMPH.

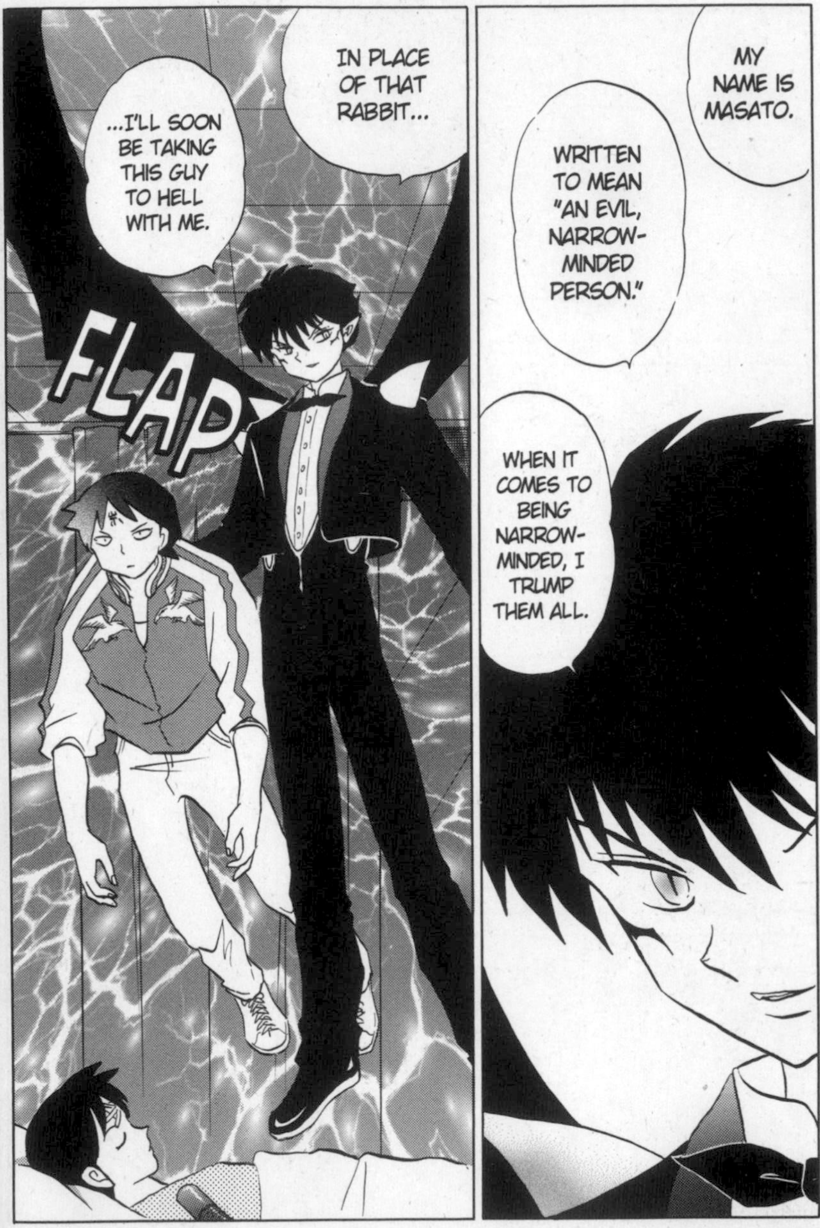
MY NAME IS MASATO.
WRITTEN TO MEAN "AN EVIL, NARROW-MINDED PERSON."
WHEN IT COMES TO BEING NARROW-MINDED, I TRUMP THEM ALL.
IN PLACE OF THAT RABBIT...
...I'LL SOON BE TAKING THIS GUY TO HELL WITH ME.
FLAP

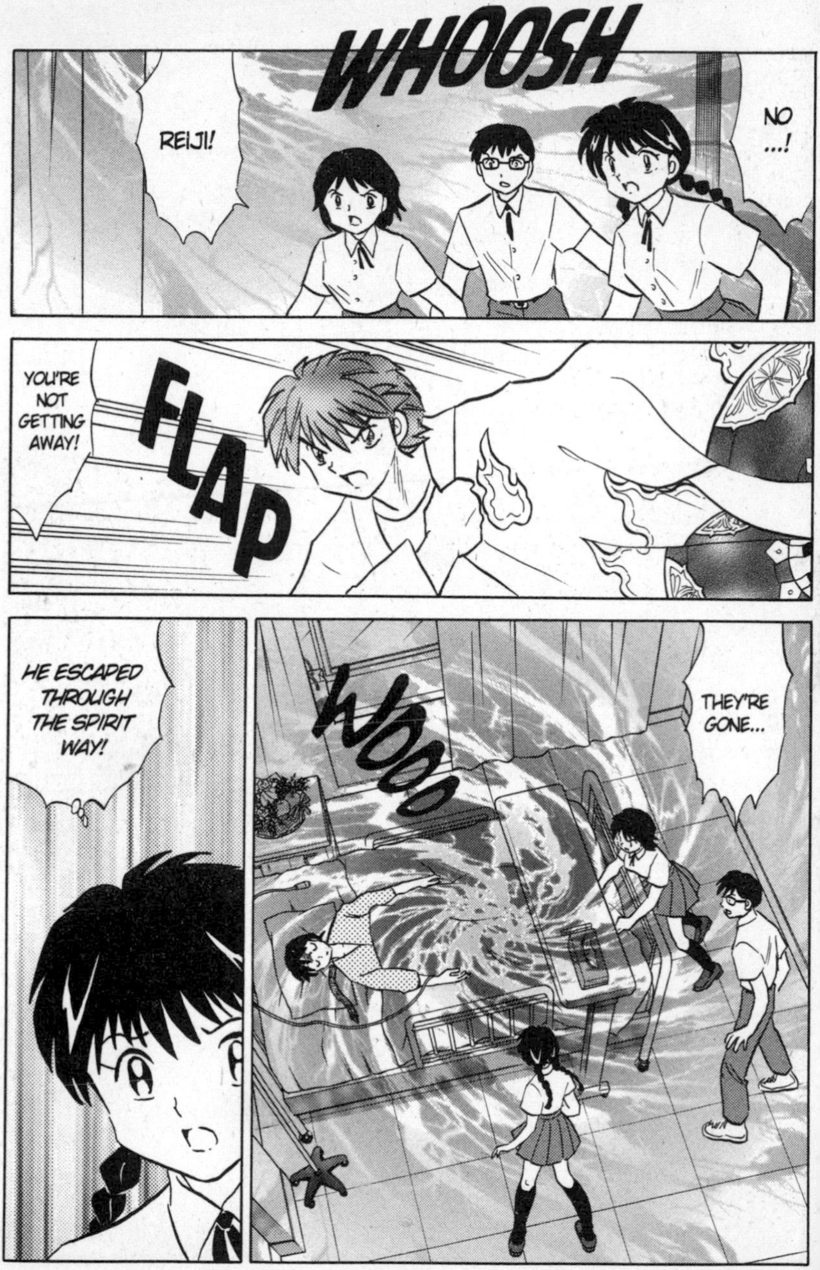
WHOOSH
NO ...!
REIJI!
FLAP
YOU'RE NOT GETTING AWAY!
THEY'RE GONE...
WOOO
HE ESCAPED THROUGH THE SPIRIT WAY!

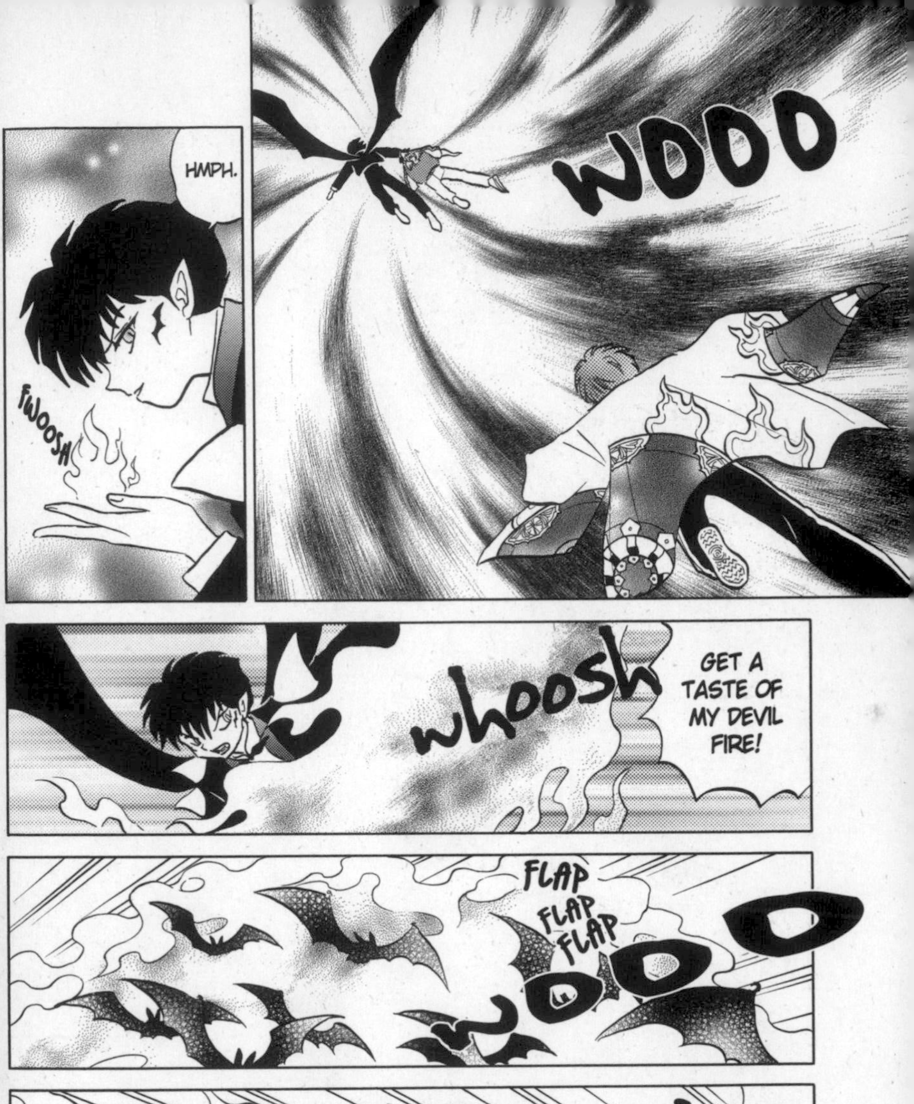
WOOO
HMPH.
FWOOSH
GET A TASTE OF MY DEVIL FIRE!
whoosh
FLAP
FLAP
FLAP
WOOOO
KUH!
FWOOSH
FWOOSH
FWOOSH

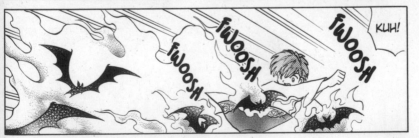

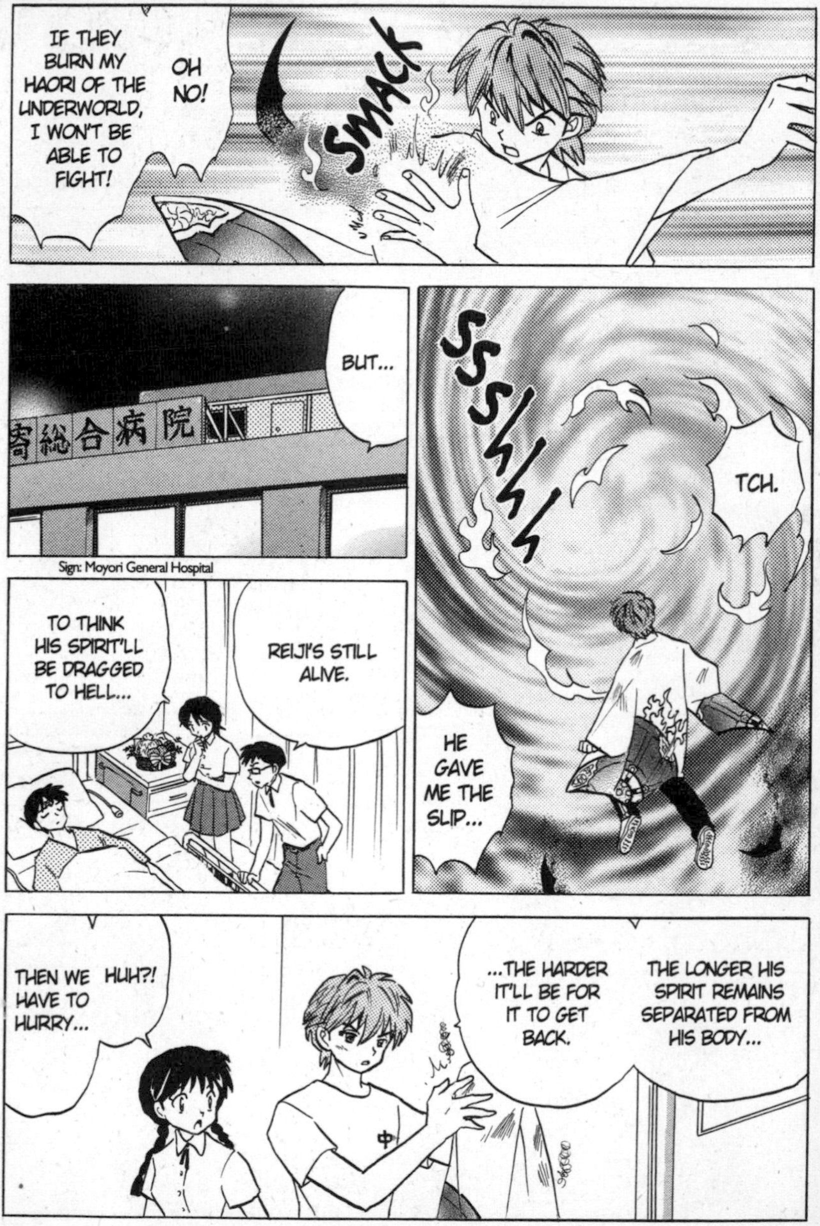
SMACK
OH NO!
IF THEY BURN MY HAORI OF THE UNDERWORLD, I WON'T BE ABLE TO FIGHT!
TCH.
SSSHHH
HE GAVE ME THE SLIP...
BUT...
Sign: Moyori General Hospital
REIJI'S STILL ALIVE.
TO THINK HIS SPIRIT'LL BE DRAGGED TO HELL...
THE LONGER HIS SPIRIT REMAINS SEPARATED FROM HIS BODY...
...THE HARDER IT'LL BE FOR IT TO GET BACK.
HUH?!
THEN WE HAVE TO HURRY...

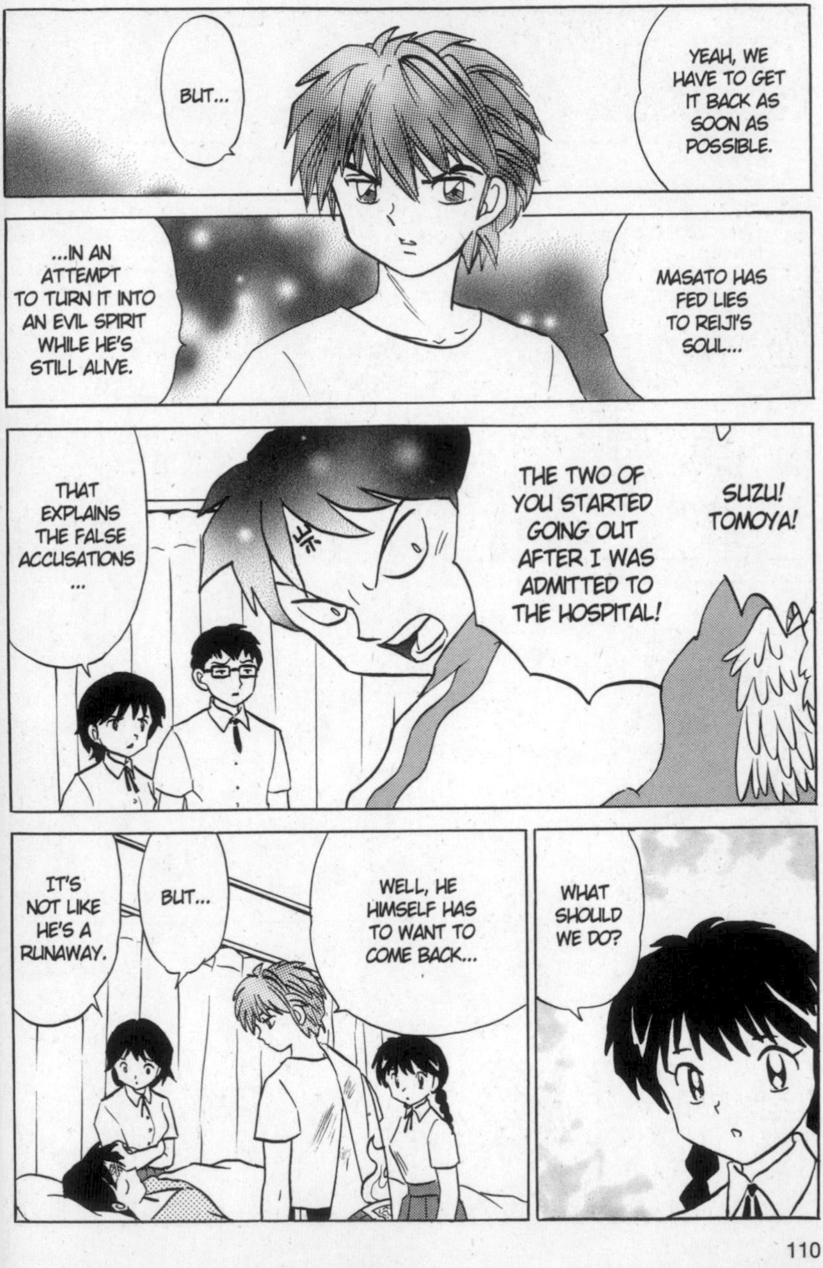
YEAH, WE HAVE TO GET IT BACK AS SOON AS POSSIBLE.
BUT...
MASATO HAS FED LIES TO REIJI'S SOUL...
...IN AN ATTEMPT TO TURN IT INTO AN EVIL SPIRIT WHILE HE'S STILL ALIVE.
SUZU! TOMOYA!
THE TWO OF YOU STARTED GOING OUT AFTER I WAS ADMITTED TO THE HOSPITAL!
THAT EXPLAINS THE FALSE ACCUSATIONS...
WHAT SHOULD WE DO?
WELL, HE HIMSELF HAS TO WANT TO COME BACK...
BUT...
IT'S NOT LIKE HE'S A RUNAWAY.

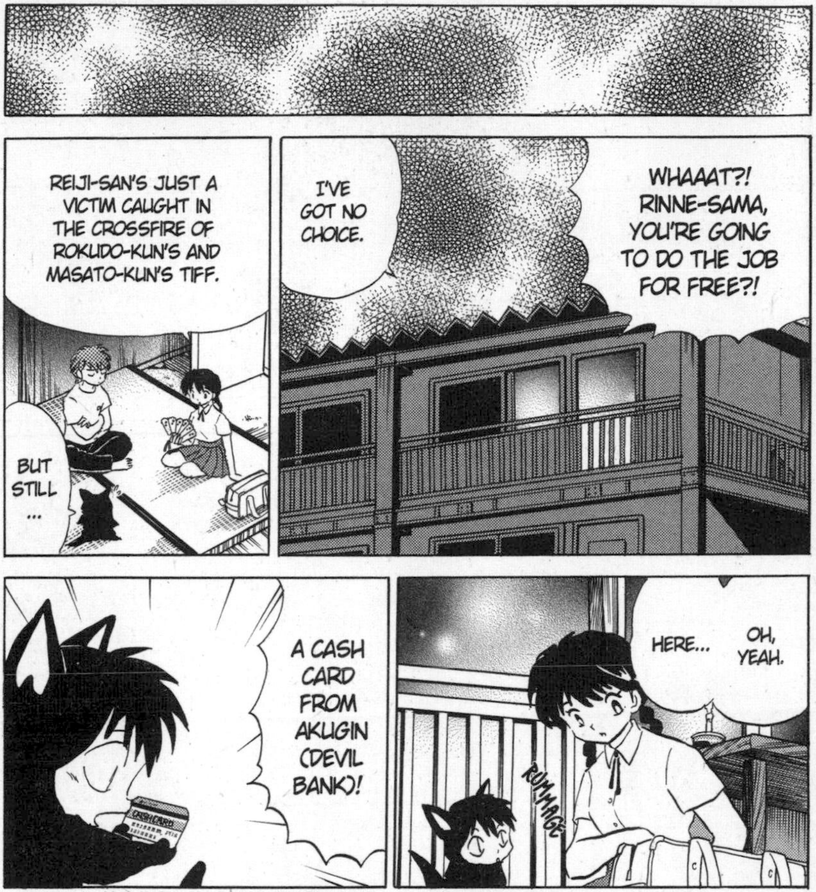
WHAAAT?! RINNE-SAMA, YOU'RE GOING TO DO THE JOB FOR FREE?!
I'VE GOT NO CHOICE.
REIJI-SAN'S JUST A VICTIM CAUGHT IN THE CROSSFIRE OF ROKUDO-KUN'S AND MASATO-KUN'S TIFF.
BUT STILL ...
OH, YEAH.
HERE...
RUMMAGE
A CASH CARD FROM AKUGIN (DEVIL BANK)!
CASH CARD

Note: AkuGin is short for *Akuma Ginko*, "Devil Bank."

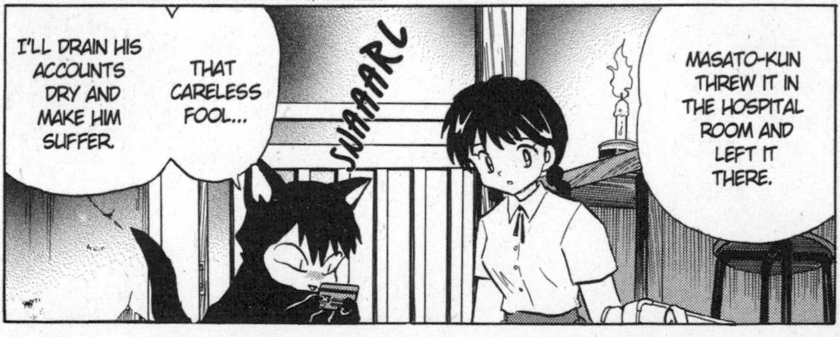
MASATO-KUN THREW IT IN THE HOSPITAL ROOM AND LEFT IT THERE.
SWAAARL
THAT CARELESS FOOL...
I'LL DRAIN HIS ACCOUNTS DRY AND MAKE HIM SUFFER.

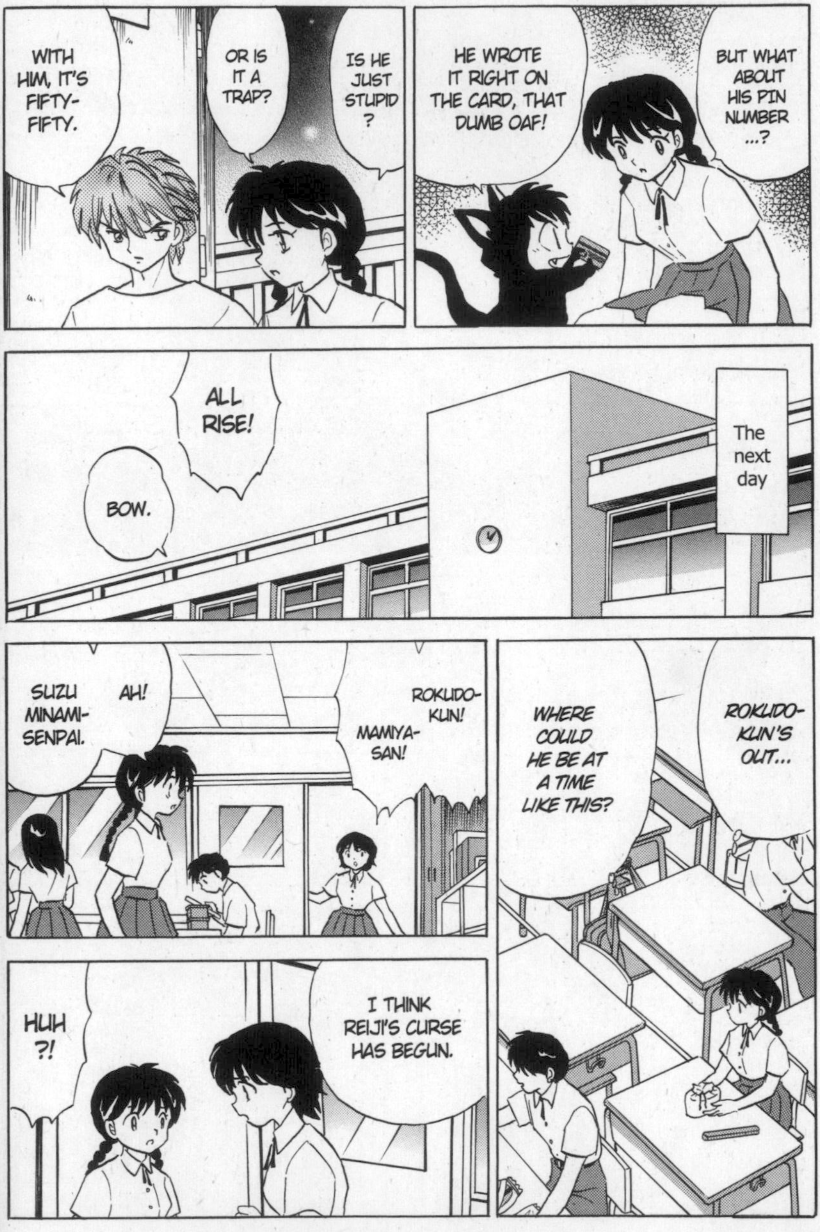
BUT WHAT ABOUT HIS PIN NUMBER ...?
HE WROTE IT RIGHT ON THE CARD, THAT DUMB OAF!
IS HE JUST STUPID ?
OR IS IT A TRAP?
WITH HIM, IT'S FIFTY-FIFTY.
The next day
ALL RISE!
BOW.
ROKUDO-KUN'S OUT...
WHERE COULD HE BE AT A TIME LIKE THIS?
ROKUDO-KUN!
MAMIYA-SAN!
AH!
SUZU MINAMI-SENPAI.
I THINK REIJI'S CURSE HAS BEGUN.
HUH ?!

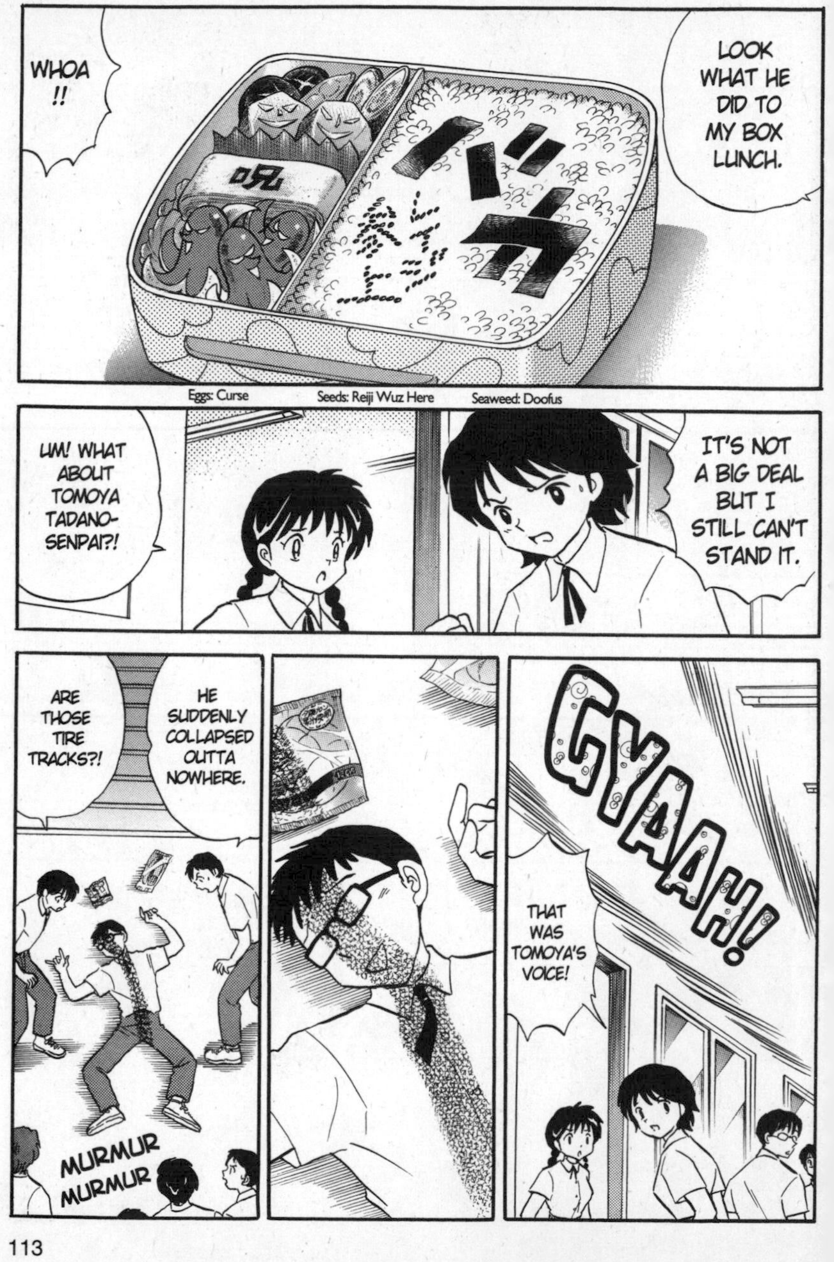
LOOK WHAT HE DID TO MY BOX LUNCH.
WHOA !!
Eggs: Curse
Seeds: Reiji Wuz Here
Seaweed: Doofus
IT'S NOT A BIG DEAL BUT I STILL CAN'T STAND IT.
UM! WHAT ABOUT TOMOYA TADANO-SENPAI?!
GYAAAH!
THAT WAS TOMOYA'S VOICE!
HE SUDDENLY COLLAPSED OUTTA NOWHERE.
ARE THOSE TIRE TRACKS?!
MURMUR MURMUR

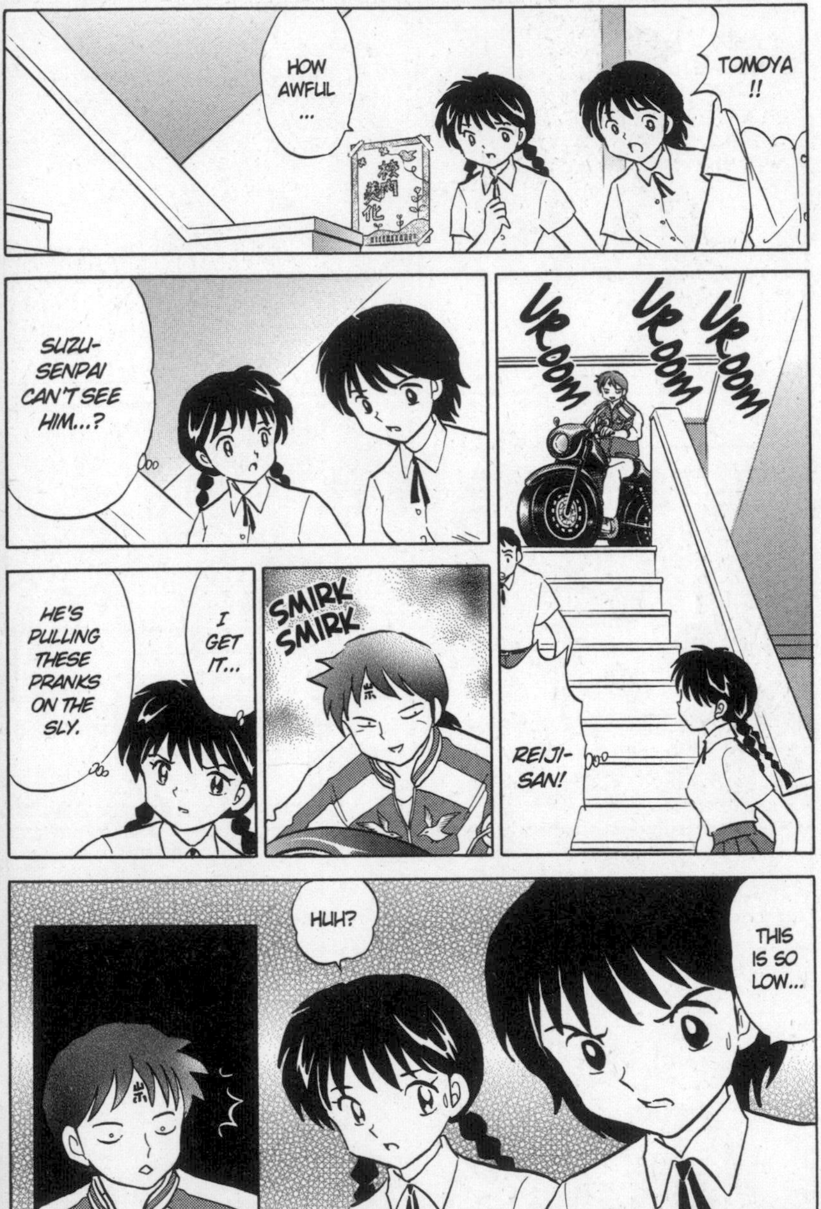
TOMOYA!!
HOW AWFUL ...
VROOM
VROOM
VROOM
REIJI-SAN!
SUZU-SENPAI CAN'T SEE HIM...?
SMIRK SMIRK
I GET IT...
HE'S PULLING THESE PRANKS ON THE SLY.
THIS IS SO LOW...
HUH?

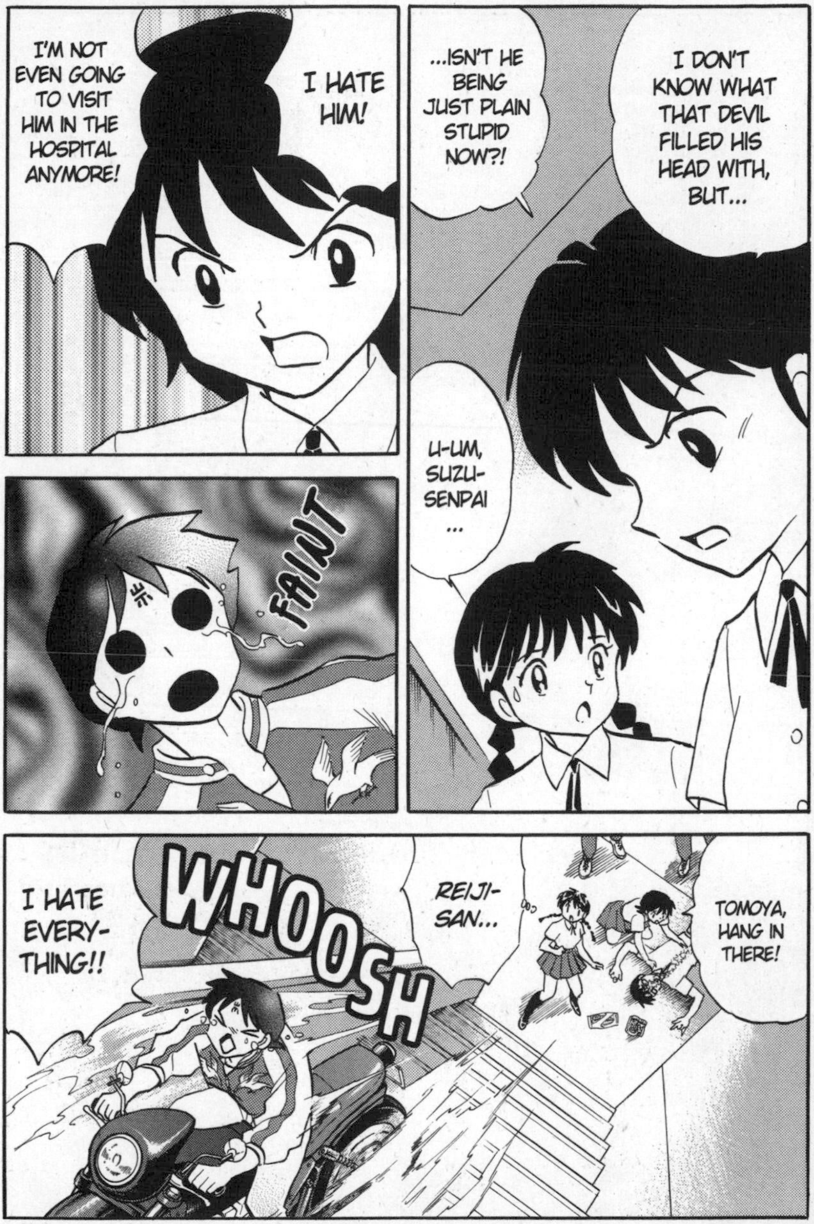
I DON'T KNOW WHAT THAT DEVIL FILLED HIS HEAD WITH, BUT...
...ISN'T HE BEING JUST PLAIN STUPID NOW?!
U-UM, SUZU-SENPAI ...
I HATE HIM!
I'M NOT EVEN GOING TO VISIT HIM IN THE HOSPITAL ANYMORE!
FAINT
TOMOYA, HANG IN THERE!
REIJI-SAN...
WHOOSH
I HATE EVERY-THING!!

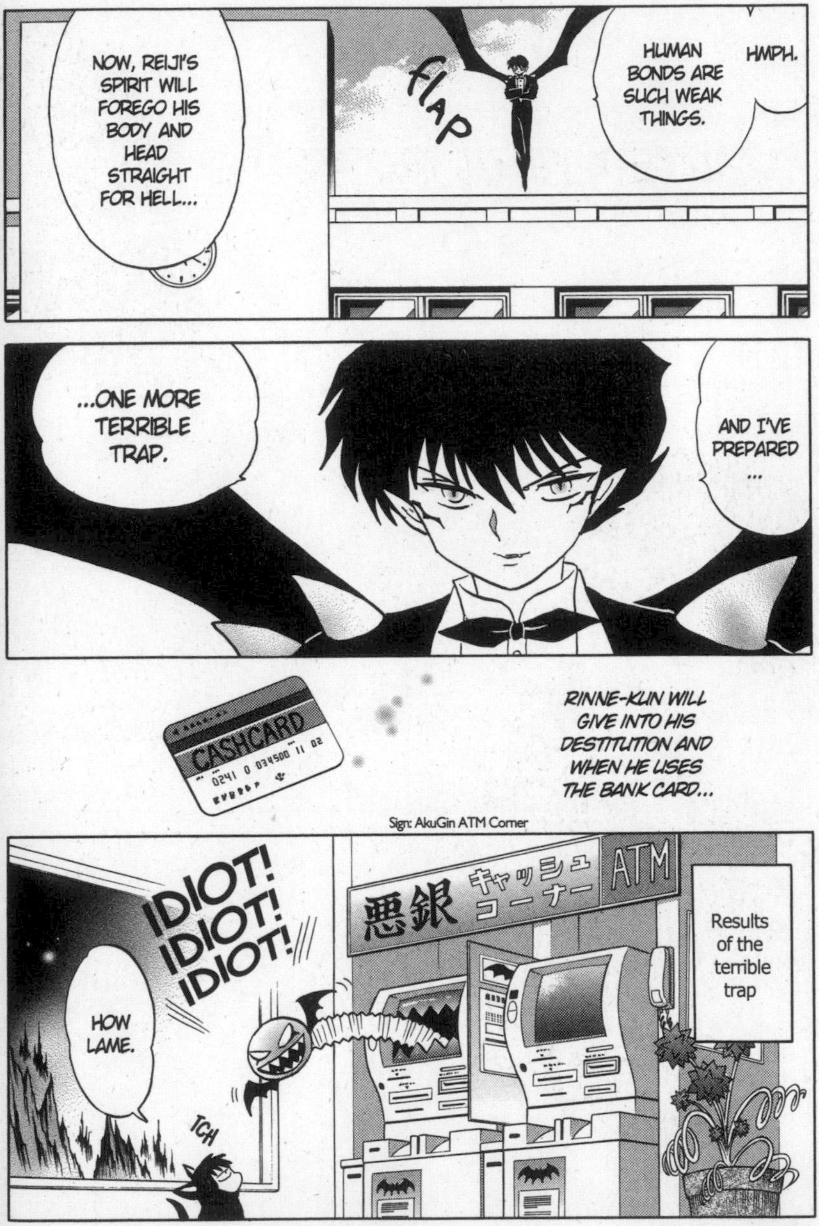
HMPH.
HUMAN BONDS ARE SUCH WEAK THINGS.
FLAP
NOW, REIJI'S SPIRIT WILL FOREGO HIS BODY AND HEAD STRAIGHT FOR HELL...
AND I'VE PREPARED ...
...ONE MORE TERRIBLE TRAP.
RINNE-KUN WILL GIVE INTO HIS DESTITUTION AND WHEN HE USES THE BANK CARD...
CASHCARD
Sign: AkuGin ATM Corner
Results of the terrible trap
悪銀 キャッシュコーナー
ATM
IDIOT! IDIOT! IDIOT!
HOW LAME.
TCH

CHAPTER 15: SPIRIT OF NO RETURN

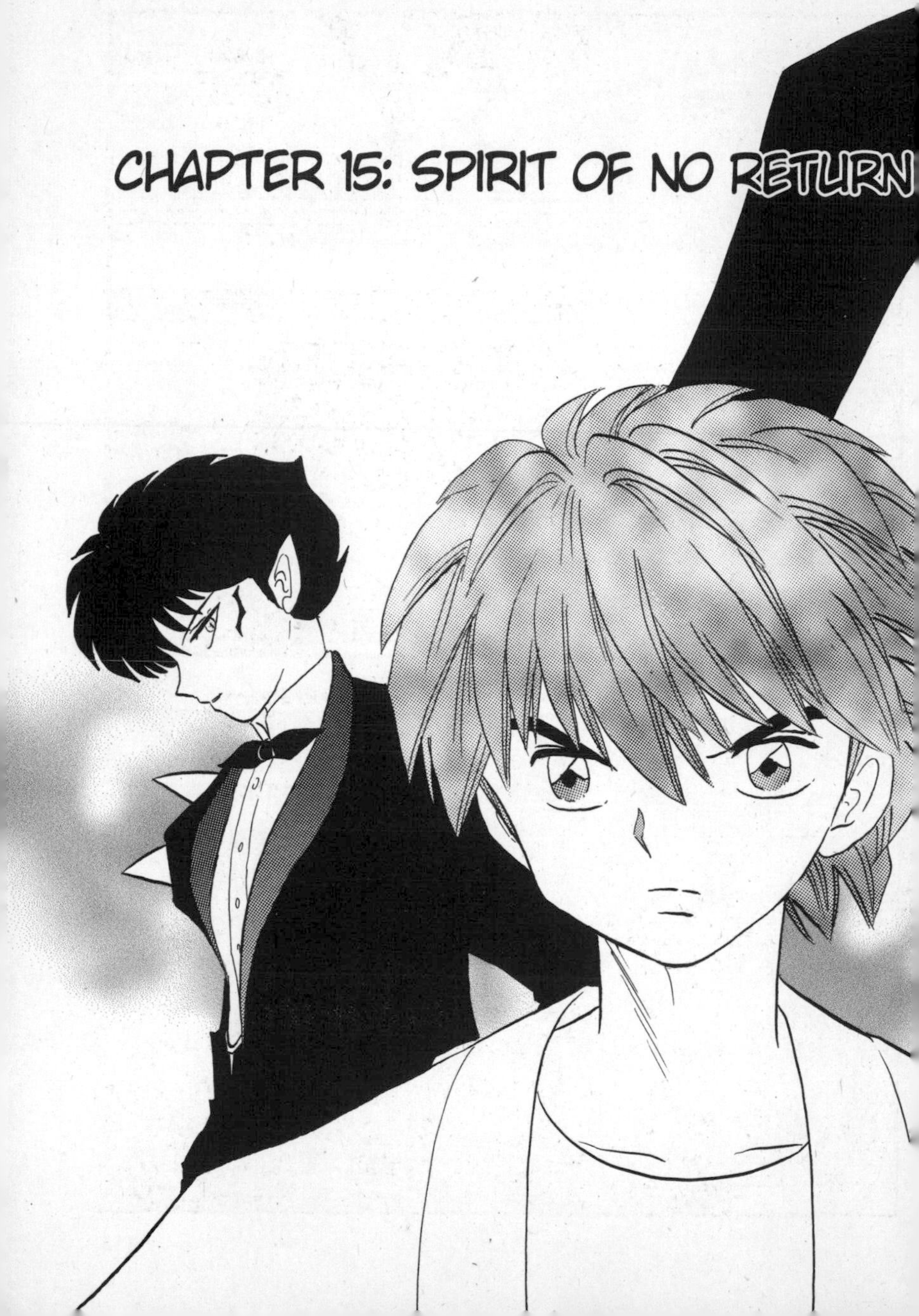

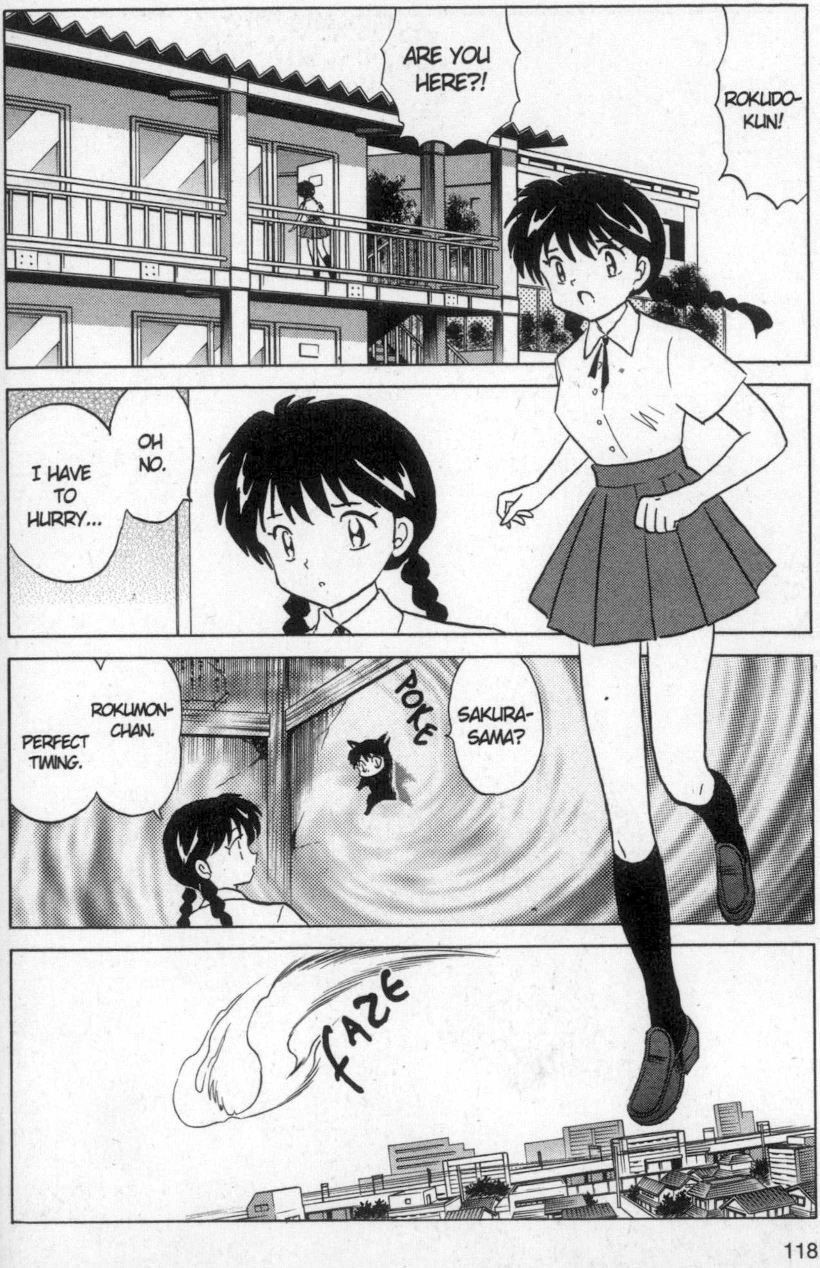
ROKUDO-KUN!
ARE YOU HERE?!
OH NO.
I HAVE TO HURRY...
SAKURA-SAMA?
POKE
ROKUMON-CHAN.
PERFECT TIMING.
FAZE

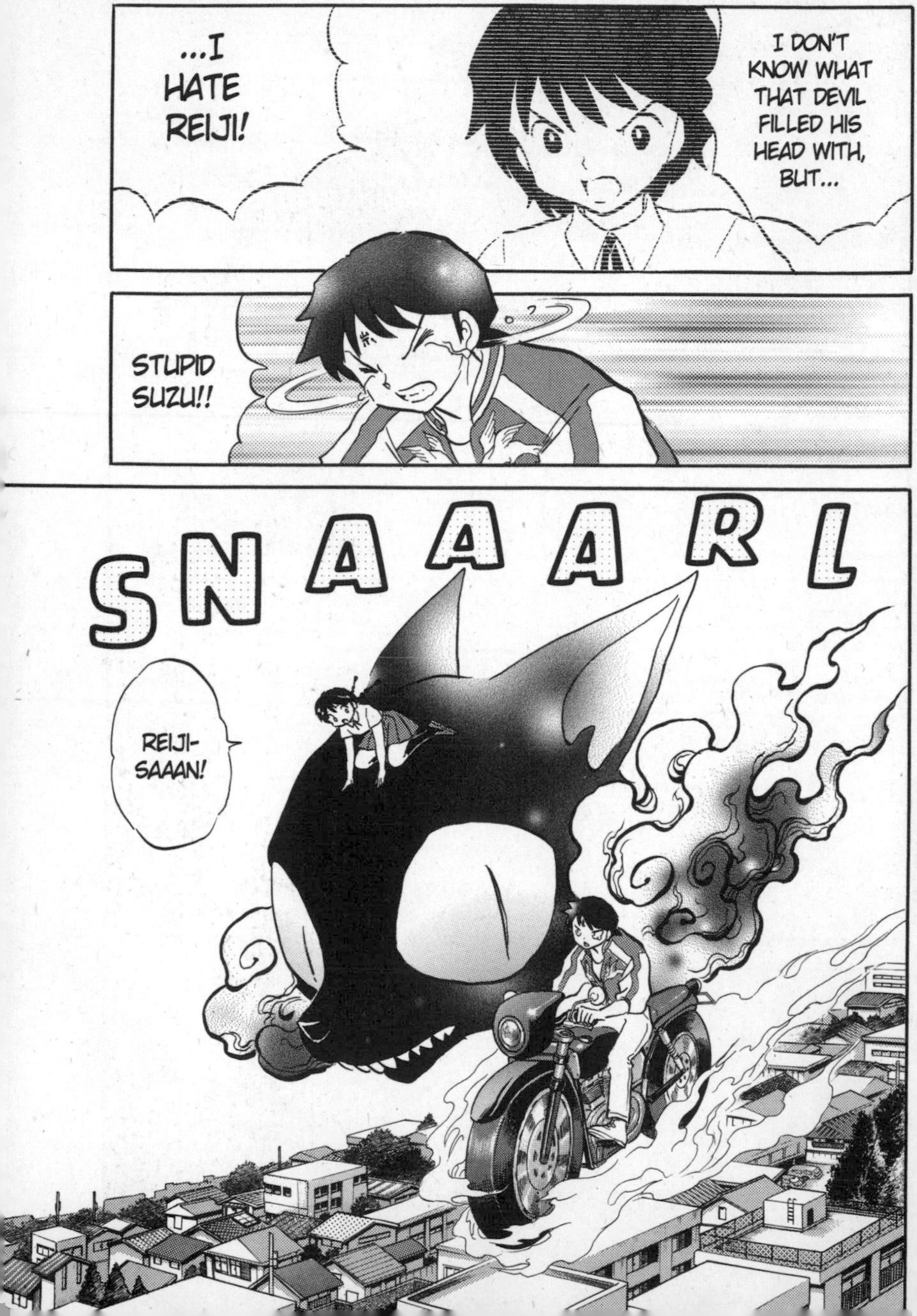
I DON'T KNOW WHAT THAT DEVIL FILLED HIS HEAD WITH, BUT...
...I HATE REIJI!
STUPID SUZU!!
SNAAARL
REIJI-SAAAN!

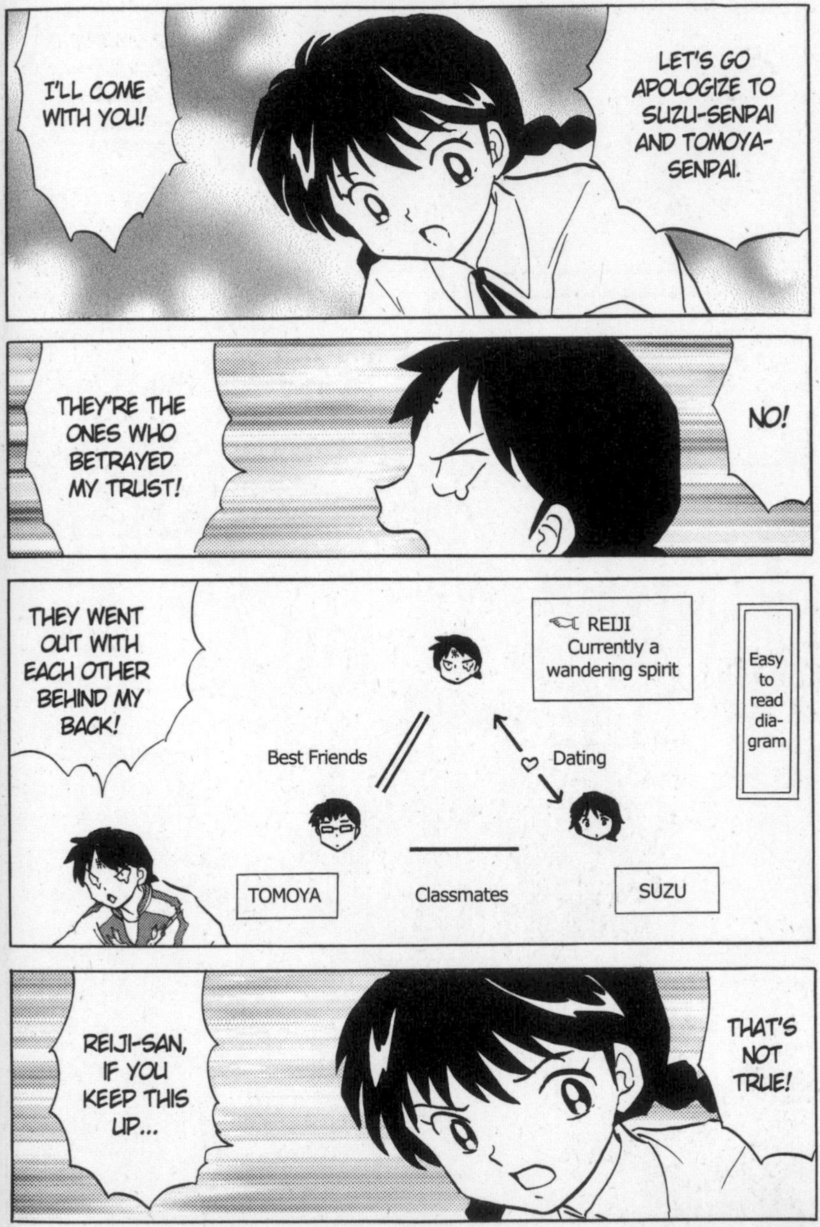
LET'S GO APOLOGIZE TO SUZU-SENPAI AND TOMOYA-SENPAI.
I'LL COME WITH YOU!
NO!
THEY'RE THE ONES WHO BETRAYED MY TRUST!
Easy to read diagram
REIJI Currently a wandering spirit
Dating
Best Friends
SUZU
Classmates
TOMOYA
THEY WENT OUT WITH EACH OTHER BEHIND MY BACK!
THAT'S NOT TRUE!
REIJI-SAN, IF YOU KEEP THIS UP...

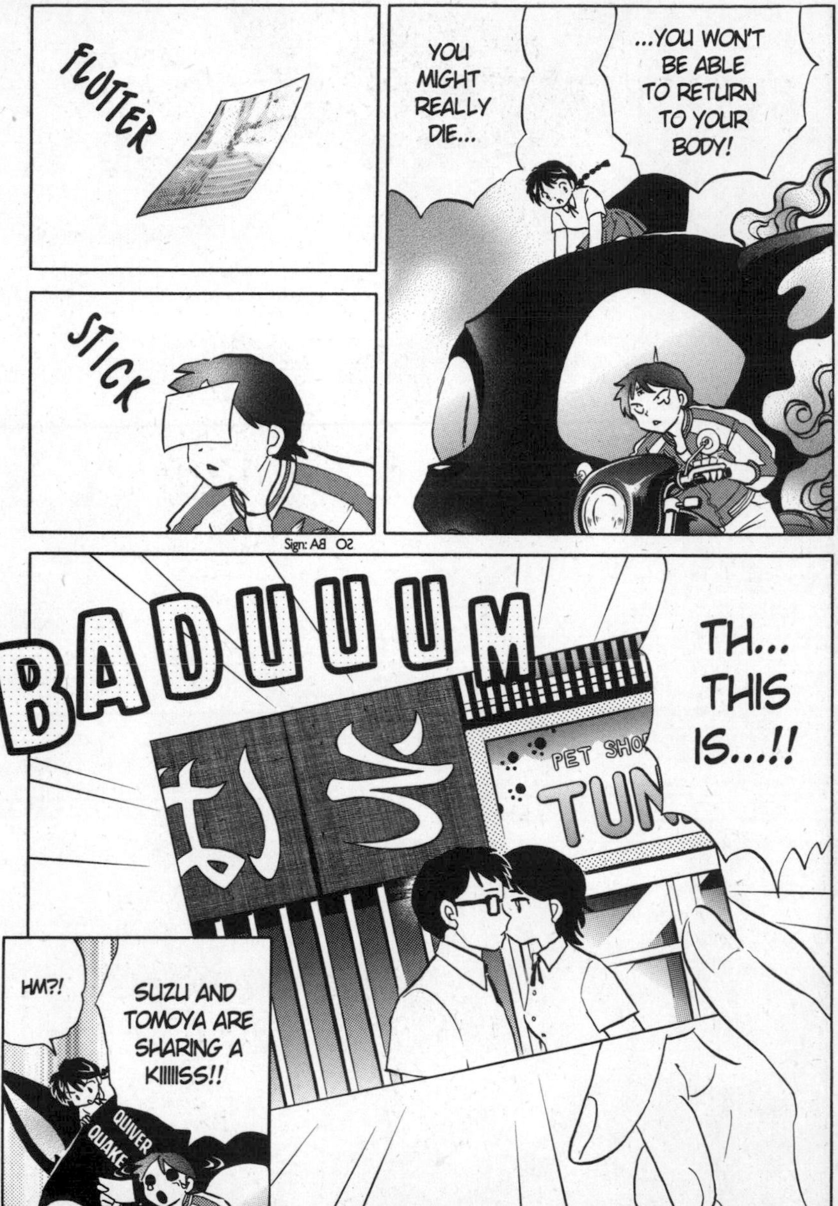
...YOU WON'T BE ABLE TO RETURN TO YOUR BODY!
YOU MIGHT REALLY DIE...
FLUTTER
STICK
Sign: AB O2
TH... THIS IS...!!
BADUUUM
PET SHOP
TUN
HM?!
SUZU AND TOMOYA ARE SHARING A KIIIISS!!
QUIVER
QUAKE

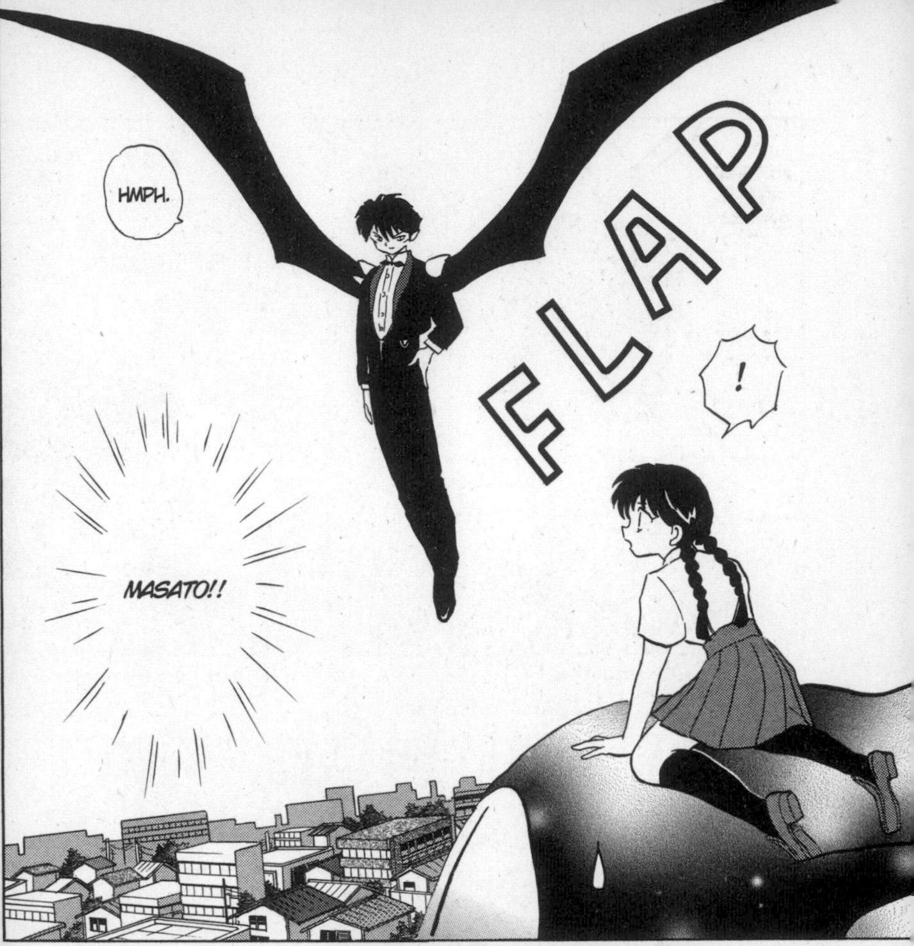
FLAP
HMPH.
!
MASATO!!

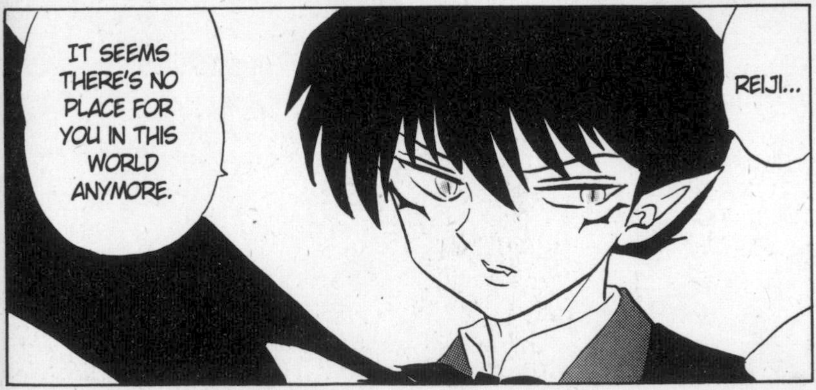
REIJI...
IT SEEMS THERE'S NO PLACE FOR YOU IN THIS WORLD ANYMORE.

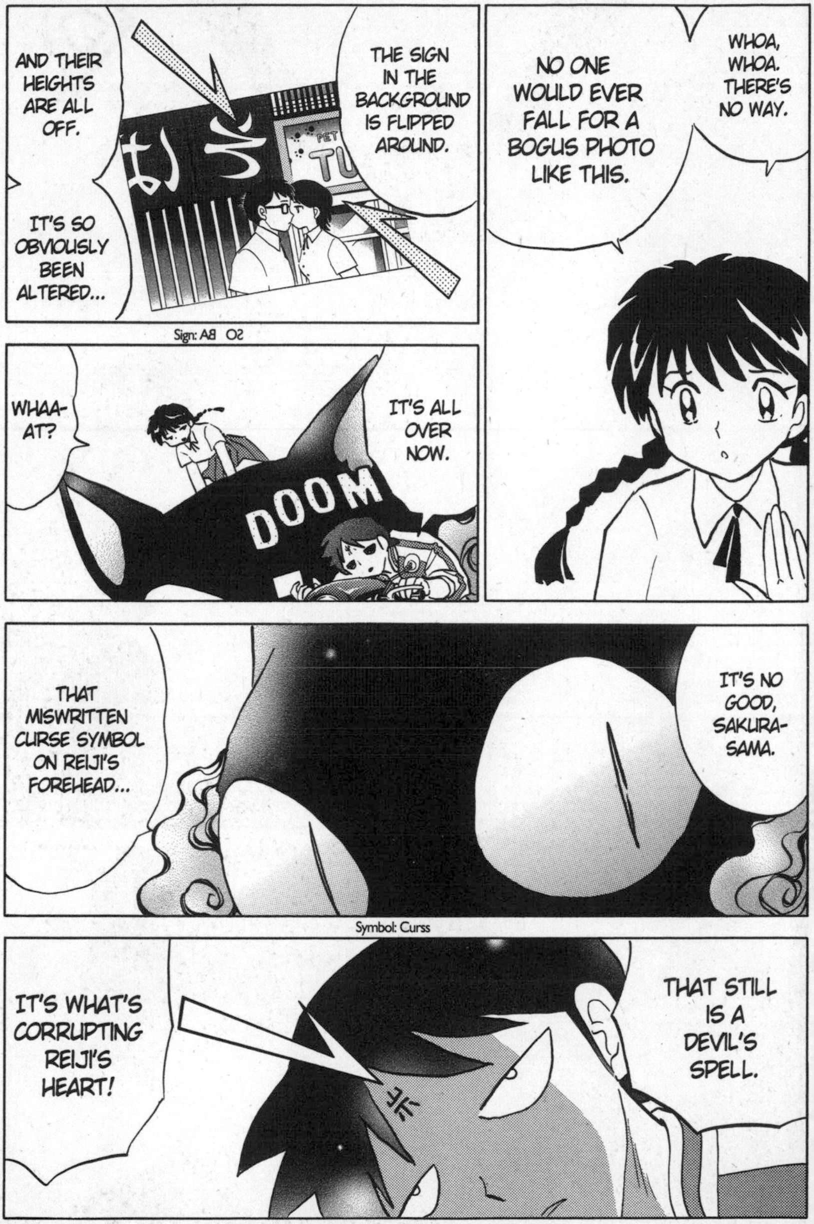
WHOA, WHOA. THERE'S NO WAY.
NO ONE WOULD EVER FALL FOR A BOGUS PHOTO LIKE THIS.
THE SIGN IN THE BACKGROUND IS FLIPPED AROUND.
AND THEIR HEIGHTS ARE ALL OFF.
IT'S SO OBVIOUSLY BEEN ALTERED...
Sign: AB OS
IT'S ALL OVER NOW.
WHAAA-AT?
DOOM
IT'S NO GOOD, SAKURA-SAMA.
THAT MISWRITTEN CURSE SYMBOL ON REIJI'S FOREHEAD...
Symbol: Curss
THAT STILL IS A DEVIL'S SPELL.
IT'S WHAT'S CORRUPTING REIJI'S HEART!

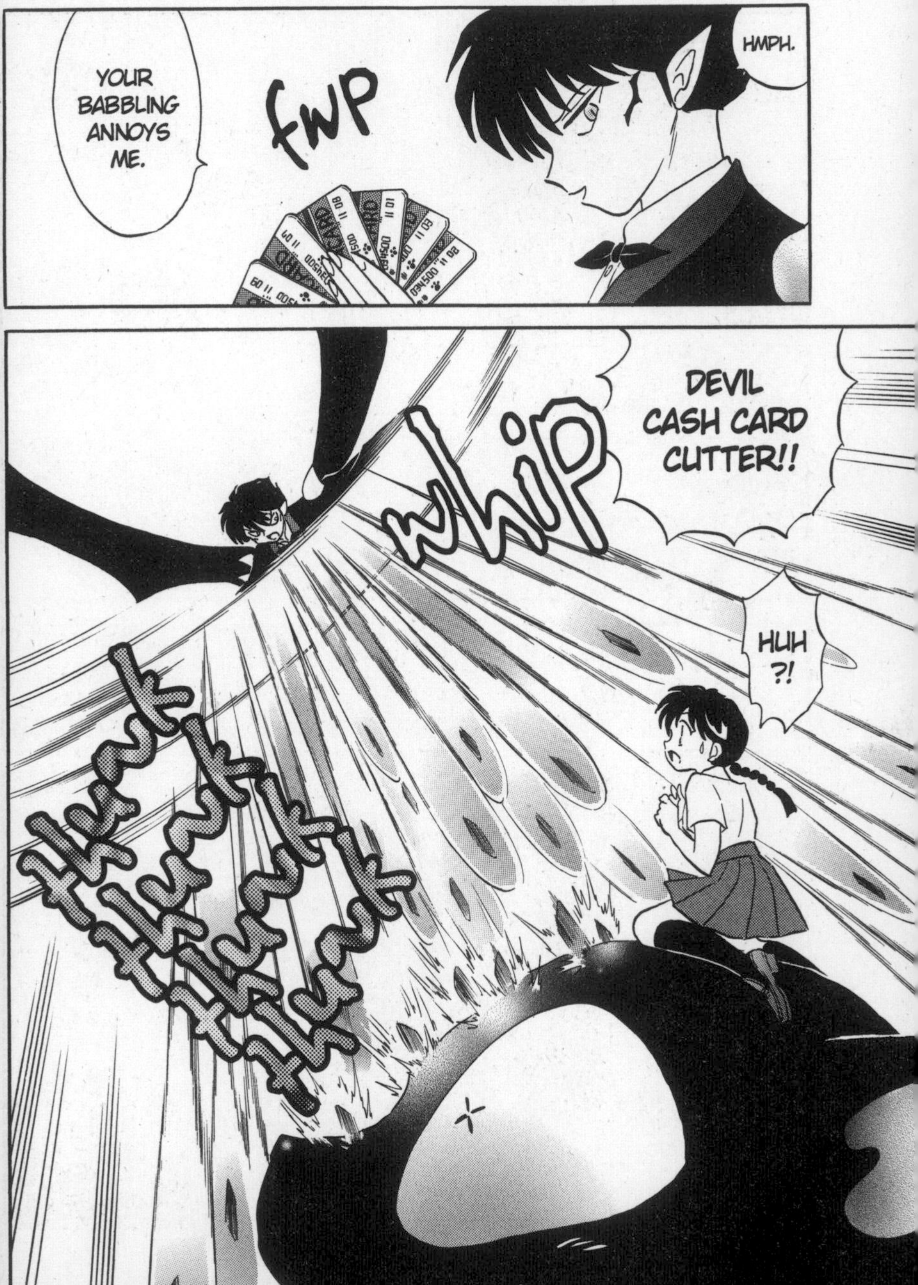
HMPH.
fwp
YOUR BABBLING ANNOYS ME.
DEVIL CASH CARD CUTTER!!
whip
HUH ?!
thunk thunk thunk thunk

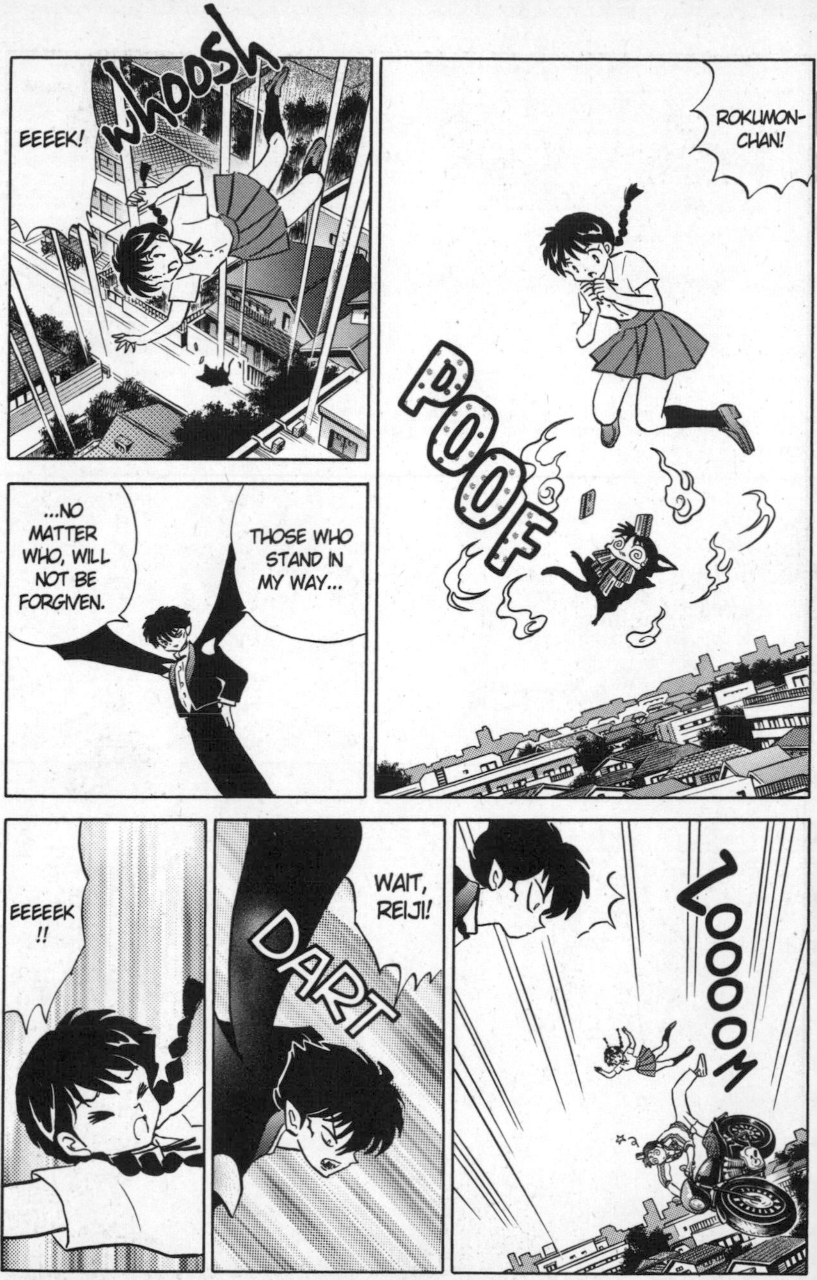
ROKUMON-CHAN!
POOF
WHOOSH
EEEEK!
THOSE WHO STAND IN MY WAY...
...NO MATTER WHO, WILL NOT BE FORGIVEN.
LOOOOOM
WAIT, REIJI!
DART
EEEEEK !!

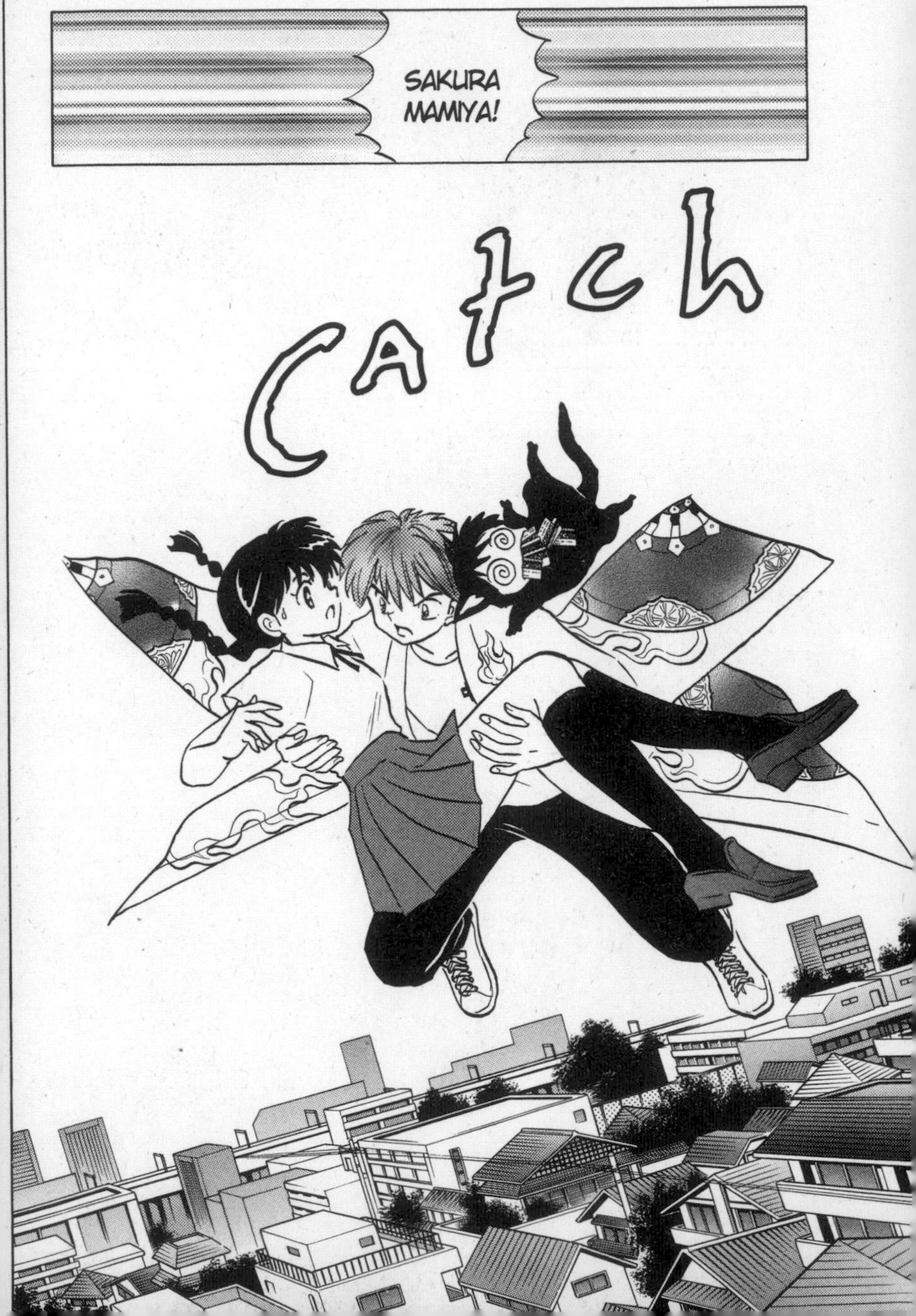
SAKURA MAMIYA!
Catch

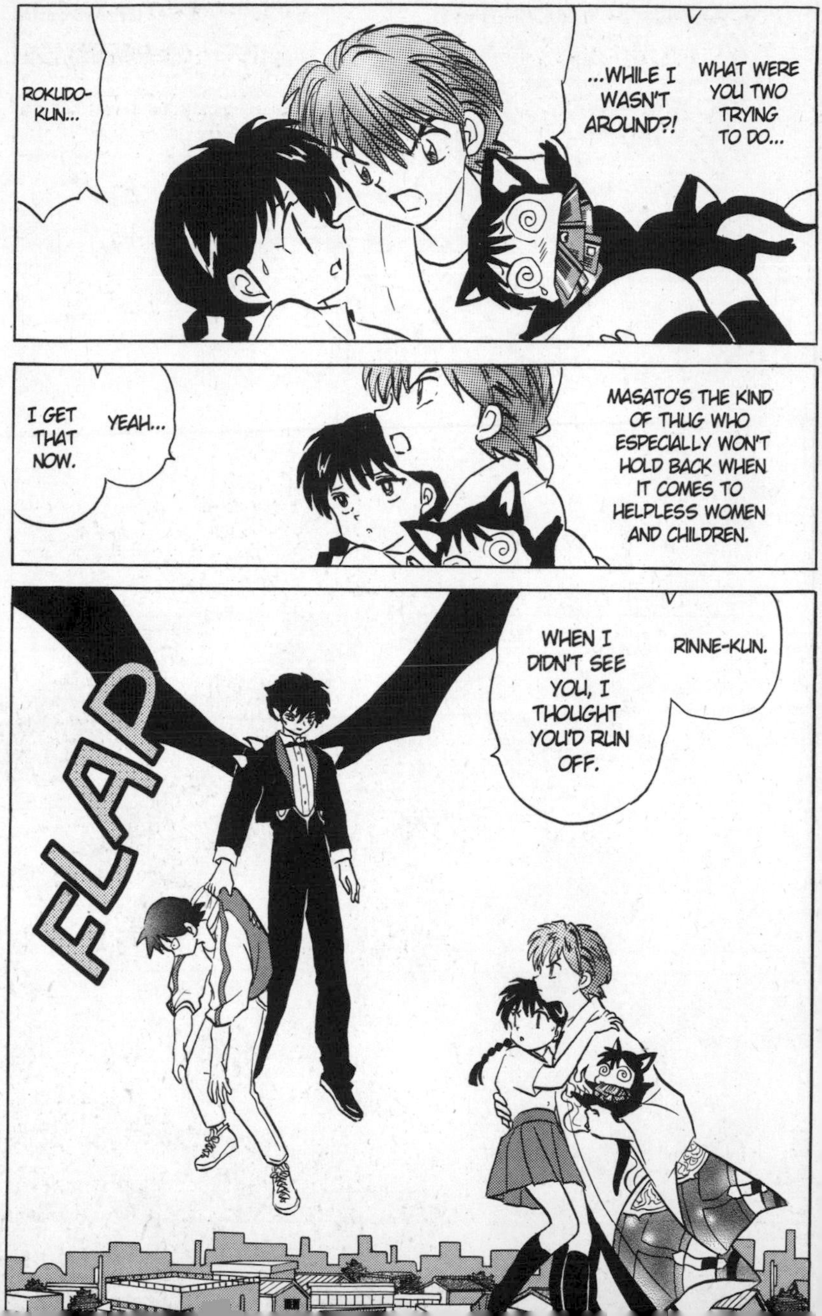
WHAT WERE YOU TWO TRYING TO DO...
...WHILE I WASN'T AROUND?!
ROKUDO-KUN...
MASATO'S THE KIND OF THUG WHO ESPECIALLY WON'T HOLD BACK WHEN IT COMES TO HELPLESS WOMEN AND CHILDREN.
YEAH...
I GET THAT NOW.
RINNE-KUN.
WHEN I DIDN'T SEE YOU, I THOUGHT YOU'D RUN OFF.
FLAP

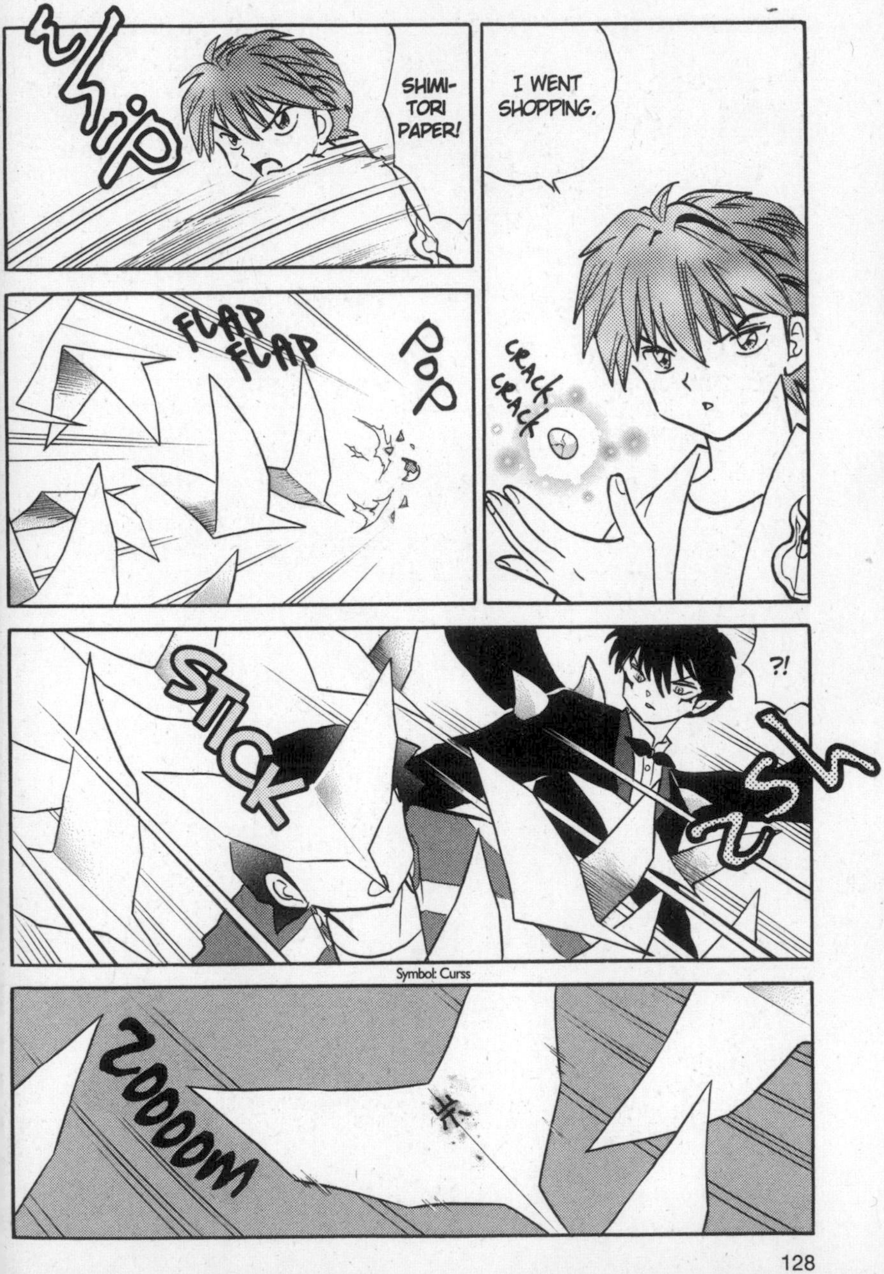
I WENT SHOPPING.
CRACK CRACK
SHIMI-TORI PAPER!
whip
POP
FLAP FLAP
?!
STICK
Symbol: Curss
ZOOOOM

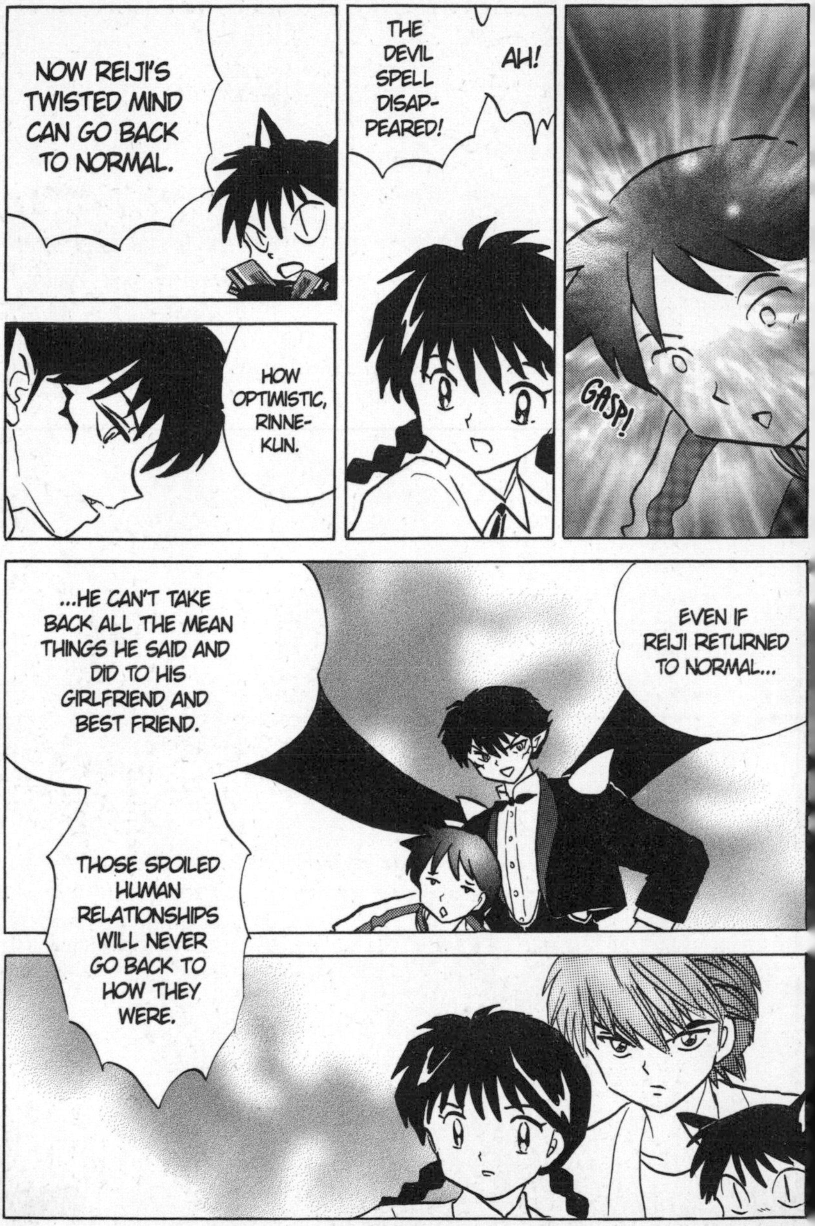
GASP!
AH!
THE DEVIL SPELL DISAP-PEARED!
NOW REIJI'S TWISTED MIND CAN GO BACK TO NORMAL.
HOW OPTIMISTIC, RINNE-KUN.
EVEN IF REIJI RETURNED TO NORMAL...
...HE CAN'T TAKE BACK ALL THE MEAN THINGS HE SAID AND DID TO HIS GIRLFRIEND AND BEST FRIEND.
THOSE SPOILED HUMAN RELATIONSHIPS WILL NEVER GO BACK TO HOW THEY WERE.

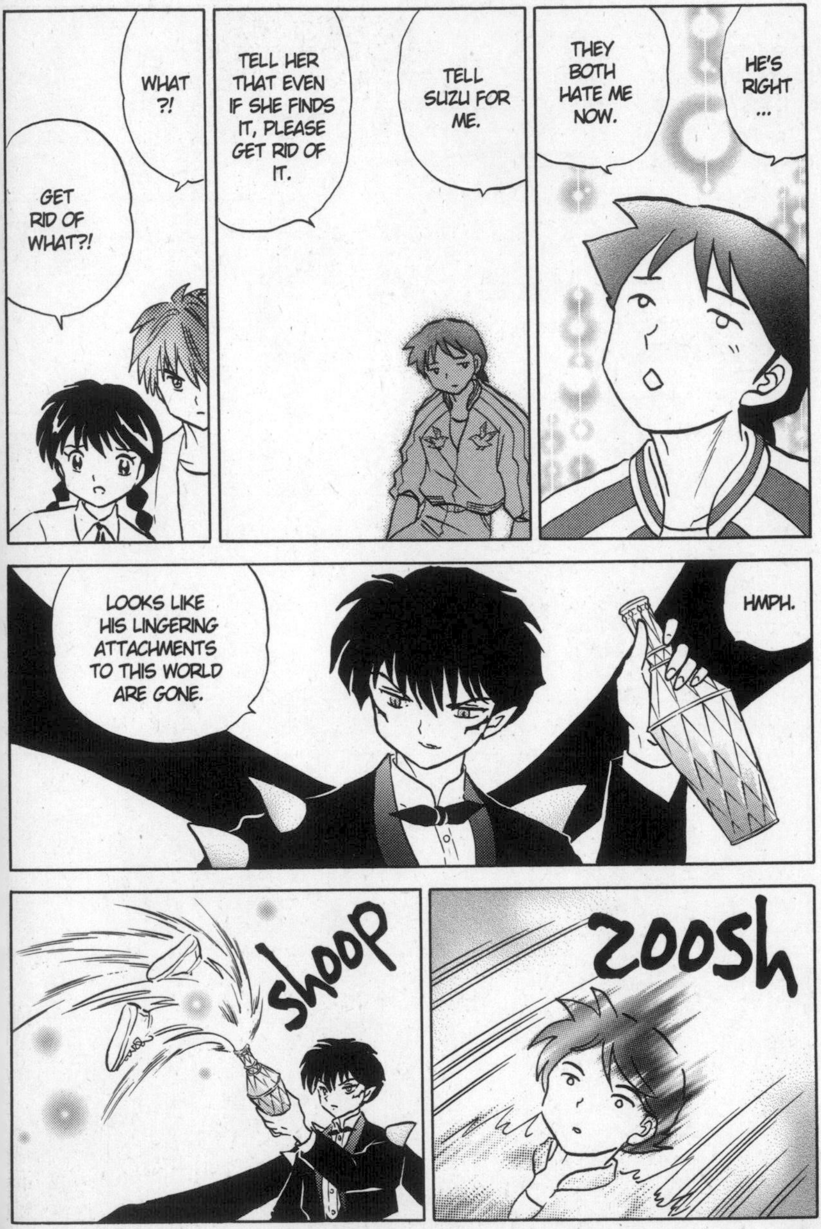
HE'S RIGHT ...
THEY BOTH HATE ME NOW.
TELL SUZU FOR ME.
TELL HER THAT EVEN IF SHE FINDS IT, PLEASE GET RID OF IT.
WHAT ?!
GET RID OF WHAT?!
HMPH.
LOOKS LIKE HIS LINGERING ATTACHMENTS TO THIS WORLD ARE GONE.
ZOOSH
SHOOP

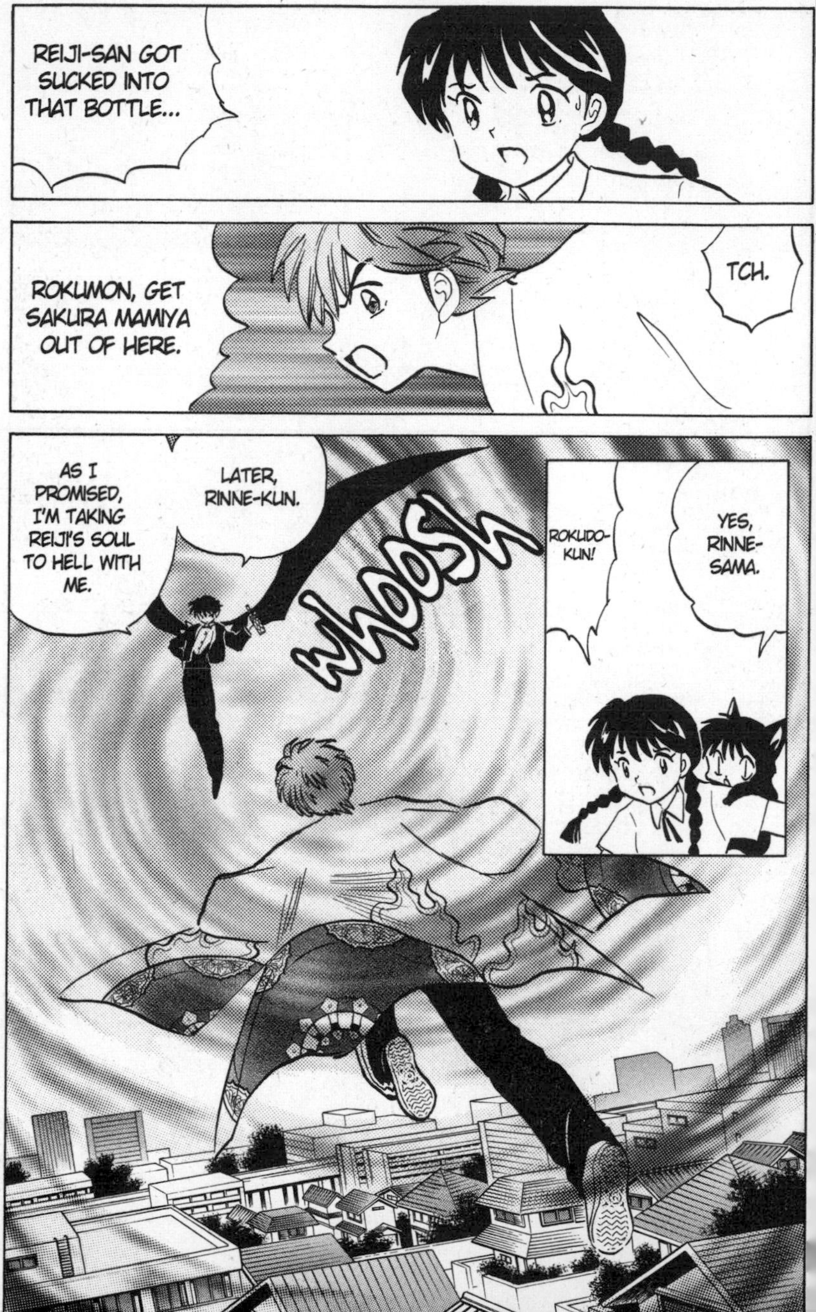
REIJI-SAN GOT SUCKED INTO THAT BOTTLE...
TCH.
ROKUMON, GET SAKURA MAMIYA OUT OF HERE.
YES, RINNE-SAMA.
ROKUDO-KUN!
LATER, RINNE-KUN.
AS I PROMISED, I'M TAKING REIJI'S SOUL TO HELL WITH ME.
WHOOSH

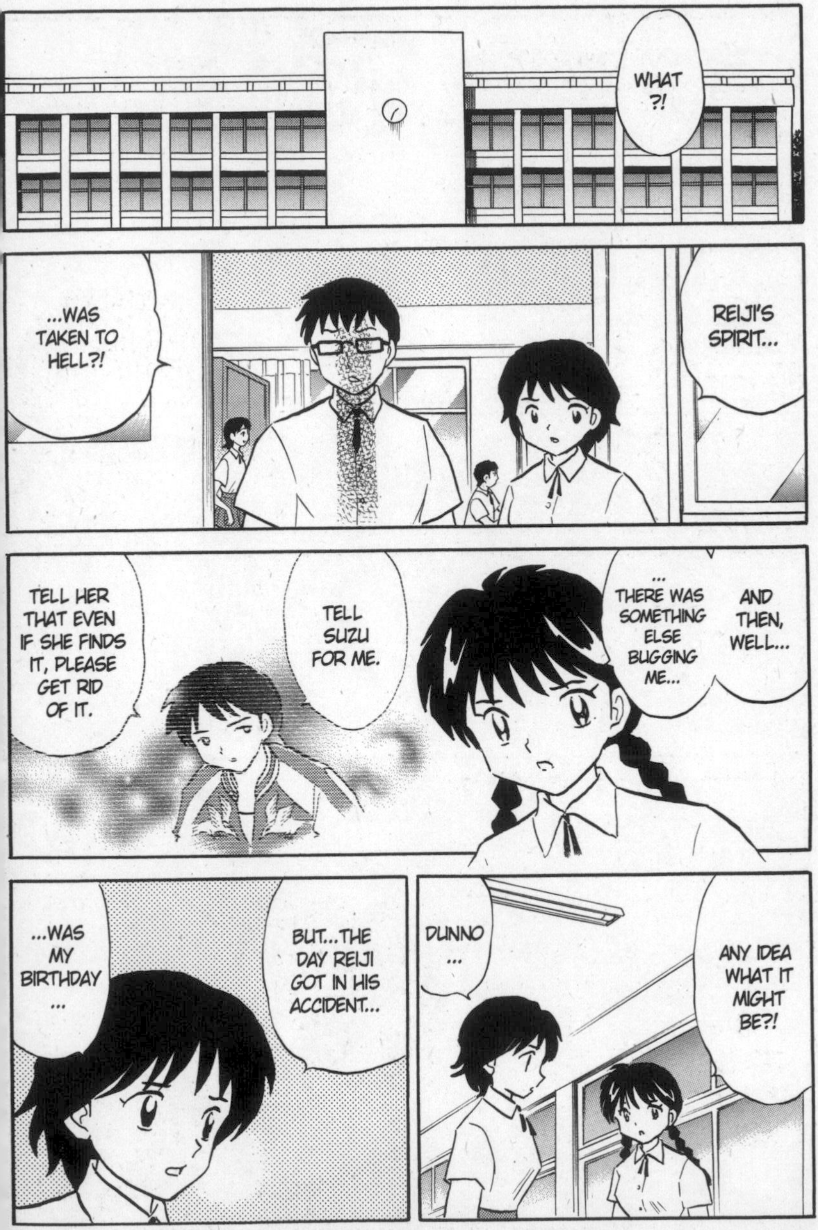
WHAT ?!
REIJI'S SPIRIT...
...WAS TAKEN TO HELL?!
AND THEN, WELL...
... THERE WAS SOMETHING ELSE BUGGING ME...
TELL SUZU FOR ME.
TELL HER THAT EVEN IF SHE FINDS IT, PLEASE GET RID OF IT.
ANY IDEA WHAT IT MIGHT BE?!
DUNNO ...
BUT...THE DAY REIJI GOT IN HIS ACCIDENT...
...WAS MY BIRTHDAY ...

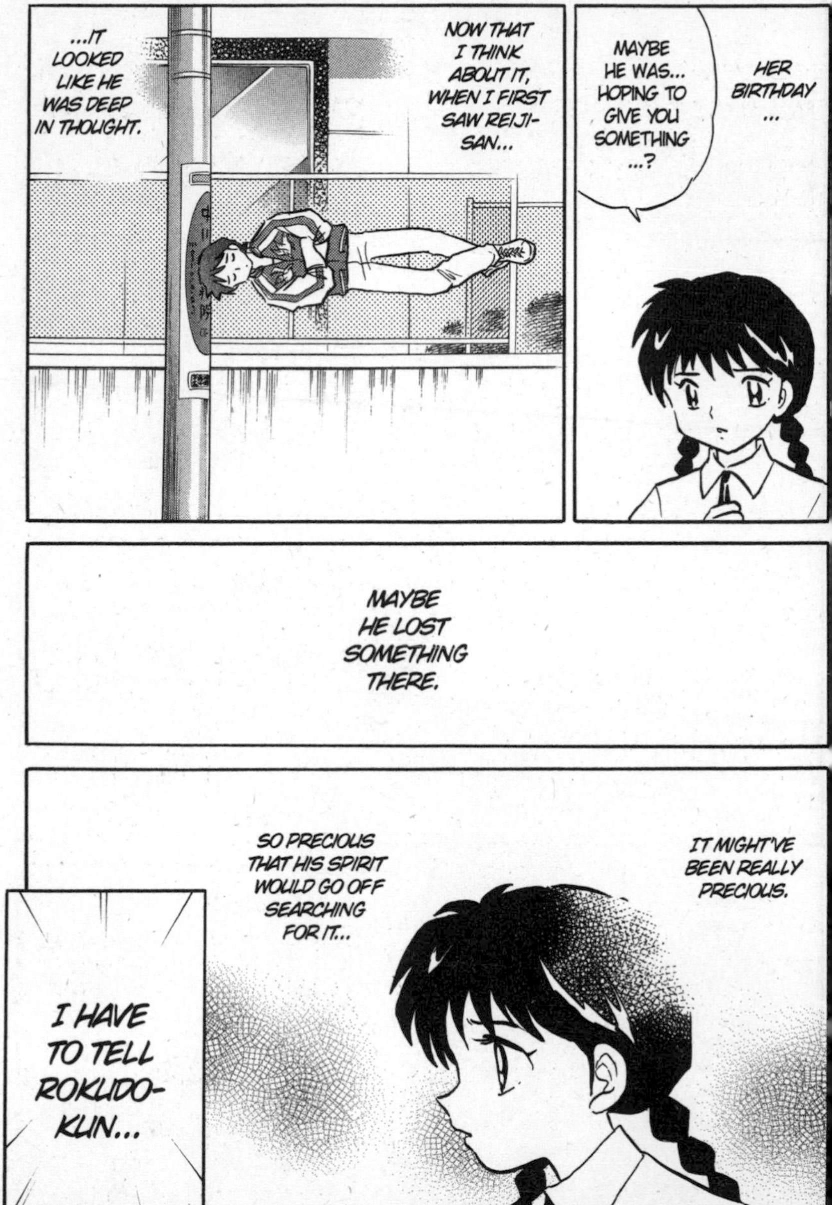
HER BIRTHDAY ...
MAYBE HE WAS... HOPING TO GIVE YOU SOMETHING ...?
NOW THAT I THINK ABOUT IT, WHEN I FIRST SAW REIJI-SAN...
...IT LOOKED LIKE HE WAS DEEP IN THOUGHT.
MAYBE HE LOST SOMETHING THERE.
IT MIGHT'VE BEEN REALLY PRECIOUS.
SO PRECIOUS THAT HIS SPIRIT WOULD GO OFF SEARCHING FOR IT...
I HAVE TO TELL ROKUDO-KUN...

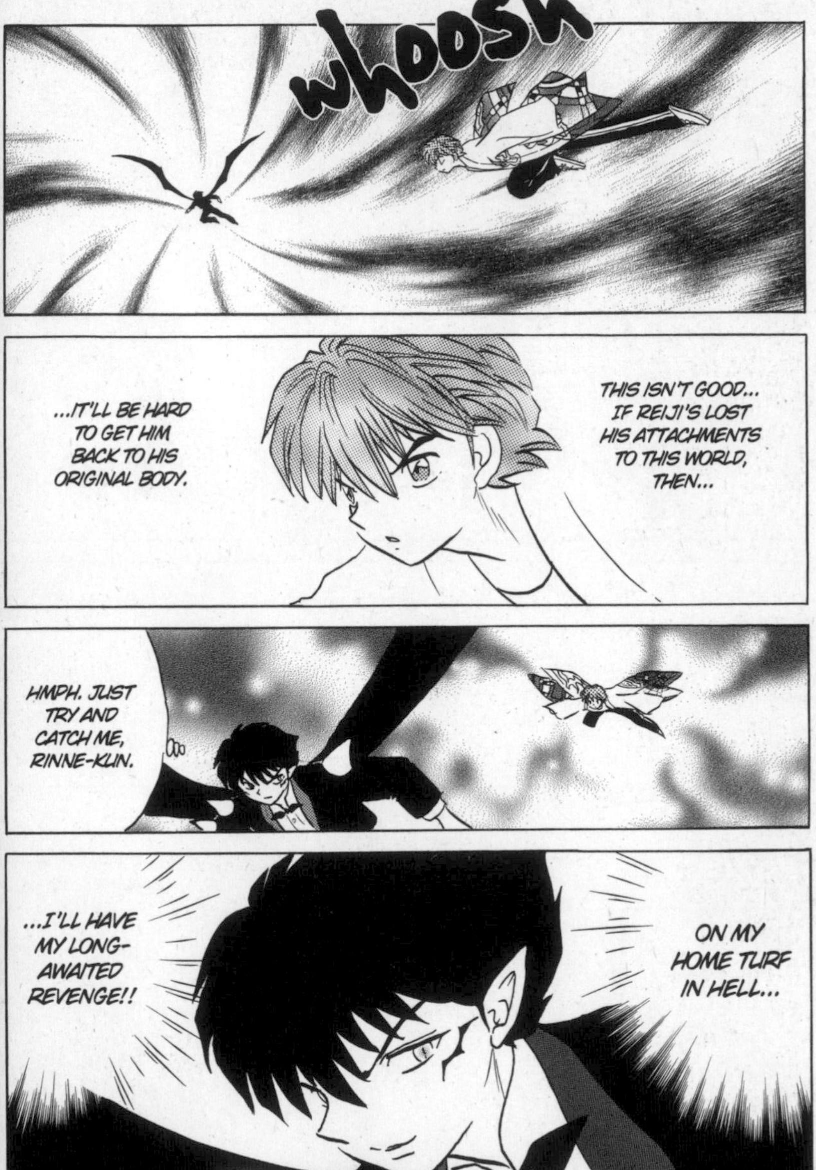
whoosh
THIS ISN'T GOOD... IF REIJI'S LOST HIS ATTACHMENTS TO THIS WORLD, THEN...
...IT'LL BE HARD TO GET HIM BACK TO HIS ORIGINAL BODY.
HMPH. JUST TRY AND CATCH ME, RINNE-KUN.
ON MY HOME TURF IN HELL...
...I'LL HAVE MY LONG-AWAITED REVENGE!!

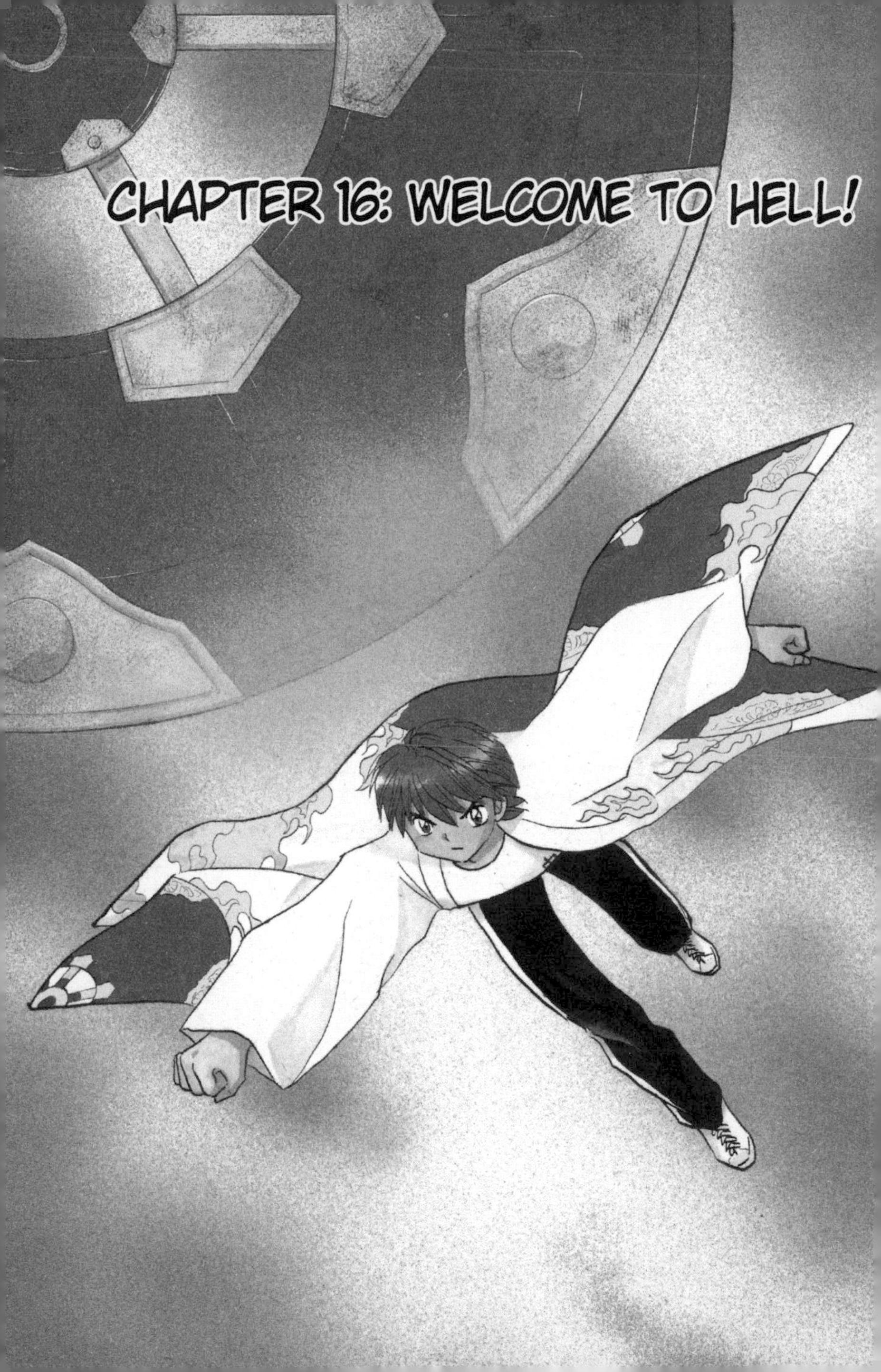
CHAPTER 16: WELCOME TO HELL!

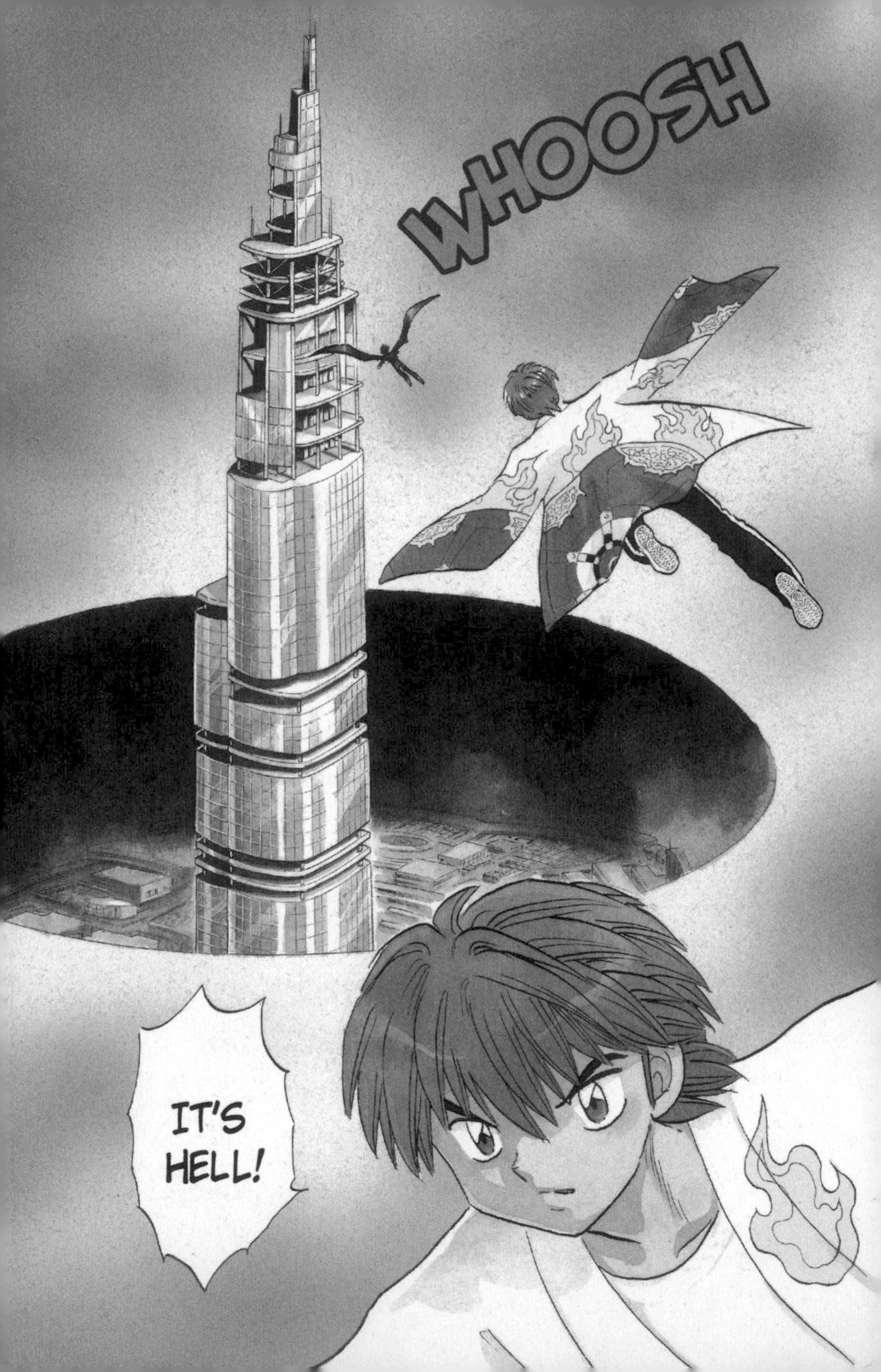
WHOOSH
IT'S HELL!

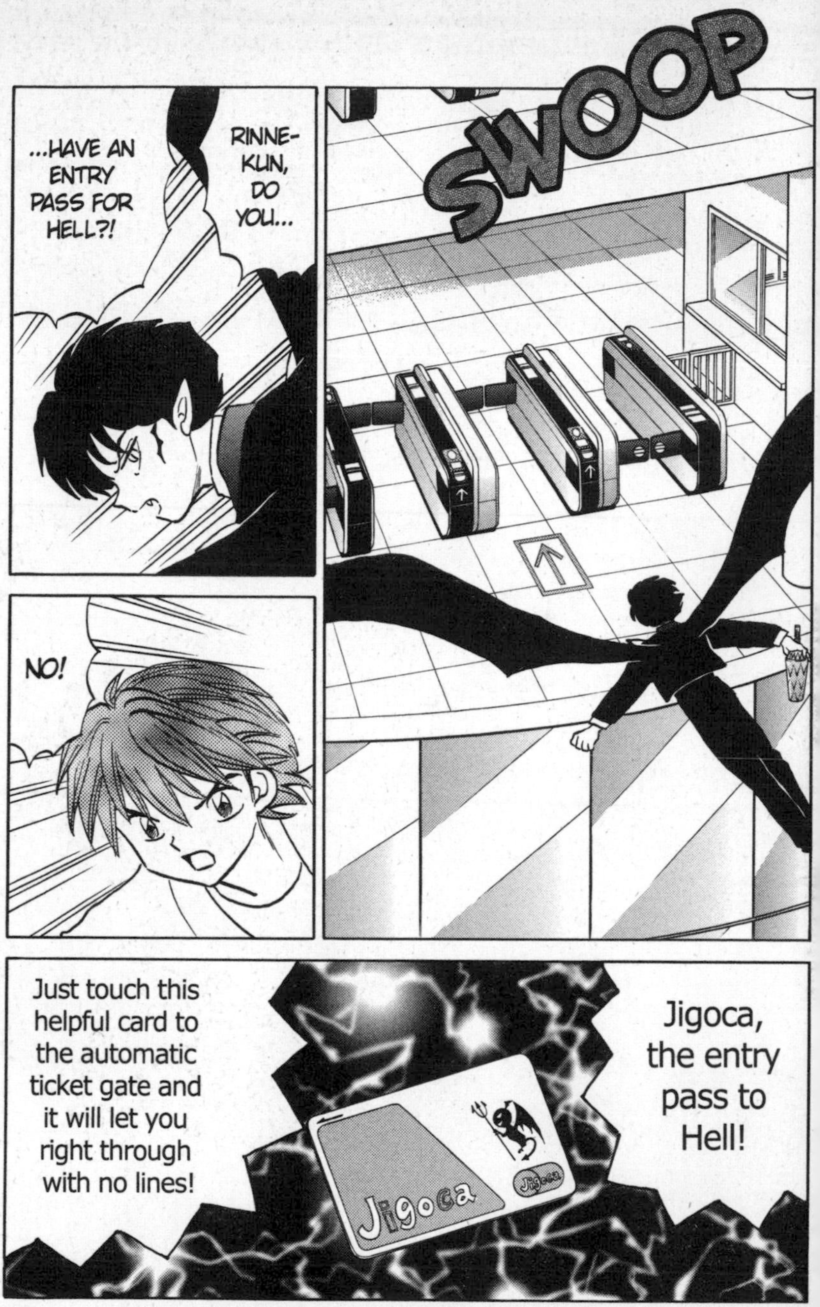
SWOOP
RINNE-KUN, DO YOU...
...HAVE AN ENTRY PASS FOR HELL?!
NO!
Jigoca, the entry pass to Hell!
Just touch this helpful card to the automatic ticket gate and it will let you right through with no lines!
Jigoca
Jigoca

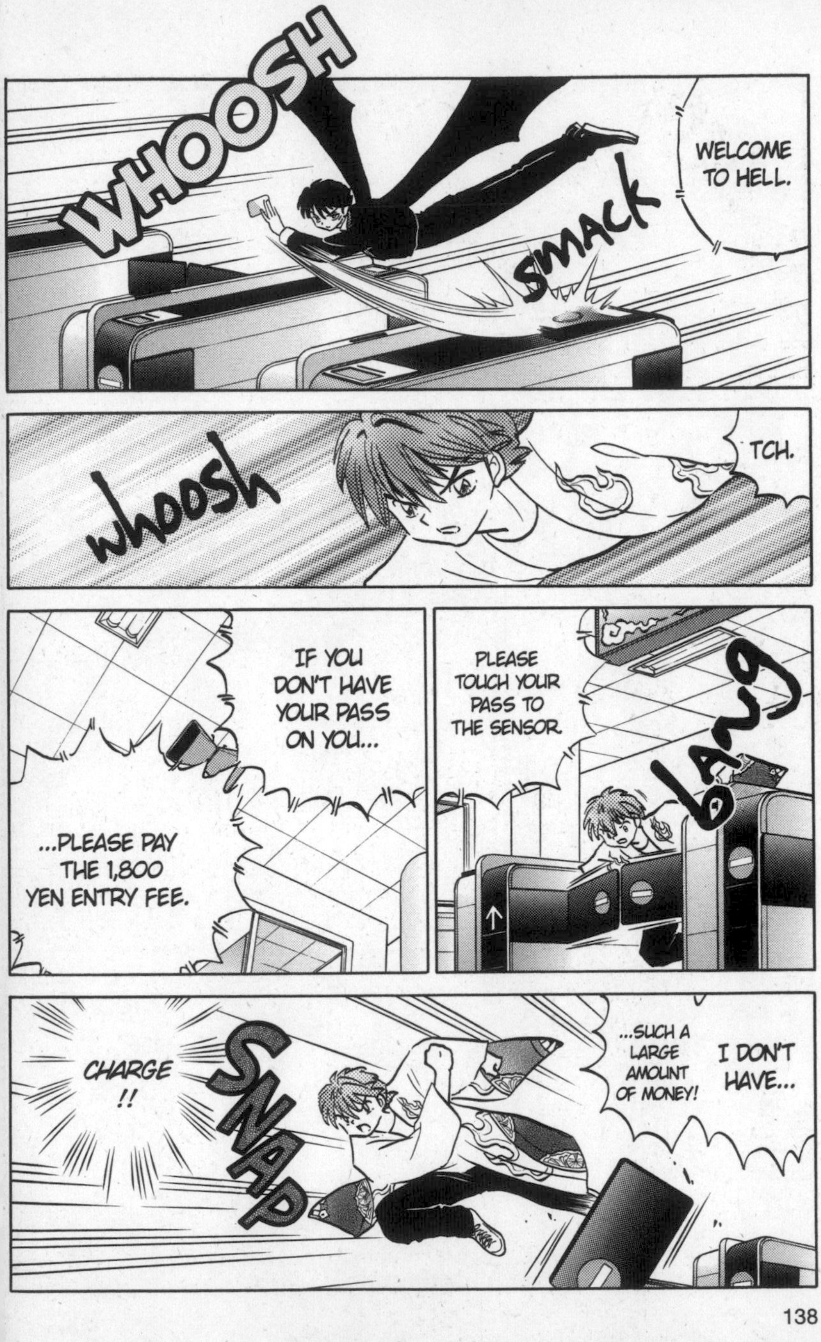
WELCOME TO HELL.
WHOOSH
SMACK
TCH.
whoosh
PLEASE TOUCH YOUR PASS TO THE SENSOR.
BANG
IF YOU DON'T HAVE YOUR PASS ON YOU...
...PLEASE PAY THE 1,800 YEN ENTRY FEE.
I DON'T HAVE...
...SUCH A LARGE AMOUNT OF MONEY!
SNAP
CHARGE !!

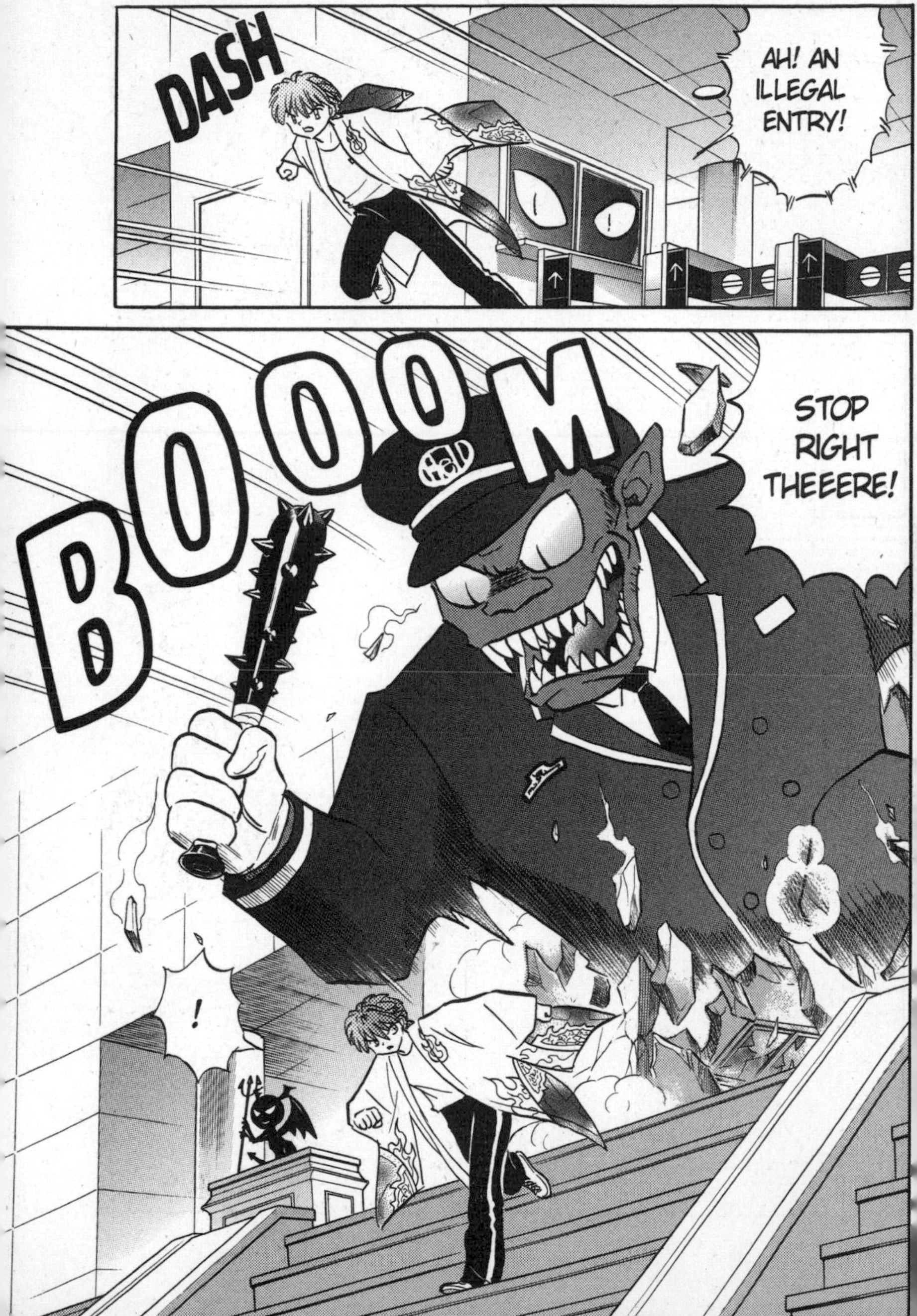
AH! AN ILLEGAL ENTRY!
DASH
STOP RIGHT THEEERE!
BOOOM
!

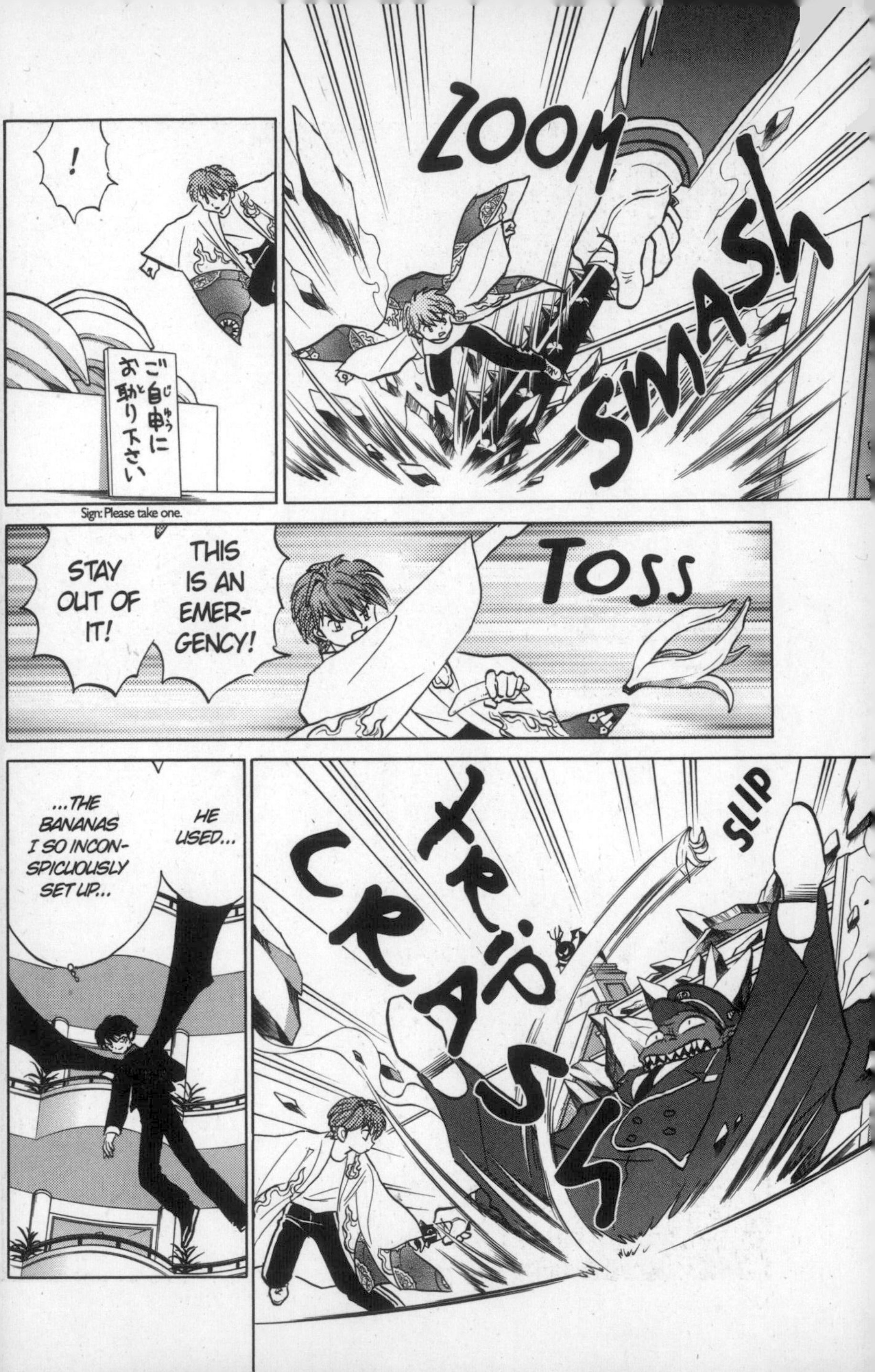
ZOOM
SMASH
!
ご自由にお取り下さい
TOSS
THIS IS AN EMERGENCY!
STAY OUT OF IT!
SLIP
TRIP
CRASH
HE USED...
...THE BANANAS I SO INCONSPICUOUSLY SET UP...
Sign: Please take one.

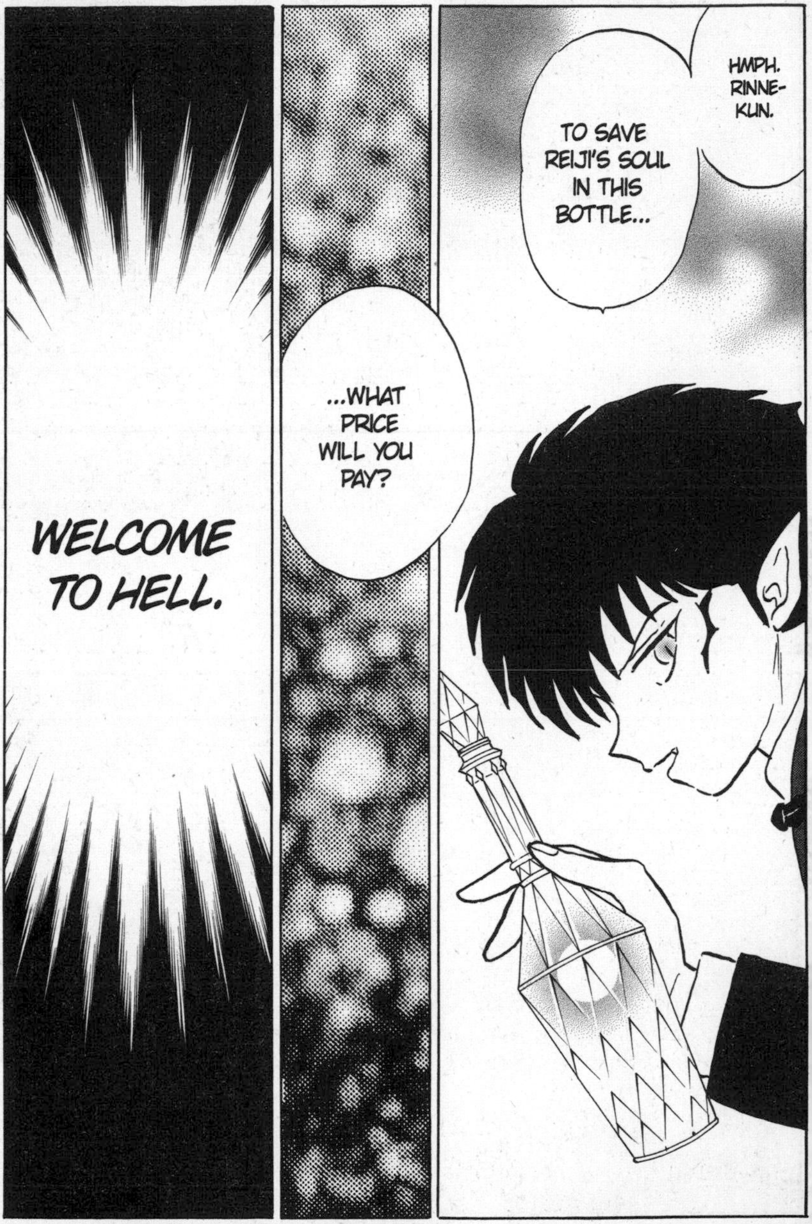
HMPH. RINNE-KUN.
TO SAVE REIJI'S SOUL IN THIS BOTTLE...
...WHAT PRICE WILL YOU PAY?
WELCOME TO HELL.

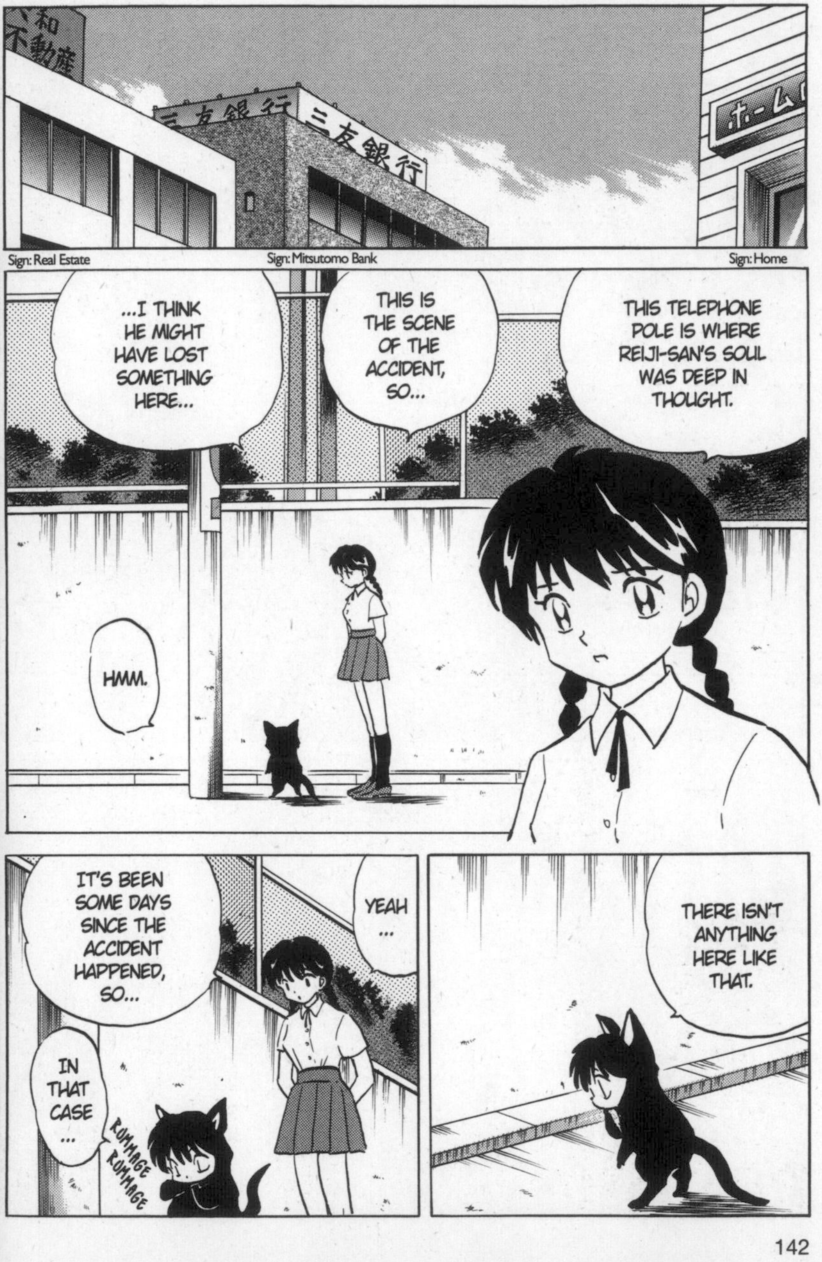
三友銀行
Sign: Real Estate
Sign: Mitsutomo Bank
Sign: Home
THIS TELEPHONE POLE IS WHERE REIJI-SAN'S SOUL WAS DEEP IN THOUGHT.
THIS IS THE SCENE OF THE ACCIDENT, SO...
...I THINK HE MIGHT HAVE LOST SOMETHING HERE...
HMM.
THERE ISN'T ANYTHING HERE LIKE THAT.
YEAH ...
IT'S BEEN SOME DAYS SINCE THE ACCIDENT HAPPENED, SO...
IN THAT CASE ...
RUMMAGE RUMMAGE

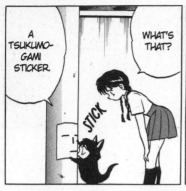

SHOW
...LET'S LISTEN TO WHAT A WITNESS HAS TO SAY.
WHAT'S THAT?
A TSUKUMO-GAMI STICKER.
STICK
A tsukumogami is an article that has survived so long, it's taken on a soul.
涼風
And a tsukumogami seal is a handy little product that instantaneously gives life to an article when applied to it. (retail price: 99 yen)
Paper: Cool Breeze
I SEE. SO THIS TELEPHONE POLE...
...SHOULD HAVE SEEN EVERYTHING THAT HAPPENED.
TRMBL TRMBL
SNARL
HM?!

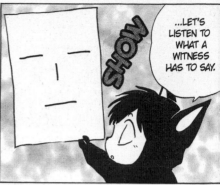

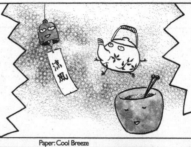

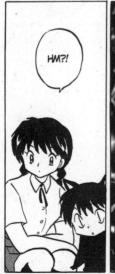

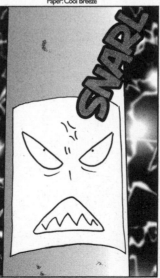

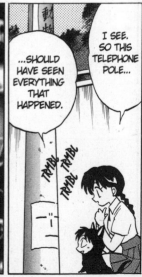

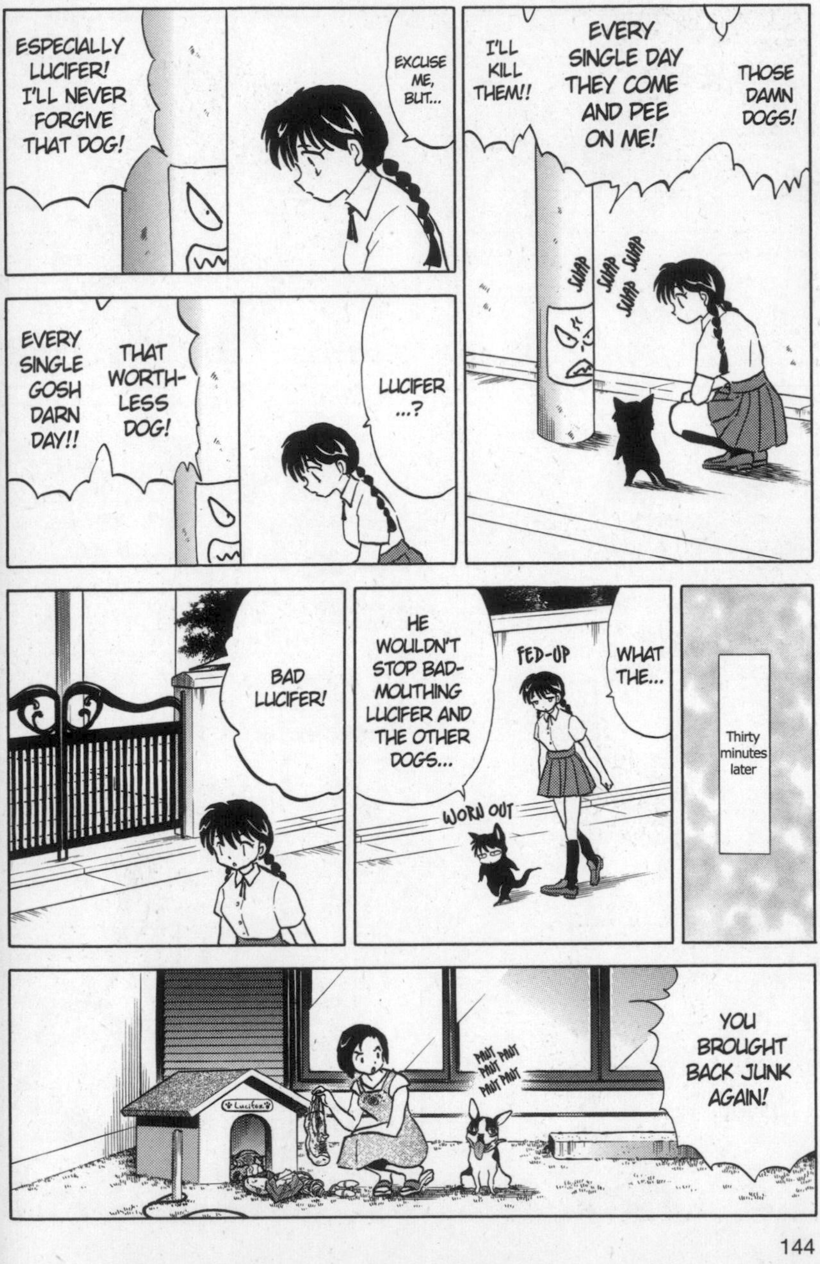
THOSE DAMN DOGS!
EVERY SINGLE DAY THEY COME AND PEE ON ME!
I'LL KILL THEM!!
EXCUSE ME, BUT...
ESPECIALLY LUCIFER! I'LL NEVER FORGIVE THAT DOG!
LUCIFER ...?
THAT WORTH-LESS DOG!
EVERY SINGLE GOSH DARN DAY!!
Thirty minutes later
WHAT THE...
FED-UP
HE WOULDN'T STOP BAD-MOUTHING LUCIFER AND THE OTHER DOGS...
WORN OUT
BAD LUCIFER!
YOU BROUGHT BACK JUNK AGAIN!
PANT PANT PANT PANT PANT PANT
Lucifer

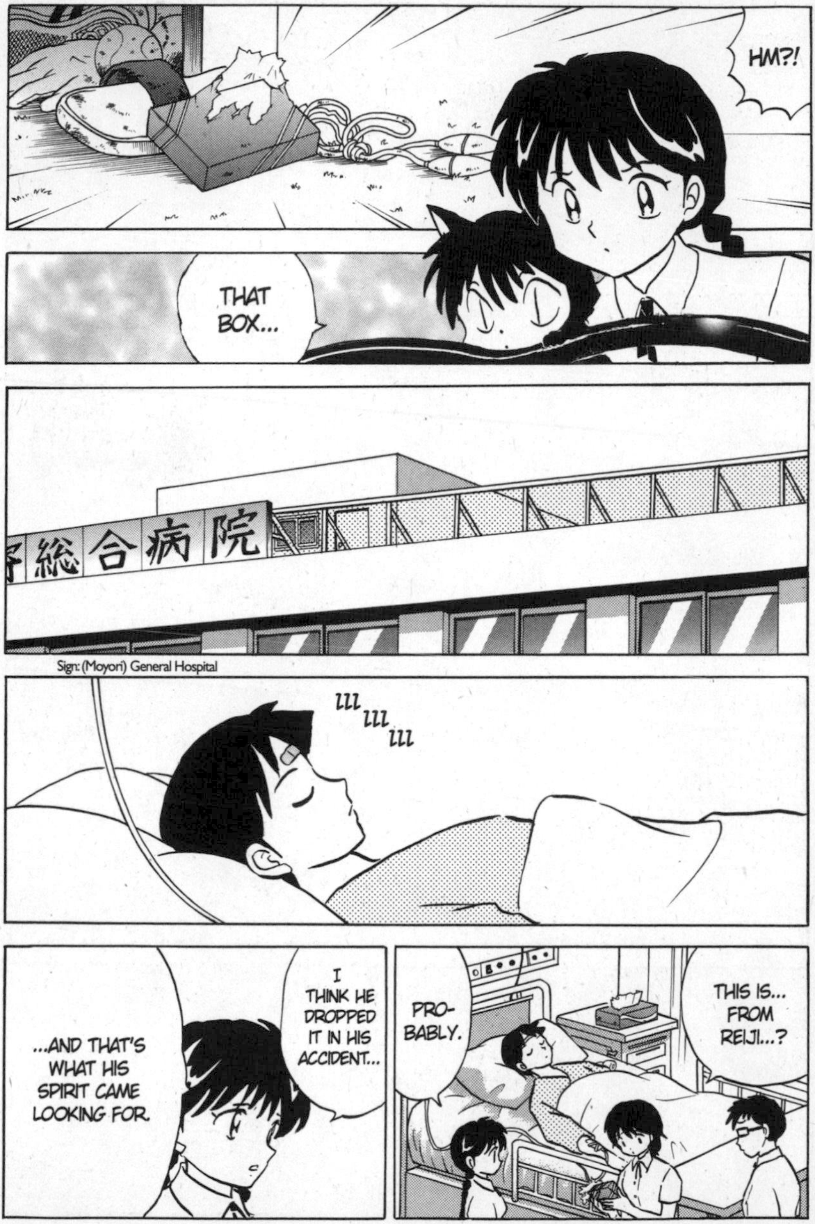
HM?!
THAT BOX...
総合病院
Sign: (Moyori) General Hospital
ZZZ ZZZ ZZZ
THIS IS... FROM REIJI...?
PRO-BABLY.
I THINK HE DROPPED IT IN HIS ACCIDENT...
...AND THAT'S WHAT HIS SPIRIT CAME LOOKING FOR.

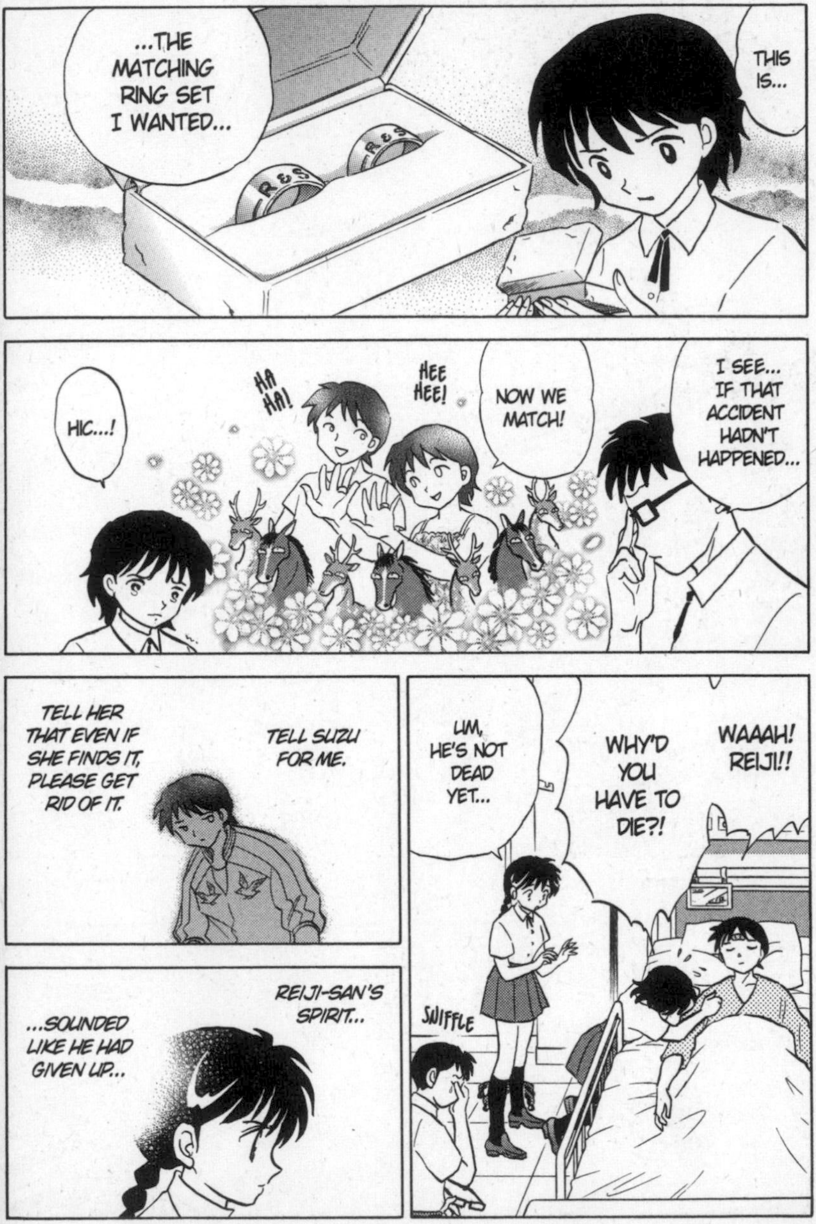
THIS IS...
...THE MATCHING RING SET I WANTED...
I SEE... IF THAT ACCIDENT HADN'T HAPPENED...
NOW WE MATCH!
HEE HEE!
HA HA!
HIC...!
WAAAH! REIJI!!
WHY'D YOU HAVE TO DIE?!
UM, HE'S NOT DEAD YET...
SNIFFLE
TELL SUZU FOR ME.
TELL HER THAT EVEN IF SHE FINDS IT, PLEASE GET RID OF IT.
REIJI-SAN'S SPIRIT...
...SOUNDED LIKE HE HAD GIVEN UP...

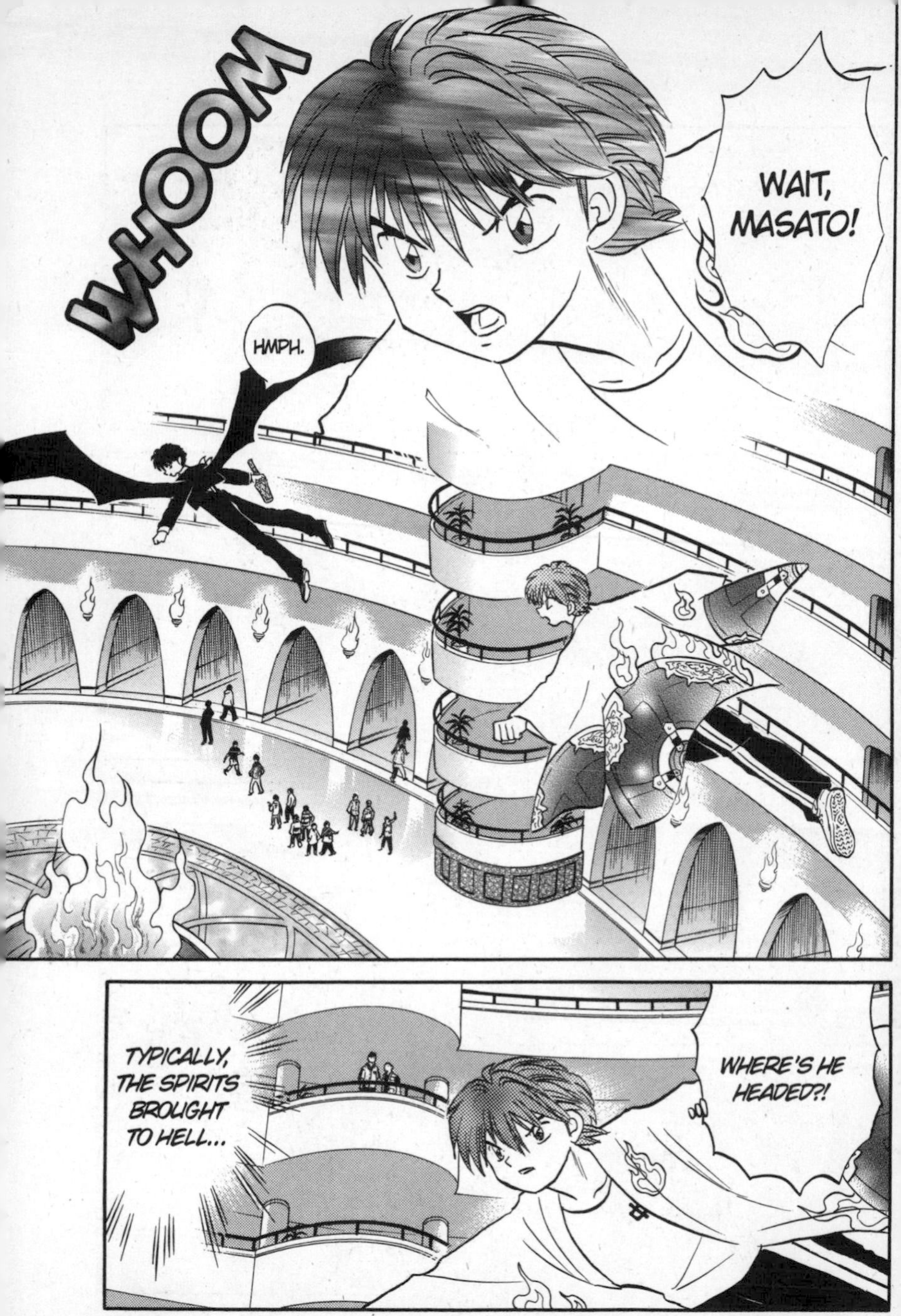
WAIT, MASATO!
WHOOM
HMPH.
WHERE'S HE HEADED?!
TYPICALLY, THE SPIRITS BROUGHT TO HELL...

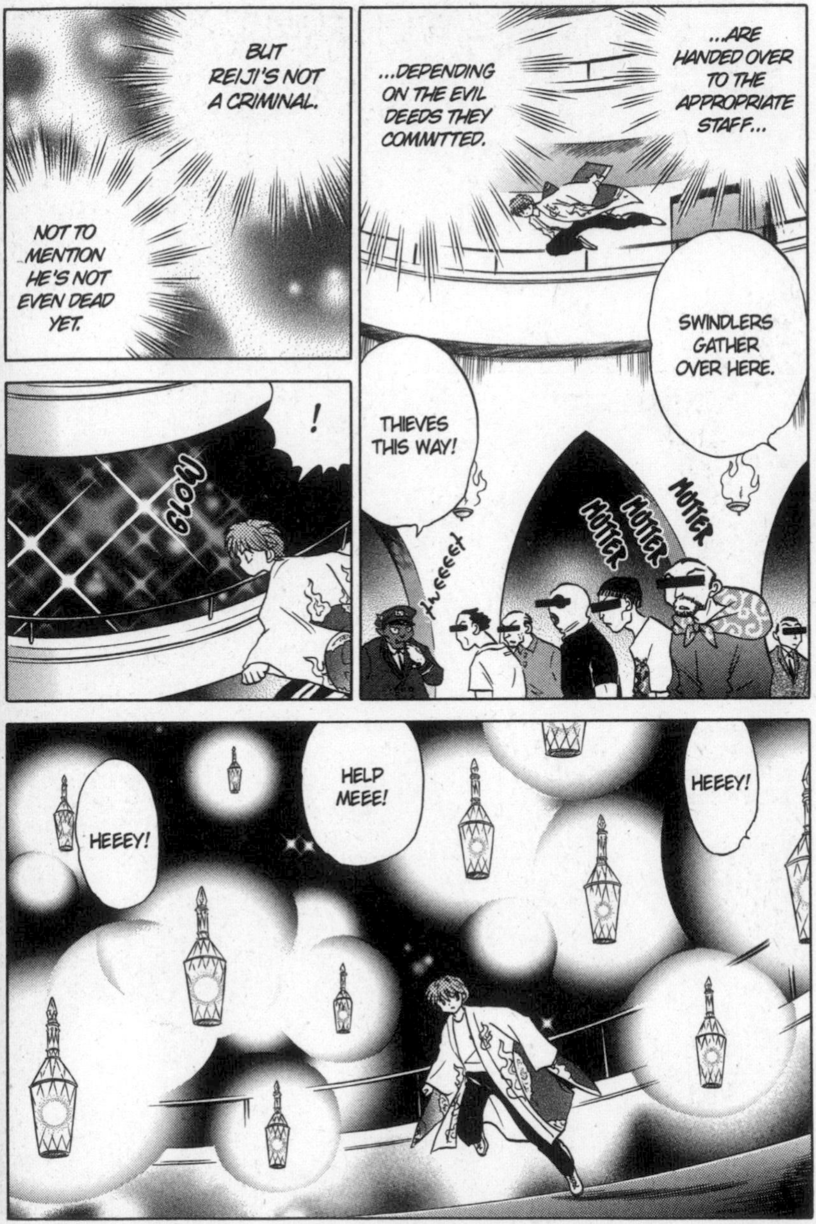
...ARE HANDED OVER TO THE APPROPRIATE STAFF...
...DEPENDING ON THE EVIL DEEDS THEY COMMITTED.
SWINDLERS GATHER OVER HERE.
MOTTER
MOTTER
MOTTER
THIEVES THIS WAY!
tweeeet
BUT REIJI'S NOT A CRIMINAL.
NOT TO MENTION HE'S NOT EVEN DEAD YET.
!
GLOW
HEEEY!
HELP MEEE!
HEEEY!

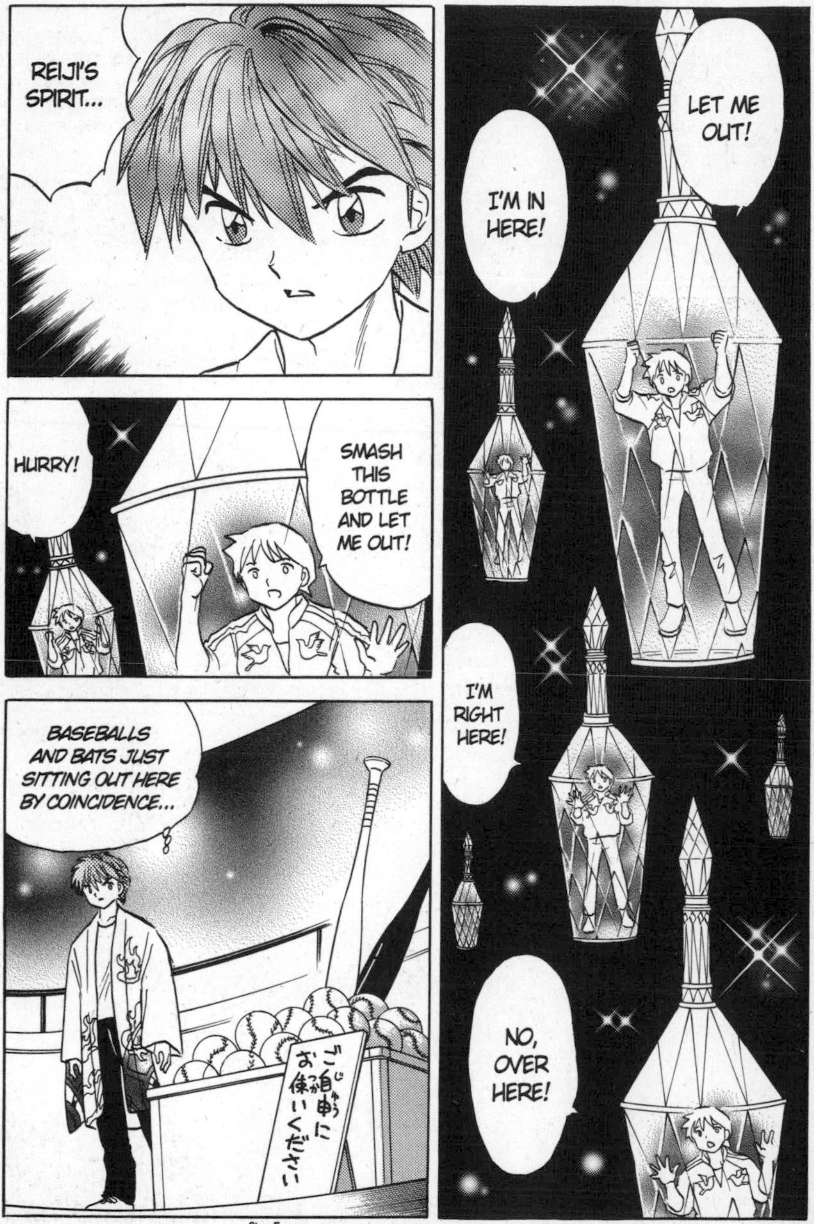
LET ME OUT!
I'M IN HERE!
I'M RIGHT HERE!
NO, OVER HERE!
REIJI'S SPIRIT...
SMASH THIS BOTTLE AND LET ME OUT!
HURRY!
BASEBALLS AND BATS JUST SITTING OUT HERE BY COINCIDENCE...
ご自由にお使いください
Sign: Free to use

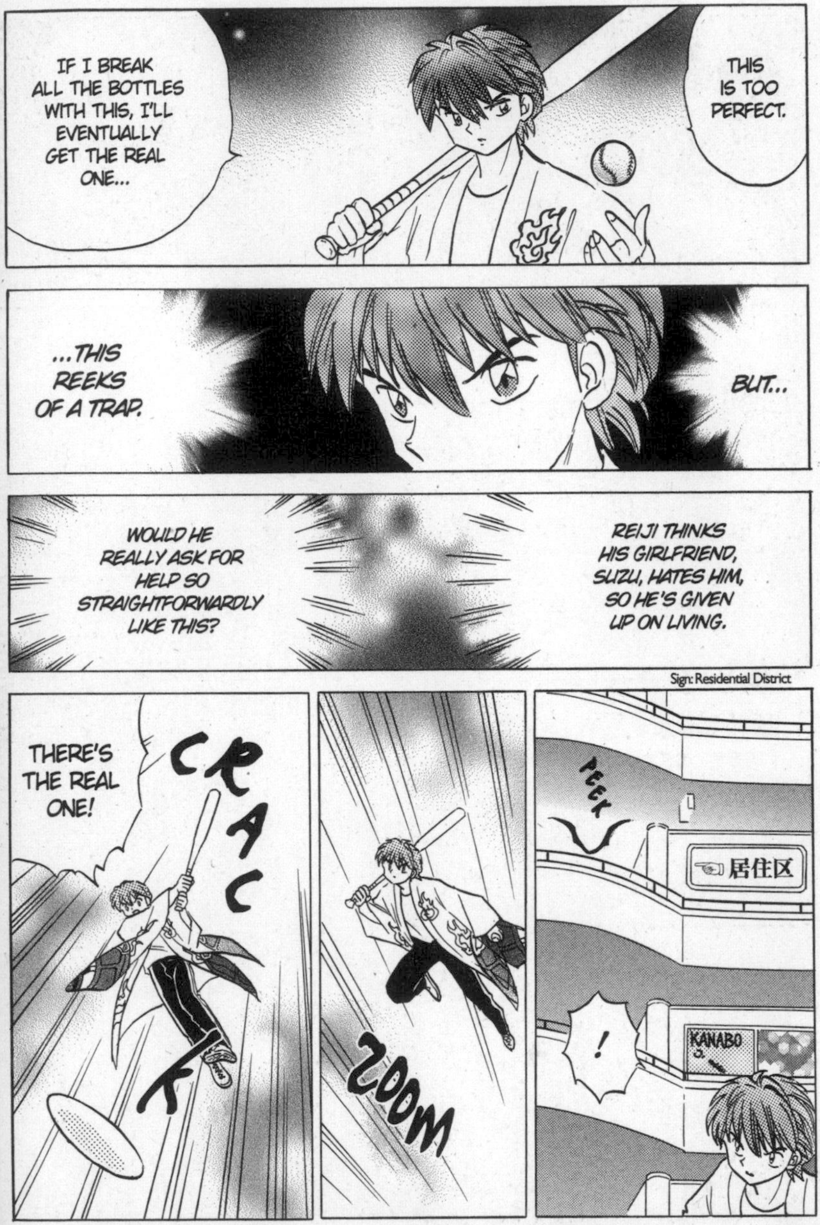
THIS IS TOO PERFECT.
IF I BREAK ALL THE BOTTLES WITH THIS, I'LL EVENTUALLY GET THE REAL ONE...
BUT...
...THIS REEKS OF A TRAP.
REIJI THINKS HIS GIRLFRIEND, SUZU, HATES HIM, SO HE'S GIVEN UP ON LIVING.
WOULD HE REALLY ASK FOR HELP SO STRAIGHTFORWARDLY LIKE THIS?
Sign: Residential District
PEEK
居住区
KANABO
!
ZOOM
THERE'S THE REAL ONE!
CRACK

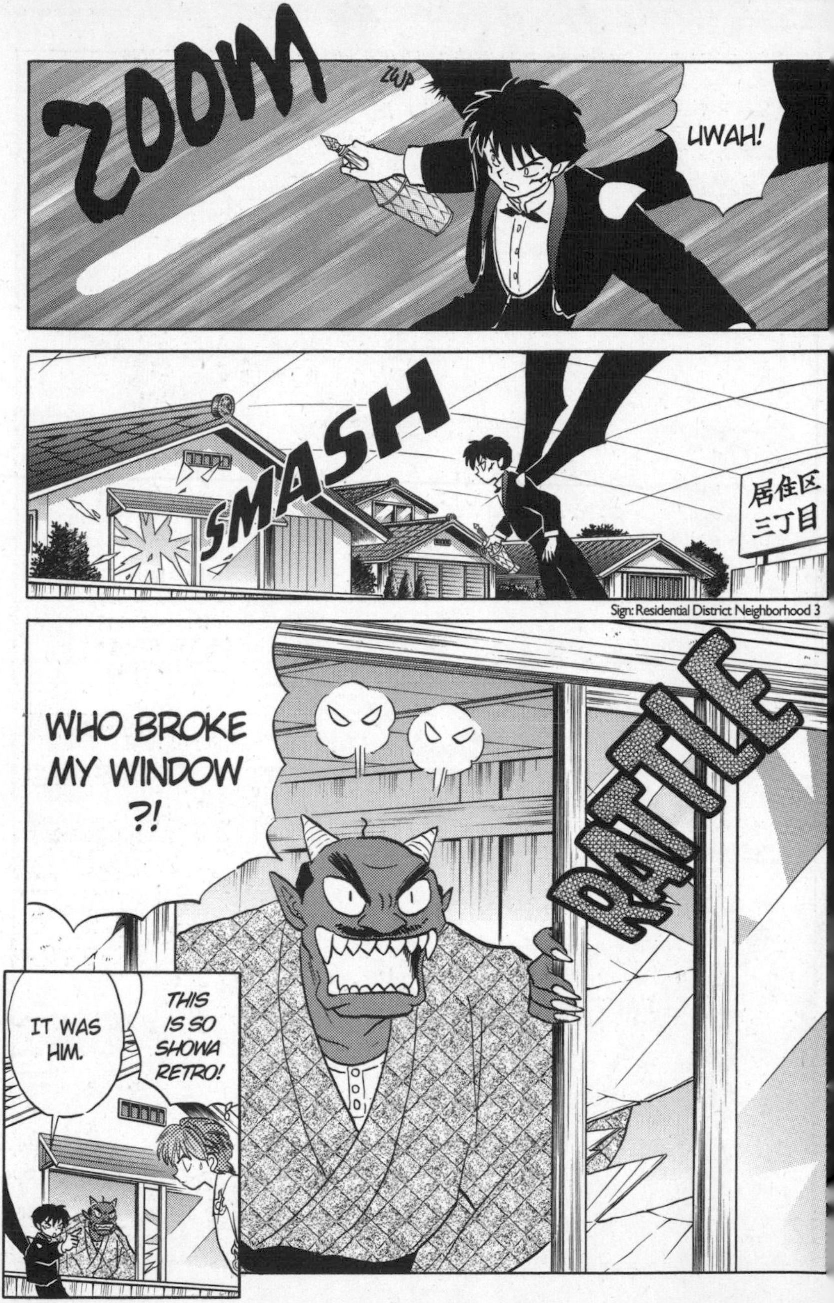
UWAH!
ZUP
ZOOM
SMASH
居住区
三丁目
Sign: Residential District Neighborhood 3
RATTLE
WHO BROKE MY WINDOW ?!
THIS IS SO SHOWA RETRO!
IT WAS HIM.

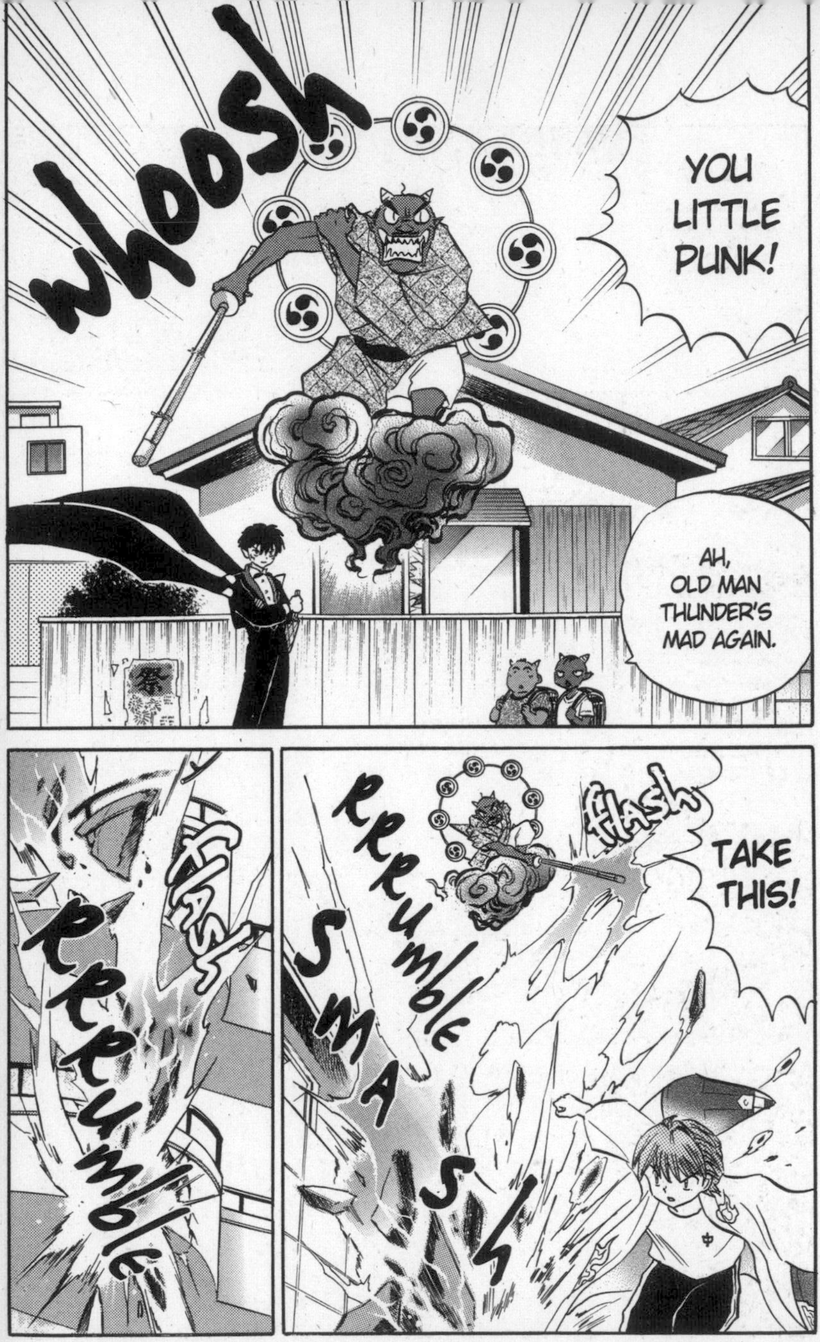
YOU LITTLE PUNK!
WHOOSH
AH, OLD MAN THUNDER'S MAD AGAIN.
TAKE THIS!
FLASH
RRRUMBLE
SMASH
FLASH
RRRUMBLE

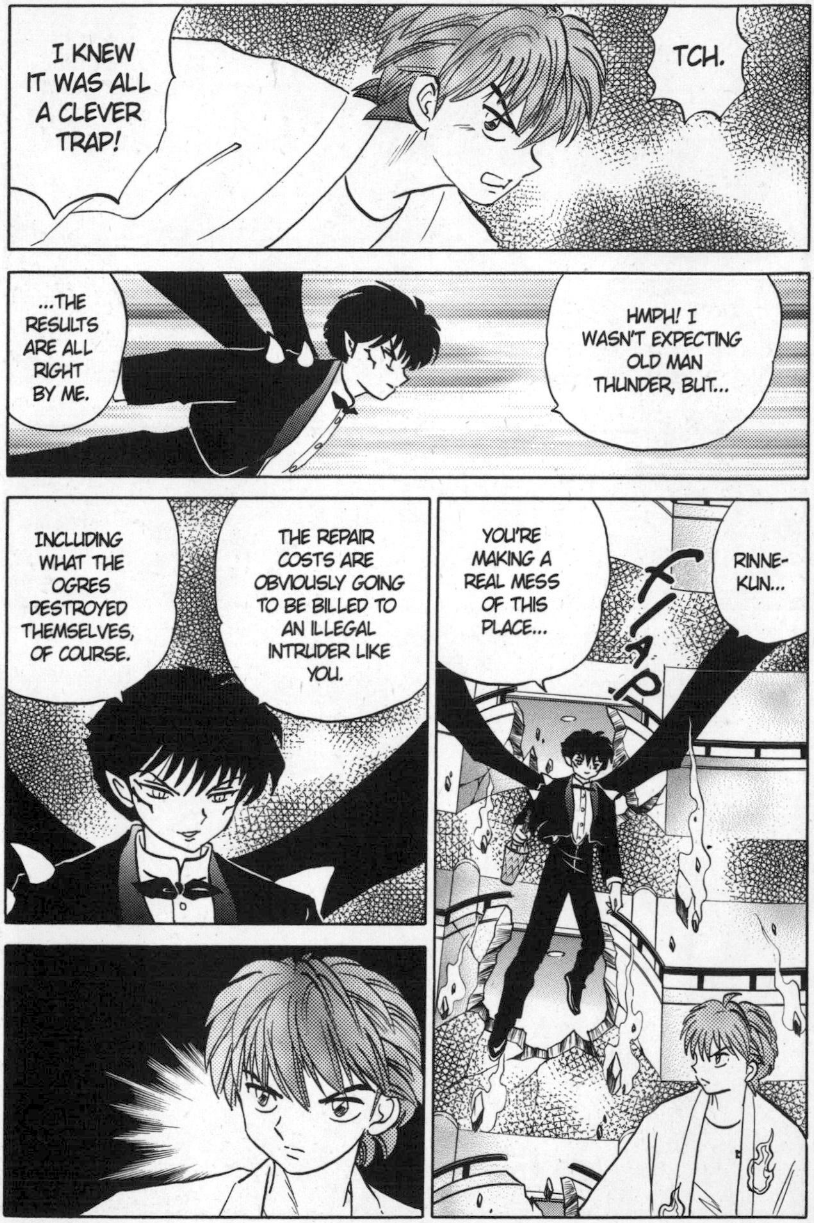
TCH.
I KNEW IT WAS ALL A CLEVER TRAP!
HMPH! I WASN'T EXPECTING OLD MAN THUNDER, BUT...
...THE RESULTS ARE ALL RIGHT BY ME.
RINNE-KUN...
FLAP!
YOU'RE MAKING A REAL MESS OF THIS PLACE...
THE REPAIR COSTS ARE OBVIOUSLY GOING TO BE BILLED TO AN ILLEGAL INTRUDER LIKE YOU.
INCLUDING WHAT THE OGRES DESTROYED THEMSELVES, OF COURSE.

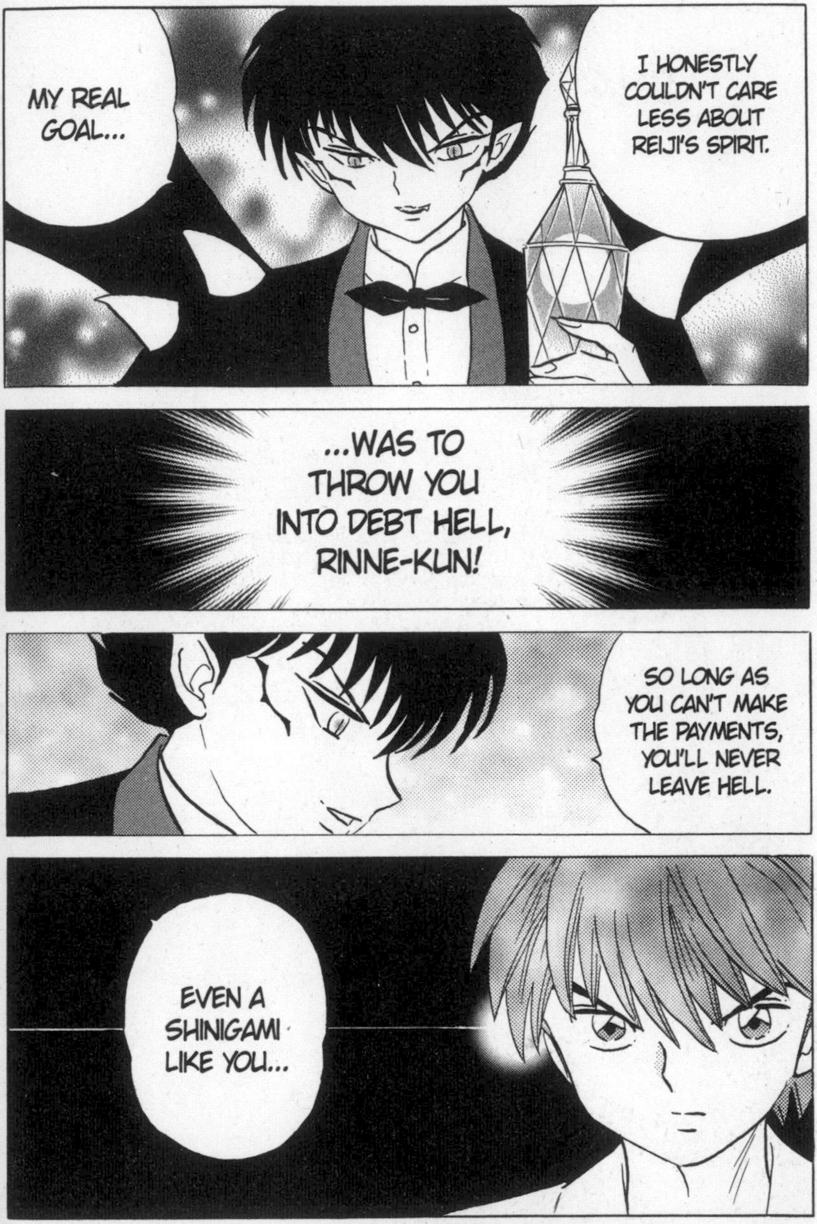
I HONESTLY COULDN'T CARE LESS ABOUT REIJI'S SPIRIT.
MY REAL GOAL...
...WAS TO THROW YOU INTO DEBT HELL, RINNE-KUN!
SO LONG AS YOU CAN'T MAKE THE PAYMENTS, YOU'LL NEVER LEAVE HELL.
EVEN A SHINIGAMI LIKE YOU...

CHAPTER 17: DEBT HELL

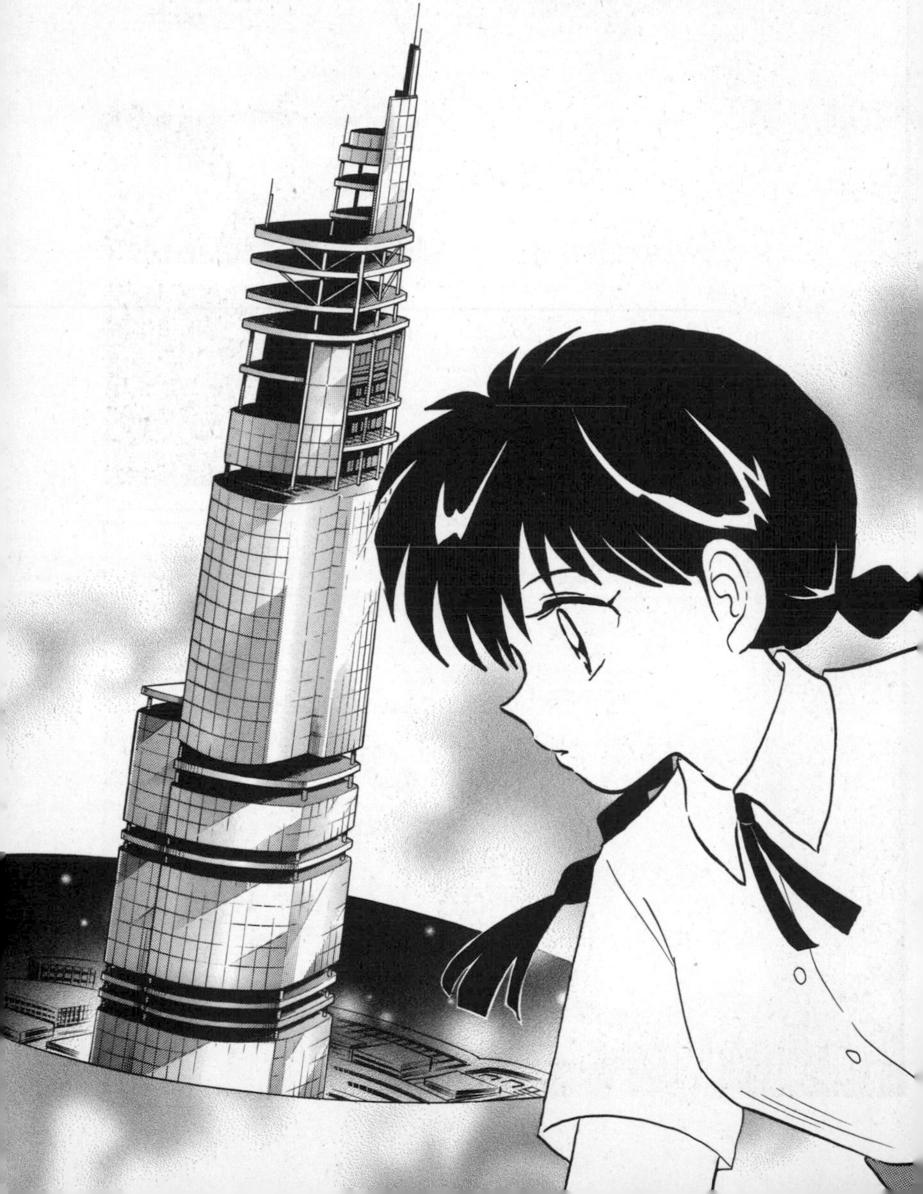

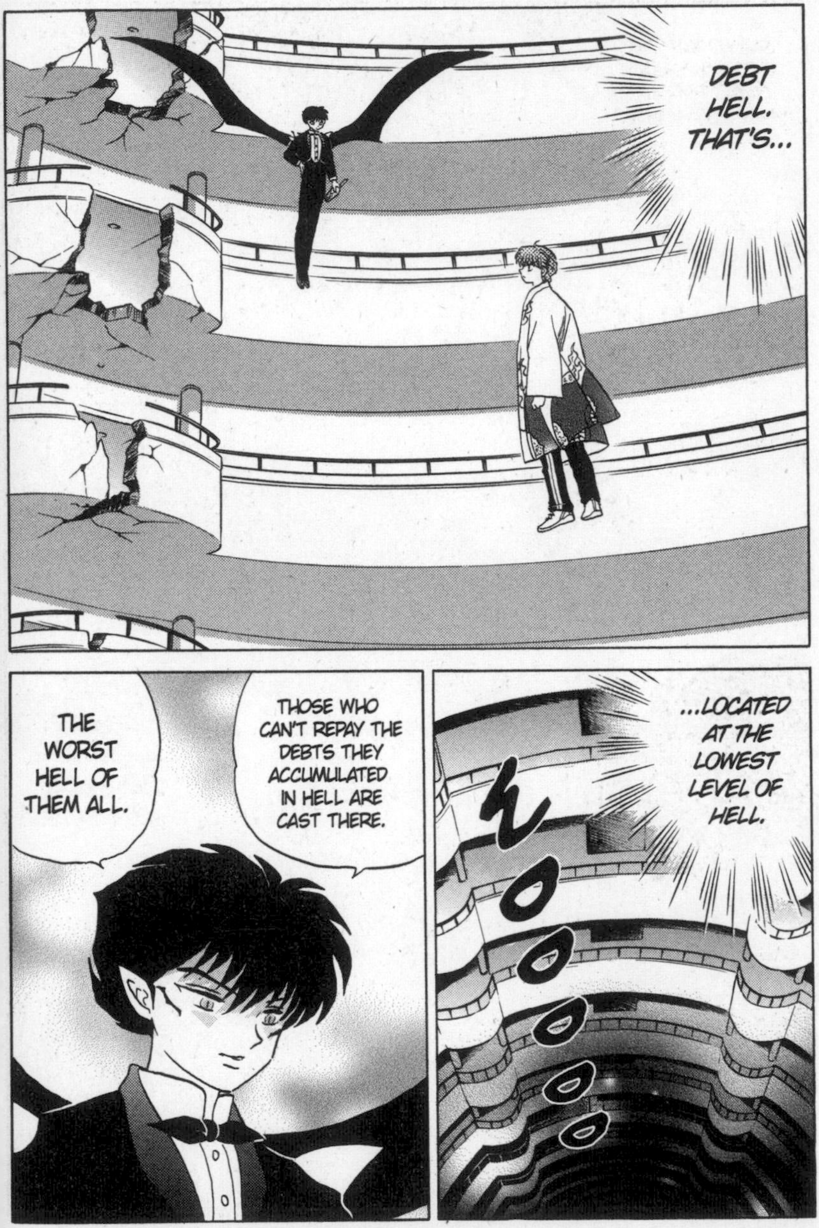
DEBT HELL. THAT'S...
...LOCATED AT THE LOWEST LEVEL OF HELL.
ZOOOOO
THOSE WHO CAN'T REPAY THE DEBTS THEY ACCUMULATED IN HELL ARE CAST THERE.
THE WORST HELL OF THEM ALL.

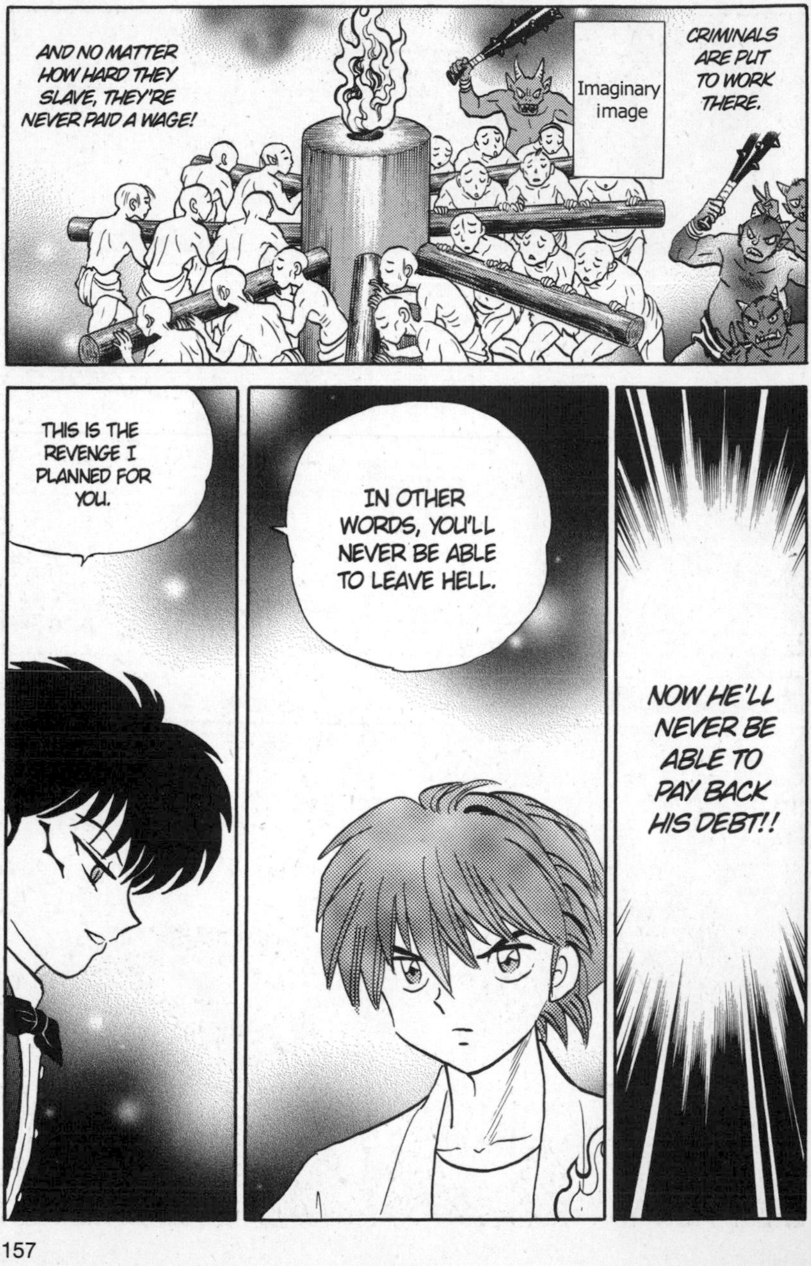
CRIMINALS ARE PUT TO WORK THERE.
Imaginary image
AND NO MATTER HOW HARD THEY SLAVE, THEY'RE NEVER PAID A WAGE!
NOW HE'LL NEVER BE ABLE TO PAY BACK HIS DEBT!!
IN OTHER WORDS, YOU'LL NEVER BE ABLE TO LEAVE HELL.
THIS IS THE REVENGE I PLANNED FOR YOU.

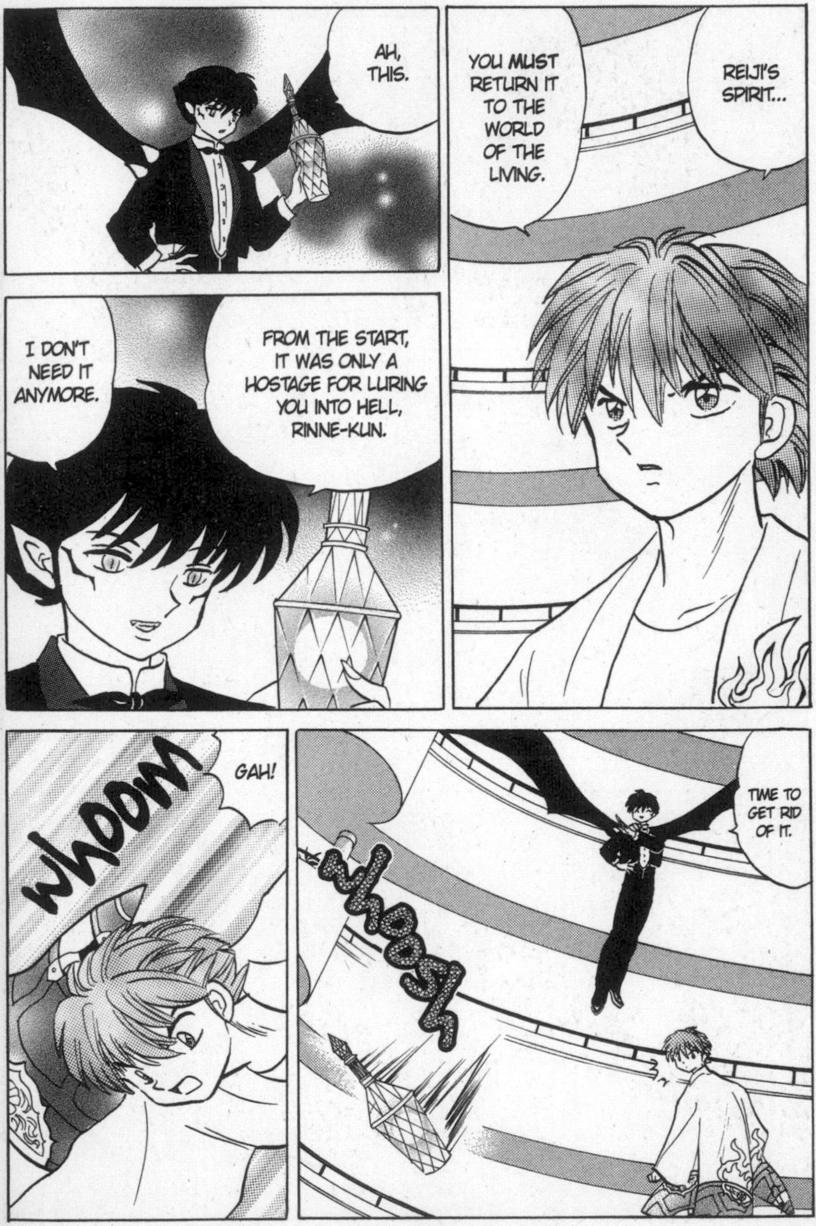
REIJI'S SPIRIT...
YOU MUST RETURN IT TO THE WORLD OF THE LIVING.
AH, THIS.
FROM THE START, IT WAS ONLY A HOSTAGE FOR LURING YOU INTO HELL, RINNE-KUN.
I DON'T NEED IT ANYMORE.
TIME TO GET RID OF IT.
WHOOSH
GAH!
WHOOM

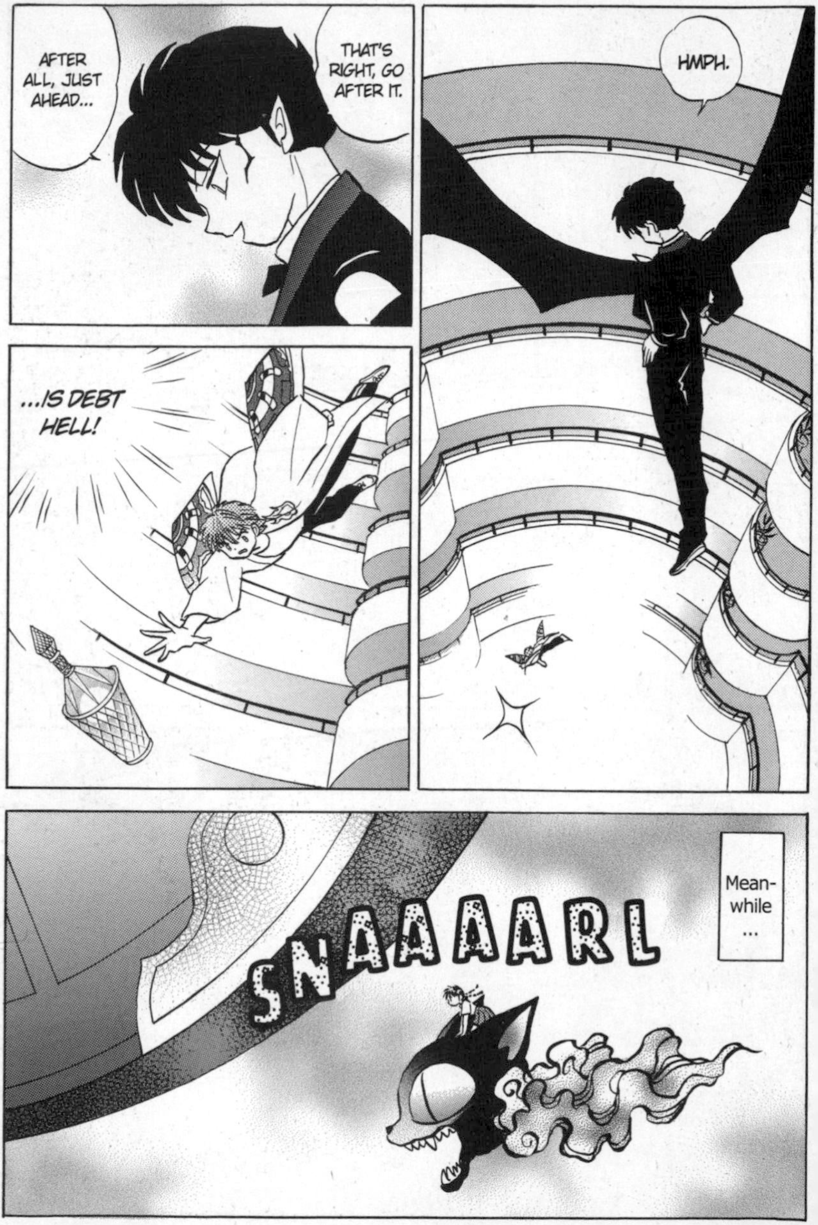

HMPH.
THAT'S RIGHT, GO AFTER IT.
AFTER ALL, JUST AHEAD...
...IS DEBT HELL!
Mean-while ...
SNAAAARL

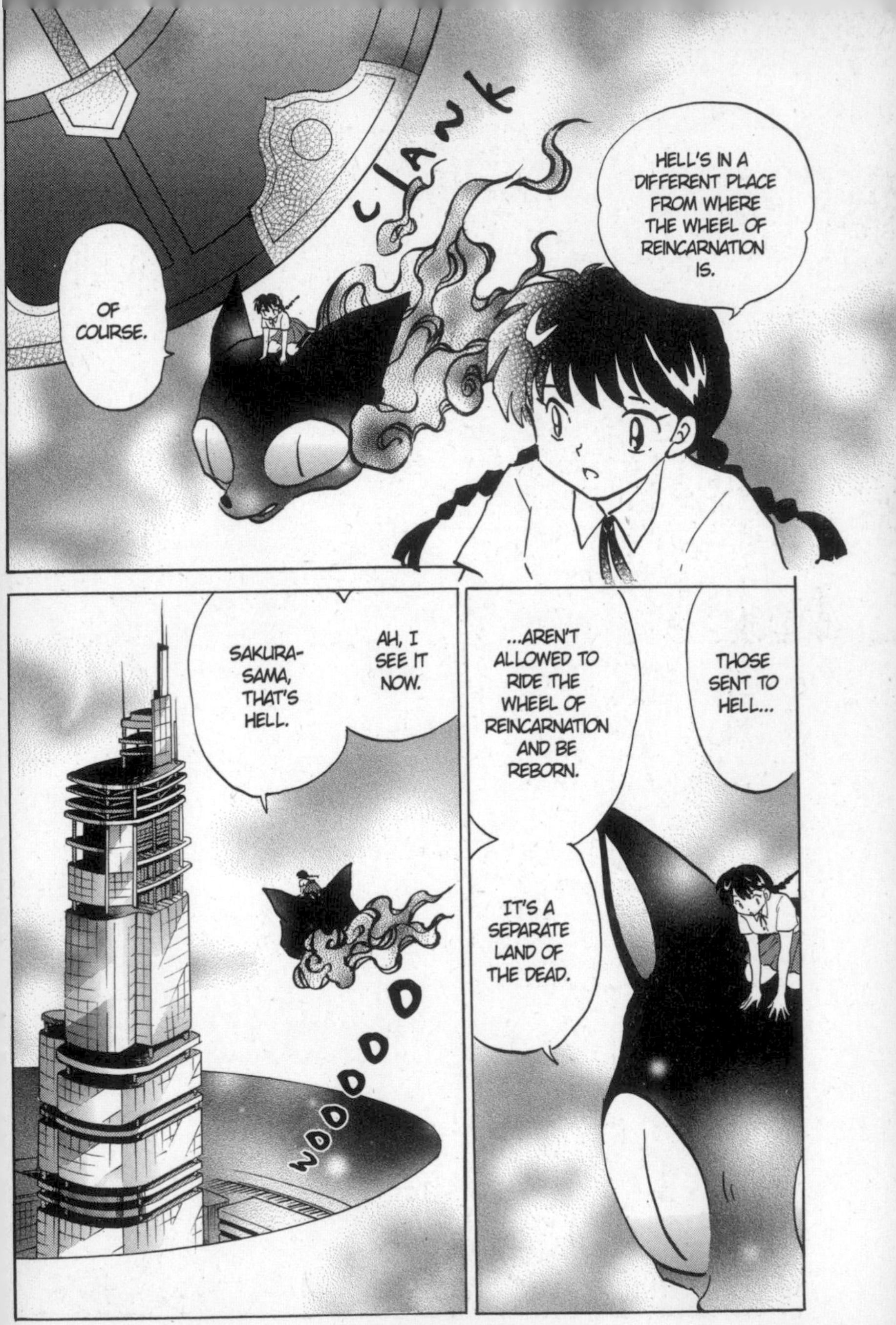

HELL'S IN A DIFFERENT PLACE FROM WHERE THE WHEEL OF REINCARNATION IS.
CLANK
OF COURSE.
THOSE SENT TO HELL...
...AREN'T ALLOWED TO RIDE THE WHEEL OF REINCARNATION AND BE REBORN.
IT'S A SEPARATE LAND OF THE DEAD.
AH, I SEE IT NOW.
SAKURA-SAMA, THAT'S HELL.
WOODDDD

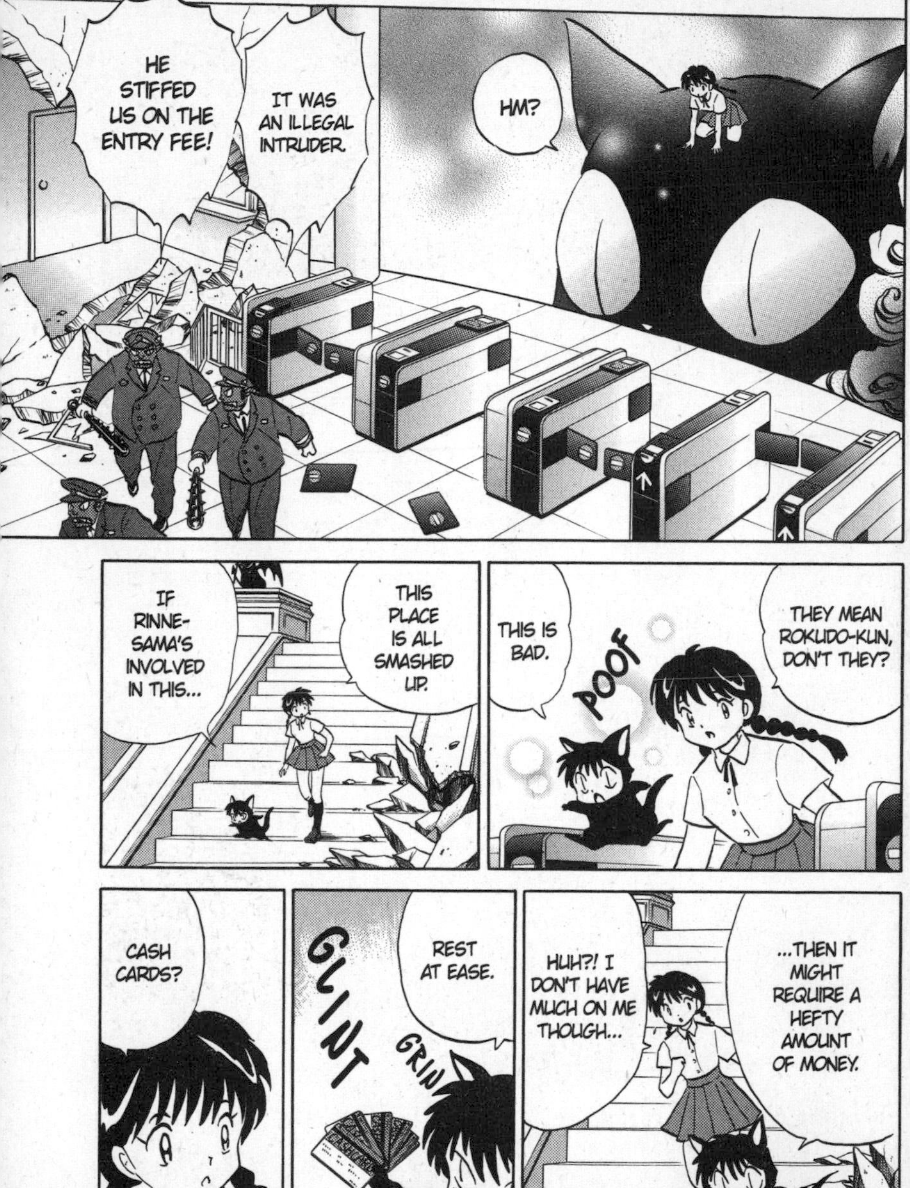
HM?
IT WAS AN ILLEGAL INTRUDER.
HE STIFFED US ON THE ENTRY FEE!
THEY MEAN ROKUDO-KUN, DON'T THEY?
POOF
THIS IS BAD.
THIS PLACE IS ALL SMASHED UP.
IF RINNE-SAMA'S INVOLVED IN THIS...
...THEN IT MIGHT REQUIRE A HEFTY AMOUNT OF MONEY.
HUH?! I DON'T HAVE MUCH ON ME THOUGH...
REST AT EASE.
GLINT
GRIN
CASH CARDS?

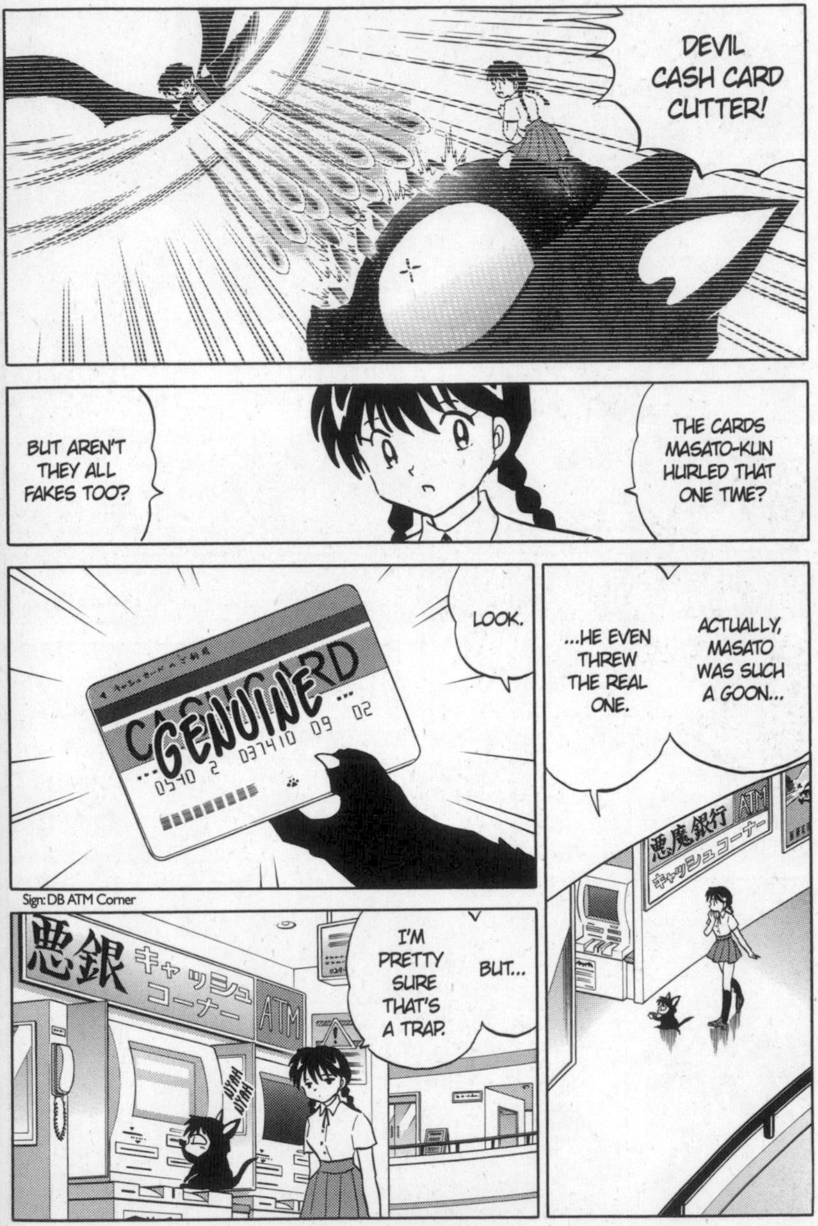
DEVIL CASH CARD CUTTER!
THE CARDS MASATO-KUN HURLED THAT ONE TIME?
BUT AREN'T THEY ALL FAKES TOO?
ACTUALLY, MASATO WAS SUCH A GOON...
...HE EVEN THREW THE REAL ONE.
悪魔銀行
ATM
キャッシュコーナー
LOOK.
CASH CARD
GENUINE
悪銀
キャッシュコーナー
ATM
I'M PRETTY SURE THAT'S A TRAP.
BUT...
NYAH NYAH
Sign: DB ATM Corner

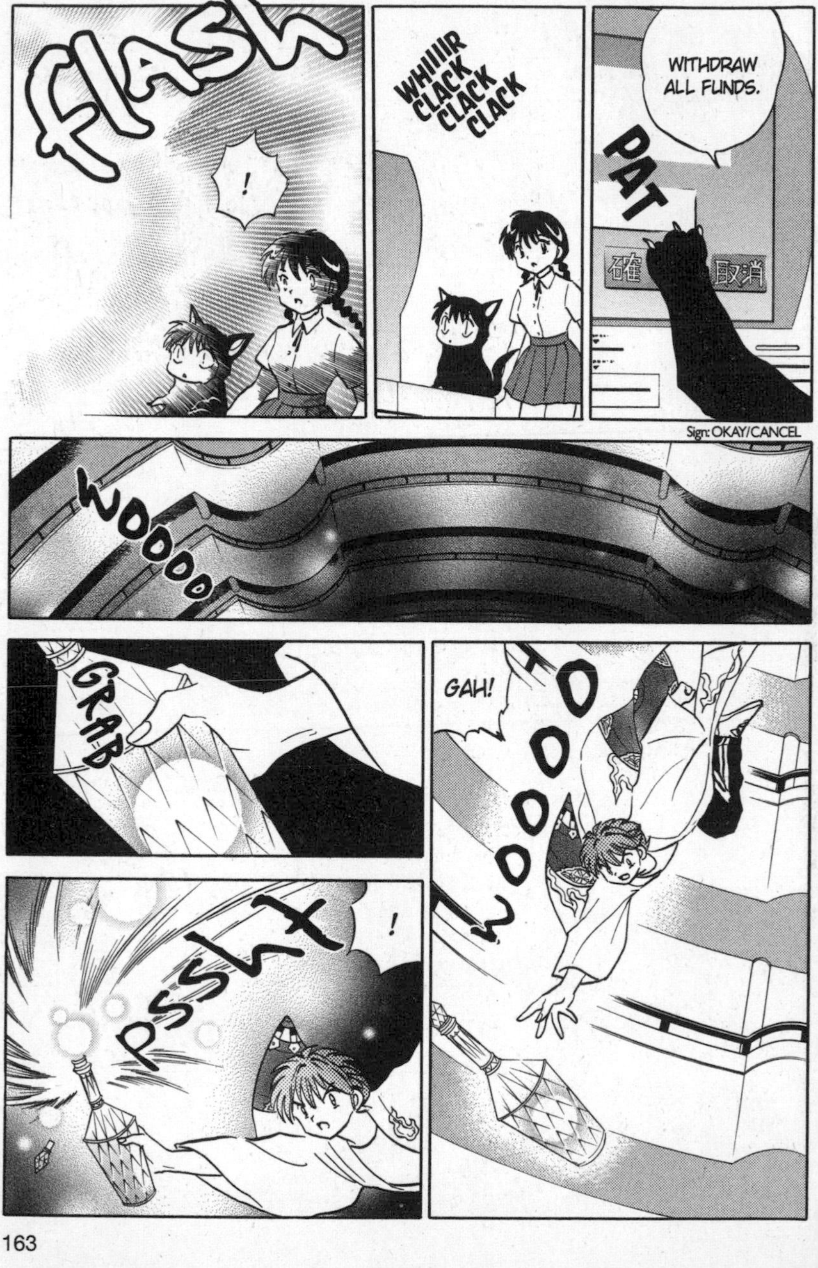
WITHDRAW ALL FUNDS.
PAT
取消
WHIIIIR CLACK CLACK CLACK
FLASH
!
WOOOOO
GAH!
WOOOOO
GRAB
PSSHT
!
Sign: OKAY/CANCEL

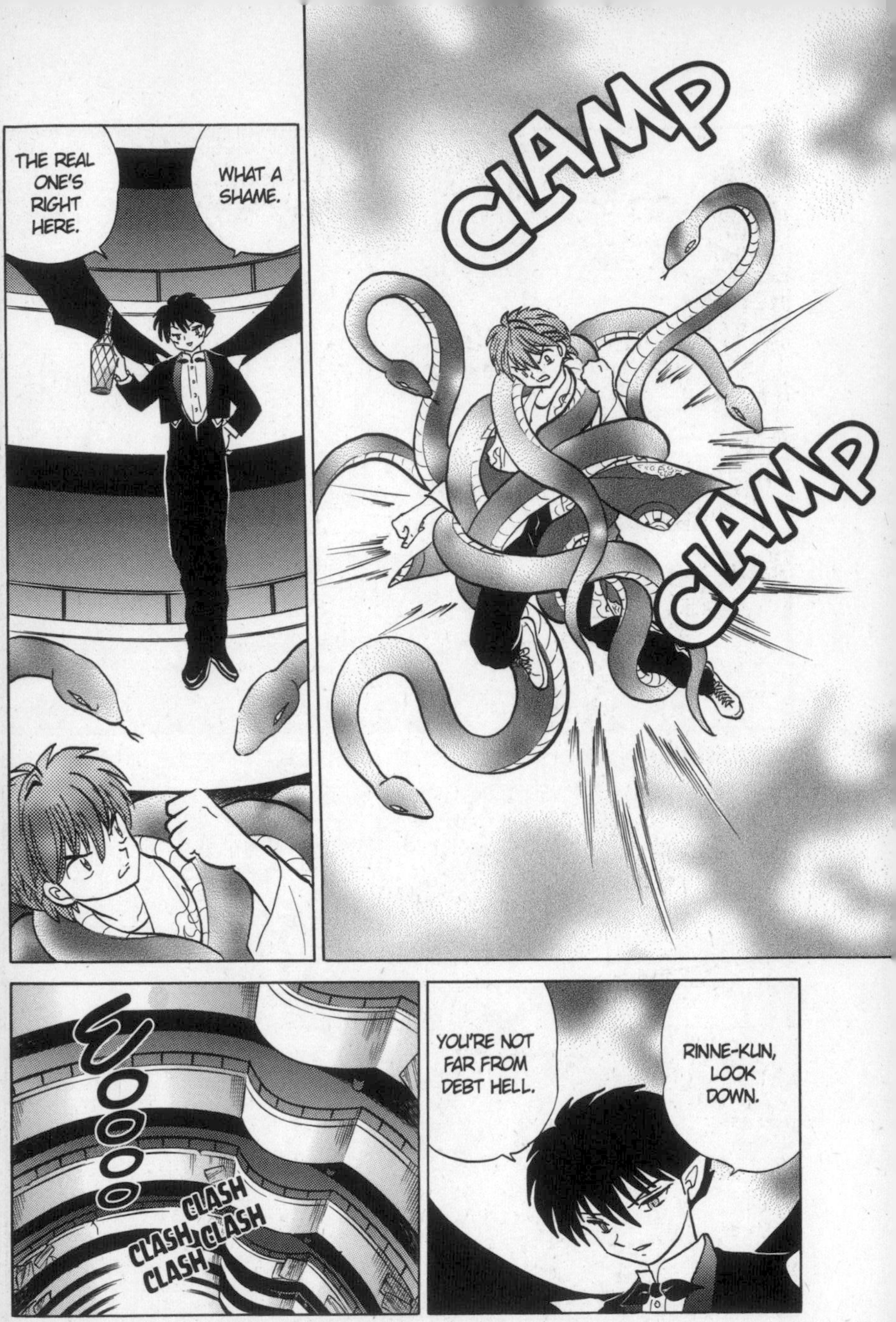
CLAMP
CLAMP
WHAT A SHAME.
THE REAL ONE'S RIGHT HERE.
RINNE-KUN, LOOK DOWN.
YOU'RE NOT FAR FROM DEBT HELL.
WOOOO
CLASH
CLASH
CLASH
CLASH

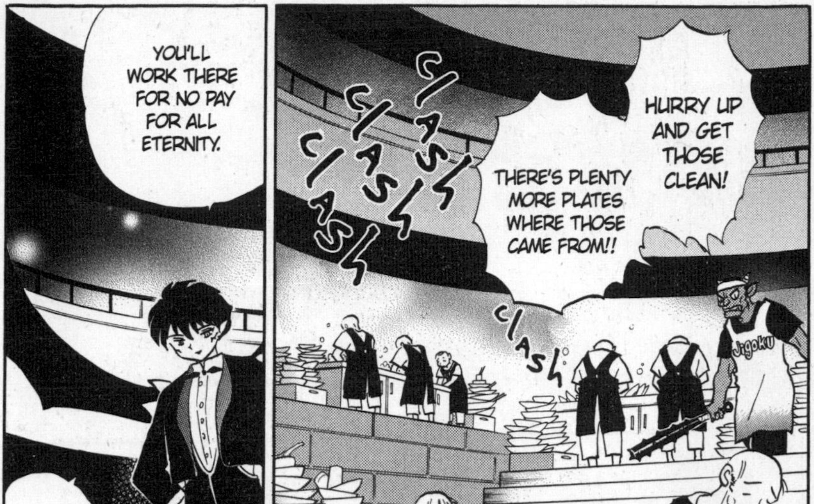
HURRY UP AND GET THOSE CLEAN!
THERE'S PLENTY MORE PLATES WHERE THOSE CAME FROM!!
CLASH CLASH CLASH
CLASH
YOU'LL WORK THERE FOR NO PAY FOR ALL ETERNITY.
BUT FIRST...
FWOOSH
SNAP
FWOOSH

Sign: Swords, Keys

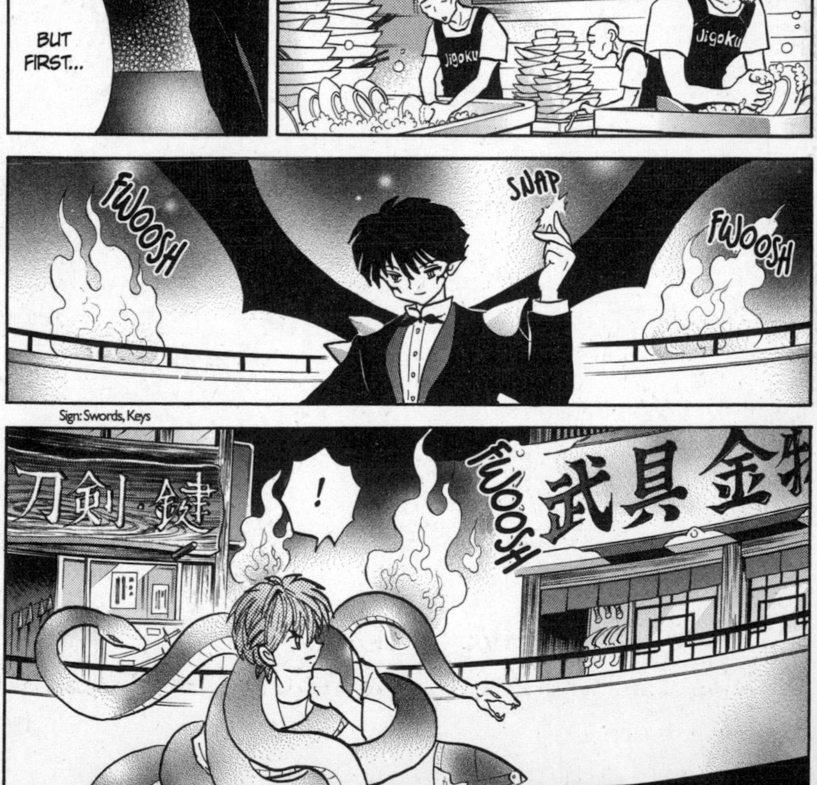
FWOOSH
!

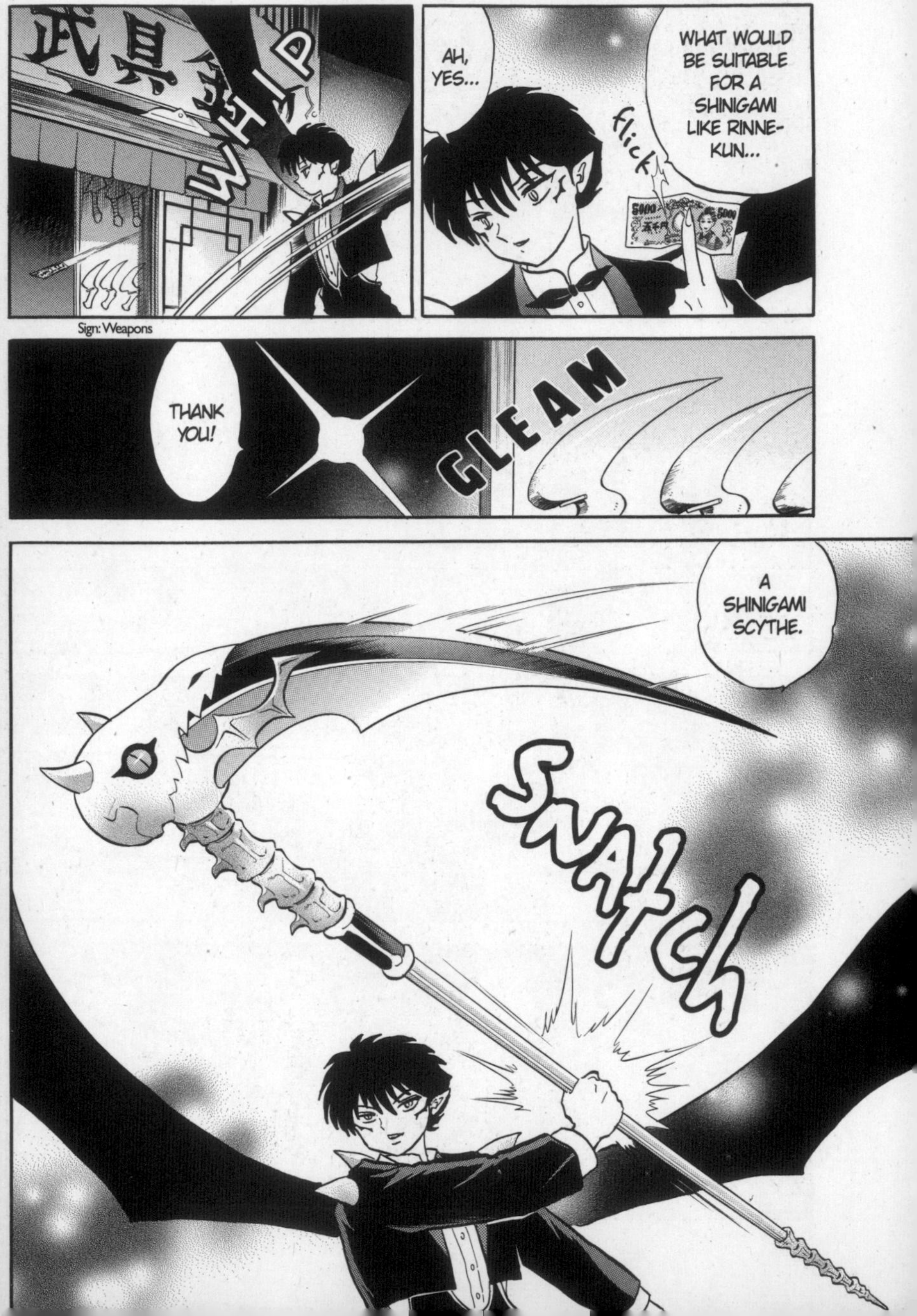
WHAT WOULD BE SUITABLE FOR A SHINIGAMI LIKE RINNE-KUN...
AH, YES...
flick
WHIP
GLEAM
THANK YOU!
A SHINIGAMI SCYTHE.
SNATCH
Sign: Weapons

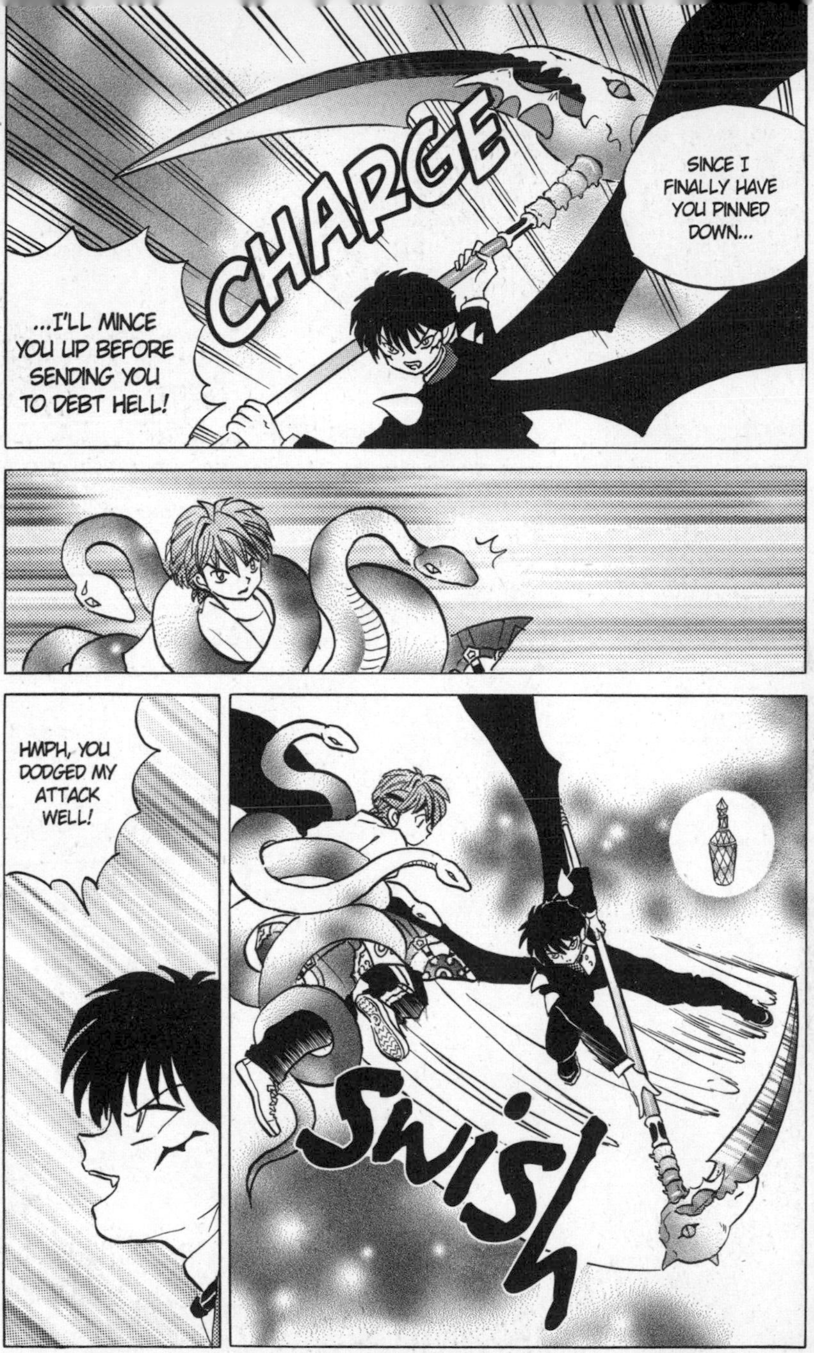
SINCE I FINALLY HAVE YOU PINNED DOWN...
CHARGE
...I'LL MINCE YOU UP BEFORE SENDING YOU TO DEBT HELL!
SWISH
HMPH, YOU DODGED MY ATTACK WELL!

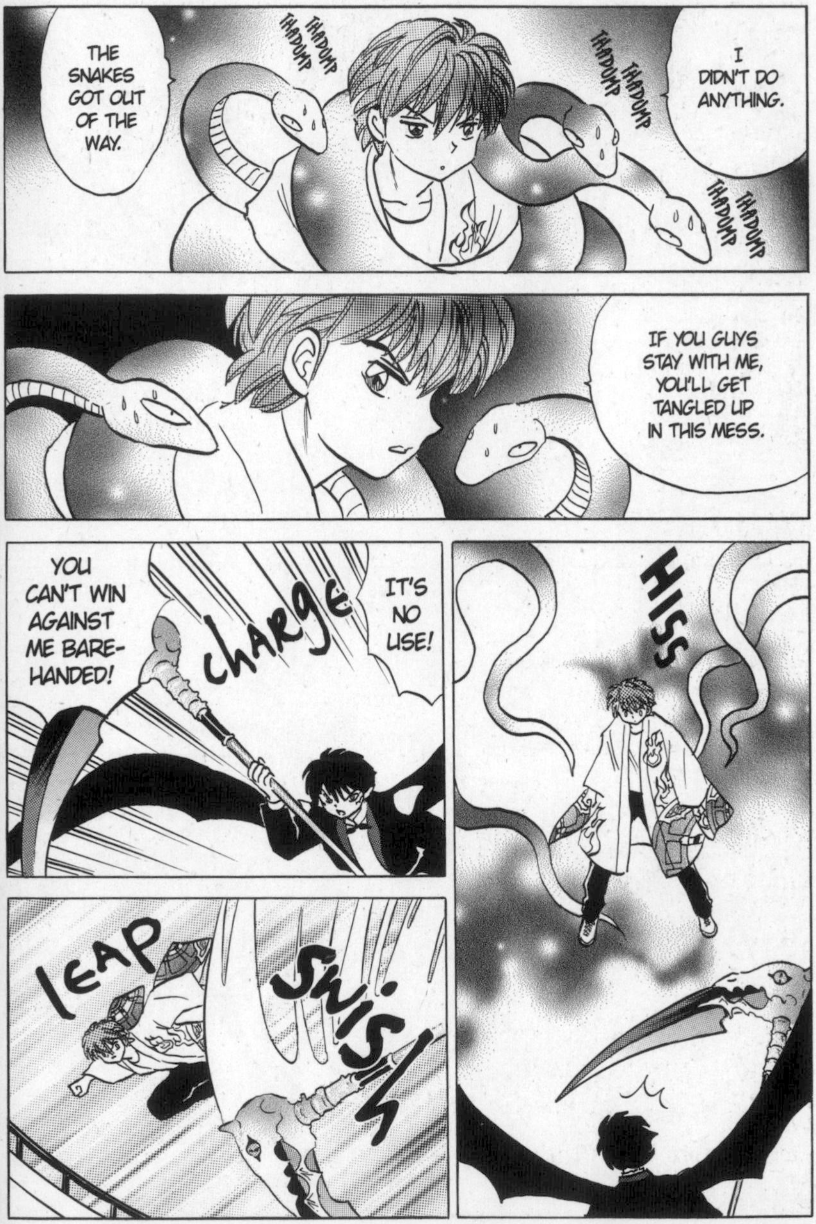
I DIDN'T DO ANYTHING.
THADUMP THADUMP
THADUMP THADUMP
THE SNAKES GOT OUT OF THE WAY.
THADUMP THADUMP
IF YOU GUYS STAY WITH ME, YOU'LL GET TANGLED UP IN THIS MESS.
HISS
IT'S NO USE!
charge
YOU CAN'T WIN AGAINST ME BARE-HANDED!
SWISH
leap

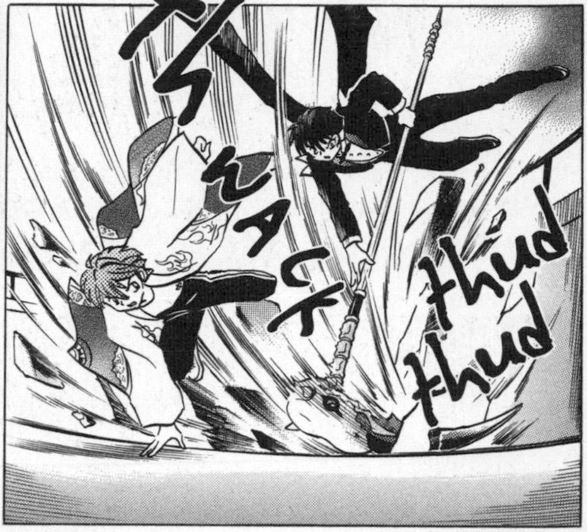
SHACK
thud thud

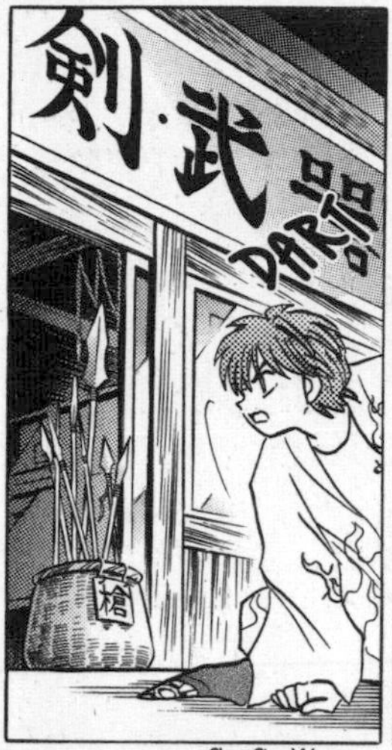
剣·武器
DARTS
槍

Shop Sign: Weapons

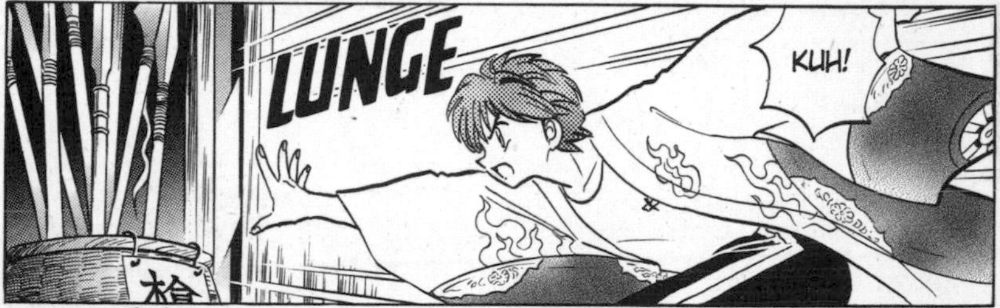
KUH!
LUNGE
槍

Sign: Spears

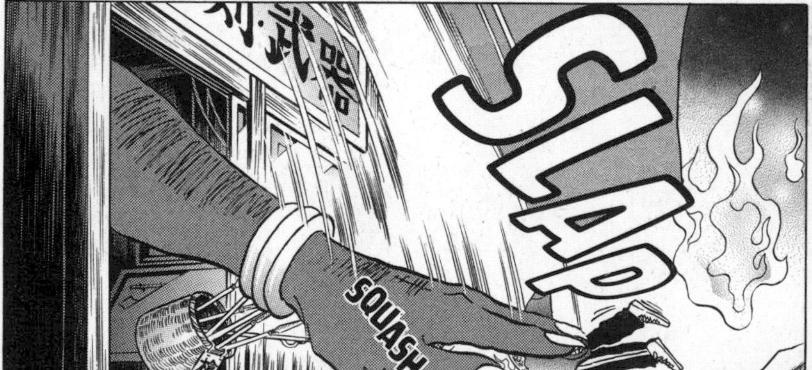
SLAP
剣·武器
SQUASH

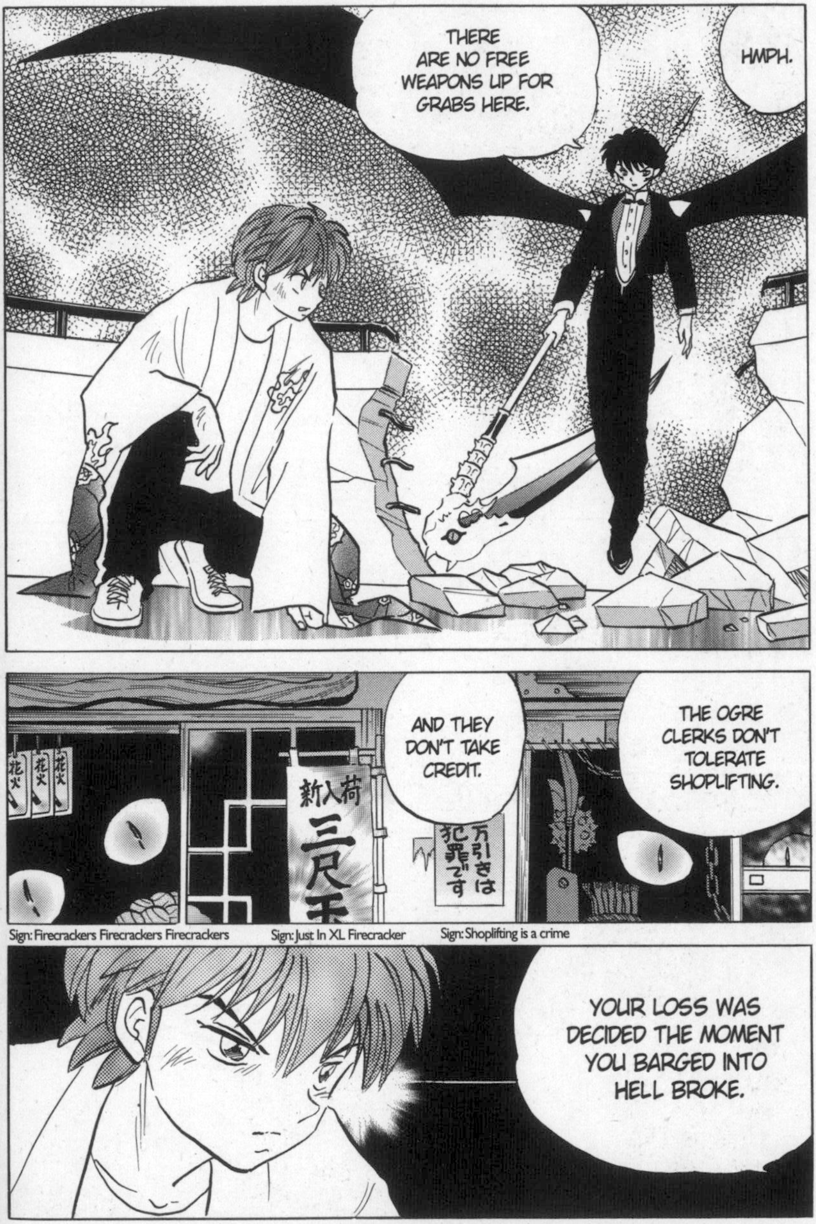
HMPH.
THERE ARE NO FREE WEAPONS UP FOR GRABS HERE.
THE OGRE CLERKS DON'T TOLERATE SHOPLIFTING.
万引きは犯罪です
AND THEY DON'T TAKE CREDIT.
新入荷
三尺
花火
花火
花火
YOUR LOSS WAS DECIDED THE MOMENT YOU BARGED INTO HELL BROKE.

Sign: Firecrackers Firecrackers Firecrackers Sign: Just In XL Firecracker Sign: Shoplifting is a crime

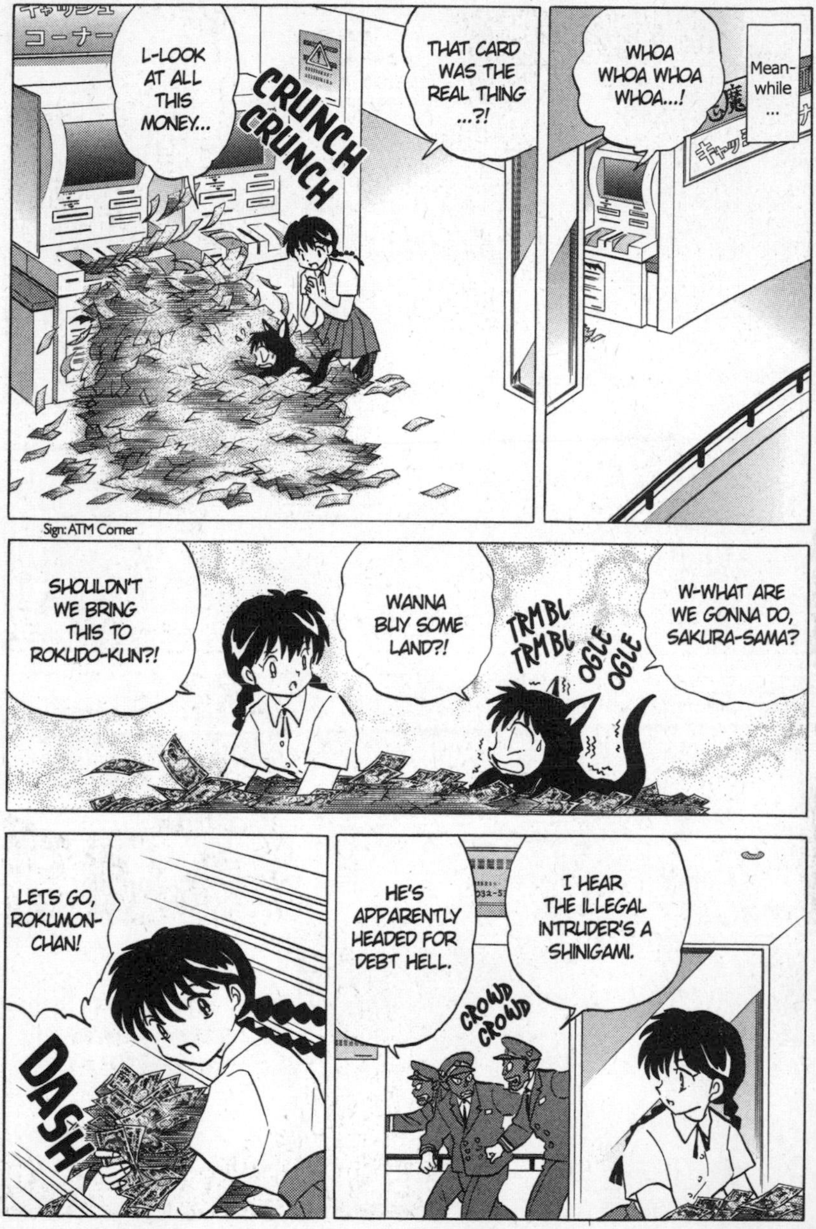
Mean-while...
WHOA WHOA WHOA WHOA...!
THAT CARD WAS THE REAL THING...?!
L-LOOK AT ALL THIS MONEY...
CRUNCH CRUNCH
W-WHAT ARE WE GONNA DO, SAKURA-SAMA?
TRMBL TRMBL
OGLE OGLE
WANNA BUY SOME LAND?!
SHOULDN'T WE BRING THIS TO ROKUDO-KUN?!
I HEAR THE ILLEGAL INTRUDER'S A SHINIGAMI.
HE'S APPARENTLY HEADED FOR DEBT HELL.
CROWD CROWD
LETS GO, ROKUMON-CHAN!
DASH

Sign: ATM Corner

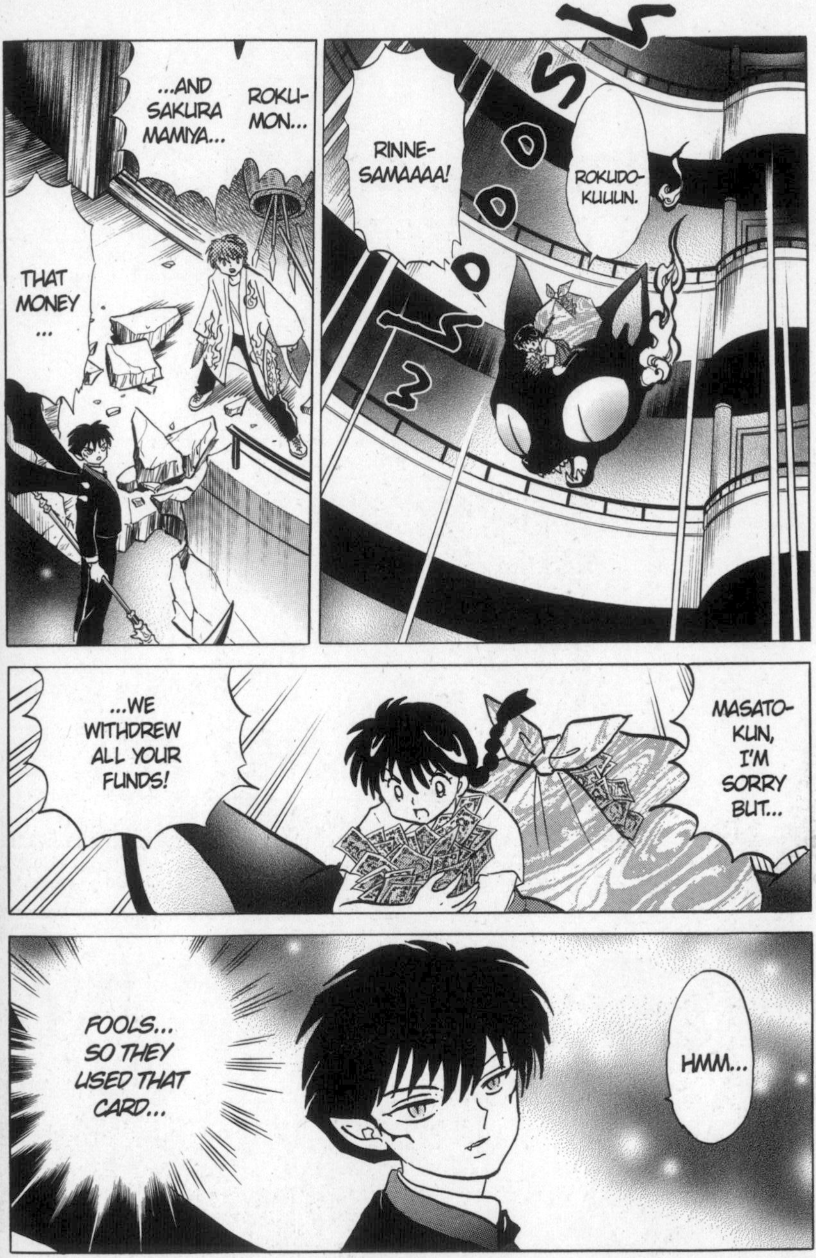
ROKUDO-KUUUN.
RINNE-SAMAAAA!
ROKU-MON...
...AND SAKURA MAMIYA...
THAT MONEY ...
MASATO-KUN, I'M SORRY BUT...
...WE WITHDREW ALL YOUR FUNDS!
HMM...
FOOLS... SO THEY USED THAT CARD...

CHAPTER 18: STREAM OF A THOUSAND WINDS

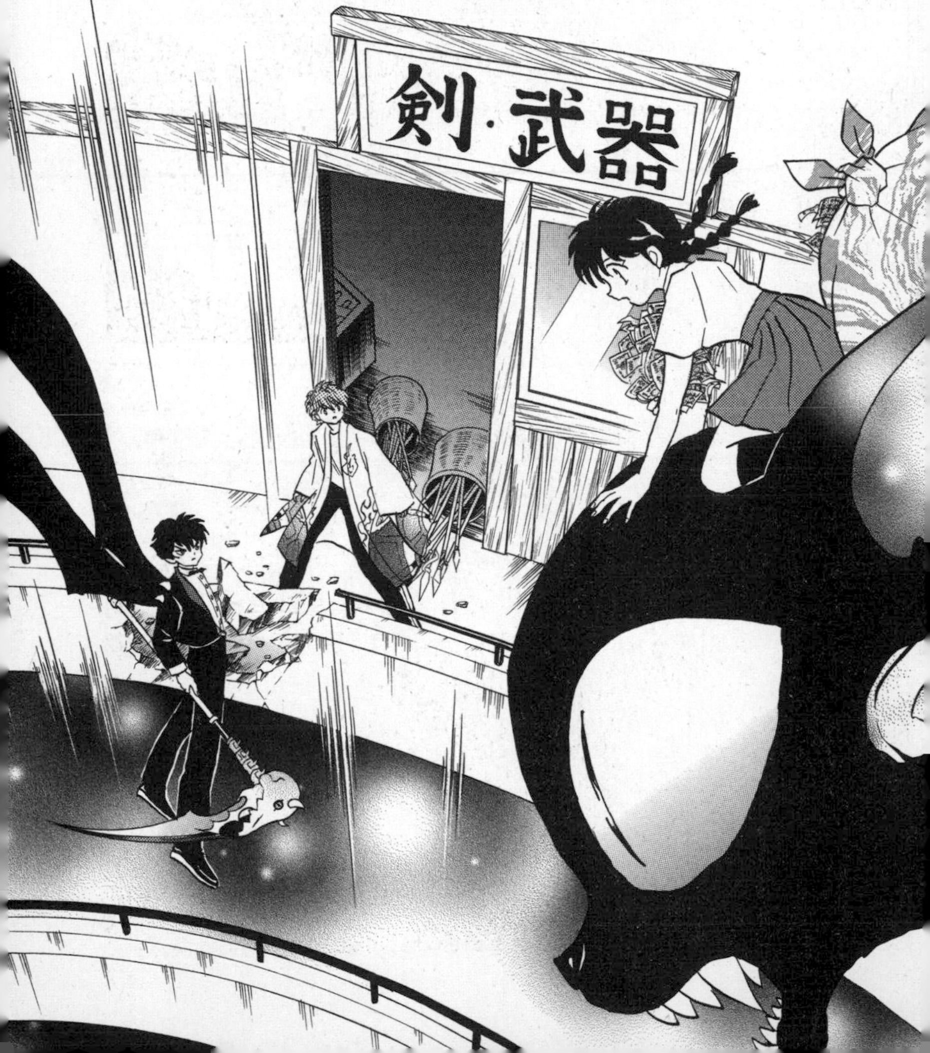
剣·武器

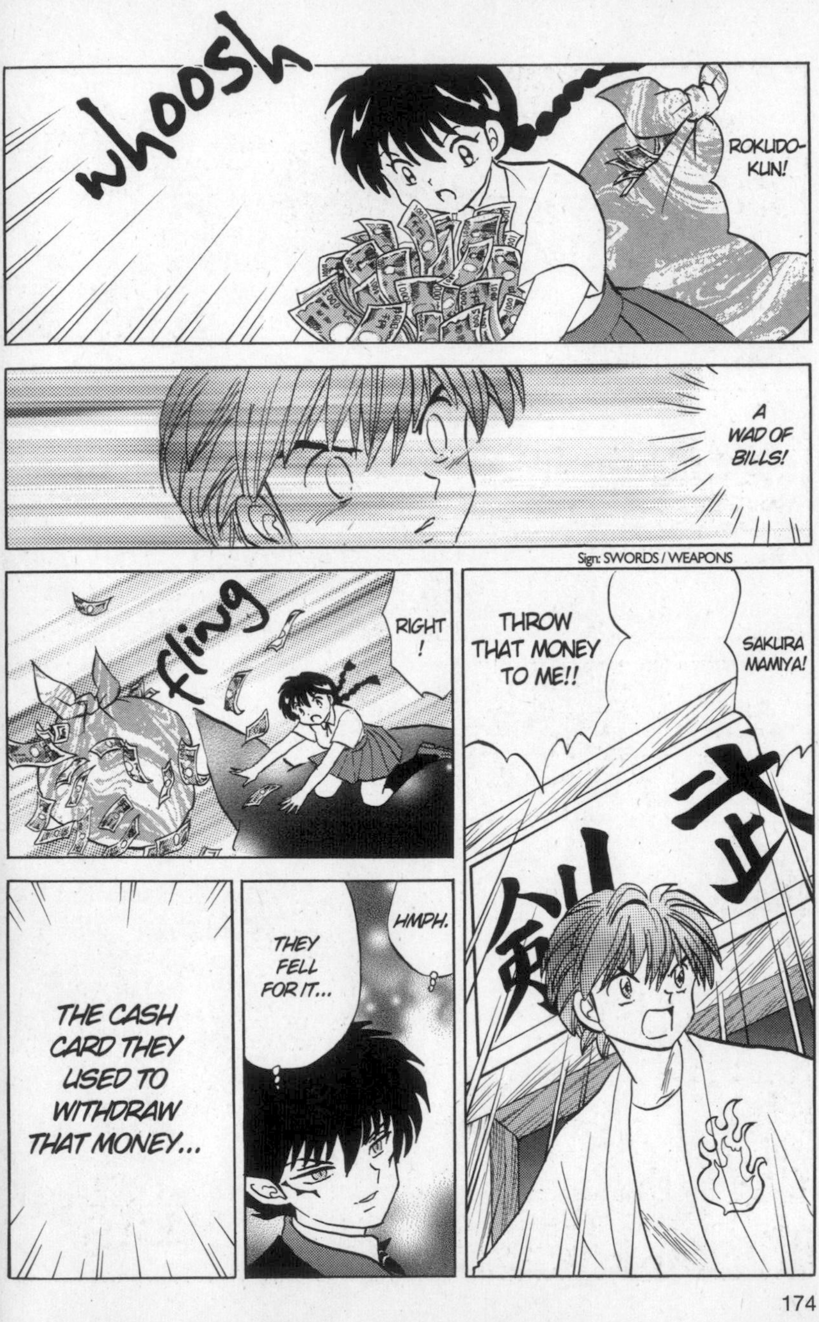
whoosh
ROKUDO-KUN!
A WAD OF BILLS!
SAKURA MAMIYA!
THROW THAT MONEY TO ME!!
RIGHT!
fling
HMPH.
THEY FELL FOR IT...
THE CASH CARD THEY USED TO WITHDRAW THAT MONEY...
Sign: SWORDS / WEAPONS

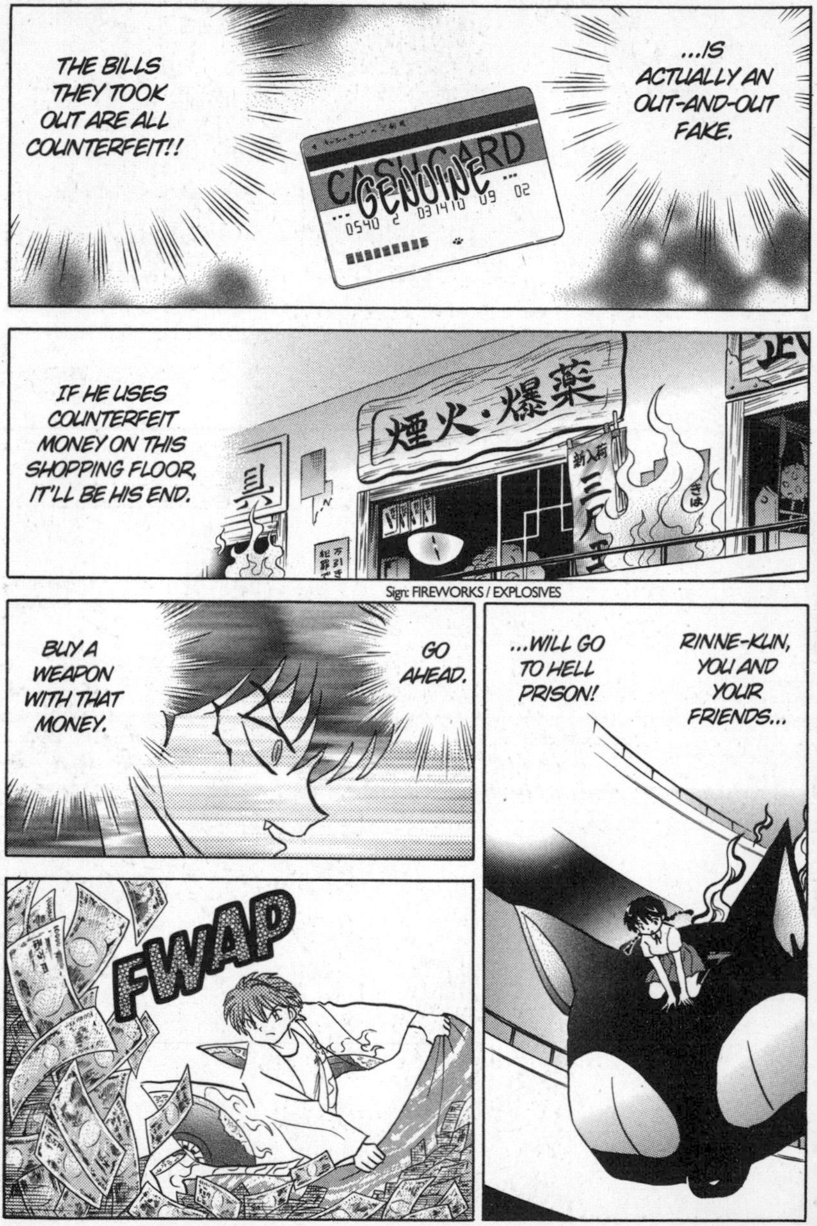
...IS ACTUALLY AN OUT-AND-OUT FAKE.
THE BILLS THEY TOOK OUT ARE ALL COUNTERFEIT!!
CASH CARD
GENUINE
IF HE USES COUNTERFEIT MONEY ON THIS SHOPPING FLOOR, IT'LL BE HIS END.
煙火・爆薬
Sign: FIREWORKS / EXPLOSIVES
RINNE-KUN, YOU AND YOUR FRIENDS...
...WILL GO TO HELL PRISON!
GO AHEAD.
BUY A WEAPON WITH THAT MONEY.
FWAP

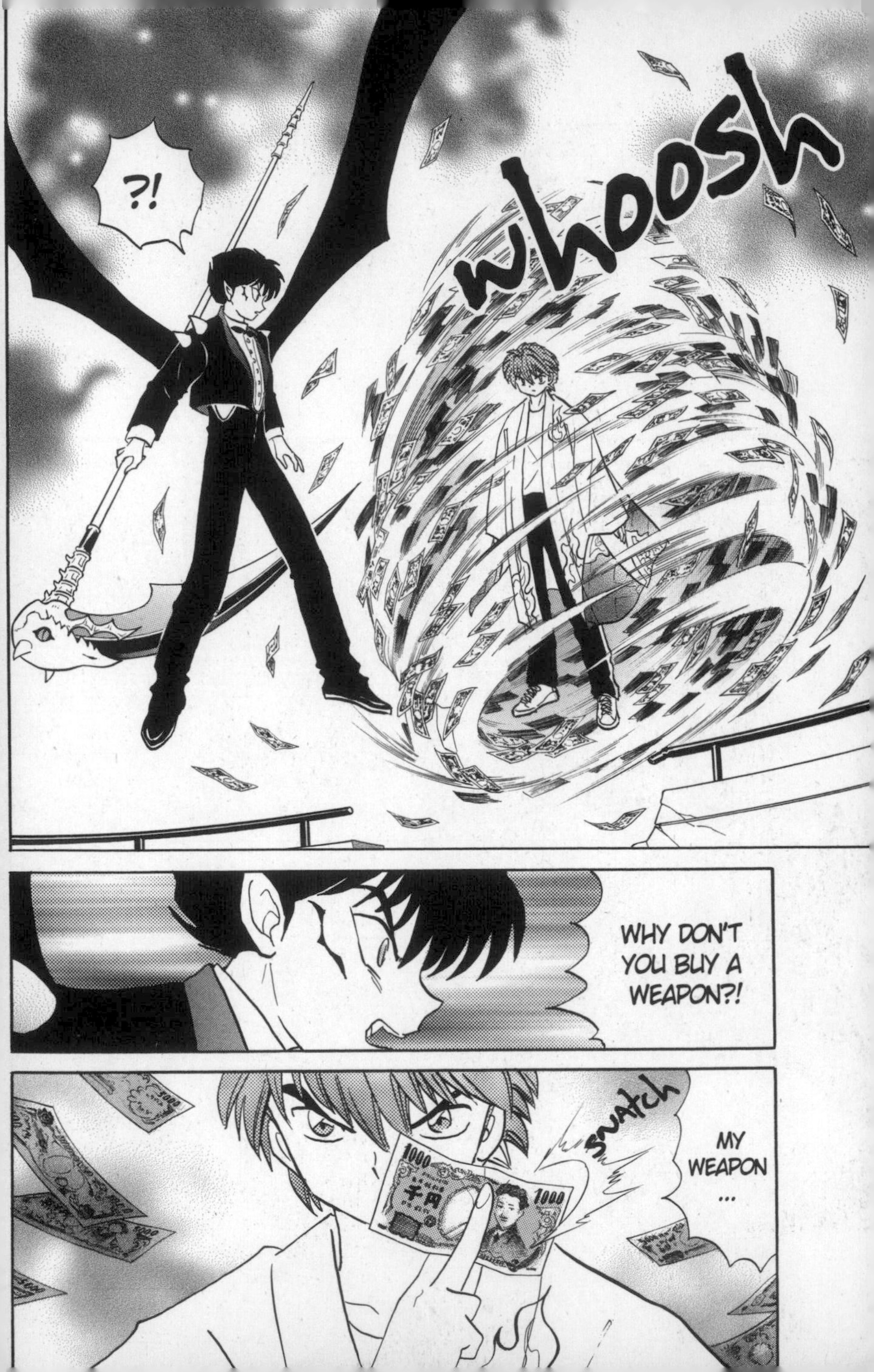
WHOOSH
?!
WHY DON'T YOU BUY A WEAPON?!
SNATCH
MY WEAPON ...

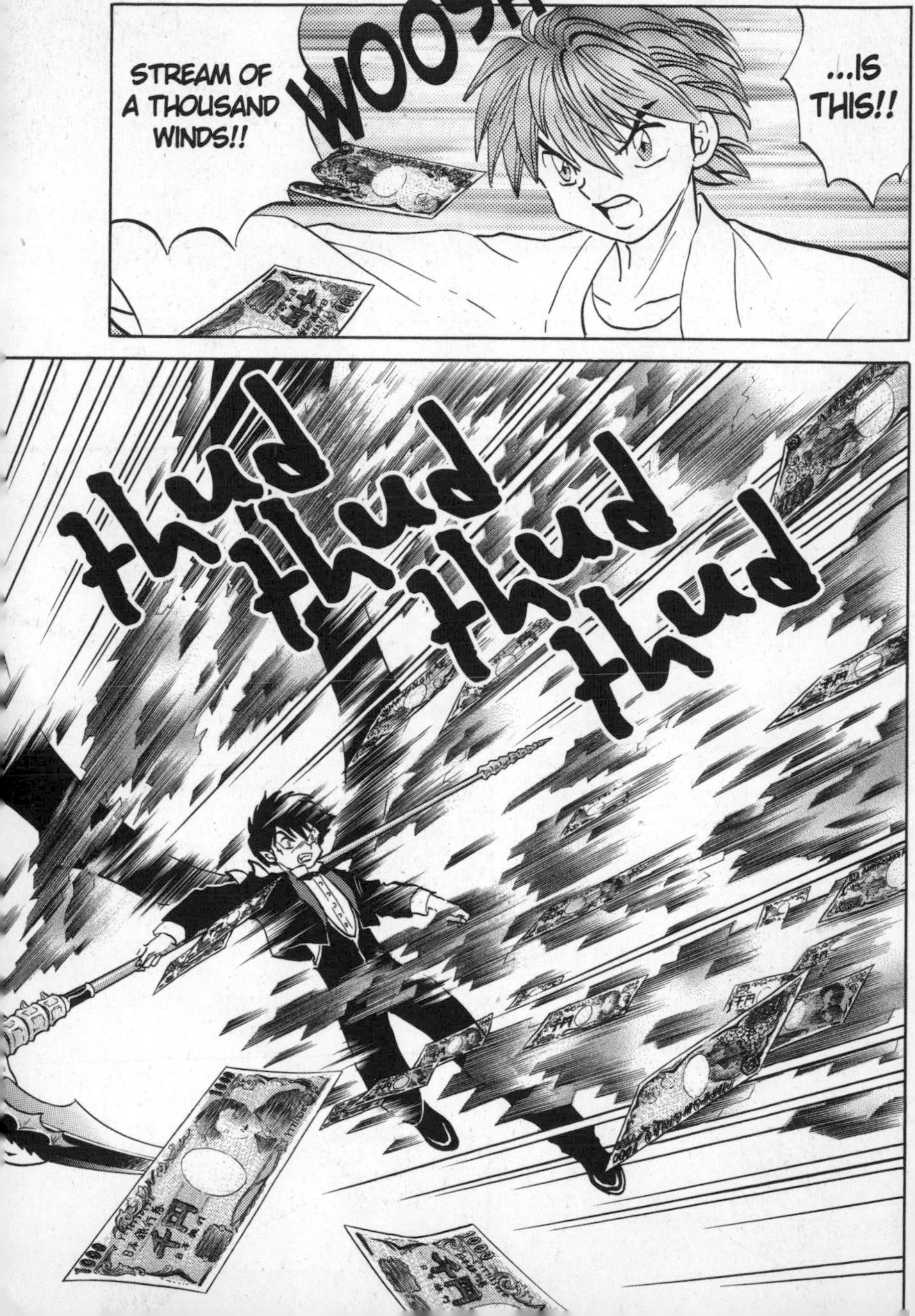
...IS THIS!!
WOOSH
STREAM OF A THOUSAND WINDS!!
thud thud thud thud

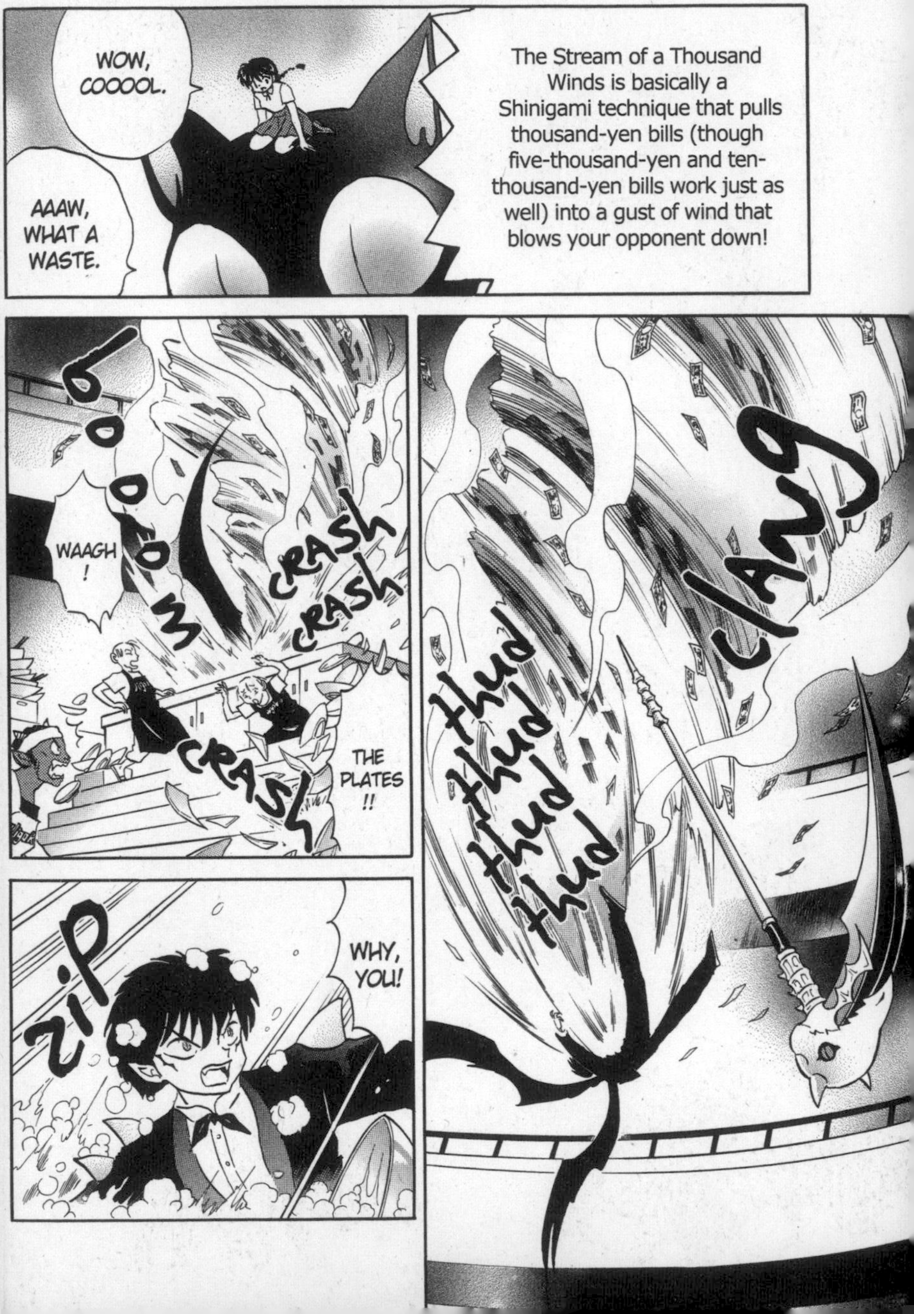
The Stream of a Thousand Winds is basically a Shinigami technique that pulls thousand-yen bills (though five-thousand-yen and ten-thousand-yen bills work just as well) into a gust of wind that blows your opponent down!
WOW, COOOOL.
AAAW, WHAT A WASTE.
clang
thud thud thud thud
BOOOOM
CRASH CRASH
WAAGH!
CRASH
THE PLATES!!
zip
WHY, YOU!

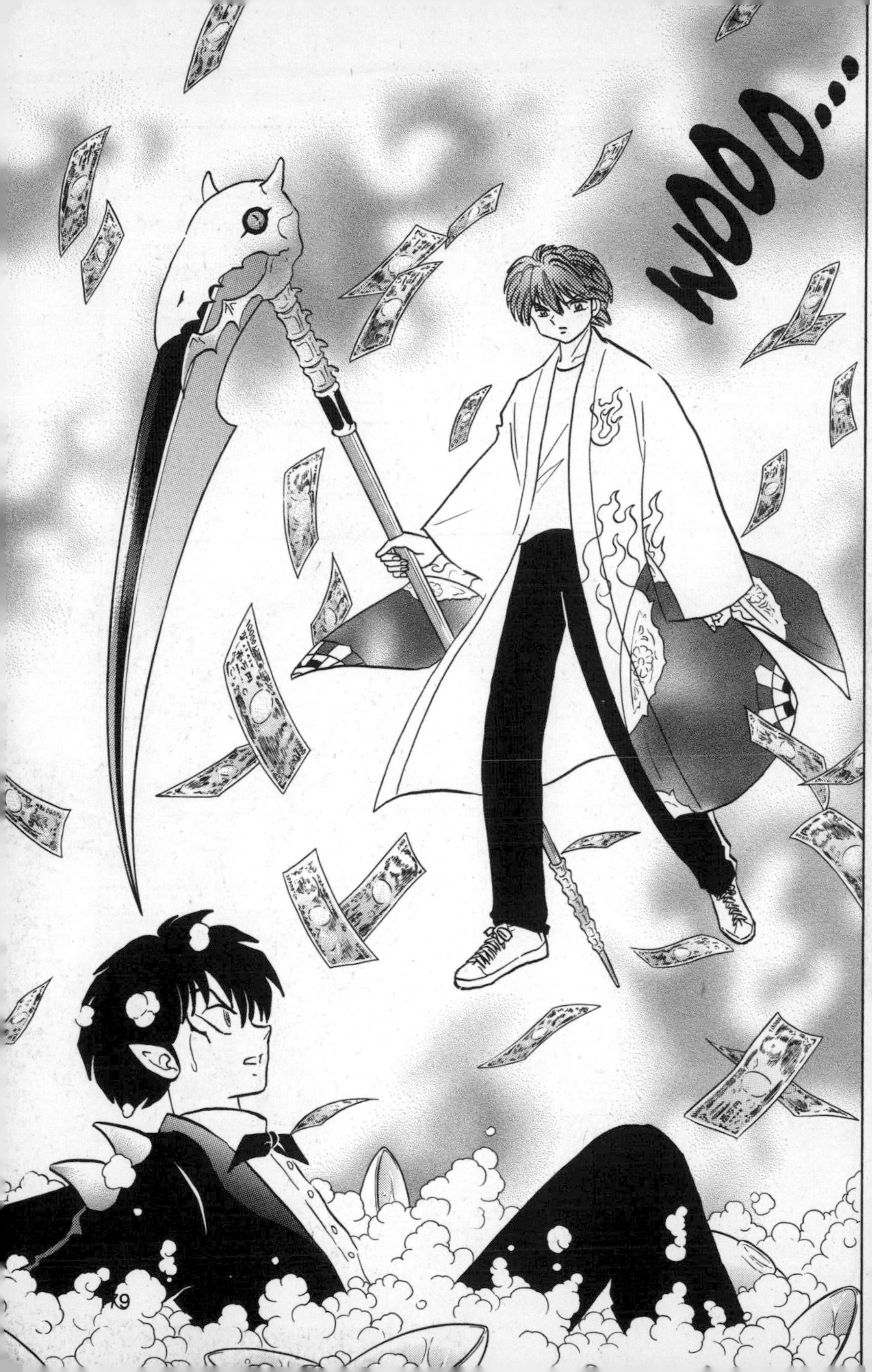
WOOO...

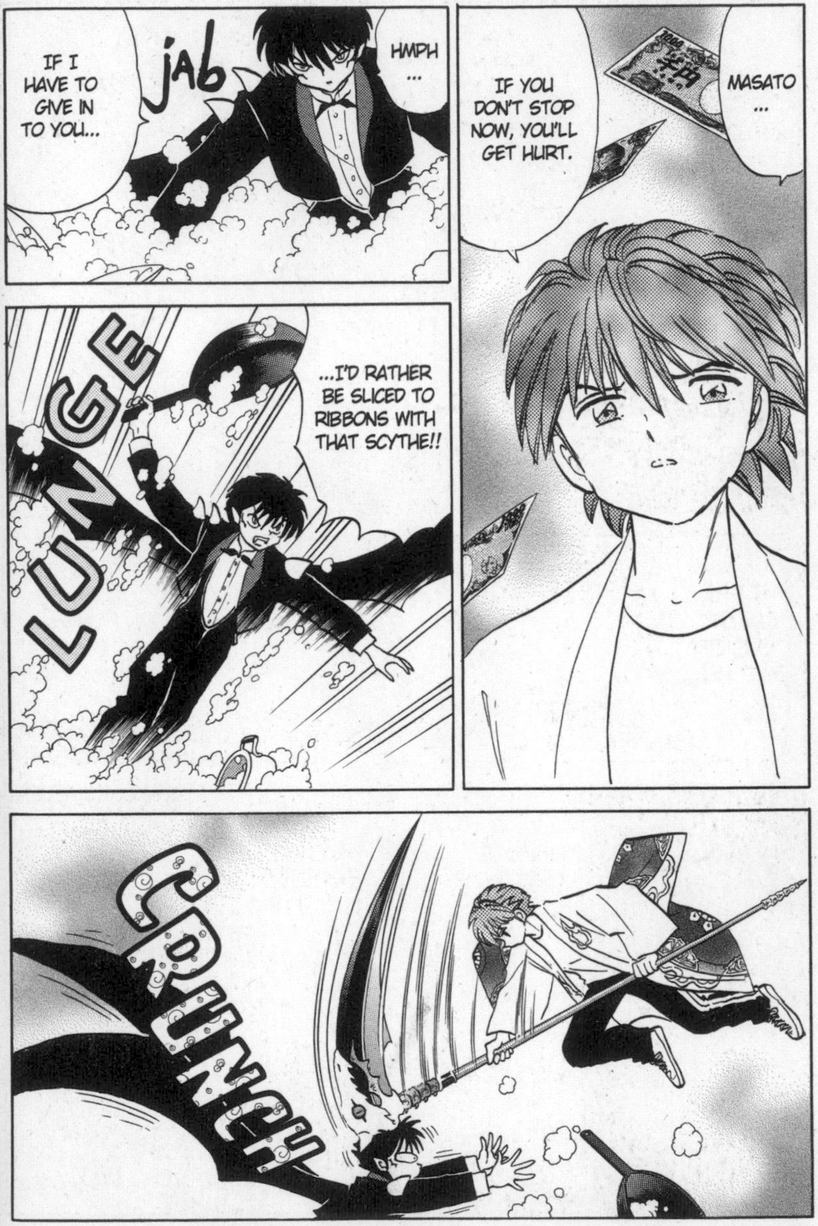
MASATO ...
IF YOU DON'T STOP NOW, YOU'LL GET HURT.
HMPH ...
jab
IF I HAVE TO GIVE IN TO YOU...
...I'D RATHER BE SLICED TO RIBBONS WITH THAT SCYTHE!!
LUNGE
CRUNCH

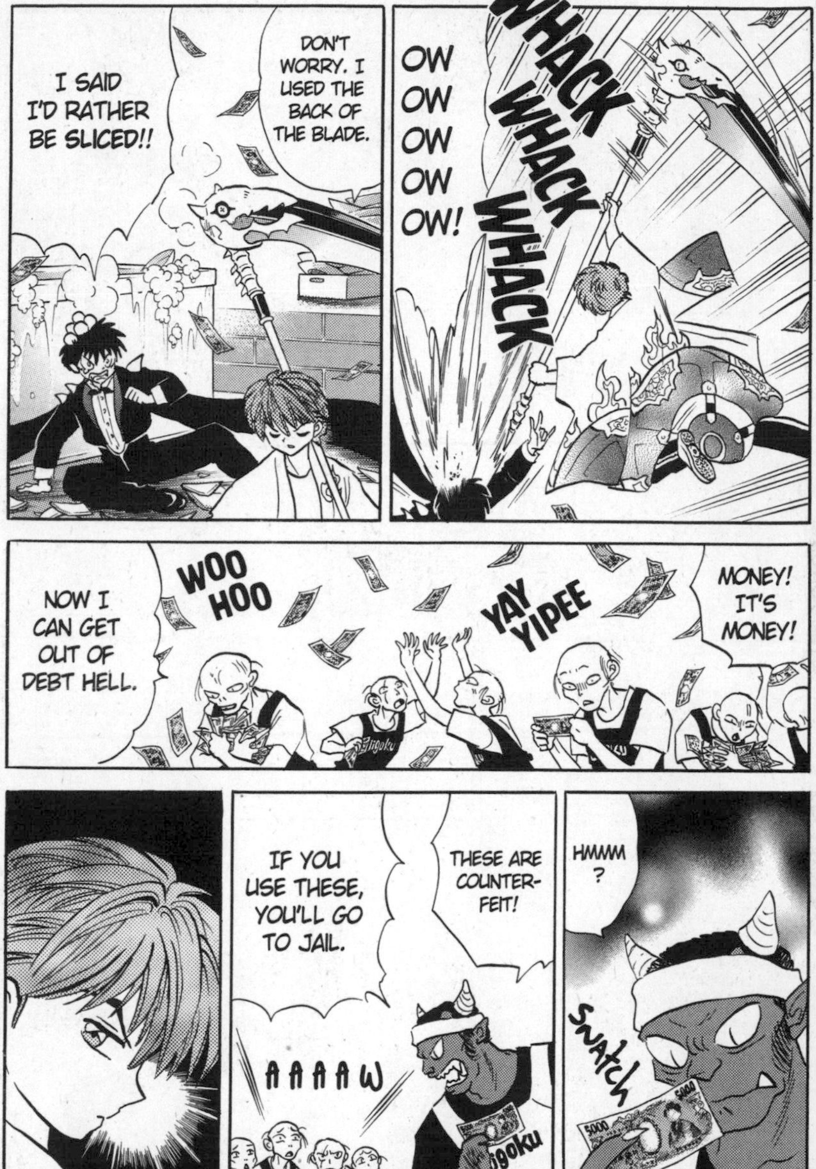
WHACK
WHACK
WHACK
OW OW OW OW OW!
DON'T WORRY. I USED THE BACK OF THE BLADE.
I SAID I'D RATHER BE SLICED!!
MONEY! IT'S MONEY!
YAY YIPEE
WOO HOO
NOW I CAN GET OUT OF DEBT HELL.
HMMM ?
Snatch
THESE ARE COUNTER-FEIT!
IF YOU USE THESE, YOU'LL GO TO JAIL.
AAAAW

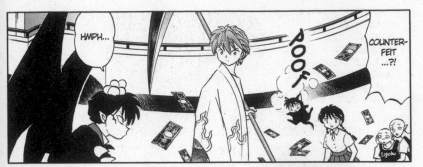

COUNTER-FEIT ...?!
POOF
HMPH...
SO YOU KNEW ALL ALONG.
THAT'S WHY YOU DIDN'T BUY A WEAPON...
NO.
THE STREAM OF A THOUSAND WINDS IS A LUXURY TECHNIQUE THAT YOU CAN'T USE WITHOUT A TON OF BILLS, SO...
I WAS SO HAPPY I COULDN'T RESIST...
HE REALLY GOT CARRIED AWAY...
AH! THERE THEY ARE!
HEY, YOU!

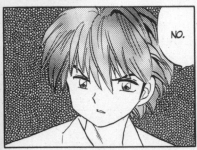

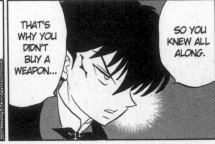

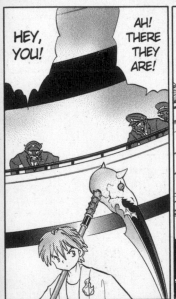

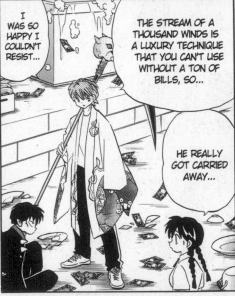

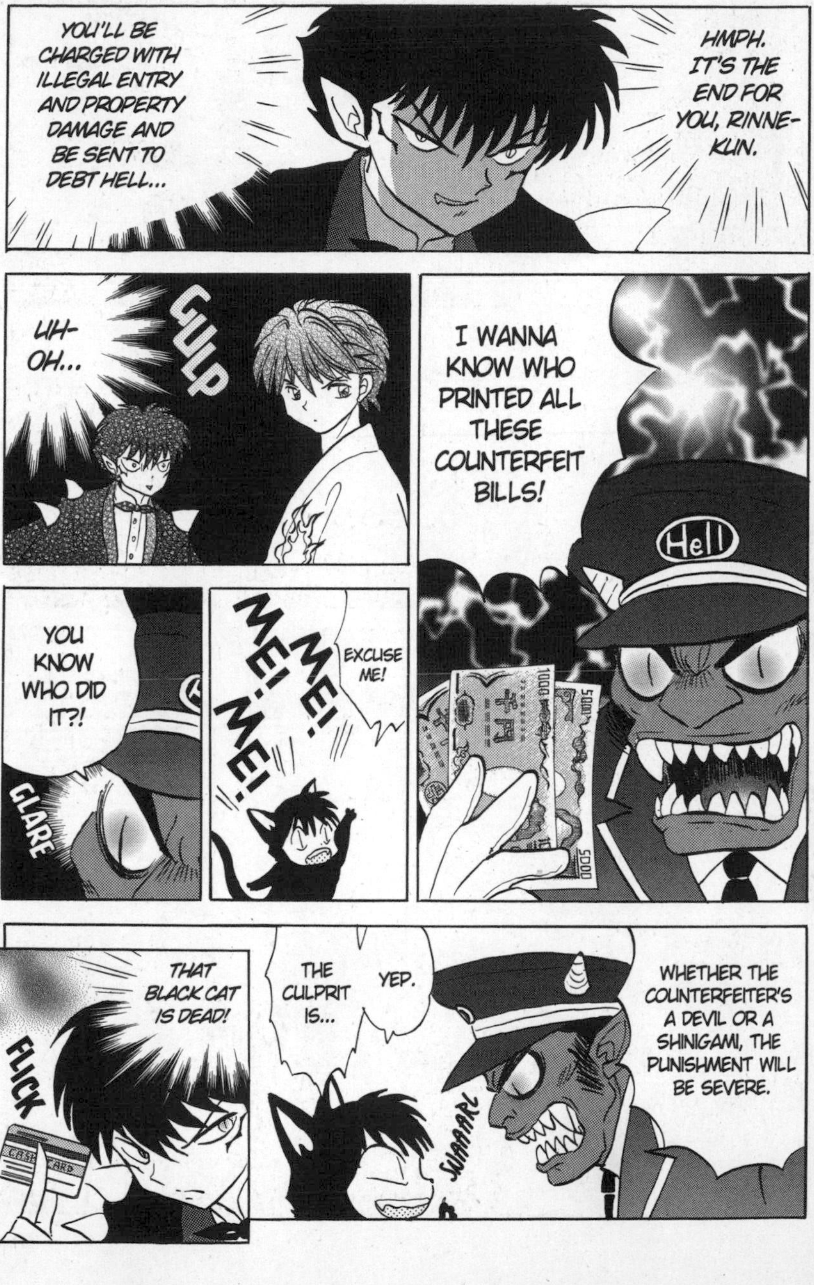
HMPH. IT'S THE END FOR YOU, RINNE-KUN.
YOU'LL BE CHARGED WITH ILLEGAL ENTRY AND PROPERTY DAMAGE AND BE SENT TO DEBT HELL...
I WANNA KNOW WHO PRINTED ALL THESE COUNTERFEIT BILLS!
Hell
GULP
UH-OH...
EXCUSE ME!
ME! ME! ME!
YOU KNOW WHO DID IT?!
GLARE
WHETHER THE COUNTERFEITER'S A DEVIL OR A SHINIGAMI, THE PUNISHMENT WILL BE SEVERE.
SNARRL
YEP.
THE CULPRIT IS...
THAT BLACK CAT IS DEAD!
FLICK

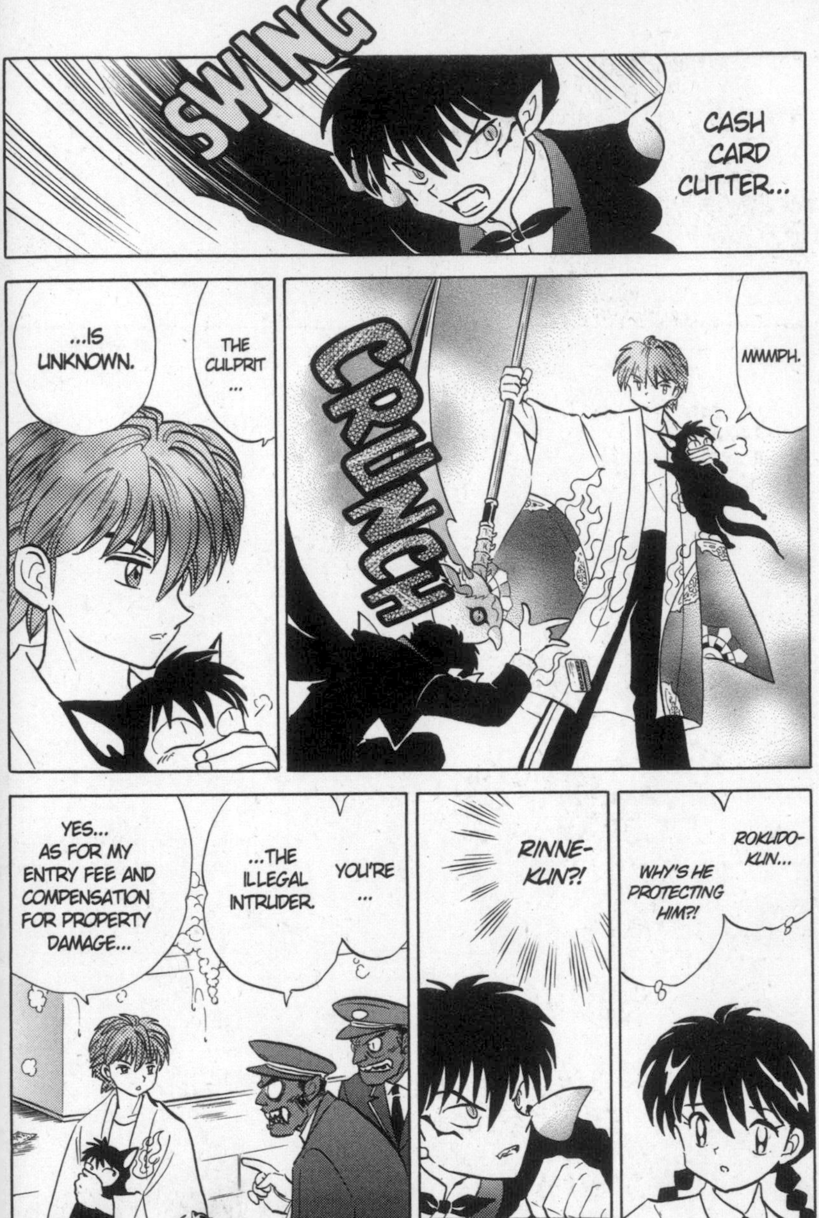
SWING
CASH CARD CUTTER...
MMMPH.
CRUNCH
THE CULPRIT ...
...IS UNKNOWN.
ROKUDO-KUN...
WHY'S HE PROTECTING HIM?!
RINNE-KUN?!
YOU'RE ...
...THE ILLEGAL INTRUDER.
YES... AS FOR MY ENTRY FEE AND COMPENSATION FOR PROPERTY DAMAGE...

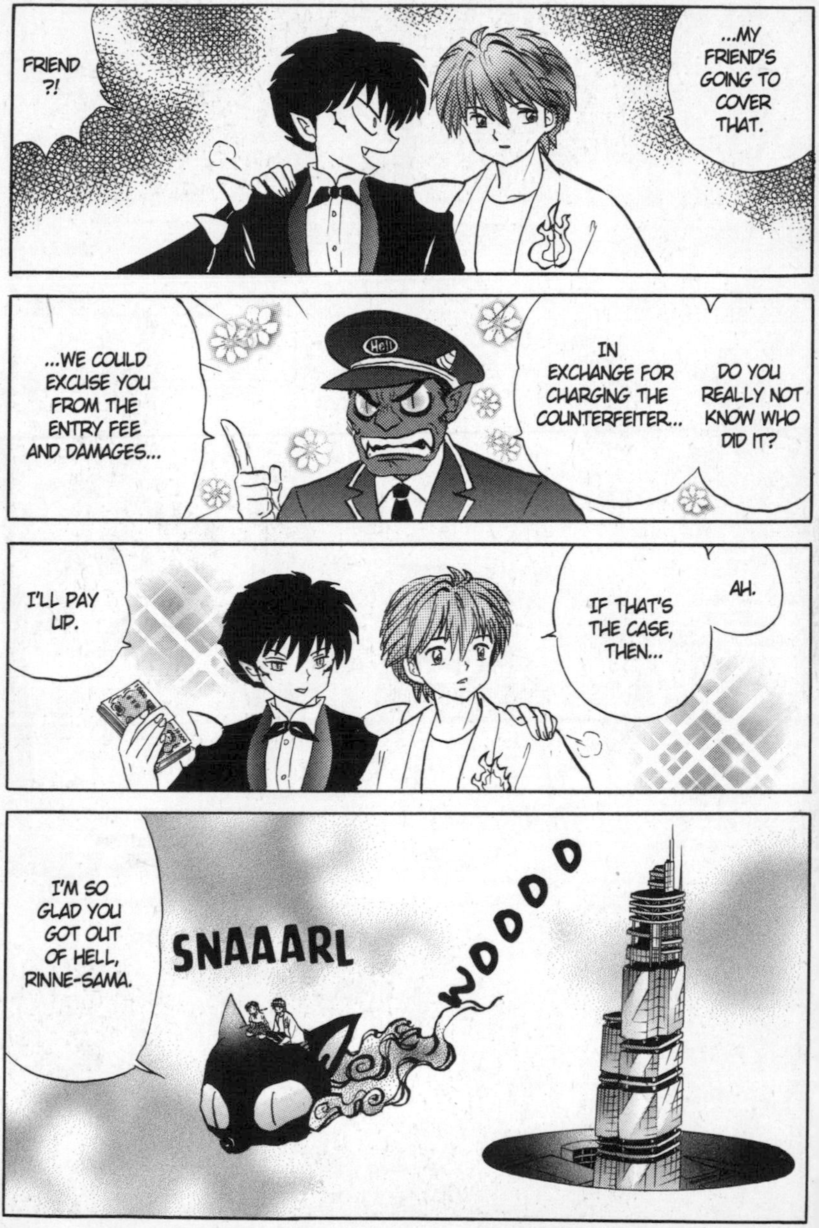
...MY FRIEND'S GOING TO COVER THAT.
FRIEND ?!
DO YOU REALLY NOT KNOW WHO DID IT?
IN EXCHANGE FOR CHARGING THE COUNTERFEITER...
...WE COULD EXCUSE YOU FROM THE ENTRY FEE AND DAMAGES...
AH.
IF THAT'S THE CASE, THEN...
I'LL PAY UP.
WDDDD
SNAAARL
I'M SO GLAD YOU GOT OUT OF HELL, RINNE-SAMA.

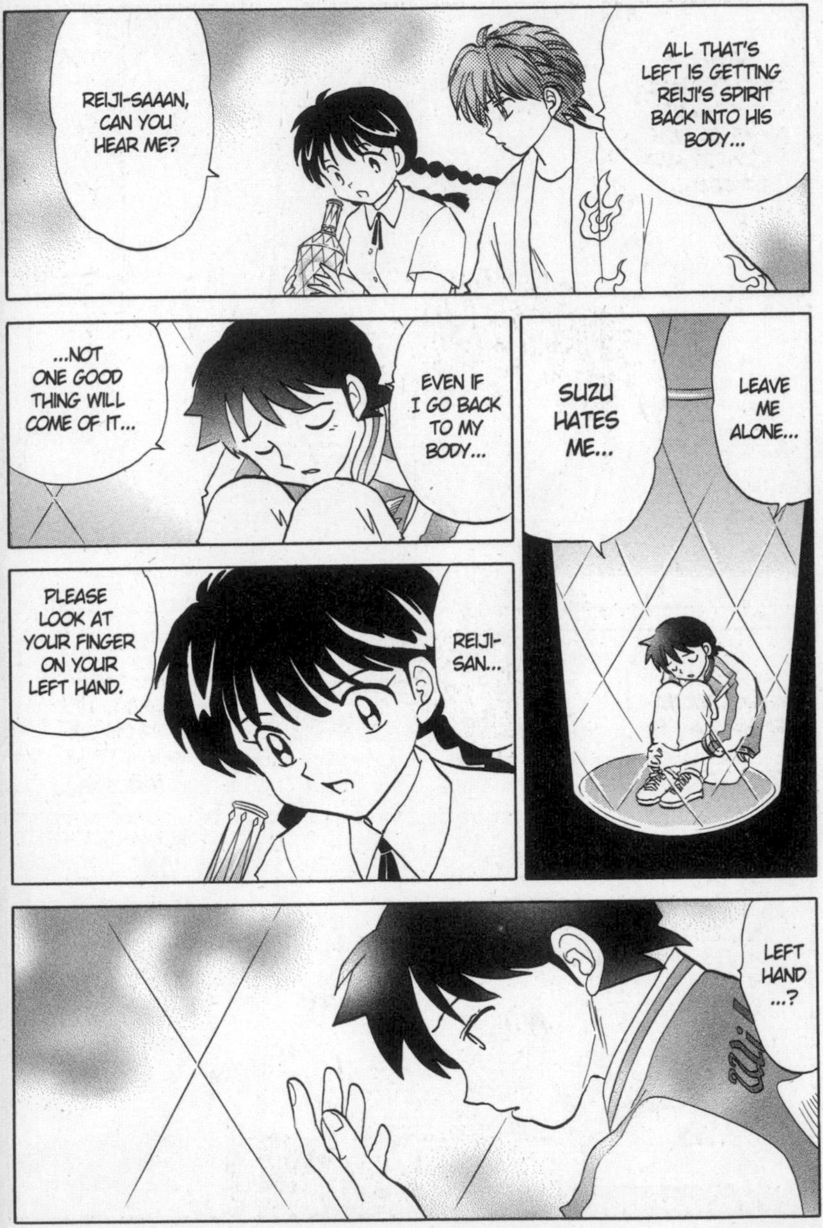
ALL THAT'S LEFT IS GETTING REIJI'S SPIRIT BACK INTO HIS BODY...
REIJI-SAAAN, CAN YOU HEAR ME?
LEAVE ME ALONE...
SUZU HATES ME...
EVEN IF I GO BACK TO MY BODY...
...NOT ONE GOOD THING WILL COME OF IT...
REIJI-SAN...
PLEASE LOOK AT YOUR FINGER ON YOUR LEFT HAND.
LEFT HAND ...?

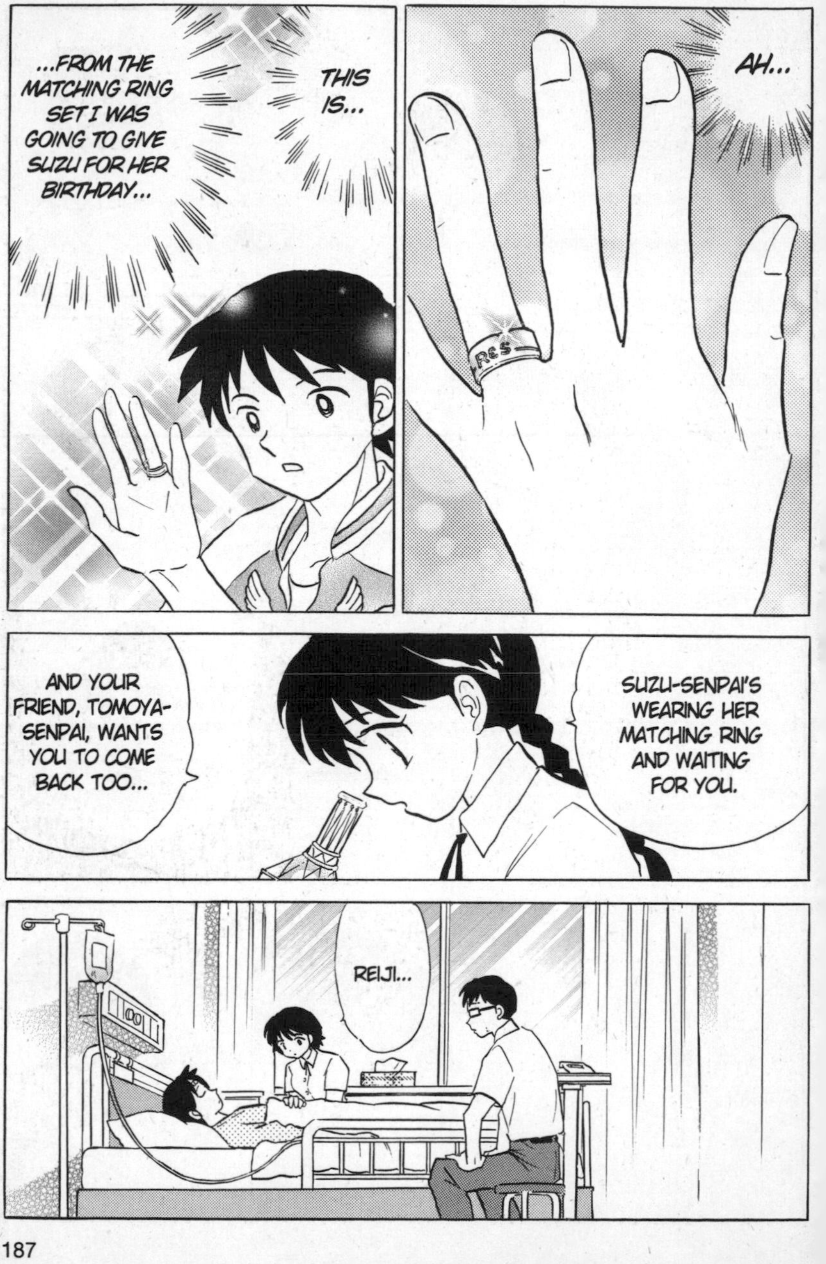
AH...
THIS IS...
...FROM THE MATCHING RING SET I WAS GOING TO GIVE SUZU FOR HER BIRTHDAY...
SUZU-SENPAI'S WEARING HER MATCHING RING AND WAITING FOR YOU.
AND YOUR FRIEND, TOMOYA-SENPAI, WANTS YOU TO COME BACK TOO...
REIJI...

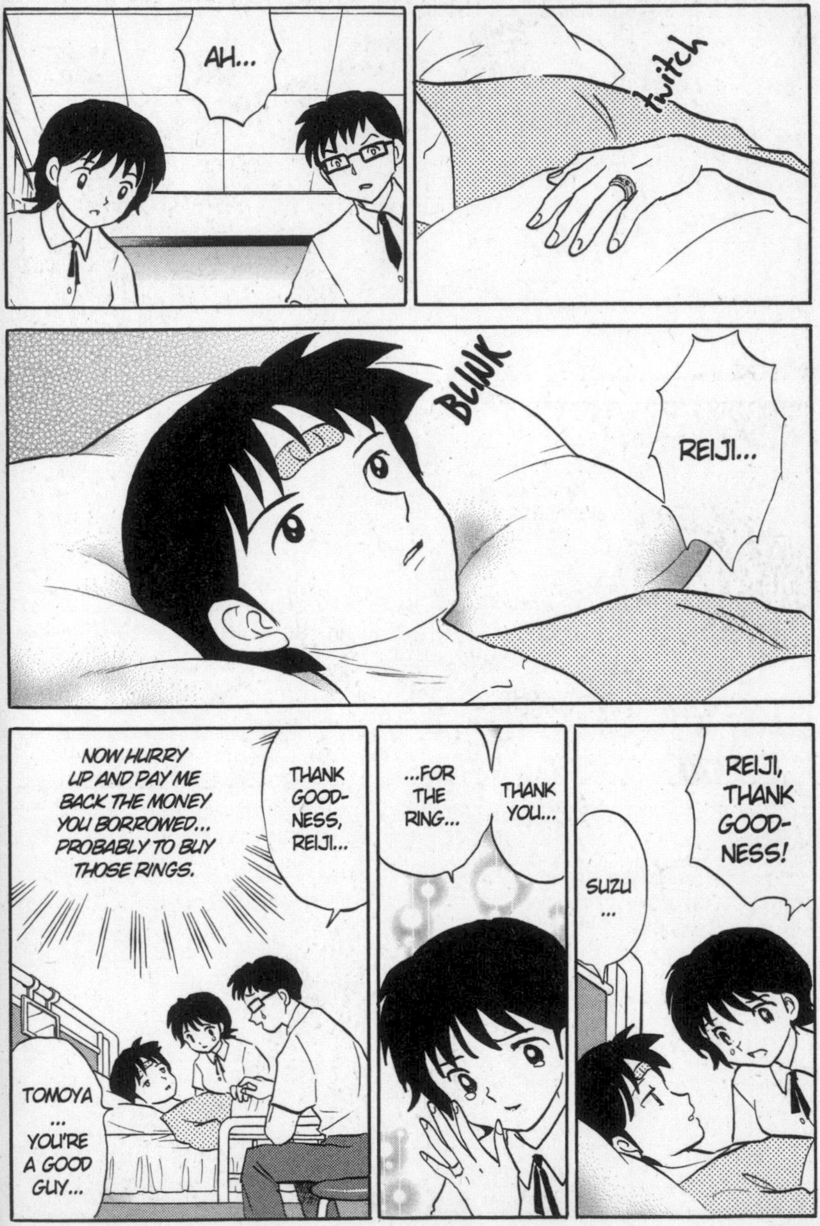
twitch
AH...
BLINK
REIJI...
REIJI, THANK GOODNESS!
SUZU ...
THANK YOU...
...FOR THE RING...
THANK GOODNESS, REIJI...
NOW HURRY UP AND PAY ME BACK THE MONEY YOU BORROWED... PROBABLY TO BUY THOSE RINGS.
TOMOYA ... YOU'RE A GOOD GUY...

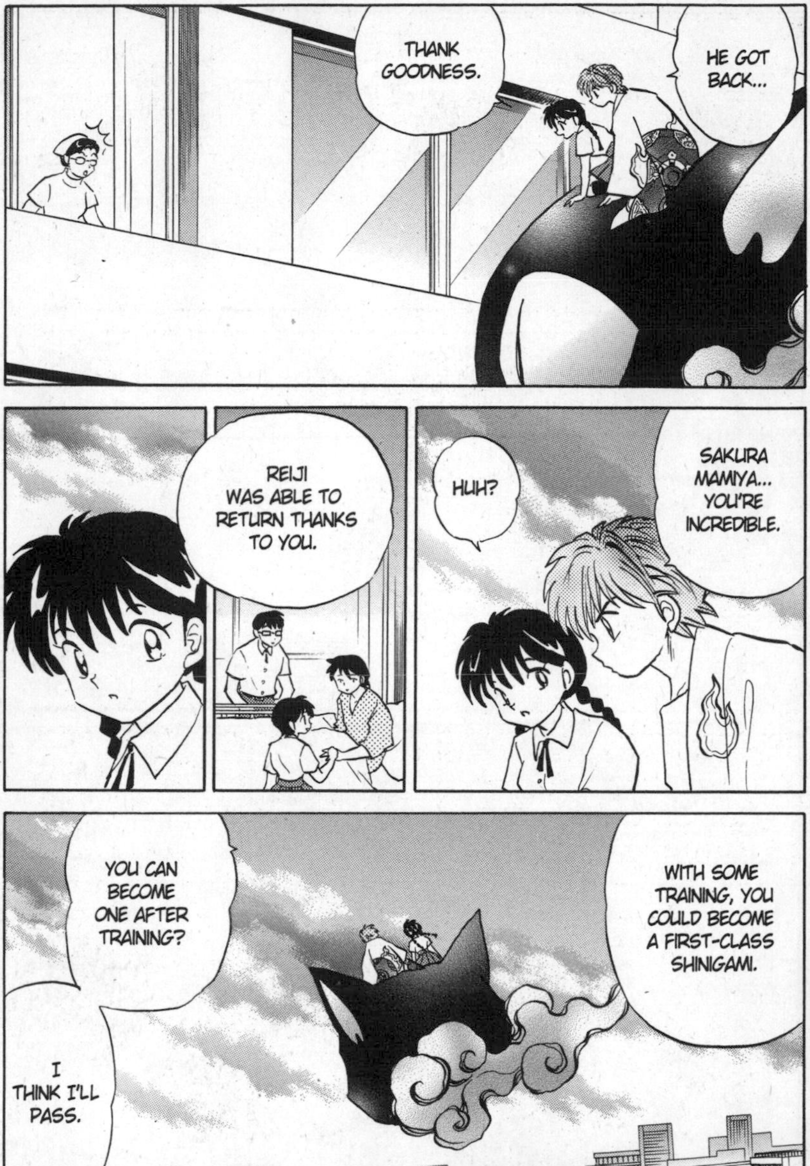
HE GOT BACK...
THANK GOODNESS.
SAKURA MAMIYA... YOU'RE INCREDIBLE.
HUH?
REIJI WAS ABLE TO RETURN THANKS TO YOU.
WITH SOME TRAINING, YOU COULD BECOME A FIRST-CLASS SHINIGAMI.
YOU CAN BECOME ONE AFTER TRAINING?
I THINK I'LL PASS.

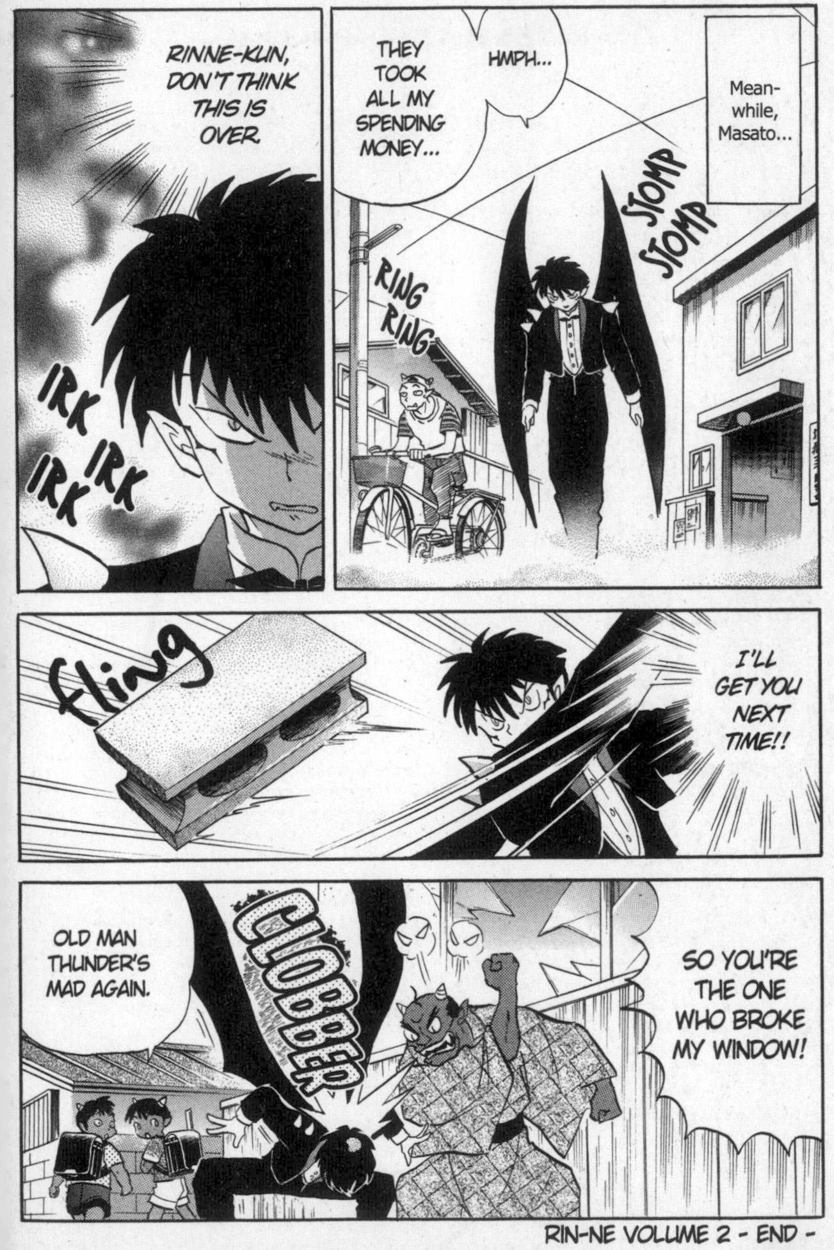
Mean-while, Masato...
HMPH...
THEY TOOK ALL MY SPENDING MONEY...
STOMP STOMP
RING RING
RINNE-KUN, DON'T THINK THIS IS OVER.
IRK IRK IRK IRK
I'LL GET YOU NEXT TIME!!
fling
SO YOU'RE THE ONE WHO BROKE MY WINDOW!
CLOBBER
OLD MAN THUNDER'S MAD AGAIN.

RIN-NE VOLUME 2 - END -

Translation and Cultural Notes

Chapter 9, page 13
In panel 6, two strange characters are showing the spirits of the dead which way to go. The character holding the banner is a *karyobinga*, a creature from Buddhist myth that is half human and half bird. It's not an angel exactly but something like one. The karyobinga sometimes appears in *gagaku* performances (gagaku is the oldest type of classical music in Japan and is associated with the Japanese imperial court). The karyobinga's assistant on the left has a whistle and a drum to catch the attention of the newly departed spirits.

Chapter 11, page 50
On this page, you'll notice that the students' faces are drawn in a rather unusual way. If you read Japanese, you'll see that they are the hiragana characters for *henohenomoheji* 「へのへのもへじ」. This is really just a playful way of drawing faces in Japan and is often seen on the faces of stick figures.

Chapter 14, page 106
When he appears, Masato explains the kanji that's used in his name. They are 「魔」 *ma*, meaning "devil" ; 「狭」 *sa*, the character used in 「狭い」 *semai*, meaning "narrow" (the *on* reading of this character is *kyou*, but when used in names is pronounced "sa"); and 「人」 *to* (this is the character for *hito*—person—but like sa, when used in names it has a different pronunciation, "to").

Chapter 16, page 137
In panel 4, Masato says Rinne needs an entry pass for hell. It's called the Jigoca. This is a contraction of two words, *jigoku* (hell) and *kaado* (card). It's also a play on the real world Suica card, which is used in Japan to get you into JR train stations. The name Suica itself stands for "Super Intelligent Urban Card" and is also a pun: *sui sui*, which means something like "whizzing through quickly" (referring to how you can quickly swipe the card over the scanner), together with the contraction for "card" gives you Suica. *Suika* also means "watermelon," by the way.

Chapter 16, page 146
Suzu and Reiji are shown surrounded by, alternately, a horse and a deer. This is a visual cue in Japanese for the word *baka* (fool, stupid, etc.), and in this case, it is suggesting that Suzu and Reiji together are *bacouple* (a word that has no English equivalent).

The word for horse is *uma*, but another pronunciation of the kanji (馬) is "ba." The word for deer is *shika*, which is where "ka" comes from. Put those together and you get *baka*. There are different theories about the origin of the word, but in this case, the pictures are used to get the point across.

Bacouple is a mash-up of the word *baka* and "couple." It's used in Japan to describe a couple who are crazy about each other, act kind of silly about it, and aren't really worried about what other people think. They'll often do things like wear exactly the same clothing (known in Japanese as the "pair look"), right down to their shoes and socks.

Chapter 16, page 151
Here Rinne says, "This is so Showa Retro!" His comment here refers to a current trend in Japan for things from the Showa period (1926–1989). And this leads to the angry "Old Man Thunder" (*kaminari oyaji* in the original Japanese). Literally, *kaminari* means "thunder" (and lightning) and *oyaji* means "old man." Taken together, this is an expression used by people who grew up in the Showa period to describe an angry and scary old man.

When "Old Man Thunder" comes after Rinne on the next page, he looks exactly like a thunder god, which you may see statues of in many Japanese temples. So in these panels, the angry old man yelling at Rinne represents both aspects of the expression—an angry old man and a thunder god!